Social Movements, Nonviolent Resistance, and the State

This volume probes the intersections between the fields of social movements and nonviolent resistance. Bringing together a range of studies focusing on protest movements around the world, it explores the overlaps and divergences between the two research concentrations, considering the dimensions of nonviolent strategies in repressive states, the means of studying them, and conditions of success of nonviolent resistance in differing state systems. In setting a new research agenda, it will appeal to scholars in sociology and political science who study social movements and nonviolent protest.

Hank Johnston is Professor of Sociology and Hansen Chair of Peace and Nonviolence Studies at San Diego State University, USA. He is the author of *What Is a Social Movement?* and *States and Social Movements*, the co-editor of *Violent Protest, Contentious Politics, and the Neoliberal State*, and the editor of *Culture, Social Movements and Protest*.

The Mobilization Series on Social Movements, Protest, and Culture

Series editor: Professor Hank Johnston

San Diego State University, USA

Published in conjunction with *Mobilization: An International Quarterly*, the premier research journal in the field, this series publishes a broad range of research in social movements, protest, and contentious politics. This is a growing field of social science research that spans sociology and political science as well as anthropology, geography, communications, and social psychology. Enjoying a broad remit, the series welcomes works on a variety of topics: social movement networks; social movements in the global South; social movements, protest, and culture; personalist politics, such as living environmentalism, anticonsumerist communities, anarchist-punk collectives; emergent repertoires of contention regional movements, and protest mobilization in different state regimes.

Social Movements and Political Activism in Contemporary Japan
Re-emerging from Invisibility
Edited by David Chiavacci and Julia Obinger

Social Movements and Organised Labour
Passions and Interests
Edited by Jürgen R. Grote and Claudius Wagemann

The Contentious Politics of Higher Education
Struggles and Power Relations within English and Italian Universities
Lorenzo Cini

Activating China
Local Actors, Foreign Influence, and State Response
Setsuko Matsuzawa

Social Movements, Nonviolent Resistance, and the State
Edited by Hank Johnston

For more information about this series, please visit: www.routledge.com/The-Mobilization-Series-on-Social-Movements-Protest-and-Culture/book-series/ASHSER1345

Social Movements, Nonviolent Resistance, and the State

Edited by Hank Johnston

Routledge
Taylor & Francis Group

LONDON AND NEW YORK

First published 2019
by Routledge
2 Park Square, Milton Park, Abingdon, Oxon OX14 4RN

and by Routledge
52 Vanderbilt Avenue, New York, NY 10017

Routledge is an imprint of the Taylor & Francis Group, an informa business

British Library Cataloguing-in-Publication Data
A catalogue record for this book is available from the British Library

Library of Congress Cataloging-in-Publication Data
Names: Johnston, Hank, 1947– editor.
Title: Social movements, nonviolent resistance, and the state / edited by Hank Johnston.
Description: 1 Edition. | New York : Routledge, 2019. | Series: The mobilization series on social movements, protest, and culture | Includes bibliographical references and index.
Identifiers: LCCN 2018044667 | ISBN 9781138606258 (hbk) | ISBN 9780429467783 (ebk) | ISBN 9780429885679 (web pdf) | ISBN 9780429885662 (epub) | ISBN 9780429885655 (mobi/kindle)
Subjects: LCSH: Social movements. | Passive resistance.
Classification: LCC HM881 .S635 2019 | DDC 303.48/4—dc23
LC record available at https://lccn.loc.gov/2018044667

ISBN: 978-1-138-60625-8 (hbk)
ISBN: 978-0-429-46778-3 (ebk)

Typeset in Times New Roman
by Apex CoVantage, LLC

Social Movements, Nonviolence, and the State is the first title in a special collection in the *Mobilization* series, The Hansen Collection of Peace and Nonviolence Research.

Hansen
Peace
Nonviolence

The study of nonviolent strategies for social change and peace movements is a subdiscipline of the contentious politics field. Funded by the Hansen Chair for Peace and Nonviolence at the College of Arts and Letters, San Diego State University, this collection aims to contribute to the social science of nonviolent social change and peace.

Contents

Figures

Tables

Contributors

Benjamin S. Case is a doctoral candidate in sociology at the University of Pittsburgh. His research interests include social movement strategy, riots, political sociology, and cultural studies, and his academic work has been published in the *Journal of Resistance Studies* and *Berkeley Journal of Sociology*. Ben is a longtime political, community, and labor organizer, and his writing has also appeared in popular venues such as *Roar Magazine, Tikkun, Popular Resistance*, and *Waging Nonviolence*. He is currently working on research looking at violent and nonviolent strategies and tactics in the South African student movement.

Erica Chenoweth is professor of public policy, Harvard Kennedy School, and Susan S. and Kenneth L. Wallack Professor, Radcliff Institute for Advanced Study, Harvard University. An internationally recognized authority on political violence and its alternatives, *Foreign Policy* magazine ranked her among the Top 100 Global Thinkers in 2013 for her efforts to promote the empirical study of civil resistance. Chenoweth received the 2014 Karl Deutsch Award, which the International Studies Association gives annually to the scholar under the age of 40 who has made the greatest impact on the field of international politics or peace research.

Killian Clarke is a PhD student in comparative politics at Princeton University. His research examines contentious politics, mobilization, and protest, with a regional focus on the Middle East. He has conducted field research in Egypt, Lebanon, Jordan, and Turkey, using a range of qualitative and quantitative research methods. His articles have appeared in *The Journal of Comparative Politics, Mobilization, European Political Science*, and *Sociology of Development*, as well as a variety of policy and news publications.

James Franklin is professor and chair of the Department of Politics and Government at Ohio Wesleyan University. His primary field is comparative politics, with research and teaching interests in contentious politics, human rights, democratization, and Latin American politics. His research has been published in a variety of social science journals, including the article "Contentious Challenges and Government Responses in Latin America," which was named the best article in *Political Research Quarterly* for 2009. One current line of research examines the effect of human rights protest on human rights records in Latin America. A separate research project is focused on cataloging and analyzing protest waves around the world, of which the current chapter is part.

Larry W. Isaac is the Gertrude Conaway Vanderbilt Professor of Sociology, professor of American Studies, and Sociology Department chair at Vanderbilt University. He is past editor of the *American Sociological Review* (2010–2015) and past president of the Southern Sociological Society. Larry has published numerous articles on topics in political sociology, social movements, labor, and social-historical change. His work has been the recipient of awards from American Sociological Association sections on Comparative-Historical Sociology, Cultural Sociology, and Labor/Labor Movement Sociology, the Southern Sociological Society, ASA/NSF Advancement of the Discipline Fund, and National Endowment for the Humanities. Larry is currently working on a co-authored book about the Nashville civil rights movement.

Hank Johnston is professor of sociology and Hansen Chair of Peace and Nonviolence Studies at San Diego State University. His research focuses on nonviolent protests in different state systems and especially their cultural dimensions. He is founding editor of *Mobilization: An International Quarterly*, the leading research journal in the field of protest and social movements. His is the author of several books, including *What Is a Social Movement? States and Social Movements*, and *Violent Protest in the Neoliberal State* (with S. Sepheriades, 2011).

David S. Meyer is professor of sociology and political science at the University of California, Irvine. He is author or editor of several books, including *The Politics of Protest: Social Movements in America*, and blogs at Politicsoutdoors.com.

Dana M. Moss is an assistant professor of sociology at the University of Pittsburgh. Dana's research investigates how collective actors experience and resist authoritarian state repression, and her current book project explains the transnational effects of regime repression and the Arab Spring revolutions on diaspora movements for democracy. Her work appears in the *American Sociological Review*, *Social Problems*, *Mobilization: An International Journal*, and *The Journal of Immigrant and Refugee Studies*, among other venues.

Sharon Erickson Nepstad is Distinguished Professor of Sociology at the University of New Mexico. Her research focuses on social movements, religion, revolution, and nonviolence. She is the author of five books: *Nonviolent Struggle: Theories, Strategies, and Dynamics* (2015, Oxford University Press), *Nonviolent Revolutions: Civil Resistance in the Late 20th Century* (2011, Oxford University Press), *Religion and War Resistance in the Plowshares Movement* (2008, Cambridge University Press), and *Convictions of the Soul: Religion, Culture, and Agency in the Central America Solidarity Movement* (2004, Oxford University Press). Her forthcoming book is *Socially Engaged*

Catholicism: Progressive Movements and Lived Religion in the United States (2018, New York University Press).

Daniel P. Ritter is assistant professor of sociology at Stockholm University and a visiting fellow, Centre for International Studies, London School of Economics. He is author of *The Iron Cage of Liberalism* (2015, Oxford University Press).

Kurt Schock is associate professor of sociology at Rutgers University, Newark. His publications include *Civil Resistance Today* (Polity, 2015), *Civil Resistance: Comparative Perspectives on Nonviolent Struggle* (editor, University of Minnesota Press, 2015), and *Unarmed Insurrections: People Power Movements in Nondemocracies* (University of Minnesota Press, 2005). *Unarmed Insurrections* was awarded Best Book of the Year by the Comparative Democratization section of the American Political Science Association and published in Spanish. He is currently completing a book manuscript on the political dynamics of land rights movements in India and Brazil.

1 Analyzing social movements, nonviolent resistance, and the state

Hank Johnston

Among sociologists and political scientists, the field of social movement and protest research has grown in a relatively short span of time to become a central and vibrant social science subdiscipline. This rise was spurred by the increase of mostly nonviolent protest in North America and Europe as a way of doing politics, that is, *contentious politics* – noninstitutional collective action that arises when politicians are unresponsive to citizen demands. Since the huge student, antiwar, and civil rights mobilizations of the 1960s and 1970s, the social movement sector has expanded greatly (Meyer and Tarrow 1998; Dalton 2002; Dodson 2011; Rucht 1999; Soule and Earl 2005). Today, the nonresponsiveness of politicians and policymakers fuels movements as diverse as Black lives movement, #MeToo, and Trumpism in the US.

Similarly, beginning with small steps about the same time, most notably with the seminal scholarship of Gene Sharp (1973) and Johan Galtung (1969), there has been a slow but steady growth of academic interest in nonviolent strategies and peaceful tactics of challenge and resistance to the state – typically repressive states that limit citizen freedoms.[1] Again, much of the interest in this area is among sociologists and political scientists and includes many scholars – like myself and most of the contributors to this volume – who bridge the field of nonviolence and social movements via research interests in resistance against repression. Studies of nonviolence have increased in recent decades as autocratic regimes have toppled worldwide, and research shows the utility of nonviolent tactics in successfully achieving regime change (Ackerman and DuVall 2000; Chenoweth and Stephan 2011; Karatnycky and Ackerman 2005; Martin 2007; Nepstad 2015a; Schock 2005, 2015). This volume brings together essays of several scholars whose important work has advanced both the nonviolence field and its intersection with social movement research.[2]

It is not coincidental that these two research foci have flourished in tandem. As Kurt Schock indicates in chapter three, they developed during a historical epoch when strategies of regime change transitioned from violent anticolonial and Marxist-Leninist-Maoist insurgencies to movements of resistance that were mostly nonviolent. Especially important were the movements that brought about the transformation of high-capacity Leninist socialist states, as well as several successful challenges to lower-capacity autocratic states in Asia and South America

(Boudreau 2004; Schock 2005). These sea changes in regime and governance have provided the social sciences with the raw data to gauge the effectiveness of nonviolent resistance. Much of these data are quantitative indicators in the international studies tradition, plus an emerging body of protest data (as the dependent variables) based on developments in database construction and machine reading of media reports, a methodological trend in the social movements field during this same period.[3] Domestically, in North American and Western European countries, democratic institutions and political norms have adjusted to broad social changes in class and economic structures to produce what have come to be called "social movement societies" (Meyer and Tarrow 1998), or the "movementization of society" (Melucci 1989), where protest is recognized and accepted as another means of doing politics – and, importantly, most of these activities are nonviolent as a matter of course. Whether they are intentionally so, as in the principled nonviolence à la Gandhi and Martin Luther King Jr., is a question we will examine in this volume as we probe different state contexts. Its second section offers several important and provocative considerations of regime contexts, how these affect mobilization, and the data used to analyze challenges.

This introductory chapter probes the intersections between these two research foci and their empirical groundings in democracies and nondemocracies, and especially this last category where so much of the nonviolence literature has focused. It is worth pointing out that repressive contexts are less studied in the literature of the social movements field. Indeed, an informed estimate would locate 80% of the field's research in Western liberal democracies and not repressive states – for obvious reasons of frequency of occurrence. Methodological risks also restrict the kinds of data available for repressive states, which tends to limit eyewitness reports from events in the streets and plazas. There are, of course, exceptions (cf., Bayat 2013; Fu 2018; Lee and Zhang 2013; Johnston 2005; O'Brien and Li 2006; Perry 2002; Stern and Hassid 2012; Straughn 2005 – plus Moss and Clarke in this volume), and by taking the two research strategies in tandem, large databases and street-level observation, we can advance the field in significant ways, as the collection of reports in this volume demonstrates. Moss's chapter six, Clarke's chapter eleven, plus my own empirical observations in this introductory essay, all take grassroots foci to engage the state side of the equation. Case's chapter deconstructs nonviolent protest events in repressive regimes with fine-grained observations about tactics, as does Isaac's in the twentieth-century US South.

More generally, the pages that follow will probe what the study of nonviolence can gain from the theoretical and methodological insights of the social movement field. Its narrative rests, above all, on the recognition that nonviolent movements are social movements, and that peaceful resistance is a form of contentious politics. The tools of analyzing the latter can and should be useful in understanding and situating the dynamics of the former. The themes of this chapter and those that follow all highlight that there is a strong syncretism between the two foci, and that that the analysis of one enriches the analysis of the other in ways that, we hope, will change conversations and research agendas for years to come. Let us begin by stepping back and making a few general observations about the overlaps between the two fields.

Dimensions of social movement analysis

Charles Tilly was a prescient analyst of the history of protest and politics and a leading theorist of contentious politics. He had little to say about nonviolence as a strategy, but a lot to say about the highly relevant concept of protest repertoires, their historical evolution, and their relation to the state – and, of course, nonviolent tactics are one element of the modern protest repertoire. In years of the field's early growth, he recognized that how analysts approach a protest movement not only shapes what they see but also directs attention to overlaps in conceptual and methodological perspectives. In his theoretical treatise on protest and the state, *From Mobilization to Revolution* (1978: 8–9), Tilly suggests that there are three fundamental dimensions to the study of social movements: (1) the protest actions that make up a movement's repertoire; (2) the ideas – including moral precepts – that define injustices, guide protests, unify members, and ultimately form the basis of collective identity; and (3) the groups and organizations that make up the movement by mobilizing and participating in the events. Forty years after Tilly penned these observations, we can broaden the scope of these three analytical dimensions to better reflect new findings and how the field has advanced, for example recognizing advances in network analysis in the organizational sphere, movement frames and collective identity in the moral-ideological sphere, and emotions and strategic adaptation in the performative sphere. There is a movement-centric quality to this three-part analysis, which we will expand in the next section by considering other actors in the field of contention, but for now, let us consider Figure 1.1 (next page), which updates Tilly's original analysis.

Groups, organizations, networks

As depicted by the top circle in the figure, a focus on mobilizing organizations must now include the fundamental network structure of a social movement (Diani 1992; Diani and McAdam 2003; della porta and Diani 2006), not just the focus on social movement organizations and their resources characteristic of the 1970s and 1980s. In other words, a focus on social movement structure means recognizing that there are numerous groups and organizations in the movement's orbit, networked by interpersonal and organizational linkages but also divergent in their overall assessment of what is to be done and how – an observation that invokes the other two dimensions. This means that, when we speak of nonviolent movements, some constituent groups may be firmly shaped by the discipline of nonviolent practice, but others may be less committed. There are empirical cases, as discussed by Benjamin Case in chapter ten, when protest movements characterized as "basically nonviolent" from a 30,000-foot perspective often have outbreaks of property destruction, fights, and violent confrontations with police. Moreover, there are outlier and renegade groups on the radical flank, whose consequences

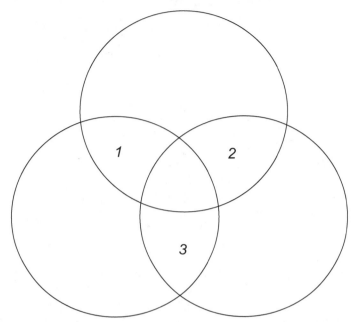

Organizational Sphere:
Relatively fixed networked relations among SMOs,
informal groups, and participants

Moral-Ideological Sphere:
Values, interests, beliefs, frames,
motivations, ideologies, identities

Performative Sphere:
Protest events as performed by
participating actors

Figure 1.1 Analytical dimensions of social movements

Source: Adapted from Tilly 1978: 9.

for the movement have been chronicled by Haines (1988). These variations are reflected by the overlapping segment two in the upper-right of Figure 1.1, which represents the intersections among the different organizations and how actions are actually performed in the street. The analyst interested in explaining these variations is invariably directed toward the center of the figure where dimensions of the ideas and meanings that unite groups and bind network configurations are brought into the analysis. Of this central intersection of ideas, organization, and performance, the chapters in this volume will have much to say.

The moral-ideological sphere

This is a dimension of social movement analysis that was underrepresented by resource mobilization and political process theories of the 1980s and 1990s, but resurrected in part by the popularity of the framing perspective (Snow and Benford 1988, 1992; Snow et al. 2014, 1986). Distinct from the theoretical concepts of the organizational dimension – social movement organizations (SMOs), their resources, structure, networked relations, ties to the state, notably elite accessibility – here we have factors such as moral and ideological commitment, collective identity, prognostic and motivational frames, and interpretative processes, that is, ways of looking at movements as mental constructs that precede action and guide it. This dimension of movement analysis was prevalent during the collective behavior phase of the field's development 50 years ago, when concepts such as grievances, relative deprivation, and social-psychological processes of meaning articulation drove the field's research. As Turner argued (1996), the rise of the resource mobilization perspective tended to obscure the moral dimension – throwing the baby out with the bathwater, so to speak – but recent dynamic and processed-oriented approaches better recognize that two dimensions are in recursive relationship, the relative importance of which is determined by the empirical case under consideration.

In the study of nonviolent movements, the realm of ideational constructs is absolutely central because herein reside the guiding principles of the struggle, whose normative guidance and moral authority vis-à-vis the state are key elements of how contention unfolds (Abu-Nimmer 2003; Barash and Webel 2009; King 1999; Magid 2005; Nepstad 2015a). Also, the role of religious beliefs in nonviolent movements resides here. Policy-oriented movement campaigns guided by faith or organized by faith-based groups are certainly not uncommon but are underrepresented when looking at the empirical distribution of contentious politics in the democratic West (but see Austin 2012; Nepstad 2004; Hondagu-Sotelo 2008; Wood 2002) and the distribution of research in the field of social movement and protest studies.

Protest performances

Tilly described the third dimension as the protest event, the performance of marches, demonstrations, and site occupations that are the defining activities of social movements and their fundamental means of attracting the attention of political elites. In my updated version of Tilly's diagram, I lay stress on the *performance* aspect of this event-action dimension to reflect developments in cultural sociology. The concept of social performance is central to the contemporary analysis of culture in the social sciences, whereby the action is analyzed in association with its interpretations among those who witness it and/or are engaged with it. This is a recursive process of creating culture, that is, the production of meaning through the interaction of the actors and the audience (Alexander and Mast 2006; Eyerman 2006; Alexander 2011; Johnston 2011a, 2016; Norton 2004). In a cultural-analytical sense, therefore, protests should not be analyzed solely in terms of movement events, but also by how they are interpreted by various audiences and onlookers, and their (performative) reactions to it.

The movement-centric character of the figure means that the full cast of players in protest performances, the onlookers, the counterprotesters, the police, the military, and other agencies of social control (especially relevant in repressive regimes) are underrepresented, and that the dynamic unfolding of movement performances is not adequately accounted for without bringing in "the other side" of the equation. In social movement analysis, the starting point of protest performances is the normative understandings of appropriate action that are part of the modern repertoire (Tilly 1978, 1995, 2006, 2008). In democracies, this includes normative understandings of the "other side" as well, most notably, the agents of social control who usually respect the right to protest – within limits, but, of course, not always. This means that the reportorial performances are dynamic and emergently interactive. These initial understandings of both sides are "brought to the street," where they are acted upon and strategically modified. Sometimes there occurs forcible constraint and even violent repression. This dynamic also holds regarding nonviolent protest, and it is in the protester-state dynamic that the power of nonviolent action most acutely unfolds in repressive states. Let us consider what social movement theory can tell us about this dark-dance performance among protesters and state agents in the protest-repression nexus as nonviolent performances unfold.

Social movement theory and nonviolence

A trend in social movement theory is the increasing emphasis on the dynamism of mobilization processes and on strategic aspects of state-challenger interactions. The seeds of this trend reach back 20 years to McAdam, Tarrow, and Tilly's program to identify the "robust processes" that operate in all episodes of political challenge (McAdam et al. 1996, 2001; McAdam and Tarrow 2011). It is fair to say that researchers of social movements and protest today increasingly recognize that important insights into collective action and its impacts come from dynamic, strategic, and processual perspectives (Alimi et al. 2012; Bosi et al. 2014; della Porta and Gbikpi 2012; Soule and King 2008).

More recent dynamic approaches include field theory (Agrikoliansky et al. 2005b; Crossley 2003; Fligstein 2001; Fligstein and McAdam 2012; Goldstone 2001; Mathieu 2012; McAdam and Boudet 2012; Péchu 2006) and a players-and-arenas perspective, recently elaborated by Duyvendak and Jasper (2015). Broadly speaking, these perspectives push the analysis toward more social-constructionist, process-oriented, and finer-grained analytical foci by emphasizing how the agentic social definition of the field unfolds among players. Duyvendak and Jasper observe (2015: 18) that a

> field's form of competition is usually taken for granted [and] . . . agreement is assumed to govern some parts of the field (cognitive understandings, goals, norms of behavior), while conflict governs others (competition for the stakes of the field), with a clear . . . boundary between them.[4]

As I will suggest in the next section, opening the door for greater diversity among players, recognizing the iterative and evolving ground rules of contention, and taking into consideration the changing stakes of political contention give the analyst not only a more accurate way of conceptualizing the resistant performances in autocratic regimes, but also sensitizes research to the complex organization of players on both the movement and states sides of the playing field. The key insight for our purposes is that these perspectives offer the analysis of nonviolent resistance some theoretical leverage to consider the interaction of multiple state agencies and elite actors, on the one hand, and a diffuse and evolving array of strategic challengers, on the other. The resulting domain of contention constitutes an empirical field in its own right, with its own emergent practices, logic, and patterns, as Isaac's chapter two analyzes in terms of the tactical adjustments of the African American civil rights movement, and as Nepstad's chapter four points out regarding the agencies of social control.

State players

The players-and-arena metaphor ideally accords equal attention to both sides of the mobilization process, as the state wields its resources to confront, channel, and control protester challenges. It is common that research in nonviolent action focuses on the tactical agency of the challengers but not so much the fine-grained adjustments on the part of state agents. A street-level perspective lays stress on the give and take of tactical adjustment, with the implicit recognition that all state agents do not necessarily march lockstep to the orders of political elites. As such, an important insight – one for which I will offer some modest examples shortly – is that there are times when the state should be deconstructed into its various players and not writ large as a monolith of counterforce and repression. Among the best research on antiauthoritarian movements (Franklin 2009, 2014, 2015; Inclán 2009, 2018; Ortiz 2013), measures of state repression tend toward generalizations of variable intensity of repression, often captured by figures on the size of security forces, state budgets on army and police, protester deaths and injuries, and similar quantifications. These studies contribute in important ways to our global understanding of nonviolent mobilization and serve as important guides to the theoretical enterprise by identifying general patterns. But they also can be informed and enriched by the finer-grained data that are characteristic of on-the-ground fieldwork, such as Moss's chapter on Jordanian activism, Clarke's chapter on Egyptian protests, and my own observations in the next section about the real-time interaction of police and protestors. Sociological studies with microdata on the repression-mobilization relationship are important complements to studies in the international-relations tradition that employ higher-level datasets. A dynamic approach to nonviolent resistance must consider the interaction between challengers and the state in all their complexity and with insights from different strategies of data collection.

As an elaboration of Tilly's rubric of social movement analysis, then, I suggest a parallel schematic to represent the "other side" of the mobilization-repression dynamic, the state in its layers of organizational, normative, and performative complexity (Figure 1.2). As Meyer's chapter points out, movements occur in state

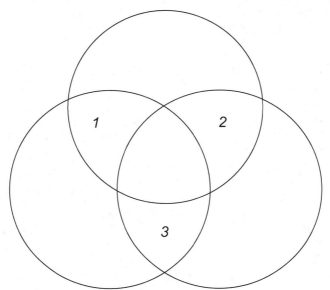

Political-Institutional Sphere:
Political parties and their civil-society ties, state institutions,
security apparatus, elite structures, military organization

Moral-Ideological Sphere:
Official state ideology, party discipline, the
interests, beliefs, motivations, and identities
of state actors

Performative Sphere:
Governance, extraction, and social control
as practiced at various administrative
levels by state actors

Figure 1.2 Dimensions of analysis for the state

contexts that have important consequences, and extending the tripartite characterization of movement analysis to the state captures the diversity of state contexts. Thus, there are three dimensions by which the analysis of the state may be
grouped and which serve as portals for the analyst's research program.

By far, the most common entry point for political science generally, and social
movement research in particular, is located at the top of the figure, which represents the institutional structures of governance, elite ties and networks, agencies
of extraction and the organization of violence, and social control – all common
themes in the social scientific analysis of political action. A much less common
focus is the lower left sphere, a dimension that represents the ideational constructs of the state, how ideologies are formed, how beliefs are disseminated and
enforced, and how meaning, morality, and normative patterns among state actors
are constructed. These are processes that influence not only the organizational
life of the state but also the commitment and engagement of state actors within
those organizations. To study the empirical reality of how the actors think about

the state and their roles in it, the analyst must confront the prospect of diversity and complexity in state institutions. As Dickson (2016) points out in his surveys of party members in China, party membership is for many a career path with luke-warm commitment, not one driven by little-red-book-waving devotion to Maoist thought. How commitment – and material interests – are distributed among actors in state and party institutions have important implications for the implementation of policy, including social control and censorship. This last observation directs the analyst to the empirical reality of the performative sphere, that is, as far as nonviolent direct action can be exerted and maintained, how exactly social control is applied "in the street."

Also included in the ideational dimension are the social-psychological forces of conformity and social pressure that foster the discipline of state actors. On the one hand, compared to social movement organizations, the moral life and interpreta-tive processes in state agencies are much more constrained, which often allows analysts to disregard the complexities therein as epiphenonemonal distractions. However, following Nepstad's analysis in chapter four and my own evidence in the next section, I suggest that there are times when the state is not a hermetically sealed leviathan of social control, with significant implications for the develop-ment of movements of oppositional challenge. When the incentives for compli-ance and the social forces of constraint and control are less relevant for state actors, that is, when moral considerations or performative discontinuities occur, things get interesting for the analyst. Let's take a closer look at the state side of the mobilization-repression equation for situations where there may be significantly less overlap and coordination, and thus openings and gaps where the opposition might flourish.

Police performing morally

The heading of this section invokes the link between thought and action, recog-nizing that actors in state and party institutions often experience a complex pull of different interpretations and commitments. In their enforcement of state policies, performance can and does deviate from institutional norms, with implications for the opposition that can be significant. We see this in a member of the Chinese Communist Party, who has family members who attend an underground Christian church. This is technically illegal for the family and ideologically unsustainable for disciplined cadres. How are they to respond? In this section, we will explore the fine-grained messiness of real life in repressive states and the effects it some-times has on the opposition. This is the microsociology of what might foment the defections and/or refusal decisions by the police and military that Nepstad so acutely chronicles in her chapter.

In the social movement literature, researchers on the mobilization-repression nexus have long recognized that the actions of both parties – the protesters and the state – vary and influence each other (Hoover and Kowalewski 1991; Lich-bach 1987; Moore 1998; Soule and Davenport 2009; Rasler 1996; Holmes 2012). We know that state elites and the security apparatus closely monitor expressions of dissent as threats to their power and privilege (della Porta 1995; della Porta and Reiter 1998). A consistent finding is that oppositional movements that pose credible challenges to the security of the state are met with strong repression (Cingranelli and Richards 1999; Davenport 2005; Regan and Henderson 2002), but the effects are variable depending on the type of regime and repressive tactics. Often, a more fine-grained focus sheds light on more complex relationships, such as how repression in authoritarian South Korea actually increased network alliances within social movements but decreased overt protests Chang (2008). In line with the blowback principle of nonviolent tactics, Loveman (1998) found that military repression stimulated protests actions in several South American authoritarian regimes. Yet the blowback threshold seems to be regime-specific and determined by many factors, as indicated by the brutal repressions in Tiananmen Square, 1989, or in Plaza de Tres Culturas, Mexico City, 1968, which stifled further mobilizations rather than encouraging them. From the perspective of the state, plotting exactly this line comprises the "dictators dilemma" (Dickson 2016; Francisco 2005), namely, applying enough social control to quell protest but not too much to cause a reaction that stirs outrage and mobilizes more intense protests.

A key factor in the repression-mobilization relationship is the loyalty of the security apparatus and the role of their defection in the success campaigns against autocratic states (Albrecht and Ohl 2016; Bayat 2017; Brooks 2013; Gelvin 2012; Hellyer 2016; Katz 2004; Nepstad 2011; Schock 2005). This is a crucial focus because the in-the-street performance of the police, army, and security apparatus directly influences nonviolent discipline among the protesters. In this section, I will argue that the loyalty of forces of social control is also a moral question, and it varies according to different actors in the security apparatus. This moral dimension and the variability among different strata and functional organization of the security forces are perspectives that are rarely pursued by researchers. Regarding the military, this involves the chain-of-command norms required to extract the obedience of (mostly) young men, who often have just recently left their villages or neighborhoods, to pursue the violent repression of peacefully protesting citizens. Whether to fire on fellow citizens – in some cases, who are just a step or two removed from friends, family, and compatriots of the security personnel – is a moral question that must be addressed by analysts seeking a comprehensive understanding.

Close investigation of the state's repressive apparatus can reveal complex moral and normative processes at work on the state side. First, to attribute actions such as defection, obedience, or following orders to just the military misses the complex organization of security services in high-capacity autocratic states. In al-Assad's Syria, prior to the civil war, there were no less than eighteen different branches of police, security, and military intelligence apparatus in the major cities. This is not to discount the military's role, which in autocratic states is often an important player in protest repression and social control (Belkin and Schofer 2003; Nepstad 2015a: ch 7; Pfaff 2006; Powell 2012; Quinlivan 1999), but rather to point out that the repressive apparatus of the state is not a homogeneous actor – a common but empirically inaccurate assumption. Different military units are located in different positions in Figure 1.2, which is to say there is divergence among them in terms of performance and moral-normative commitment to the regime.

There are typically special units, elite divisions, and republican guards chosen for loyalty to the president. These often play different roles in protecting the regime, and it is not uncommon that there are competing forces among them to guide their decisions of the commanders. Commitments to remain loyal to the existing regime and the premier, president, or party chairman, for many, are moral ones, but there may also be strong elements of self-interest that guide actions of top military leaders and praetorian guards and presidential units. The division between the military and special units and militias or elite security units gives rise to spaces of opportunity for the opposition. During the Arab Spring protests in Egypt, the army refused to fire on protesters, but security forces and hired party thugs waded into protests on Friday, January 29, 2011. In the next two days, the Egyptian army stood between protesters and the *mukhabarat* and armed supporters of the regime who had been called out by the ruling party (see Moss's chapter on Jordan). The military's role in the fall of the Mubarak regime in 2011 was crucial.

Apropos of the composition of these military units, officers must take caution in ordering conscripts to fire on protesting youth with whom they can identify strongly, risking breakdown in chain of command. This occurred numerous times in the radicalization of Syrian protests and their descent into civil war. In the northern Syria town of Jisr al-Shoughour, lower-level desertions had been reported for weeks in 2011 as the regime mobilized the army against the protesters. A large military operation against this Sunni stronghold meant that many Sunni conscripts were ordered to fire on townspeople. Scores refused, and some officers defected to aid the townspeople in their resistance (Zoeph and Shadid 2011). In Syria, compounding desertions were sectarian divisions in the military, whose officer corps was strongly composed by the Alawite minority – a Shiite sect – to which the al-Assad clan belonged. Recognition of potential breeches of loyalty is one of the main reasons for the multilayered organization of military force in authoritarian states, to which I referred earlier. Also (and often uncharted by researchers), these tribal and sectarian divisions and their effects on troop loyalty are frequently the reason for the use of mercenary thugs, ruffians, and vigilantes in autocratic states to repress resistance. The morality of patriotism and/or normative restraints on the chain of command are not present here, but financial compensation and mercenary self-interest take their place.

This diverse group of actors perform on the "unofficial" state side, and are often overlooked in comparative approaches to repression and regime change. I include here far less "moral actors" (although there are normative codes among them) such as thugs, ruffians, vigilantes, local militias, and even foreign mercenaries, who are commonly employed as enforcers and protectors of spheres of corruption among officials in the everyday, mundane business of the autocratic state[5] and can be mobilized to threaten activists and disrupt protest gatherings. These groups include gangsters, party members, and off-duty policemen known for their brutality, physical intimidation, and violent efficiency (Ong 2015; Volkov 2002). In any population, it is axiomatic that there is a proportion of people like this, known for their violent dispositions and amorality (or immorality), who are motivated by payment for their services rather than a principled defense of the regime or party. They are used as agents of enforcement and fear, especially during periods of increased dissident activity, or to terrorize individual citizens whose actions pose threats to political elites. Kaddafi armed his supporters in Tripoli to intimidate citizens from protesting and brought in paid thugs from Chad for enforcement (Therolf 2011). Thugs, rather than the police, are often used to intimidate reporters whose stories challenge political elites, as in the case of Mikhail Beketov, a newspaper editor who had often written about corrupt officials in Russia. His car was blown up, and he was badly beaten by armed thugs. Although the police promised an investigation, the case remains unsolved. According to one observer:

> These types of attacks or other means of intimidation . . . serve as unnerving deterrents [in Russia]. And in a few cases, in recent years the violence in the country has escalated into contract killings. Corruption is widespread and the government functions poorly, but [for obvious reasons] most journalists and nonprofit groups shy away from delving deeply into these problems.
>
> (Levy 2010)

One plausible estimate holds that over 100 newspaper reporters and editors have been murdered since 2000 in Russia for pursuing stories of regime corruption.[6]

That thugs and enforcers are available for hire should not obscure the fact that *Homo sapiens* are fundamentally moral species. This recognition brings us back to observations about moral and interpretative processes among the forces of social control and how they affect the performance dimension of state actors (Figure 1.2). I would like to close this section with some microsociological observations about the organization of the state that relates directly to the points about free spaces in the last section. In one of my earlier field studies (Johnston 2005), I interviewed a former Communist Party member who had worked as a censor for the Ministry of Information in a former Soviet Republic. The encounter occurred six years after the dissolution of Soviet Union and the subsequent independence of its autochthonous non-Russian republics that had made up the USSR. I had received the respondent's name by other oppositional activists, with the clear implication that he was known for his quiet activism within the ministry. In the party member's own words:

> I did what I could. There were people we answered to, and we were watched and had to be careful. But, for example, when, my boss was on vacation or had other projects, I could let things pass that otherwise would not go [books, collections of poetry, magazine articles]. I had to be cautious. One did what one could. I was not a hero. Some people were without fear, but I had a family and children and had to take care of them, but I did what I could within the system. I had decided that I could be more use working within the system.
>
> (Johnston 2005)

The quote was initially used to support observations about the forms of hidden resistance in repressive states (Johnston 2005, 2011b, 2014) in the vein of Scott (1985, 1990) and Bayat (2013, 2017). It remains a poignant statement, yet, at the time, comprised but one piece of the evidence for the claim of a small but pervasive subterranean opposition. But I now see there was much more going on, namely, the regime and its opposition exist in a dynamic relationship that extends to microscopic, quotidian levels of individual agency within agencies of social control.

I encountered this again several years later, in the context of a different project, during a conversation with a Syrian democratic activist (Johnston 2015). He was a physician who lived comfortably in his Damascus neighborhood. He had not hidden his dissident activism against the al-Assad regime, and his anti-regime activities were known to the *mukhabarat*. One evening, an agent of the secret service (and neighbor) came to his house and told him that he would be arrested soon, and that he should flee as soon as possible, which he did. Now a resident of the US, he owes his safety, and that of his family, to this example of what might be characterized as the "porousness" of the social control apparatus and the complexity of defection/refusal decisions. My research in the former Soviet Union offered another example: one respondent described a member of the *nomenklatura* who sometimes participated in discussions in an intellectual circle. When the talk went "too far" politically, the official would warn participants not to cross the line and put him in an awkward position.

Although anecdotal, these microlevel cases of conflicting performances reflect ambivalent moral stances among agents of social control. I suggest they are not uncommon. Police and army officers go home after work and have families and neighborhood friends. These are social relations that present a different way of viewing the moral choices they face. The duplicity that characterizes a lot of oppositional activism among dissidents – their public lies but private truths – in autocratic states, at least in early stages, is replicated among the actors on the other side, raising the consideration that there are moral agents for change in the state too. A Polish KOR activist mentioned that border officers helped transport dissident literature for them (Szporer 2012: 29). And to repeat an earlier example from a current project of mine: a Chinese Party official's mother and aunt's family attended an underground Christian church (see also Vala and O'Brien 2007). The cadre must live with this contradiction – party members must avow their atheism and are aware of the party's policy about illegal churches. She cannot speak of her family's faith – or perhaps more accurately – can only carefully and, at first, circumlocutiously mention it only among her most trusted friends, because, after all – the point of this section – the state is not all goose-stepping conformity, and others too know that life is messy and can give a bit of grace to a close friend, despite the party line. Obviously, this messiness is not enough to bring down a regime, or even, by themselves, precipitate mass refusals among security apparatus, but they do represent small areas – microareas might be a more appropriate term – where acts of resistance can bubble to the surface of daily life. For many citizens in autocratic states, daily life is nonpolitical and appears to be superficially quiescent about political resistance, yet a plausible hypothesis is that such messiness creates an ambience that (1) allows actions that can trigger more widespread resistance; and, regarding the "other side," (2) can play a role in disobedience and desertions among security forces by laying foundations of doubt and ambivalence.

The key insight is that authoritarian social control embraces multiple dimensions of commitment within a multileveled administrative apparatus. Most conspicuously, as the last examples demonstrate, it is incorrect to conceive high-capacity autocratic states as hermetically sealed juggernauts of social control and repression. Rather, the porousness suggested by these examples directs the analyst's attention to consider a continuum that runs from compromised service (the censor and the Syrian *mukhaharat* agent) to desertion, to disobedience, and then finally to mass defections à la Nepstad's chapter. The examples cited here document the insight of conflicted normative systems among some in the security forces and how they affect performance (area three in Figure 1.2). It is incorrect to assume the military, the security apparatus, and the police are homogeneous actors. It is an empirical question if variations in their performance can be dismissed as outlying anomalies when analyzing nonviolent resistance against the state.

Looking ahead

The chapters that follow are grouped into two sections. The first contains contributions that elaborate the nonviolence paradigm and advance our understanding, especially regarding its strategic implementation and effectiveness. The second section brings together essays and research reports that engage the paradigm and challenge it. The goal is to move the field forward, as I hope the modest observations of this introduction have done, by probing the intersection between movement studies and nonviolence studies. In both sections, the analytical foci alternate between the two sides of the mobilization-repression equation: activist strategies to confront the repressive state and state strategies that, in the complexity of its performance, are charged to maintain the status quo of power in the face of mounting protest challenges.

Appropriately, Larry Isaac's contribution begins the first section with a study of prototypical nonviolent movement in North America, the African American civil rights struggle of the twentieth century. He presents a fine-grained movement-focused analysis of how the nonviolent strategy of the southern civil rights movement established itself and evolved in the face of heavy repression from local police apparatus. Rather than assuming nonviolence as the only way the civil rights struggle could have unfolded, Isaac analyzes the tactical interaction of insurgents and how they responded creatively to push the movement's momentum in Southern states during the early 1960s. His analysis develops the important concept of *insurgent quality* to explain effective tactical adaptation. The chapter explores the synergy between social movement perspectives and nonviolence studies with a tactical focus on activist responses to street-level repression. Its data offer an on-the-ground view of strategic development that makes important contributions to both the history of the African American civil rights movement as well as to the nonviolence literature on activist choice and agency. Isaac's fine-grained data complement and enrich the findings of chapters that rely on aggregated datasets, which, if used exclusively, limit the methodological dimensions of Figure 1.1.

Chapter three by Kurt Schock also pursues tactical issues by shifting the regional context to the global South and the strategic focus to "rightful resistance" variations of nonviolent action by looking at land rights campaigns in Brazil and India. Just as organizations in the US civil rights movement pursued legal avenues to uphold federal antisegregation laws, Schock notes a similar legal strategy among nonviolent land rights movements. These movements seek to leverage existing laws and reform old ones about land ownership, usage, and equality – a strategy he notes that is linked to a decrease over the last 50 years in armed insurgencies pursuing agrarian-revolutionary strategies. Through comparisons of two contemporary movements, the Movement of Landless Rural Workers (Movimento dos Trabalhadores Rurais Sem Terra) in Brazil and India's Unity Forum (Ekta Parishad – founded by Gandhian activist Rajagopal P. V.), Schock analyzes similarities in the two movements' strategies to gauge their effectiveness. This chapter highlights how nonviolent "rightful resistance" leverages the legal sphere against the powerful forces that resist land reform. Schock closes by exploring the shape of the state dimension that may be conducive to these strategies.

The next chapter also pursues the intersection of activist strategy and state structure. Sharon Erickson Nepstad approaches it from the state's side of the equation, with a focus on the organization of social control. As I have discussed, scholars have identified the defection of security forces as increasing the likelihood of regime change. Nepstad examines the options available to the security apparatus at the apex of nonviolent mobilization and the consequences of those choices. A key contribution of the chapter lies in its application of Gandhi's call for a "constructive program" of building alternative institutions to the state's social control apparatus. Nepstad observes that nonviolent activists often promote defections rather than encourage a different view of security's institutional mission and culture. On a practical level, this means encouraging police and troops to refuse orders to repress protestors and uphold ideals of state institutions. In this sense, this chapter parallels the previous two by its contribution to strategic thinking about nonviolence. Neutralizing the state's repressive force by reframing the military's role opens the field for movement growth and strengthens the movement's autonomy. Similar to Schock's comparative approach, Nepstad's observations are based upon contrasting cases: where the military refused to interfere (Serbia in 2000 and Tunisia in 2011) and where the military defected to side with protestors (Philippines in 1986 and Egypt in 2011). This chapter is a contribution that develops a dynamic perspectives characteristic of the social movements literature. Importantly, it offers mesolevel insights about the state side of the equation, which are often missed by aggregated measures of state strategies.

Our next study also follows in the comparative-politics tradition with a comprehensive analysis of ten nonviolent protest waves and their outcomes in authoritarian regimes. Author James Franklin reinforces the volume's focus on the state by analyzing characteristics conducive to regime change. He finds that authoritarian governments that are internally divided or limited by semidemocratic institutions are most vulnerable (cf., Moss's chapter that follows, and later, Clarke's chapter) and then explores patterns of the state's repressive strategy, for example, when repression rises over time to meet mobilization levels. He finds that under these circumstances, backfire effects are mitigated and protests are less successful. Franklin's data also allow him to analyze the strategic adaptation of protesters, showing that state efforts to target dissident organizations tend to wear off over time. On this side of the playing field, he also identifies successful oppositional strategies: spatially focused confrontations in a central location and extended occupations yield high payoffs regarding regime change, but they also carry high risks because protest centralization allows for repressive concentration as well. Another strategy is serial protest, where protest events of short duration occur in a wave that, as a whole, lasts longer. Importantly, democratic reform is the most common outcome for these kinds of protest waves.

Dana Moss's chapter concludes the first section by examining an understudied but important aspect of the state-movement dynamic. For various reasons concerning their domestic and international legitimacy, authoritarian regimes often permit limited protest to occur aboveground – typically on a limited range of issues (as in Clarke's chapter eleven). She notes that the jury is still out regarding the impact of such protest campaigns on the overall march to regime change. Some researchers have argued that limited protests are but window dressing to legitimize authoritarian rule, and, ultimately, such protests are ineffective. A different perspective holds that moderate protests can accumulate and have significant effects. Moss is a political sociologist and movement researcher whose fieldwork on activism and repression focuses on the Kingdom of Jordan. Importantly, the on-the-ground data she gathers offer evidence that protests within regime-delimited civic spaces engage in a dynamic process of discovering, testing, and contesting. In Moss's terminology, they push the "red lines" of what is permissible, challenging regime practices and undermining sociopolitical norms that restrict dissent. Moss argues that moderate mobilization is an important and often neglected mechanism of peaceful change because activists (1) defend and expand the liberalizing the promises that authoritarian elites often used to legitimate their rule, even when there is little apparent progress toward democratization; and significantly, such practices (2) strengthen norms of citizenship in nondemocracies. The chapter concludes by outlining the implications of these mechanisms for the study of mobilization, authoritarianism, and social change more broadly.

Chapters in the first section are significant contributions to the ongoing development of nonviolent strategic action as a subfield of social scientific study and its impacts on the repressive state. Importantly, they mix methodologies typical of comparative international analysis and fine-grained fieldwork-based analysis to refine our understandings of nonviolence. The next section also elaborates methodological themes, posing questions about paradigm and data to ponder where the field may be headed. It brings both movement sociologists and political scientists of nonviolent strategies together in dialogue to push the field forward.

David Meyer, an eminent social movement scholar, opens this section with important questions about the broader political and social contexts in which non-violent campaigns develop. His essay ponders if the findings about the effectiveness of direct nonviolent resistance – that have recently animated so much interest in the field – are generalizable to all political contexts and all tactical arenas. Indeed, he provocatively asks whether nonviolent effectiveness is the correct question at all. Meyer identifies several factors that make nonviolent action attractive to social change advocates – among them, its persuasive moral force – and others factors that seem to make it especially effective. He spins a thread that runs through both this section and the previous one, namely, the diversity of actors in any movement campaign, including the targets, and the difficulties of ascribing causal influence to one particular actor or strategy. Apropos of this volume's central theme, state contexts are especially relevant in the success of any particular collective action strategy. He asserts that the broader social and political context strictly limits the extent to which nonviolent action can promote social change, and that the focus on efficacy of the tactic misses the point.

Erica Chenoweth, whose groundbreaking work with colleague Lynn Stephan has significantly shaped the nonviolence paradigm, contributes to the volume by reviewing three major objections lodged by various scholars to recent empirical work on the strategic effectiveness of nonviolent resistance. Importantly, her narrative elaborates some of the theoretical, empirical, or methodological advances that have been provoked by these challenges – most of which significantly advance the study of civil resistance. These ongoing debates provide fertile soil for the study of mobilization and resistance more generally, and are reminiscent of the methodological debate over event data and media biases among a past generation of movement researchers. This chapter is an important contribution to the volume, introducing a new thread of methodological critique into the book's conversation and engagement, which continues in the chapter that follows. Controversies about data help push for greater rigor, can provoke methodological innovations in the field through dialogue, and open new resources and data from which to further study the causes, dynamics, and outcomes of mass mobilization.

Daniel Ritter follows up on Meyer's opening observations about the complexity of causal influence. Ritter's study argues that in order to understand why some unarmed revolutionary movements fail to oust repressive regimes – that is, why civil resistance fails – it is necessary to consider, above all, the structural contexts in which such movements occur. Building on recent insights from the study of revolutions and focusing on the case of the popular Bahraini challenge against the authoritarian rule of the Khalifa monarchy in 2011, this chapter proposes that one particular structural context is especially important, namely the international relations of the country facing an unarmed insurrection. By laying stress on the centrality of macrostructural factors, the chapter explicitly challenges the dominant, agency-based conception of civil resistance success. Rather than depending on the protesters' ingenuity and preparedness for effective struggle, Ritter argues that certain transnational contexts constitute immense barriers to success that make unarmed revolutionary success highly improbable.

Benjamin Case poses questions about the relationship between violence and the success or failure of social movements. Recalling Gamson's (1990) and Piven and Cloward's (1977) seminal studies of movement strategies (see also Piven 2012), some scholars – and activists – claim that violence, or at the minimum, intense disruption, is necessary for regime change struggle. Advocates of nonviolence counter with the observation that violence undermines democratic transitions, and there have been strides in demonstrating the comparative efficacy of "nonviolent" tactics to challenge repressive regimes. This body of research has become a major force in shaping social movement strategy today, and in making practical calls for nonviolent discipline among movement strategists. This chapter argues that these arguments narrowly interpret the data and uphold a violence-nonviolence dichotomy that ignores low-level protestor violence that does not reflect the strategies and tactics of real social movements in the street. Case combines data on contentious political actions with data on civil resistance to find evidence that riots and property destruction co-occur in the vast majority of revolutions coded as "nonviolent." His findings demonstrate the need for a more rigorous operational definition of the nonviolent movement. Case provocatively suggests that scholars must move beyond the nonviolence paradigm as it is constituted so that analyses of unarmed movements include a broader range of collective actions that more accurately reflect the complexity of movement repertoires.

The final chapter by Killian Clarke completes the social movement-nonviolence circle by demonstrating how the study of nonviolent mobilization in repressive states can contribute to social movement theory generally. This is accomplished, not by identifying macrolevel structural factors as Ritter does, but by discovering mesolevel mechanisms through on-the-ground fieldwork. Like Moss's contribution in chapter six, Clarke's study is based on a method more commonly employed in social movement research, qualitative fieldwork and intensive interviewing. He uses thirty-five interviews with leaders, members, and affiliates of the Kefaya (Enough!) movement in Egypt, which mobilized six years prior to the January 25 (mostly) nonviolent uprising that toppled Mubarak. Kefaya was a nonviolent movement that faced significant threats and challenges from the regime, yet it overcame obstacles to make a sustained, reformist, and nonviolent challenge to the regime's status quo.

Significantly, Clarke's analysis identifies three mechanisms of coalition formation that operate in both democratic and nondemocratic settings and shows how characteristics of liberal authoritarianism – a regime structure also explored earlier by Moss – can accentuate their role. His analysis also leads to the counterintuitive proposition that liberal authoritarianism can actually facilitate nonviolent reformist mobilization by (1) accentuating "least-common-denominator goals" that unite different groups, (2) incentivizing involvement for existing civil society groups, and (3) enhancing the role of protest events in building cohesion among participants. This is an important study of how reform movements in repressive states get off the ground. In addition to showing the contributions of intensive fieldwork as a complementary method for the study of nonviolence in repressive regimes, his research report underlines the synergy between the social movement field and the nonviolent field – a key thread that is woven throughout our volume.

Notes

1 The social science of nonviolence studies developed out of interest in Gandhi's success-ful efforts to win independence from Great Britain. Gregg (1935) probed the moral basis of the tactic's efficacy in the movement's development, and Bondurant (1965) analyzed Gandhian thinking in terms of political science concepts. However, despite these early treatments, Nepstad (2011a) points out that the field of nonviolence studies remained marginal in sociology and political science until Sharp's systematic analysis of its practi-cal logic (1973) rather than its moral foundations.
2 Their chapters have evolved from a conference on nonviolent strategies and the state sponsored by the Hansen Foundation for Peace and Nonviolence at San Diego State University.
3 The growth of the social movements field similarly coincided with a methodological shift. An emphasis was placed on resources and organization in the 1970s and 1980s, which, in turn, brought greater ease quantifying these variables. The establishment of the field, and its scholarly reputation in sociology and political science in the second part of the last century, rested to a great extent on these methodological trends (see Crist and McCarthy 1996; Johnston 2014: 38–43, 131–136).
4 Duyvendak and Jasper (2015: 22–23) stress the importance the diversity of players, the players' definitions of what is occurring, and the changing rules of the game. Thus, they refer to speak of arenas rather than fields. This shift in terms emphasizes the more fluid elements of membership, goal definition, rules of the game, and spatialization, elements that Isaac stresses in his chapter two discussion of nonviolent tactics in the civil rights movement.
5 Official corruption and autocratic state regimes go hand in hand because of the lack of oversight and rule of law, which open opportunities for self-enrichment and venality among political elites.
6 We cannot authoritatively say that all these murders have been by local, low-level thugs. According to some observers, cases of poisoning suggest government agents with tools not commonly associated with hoodlums.

References

Abu-Nimmer, Mohammed. 2003. *Nonviolence and Peace Building in Islam: Theory and Practice*. Gainesville: University of Florida Press.

Ackerman, Peter, and Jack DuVall. 2000. *A Force More Powerful*. New York: St. Martin's Press.

Agrikoliansky, Eric, Olivier Fillieule, and Nona Mayer. 2005. *L'altermondialisme en France. La longue histoire d'une nouvelle cause*. Paris: Flammarion.

Albrecht, Holger, and Dorothy Ohl. 2016. "Exit, Resistance, Loyalty: Military Behavior during Unrest in Authoritarian Regimes." *Perspectives on Politics* 14(1): 38–52.

Alexander, Jeffery C. 2011. *Performative Revolution in Egypt: An Essay in Cultural Power*. London: Bloomsbury Academic.

Alexander, Jeffery C., Bernhard Giesen, and Jason L. Mast. 2006. *Social Performance: Symbolic Action, Cultural Pragmatics and Ritual*. New York: Cambridge University Press.

Alimi, Eitan Y., Lorenzo Bosi, and Chares Demetriou. 2012. "Relational Dynamics and Processes of Radicalization: A Comparative Framework." *Mobilization: An International Quarterly* 17: 7–26.

Austin, Allan W. 2012. *Quaker Brotherhood: Interracial Activism and the American Friends Service Committee, 1917–1950*. Urbana: University of Illinois Press.

Barash, David P., and Charles P. Webel. 2009. *Peace and Conflict Studies*. London: Sage.

Bayat, Asef. 1997. *Street Politics: Poor People's Movements in Iran*. New York: Columbia University Press.

Bayat, Asef. 2003. "The Street and Politics of Dissent in the Arab World." *Middle East Report* 226: 10–17.

Bayat, Asef. 2013. *Life as Politics*. Stanford, CA: Stanford University Press.

Bayat, Asef. 2017. *Revolution without Revolutionaries: Making Sense of the Arab Spring*. Stanford: Stanford University Press.

Belkin, Aaron, and Evan Schofer. 2003. "Towards a Structural Understanding of Coup Risk." *Journal of Conflict Resolution* 47(5): 594–620.

Bondurant, Joan. 1965. *Conquest of Violence: The Gandhian Philosophy of Conflict*. Berkeley: University of California Press.

Bosi, Lorenzo, Chares Demetriou, and Stefan Malthaner. 2014. *The Dynamics of Radicalization: A Processual Perspective*. Farnham, UK: Ashgate.

Boudreau, Vincent. 2004. *Resisting Dictatorship: Repression and Protest in Southeast Asia*. New York: Cambridge University Press.

Brooks, Risa. 2013. "Abandoned at the Palace: Why the Tunisian Military Defected from the Ben Ali Regime in January 2011." *The Journal of Strategic Studies* 26(2): 205–220.

Chang, Paul Y. 2008. "Unintended Consequences of Repression: Alliance Formation in South Korea's Democracy Movement (1970–1979)." *Social Forces* 87(2): 651–677.

Chenoweth, Erica, and Maria J. Stephan. 2011. *Why Civil Resistance Works: The Strategic Logic of Nonviolent Conflict*. New York: Columbia University Press.

Cingranelli, David L., and David Richards. 1999. "Respect for Human Rights after the End of the Cold War." *Journal of Peace Research* 44: 669–687.

Crist, John, and John McCarthy. 1996. "If I Had a Hammer: The Changing Methodological Repertoire of Collective Behavior and Social Movement Research." *Mobilization: An International Quarterly* 1(1): 87–102.

Crossley, Nick. 2003. "From Reproduction to Transformation: Social Movement Fields and the Radical Habitus." *Theory, Culture and Society* 206: 43–68.

Dalton, Russell. 2002. *Citizen Politics: Public Opinion and Political Parties in Advanced Industrial Democracies*, 3rd edition. New York: Chatham House Publishers.

Davenport, Christian. 2005. "Repression and Mobilization: Insights from Political Science and Sociology." Pp. vii–xvi in *Repression and Mobilization*, edited by Christian Davenport, Hank Johnston, and Carol Mueller. Minneapolis: University of Minnesota Press.

della Porta, Donatella. 1995. *Social Movements, Political Violence, and the State: A Comparative Analysis of Germany and Italy*. New York: Cambridge University Press.

della Porta, Donatella, and Mario Diani. 2006. *Social Movements: An Introduction*, 2nd edition. Malden, MA: Blackwell Publishing.

della Porta, Donatella, and Bernard Gbikpi. 2012. "Riots: A Dynamic View." Pp. 87–100 in *Violent Protest, Contentious Politics and the Neoliberal State*, edited by Hank Johnston and Seraphim Seferiades. Farnham, UK: Ashgate.

della Porta, Donatella, and Herbert Reiter. 1998. *Policing Protest: The Control of Mass Demonstrations in Western Democracies*. Minneapolis: University of Minnesota Press.

Diani, Mario. 1992. "The Concept of Social Movement." *Sociological Review* 40: 1–25.

Diani, Mario, and Doug McAdam. 2003. *Social Movements and Networks: Relational Approaches Collective Action*. New York: Oxford University Press.

Dickson, Bruce J. 2016. *The Dictators Dilemma*. New York: Oxford University Press.

Dodson, Kyle. 2011. "The Social Movement Society in Comparative Perspective." *Mobilization: An International Quarterly* 16(4): 475–495.

Duyvendak, Jan Willem, and James M. Jasper, eds. 2015. *Players and Arenas: The Interactive Dynamics of Protest*. Amsterdam: University of Amsterdam Press.

Eyerman, Ron. 2006. "Performing Opposition, or How Social Movements Move." Pp. 193–217 in *Social Performance: Symbolic Action, Cultural Pragmatics and Ritual*, edited by Jeffrey Alexander, Bernhard Giesen, and Jason L. Mast. New York: Cambridge University Press.

Fligstein, Neil. 2001. "Social Skill and the Theory of Fields." *Sociological Theory* 19: 2.

Fligstein, Neil, and Doug McAdam. 2012. *A Theory of Fields*. New York: Oxford University Press.

Francisco, Ronald A. 2005. "After the Massacre: Mobilization in the Wake of Harsh Repression." *Mobilization: An International Quarterly* 9: 107–126.

Franklin, James C. 2009. "Contentious Challenges and Government Responses in Latin America." *Political Research Quarterly* 62(4): 700–714.

Franklin, James C. 2014. "Democratic Revolutions and Those That Might Have Been: Comparing the Outcomes of Protest Waves under Authoritarian Rule." Paper prepared for delivery at the 2014 Annual Meeting of the American Political Science Association, Washington, DC, August 28–31.

Franklin, James C. 2015. "Persistent Challengers: Repression, Concessions, Challenger Strength, and Commitment in Latin America." *Mobilization: An International Quarterly* 20(1): 61–80.

Fu, Diana. 2018. *Mobilizing without the Masses: Control and Contention in China*. New York: Cambridge University Press.

Galtung John. 1969. "Violence, Peace, and Peace Research." *Journal of Peace Research* 6: 167–191.

Gamson, William A. 1990 [1975]. *The Strategy of Social Protest*, 2nd edition. Belmont, CA: Wadsworth.

Gelvin, James L. 2012. *The Arab Uprisings: What Everyone Needs to Know*. New York: Oxford University Press.

Goldstone, Jack. 2001. "More Social Movements or Fewer? Beyond Political Opportunity Structures to Relational Fields." *Theory and Society* 33: 333–365.

Gregg, Richard. 1935. *The Power of Nonviolence*. London: George Routledge.

Haines, Herbert. 1988. *Black Radicals and the Civil Rights Mainstream 1954–1970*. Knoxville: University of Tennessee Press.

Hellyer, H. A. 2016. *A Revolution Undone: Egypt's Road Beyond Revolt*. New York: Oxford University Press.

Holmes, Amy Austin. 2012. "There Are Weeks When Decades Happen: Structure and Strategy in the Egyptian Revolution." *Mobilization: An International Quarterly* 17: 391–410.

Hondagu-Sotelo, Pierette. 2008. *God's Heart Has No Borders*. Berkeley: University of California Press.

Hoover, Dean, and David Kowalewski. 1991. "Dynamic Models of Dessent and Repression." *Journal of Conflict Resolution* 36(2): 150–182.

Inclán, María. 2009. "The Sliding Doors of Opportunity: The Zapatistas and Their Cycle of Protest." *Mobilization: An International Quarterly* 14(1): 85–106.

Inclán, María. 2018. *The Zapatista Movement and Mexico's Democratic Transition*. New York: Oxford University Press.

Johnston, Hank. 2005. "Talking the Walk: Speech Acts and Resistance in Authoritarian Regimes." Pp. 108–137 in *Repression and Mobilization*, edited by Christian Davenport, Hank Johnston, and Carol Mueller. Minneapolis: University of Minnesota Press.

Johnston, Hank. 2011a. "Cultural Analysis of Political Protest." Pp. 327–347 in *Handbook of Politics*, edited by Kevin T. Leicht and J. Craig Jenkins. New York: Springer.

Johnston, Hank. 2011b. *States and Social Movements*. London: Polity.

Johnston, Hank. 2014. *What Is a Social Movement?* London: Polity.

Johnston, Hank. 2015. "Theory, Method, and the Robust Mechanism of Framing: Reflections on Syria and Palestine." *Civil Wars* 17(2): 1–24.

Johnston, Hank. 2016. "Dimensions of Culture in Social Movement Research." Pp. 414–428 in *The Sage Handbook of Cultural Sociology*, edited by David Inglis and Anamaria Almila. London: Sage.

Karatnycky, Adiran, and Peter Ackerman. 2005. *How Freedom Is Won: From Civil Resistance to Durable Democracy*. Washington, DC: Freedom House.

Katz, Mark N. 2004. "Democratic Revolutions: Why Some Succeed, Why Others Fail." *World Affairs* 166(3): 163–170.

King, Mary. 1999. *Mahatma Gandhi and Martin Luther King, Jr.: The Power of Nonviolent Action*. Paris: UNESCO.

Lee, Ching Kwan, and Yonghong Zhang. 2013. "The Power of Instability: Unraveling the Microfoundations of Bargained Authoritarianism in China." *American Journal of Sociology* 118(6): 1475–1508.

Levy, Clifford. 2010. "In Culture of Graft and Impunity, Russian Journalists Pay in Blood." *New York Times*. May 18: A1–A4.

Lichbach, Mark Irving. 1987. "Deterrence or Escalation? The Puzzle of Aggregate Studies of Repression and Dissent." *Journal of Conflict Resolution* 31: 266–297.

Loveman, Mara. 1998. "High-Risk Collective Action: Defending Human Rights in Chile, Uruguay, and Argentina." *American Journal of Sociology* 104(2): 477–525.

Magid, Shaul. 2005. "A Monk, a Rabbi, and the Meaning of This Hour: War and Nonviolence in Abraham Joshua Heschel and Thomas Merton." *Cross Currents* 552: 184–213.

Martin, Brian. 2007. *Justice Ignited: The Dynamics of Backfire*. Lanham, MD: Rowman and Littlefield.

Mathieu, Lilian. 2012. *L'espace des mouvements sociaux*. Paris: Editions du Croquant.

McAdam, Doug, and Hillary Boudet. 2012. *Putting Social Movements in Their Place*. New York: Cambridge University Press.

McAdam, Doug, and Sidney Tarrow. 2011. "Dynamics of Contention Ten Years On: A Special of Mobilization." *Mobilization: An International Quarterly* 16: 1–116.

McAdam, Doug, Sidney Tarrow, and Charles Tilly. 1996. "To Map Contentious Politics." *Mobilization: An International Quarterly* 1(1): 17–34.

McAdam, Doug, Sidney Tarrow, and Charles Tilly. 2001. *Dynamics of Contention*. New York: Cambridge University Press.

Melucci, Alberto. 1989. *Nomads of the Present*. Philadelphia: Temple University Press.

Meyer, David S., and Sidney Tarrow. 1998. "A Movement Society: Contentious Politics for the New Century." Pp. 1–28 in *The Social Movement Society: Contentious Politics for the New Century*, edited by David S. Meyer and Sidney Tarrow. Lanham, MD: Rowman and Littlefield.

Moore, Will. 1998. "Repression and Dissent: Substitution, Context and Timing." *American Journal of Political Science* 42: 851–873.

Nepstad, Sharon Erickson. 2004. *Convictions of the Soul*. New York: Oxford University Press.

Nepstad, Sharon Erickson. 2011. *Nonviolent Revolutions: Civil Resistance in the Late 20th Century*. New York: Oxford University Press.

Nepstad, Sharon Erickson. 2015a. *Nonviolent Struggle: Theories, Strategies and Dynamics*. New York: Oxford University Press.

Nepstad, Sharon Erickson. 2015b. "Nonviolent Resistance Research." *Mobilization: An International Quarterly* 204: 415–426. A special issue on Nonviolence and Social Movements.

Norton, Ann. 2004. *Ninety-Five Theses on Politics, Culture, and Method*. New Haven, CT: Yale University Press.

O'Brien, Kevin J., and Lianjiang Li. 2006. *Rightful Resistance in Rural China*. New York: Cambridge University Press. 8(1): 51–64.

Ong, Lynette. 2015. "Thugs for Hire: State Coercion and Everyday Repression in China." Paper prepared for the workshop, Collective Protest and State Governance in China's Zi Jinping, Harvard-Yenching Institute, Harvard University, May 18.

Ortiz, David. 2013. "Rocks, Bottles, and Weak Autocracies: The Role of Political Regime Settings of Contention-Repression Interaction." *Mobilization: An International Quarterly* 183: 289–312.

Péchu, Cécile. 2006. *Droit au logement, genèse et sociologie d'une mobilisation*. Paris: Dalloz.

Perry, Elizabeth J. 2002. *Challenging the Mandate of Heaven: Social Protest and State Power in China*. New York: M. E. Sharpe.

Pfaff, Steven. 2006. *Exit-Voice Dynamics and the Collapse of East Germany*. Durham, NC: Duke University Press.

Piven, Frances Fox. 2012. "Protest Movements and Violence." Pp. 19–28 in *Violent Protest, Contentious Politics, and the Neoliberal State*, edited by Seraphim Seferiades and Hank Johnston. Farnham, UK: Ashgate.

Piven, Frances Fox, and Richard Cloward. 1977. *Poor People's Movements*. New York: Pantheon.

Powell, Jonathan. 2012. "Determinants of the Attempting and Outcome of Coups d'Etat." *Journal of Conflict Resolution* 56(6): 1017–1040.

Quinlivan, James T. 1999. "Coup-Proofing: Its Practices and Consequences in the Middle East." *International Security* 24(2): 131–165.

Rasler, Karen. 1996. "Concessions, Repression, and Political Protest in the Iranian Revolution." *American Sociological Review* 61(1): 132–152.

Regan, Patrick M., and Errol Henderson. 2002. "Democracy, Threats and Political Repression in Developing Countries: Are Democracies Internally Less Violent?" *Third World Quarterly* 23(1): 119–136.

Rucht, Dieter. 1999. "The Impact of Environmental Movements in Western Societies." Pp. 204–224 in *How Movements Matter: Theoretical and Comparative Studies on the Consequences of Social Movements*, edited by Marco Giugni, Doug McAdam, and Charles Tilly. Minneapolis: University of Minnesota Press.

Schock, Kurt. 2005. *Unarmed Insurrections: People Power Movements in Nondemocracies*. Minneapolis: University of Minnesota Press.

Schock, Kurt. 2015. "Rightful Radical Resistance: Mass Mobilization and Land Struggles in India and Brazil." *Mobilization: An International Quarterly* 20(4): 493–515.

Scott, James C. 1985. *Weapons of the Weak*. New Haven, CT: Yale University Press.

Scott, James C. 1990. *Domination and the Arts of Resistance*. New Haven, CT: Yale University Press.

Sharp, Gene. 1973. *The Politics of Nonviolent Action*. Boston: Porter Sargent Publishers Inc.

Snow, David A., and Robert D. Benford. 1988. "Ideology, Frame Resonance, and Participant Mobilization." Pp. 197–217 in *International Social Movement Research*, edited by Bert Klandermans, Hanspeter Kriesi, and Sidney Tarrow. Greenwich, CT: JAI Press.

Snow, David A., and Robert D. Benford. 1992. "Master Frames and Cycles of Protest." Pp. 133–155 in *Frontiers of Social Movement Theory*, edited by Aldon D. Morris and Carol McClurg Mueller. New Haven, London: Yale University Press.

Snow, David A., Robert D. Benford, Holly J. McCammon, Lyndi Hewett, and Scott Fitzgerald. 2014. "The Emergence, Development, and Future of the Framing Perspective: 25+ Years since Frame Alignment." *Mobilization: An International Quarterly* 19(1): 23–45.

Snow, David A., E. Burke Rochford, Jr., Steven K. Worden, and Robert D. Benford. 1986. "Frame Alignment Processes, Micromobilization, and Movement Participation." *American Sociological Review* 51: 464–481.

Soule, Sarah A., and Christian Davenport. 2009. "Velvet Glove, Iron Fist or Even Hand?" *Mobilization: An International Quarterly* 14: 1–22.

Soule, Sarah A., and Jennifer Earl. 2005. "A Movement Society Revisited: The Character of American Social Protest, 1960–1986." *Mobilization: An International Quarterly* 10: 345–364.

Soule, Sarah A., and Brayden G. King. 2008. "Competition and Resource Partitioning in Three Social Movement Industries." *American Journal of Sociology* 113: 1568–1610.

Stern, Rachel E., and Jonathan Hassid. 2012. "Amplifying Silence: Uncertainty and Control Parables in China." *Comparative Political Studies* 45(10): 1230–1254.

Straughn, Jeremy Brooke. 2005. "'Taking the State at Its Word': The Art of Consentful Contention in the German Democratic Republic." *American Journal of Sociology* 110(6): 1598–1650.

Szporer, Michael. 2012. *Solidarity: The Great Workers Strike of 1980*. Lanham, MD: Lexington Books.

Therolf, Garrett. 2011. "Kadafi Using Civilian Supporters to Clear Away Libyan Protesters." *Los Angeles Times*. February 26. www.latimes.com/news/nationworld/world/middleeast/la-fg-libya-kadafi-20110227.0.6062616.story

Tilly, Charles. 1978. *From Mobilization to Revolution*. Reading, MA: Addison-Wesley.

Tilly, Charles. 1995. *Popular Contention in Great Britain 1758–1834*. Cambridge, MA: Harvard University Press.

Tilly, Charles. 2006. *Regimes and Repertoires*. Chicago: University of Chicago Press.

Tilly, Charles. 2008. *Contentious Performances*. New York: Cambridge University Press.

Turner, Ralph. 1996. "The Moral Issue in Collective Behavior and Collective Action." *Mobilization:* 1(1): 1–15.

Vala, Carsten T., and Kevin J. O'Brien. 2007. "Attraction without Networks: Recruiting Strangers to Unregistered Protestantism in China." *Mobilization: An International Quarterly* 12: 79–94.

Volkov, Vadim. 2002. *Violent Entrepreneurs*. Ithaca, NY: Cornell University Press.

Wood, Richard L. 2002. *Faith in Action*. Chicago: University of Chicago Press.

Zoeph, Katherine, and Anthony Shadid. 2011. "Assad Brother Plays Big Role in Ruling Syria." *New York Times*. June 8: A1.

Part I

Nonviolence and social movements

Elaborations

2 Performative power in nonviolent tactical adaptation to violence

Evidence from US civil rights movement campaigns

Larry W. Isaac

The sociology of the US civil rights movement has emphasized the structural conditions and organizational infrastructures that help account for the movement's emergence, trajectory, and impact (e.g., McAdam 1982; Morris 1984; Andrews 2004; Luders 2010). Underplayed in this work is the agency and power of nonviolent praxis itself. It is, of course, well known that the southern civil rights movement employed nonviolent direct action and is in many ways a poster child for the strategy. It is less well understood how that came to be, how nonviolence was employed in the face of brutal repression from white supremacist opposition, and the form of power inherent in it. In fact, much of the otherwise excellent research on the movement never problematizes the use of nonviolent strategy. Too often we are left with the tacit view that there was only one way to challenge Jim Crow institutions, or that nonviolence was inevitable, it could be no other way.

My purpose here is to focus on tactical adaptation to counter-violence. Simply put, I ask how nonviolent insurgents responded when assaulted with violence by white supremacist counterforces. How did movement agents adapt nonviolent strategy in concrete tactical form when faced with violent assault?

The expectation of counter-violence is a presupposition for this question, as it is in the nonviolence studies literature (e.g., Sharp 1973; Schock 2005; Chenoweth and Stephan 2011; Nepstad 2015) and as it was for movement participants. The Jim Crow system was built upon and reproduced by repression and violence, so one should not expect that it would concede readily and peacefully to any sort of insurgent challenge, nonviolent or not. The long process of developing nonviolent strategy and the ways it was deployed tactically are both a function, in part, of the violent social system within which it was embedded.

Effective nonviolent tactical adaptation to violent counterassault is an exercise in a particular form of power, performative power (Alexander 2011; Reed 2013). However, before nonviolent praxis could be exercised in a militant, effective form of performance, there were decades of strategic development that took place in various kinds of social movement schools and through experimental practice outside the South (see Isaac et al. 2012, 2017; Chabot 2012). These schools cultivated movement intellectuals (Eyerman and Jamison 1991) and high-quality movement cadre.

My analysis illustrates how effective tactical adaptation to violence was deployed in five major movement campaigns. It also makes clear that core cadre, trained in a premier movement school in Nashville, were instrumental in all five of these key campaigns during the movement heyday (1960–1965). Evidence also shows, at least during this period, that violent repression sometimes worked to temporarily slow movement actions, but never fully defeated the movement.[1] As insurgents adapted – sometimes quickly on the fly, sometimes more gradually – to forms of violent repression, they produced important lessons and a defensive tactical repertoire in addition to the more offensive repertoire featured in the literature (e.g., McAdam 1983; Morris 1984).

The creative and effective tactical adaptation to violence in these campaign episodes suggests several important implications that contribute to our understanding of (1) nonviolent praxis in the southern civil rights movement, (2) movement tactical interactions with violent adversaries, (3) the importance of making power explicit in social movement studies, in this case performative power, and (4) how the repertoire of nonviolent direct action was augmented by innovation on the defensive side of insurgent actions.

Social movement scholars have studied cases of strategic shifts away from nonviolence to violence (e.g., McAdam 1982, 1988; Maney 2012; Santaro and Fitzpatrick 2015). I take a different approach by focusing on tactical adaptation to violence in major campaigns throughout the movement's heyday. When faced with a major violent assault or a series of highly repressive acts, how did movement agents tactically adjust their direction? And who conceived of the tactical response? In this way, I gain leverage on (1) adaptations that insurgents created in response to violent repression and (2) conditions that may structure the efficacy of such tactical adaptations, especially insurgent quantity and quality (products of strategic development) as elements of tactical adaptation.[2]

Nonviolent tactical adaptation to violent repression

Nonviolent collective action is contentious action consisting of strategy and tactics designed for producing social change, "a method for fighting oppression and injustice" (Nepstad 2015: 2). It is a civilian-based form of struggle that activates social, economic, and political power sources without resorting to violence or the threat of violence (Nepstad and Kurtz 2012; Sharp 2005). While some pacifists gravitated to the making of the nonviolent repertoire in the mid-twentieth century, nonviolence should not be confused with pacifism, which is the "principled opposition to war and the use of violence for political purposes" (Nepstad 2015: 2).

Nonviolent collective action typically moves outside institutional channels and can assume a variety of different forms that carry varying degrees of transgression and disruptive impact, including (1) persuasion through protest, (2) withdrawal of cooperation (e.g., boycotts, strikes), (3) disruptive interventions (e.g., sit-ins, freedom rides), and (4) building alternative or parallel institutions (e.g., Mississippi Freedom Democratic Party). In the long history of nonviolent collective action, some activists developed into "principled" (e.g., Gandhi), often religiously grounded, and others into "pragmatic" (e.g., Sharp) practitioners (Nepstad 2015: 5), what was often referred to during the civil rights movement as "nonviolence as a way of life" versus "nonviolence as a tactic." In either case, if nonviolence is to have a chance of producing significant social change, it requires careful attention to strategy and tactics, and the performance quality of its agents.

A perennial debate within and outside nonviolent movements, especially those of substantial size and with participants who think of nonviolence solely in tactical terms, is the question of nonviolent efficacy in the face of persistent violent repression. Can nonviolent insurgents maintain movement momentum when faced with heavy repression and violence? If so, how do they respond to such countermeasures?

To answer this question, I draw on conceptual insights from social movement scholarship on strategy and tactics and from nonviolence and civil resistance scholarship. Per nonviolence scholarship, I focus on how nonviolent insurgents actually responded to violent repression. This question is movement-significant because (1) nonviolent movements should expect to face violent repression,[3] (2) how nonviolent agents respond to violence plays an important role in activating the power of nonviolent praxis, and (3) movement resilience in the face of such repression is a major predictor of the likelihood of success (Nepstad 2015; Schock 2005).

On the other hand, sociological movement scholarship has less to say about nonviolence per se, but is useful for conceptualizing strategy and tactics (e.g., McAdam 1983; Ganz 2000; Andrews 2004; McCammon 2012). For my question, a modest extension of McAdam's theory of tactical innovation will serve as a starting point:

> Lacking institutionalized power, challengers must devise protest techniques that offset their powerlessness. This is referred to as a process of *tactical innovation*. Such innovations, however, only temporarily afford challengers increased bargaining leverage. In chess-like fashion, movement opponents can be expected, through effective tactical adaptation, to neutralize the new tactic, thereby reinstituting the power disparity between themselves and the challenger.
>
> (McAdam 1983: 735)

Tactical innovation is defined as "the creativity of insurgents in devising new tactical forms" (McAdam 1983: 736). On the other side, *tactical adaptation* is "the ability of opponents to neutralize these moves through effective tactical counters." The two-sided combination of acts define the ongoing process of *tactical interaction*. McAdam argues that the tactical innovation side of this interaction was responsible, at least in part, for driving the pace of insurgency during the civil rights movement's heyday (p. 736).

While McAdam's (1983) interest was how innovation in tactical forms – shifts from say boycotts to sit-ins to freedom rides to community campaigns – could serve to hasten the pace of the movement generally, my focus is on tactical adaptation by nonviolent insurgents to violent assaults on them. In McAdam's (1983) usage, tactical adaptation refers to how opponents – white supremacist forces

Table 2.1 Partial models of movement – countermovement tactical interaction

Panel A: McAdam (1983): quantitative probabilistic assessment		
insurgent tactical innovation (shift to new tactical form) →	counter tactical adaptation (unobserved) →	pace of movement actions
Panel B: Present focus: qualitative case assessment		
counter movement acts of repression and violence →	insurgent nonviolent tactical adaptation →	movement momentum and campaign outcome

in this case – responded to forms of collective action deployed by movement activists. Panel A of Table 2.1 illustrates his focus. I shift the emphasis of tactical adaptation from the opposition to that of the nonviolent civil rights insurgents in Panel B. Therefore, by "tactical adaptation" in this context, I mean "nonviolent movement tactical adaptation" as the ability of movement agents to creatively adapt when they face violent repression from the opposition.[4] In light of one of the core principles of nonviolent action – i.e., that a violent assault must always be answered nonviolently (e.g., Lawson 1961) – the question of tactical adaptation to violence is crucial on practical grounds and an important window into the operation of a particular kind of power.

Strategic development of nonviolent performative power

Movement strategies are broad, usually long-term methodological plans of action for attaining social change goals. Sometimes nascent movements begin in rather spontaneous fashion without clear strategy; but others unfold over long stretches of history and in the process produce a powerful transformation in contentious repertoire, what I refer to as strategic development. The long-term strategic development of nonviolent praxis in the civil rights movement was crucial to the major take-off in 1960, and also necessary for full understanding of the cases of tactical adaptation analyzed below.

An important part of strategic development in the long civil rights movement[5] required that nonviolence become the modal strategy within a repertoire (Tilly 2006) of several other major contenders. The pre-WWII repertoire of contention consisted of several major forms of action including: armed self-defense (e.g., Tyson 1998; Hill 2004; Strain 2005; Jeffries 2009; Cobb 2014); institutionalized strategies, namely electoral politics (outside the South) and legal approaches best exemplified by the National Association for the Advancement of Colored People's (NAACP's) court battles against lynching and school desegregation since its founding in 1909; and aesthetic or artistic activism practiced by black writers, poets, musicians, artists, actors, and athletes who turned their art, their aesthetic labor, toward movement ends.[6]

During the later nineteenth and early twentieth centuries, nonviolent direct action was also part of the protest repertoire directed at segregated schools and transit (e.g., horse-drawn travel cars, trolley cars), and by the Great Depression, hiring practices became targets in some businesses (Meier and Rudwick 2007). But prior to the 1950s, these actions did not give rise to

> a nonviolent movement or even envisioned one, either the protest was a spontaneous and localized expression of black anger at the growth of segregation or it was simply one tactic of a group or organization that had no special commitment to nonviolence.
>
> (Fredrickson 1995: 231)

Protests were small-scale, isolated, episodic, outside the South, unchained or uncoupled to any communities of insurgent development, and prior to the 1940s, owed virtually nothing to Gandhi (Meier and Rudwick 2007). In short, there was no strategic development guiding these early nonviolent protests. Too often contemporary scholarship misses this process, thereby producing an ahistorical conception of nonviolent protest.

By *strategic development*, I mean the long-term, struggle-laden process of learning and experimentation associated with producing clarity on strategic direction and enhancing strategic capacity. My meaning of strategic development is consistent with the idea of movement strategizing as developmental learning, enchaining of strategic knowledge and social relations that is both path dependent and cumulative. Because these decisions are cumulative and often innovative, they can lead to transformative events (Sewell 2005) or moments that signal new directions and possibilities for collective action.

The process of strategic development in the civil rights movement involved diffusion of ideas about strategy that moved not only within the US but internationally, namely from Gandhi's struggles in India. Chabot (2010) and Isaac et al. (2012) have featured the role of dialogical diffusion in the flow and reconfiguration of the Gandhian repertoire in the US. This is diffusion involving face-to-face interaction, intellectual struggle over strategy as understood in one context and its potential resonance and adaptability in another context. In short, it involved a long-term process of collective learning (Chabot 2012: 4) about the Gandhian repertoire and how it might be used, in combination with other indigenous cultural materials, to shape a nonviolent strategy capable of attacking southern Jim Crow in an effective manner.

This process of dialogical, learning-based diffusion was most effectively fostered and developed within "social movement schools" (Isaac et al. 2012), those organizational spaces deliberately created to educate, mentor, train, and otherwise seek to prepare individuals for work as effective movement agents (Isaac et al. 2017). Over the long civil rights movement, these schools took on a variety of different forms (Isaac et al. 2017), including (1) critical communities (Rochon 1998) such as black intellectuals at Howard University engaged in early discussion, debate, teaching, and writing about Gandhian strategy and its potential appropriateness for the assault on Jim Crow (Isaac et al. 2012); (2) interracial institutes on strategy that grew out of the coalition between A. Philip Randolph's March on Washington Movement (MOWM) affiliates with Bayard Rustin and Fellowship of

Reconciliation (FOR) and Congress of Racial Equality (CORE) chapters (Gilmore 2008; Siracusa 2017); (3) movement halfway houses such as the Highlander Folk School (Morris 1984); (4) FOR traveling workshops; and (5) local organic movement workshops such as the Lawson-run Nashville workshops (Isaac et al. 2012, 2016). The point is that the potential power of Gandhian strategy had to go through a difficult process of translation, experimentation, and finally full-scale implementation (Chabot 2012), a trajectory punctuated by several major moments that transformed and extended the repertoire and, in the process, shaped the movement. These moments included the (1) mass Americanization of Gandhian strategy brought about by the coalition between A. Philip Randolph's MOWM with Bayard Rustin and FOR and CORE chapters[7] (Gilmore 2008; Siracusa 2017); (2) the personal transformation of Martin Luther King to nonviolence as a way of life in and the success of the Montgomery bus boycott campaign in 1955 (see Carson 2010); and (3) the role of the Nashville movement launched in the context of and contributing to sit-in fever of spring 1960 (see Isaac et al. 2012). This third transformation in strategic development sets the stage for the following analysis of tactical adaptation and, therefore, requires further comment.

In the winter-spring of 1960, the third major moment in strategic development of nonviolent strategy unfolded with the student-led sit-in campaigns. While Montgomery signaled the potential for nonviolent movement impact, in fact very little movement action happened in the years between Montgomery and 1960. There were a few other bus boycotts and the school desegregation confrontation in Little Rock, but nothing that was energizing or driving the movement forward. To many, the movement appeared to have stalled. In the words of James Lawson (1961) – one of the master tacticians of the movement – it was now necessary to build on and "make many Montgomerys" and to do so by training a "nonviolent army."

The sit-in fever that confronted Jim Crow segregation at lunch counters, movie theaters, and other businesses across scores of southern cities accelerated the pace of the movement. This was a major turning point because it (1) produced massive youth participation in the movement for the first time (along with subsequent founding of the Student Nonviolent Coordinating Committee), (2) used a more daring militant and transgressive tactic than the earlier boycotts, (3) generated new energy associated with the innovative tactic that spawned related mimicking tactics (jail-ins, stand-ins, swim-ins, lay-ins), and (4) sparked preparation in some locations (like Nashville) that produced a special cadre of committed activists (Isaac et al. 2012, 2016). All of this helped increase the pace of actions over the heyday of the movement.

These prior developments and collective learning that grew from them were necessary not only for advancing strategy but also for learning how to execute concrete tactics in a way that could tap the full power of nonviolence. Power is certainly implicit in many accounts of the civil rights and other movements, but it is not conceptualized in a direct and explicit manner. For example, when analysts point to the need for mobilizing material resources relative to the opposition, a material relational power is being implicitly invoked. Alternatively, when analysts highlight the importance of framing the movement's message for a wider audience, a form of discursive power is being signified. These are both, without a doubt, important forms of power in social movement dynamics.

The dimension of power that forms the central axis of nonviolent direct action in the analysis which follows is that of performative power. By *performative power*, I mean (following Reed 2013: 203) "how situated action and interaction exerts control over actors and their future actions." Performative power is often at the heart of what social movement actors do in public. In the nonviolent civil rights movement, it was absolutely essential. One way we can see performative power at work is to examine how movement activists responded to violent assaults designed to mute and destroy their message and actions.

If the civil rights movement can be understood as a struggle for "civic repair," the attempt to include the excluded within the equalizing promise of democratic civil society (as Alexander 2011: 147 puts it), then effective nonviolent tactical adaptation to violent assault would be crucial. As movement agents acquired more and more experience in directly confronting violent adversaries in a creative manner, they accumulated a repertoire of tactical adaptations that was informed by and expanded nonviolent praxis. These performances of tactical adaptation, when effectively executed, contributed to persuasion that had a power to (1) both energize participants and maintain movement momentum, (2) facilitate emotional and moral identification of a wider audience, often whites located outside the South,[8] (3) produce change by removing Jim Crow arrangements, and (4) do so in a way that prefigured the desired new society. Tactical adaptation is not only a creative action in response to repressive violence, it is also an important vehicle for symbolic communication associated with the nonviolent performance, performative power.

Next I follow a key thread of nonviolent performance in the southern movement, one that was launched from Nashville and propelled through a series of major campaigns between 1960 and 1965. The core of my argument is that effective nonviolent tactical adaptation generated performative power for the movement, and that was heavily dependent on high-quality insurgents who had learned how to live nonviolently and/or use nonviolent direct action for social change. Performative power in the sense deployed here is shown to be autonomous from or not simply parasitic on other dimensions of power such as relational or discursive power.

Methods and case selection

Since my concern is nonviolent movement tactical adaptation to violent repression, I focus on campaign interaction sequences, sequences of struggle in which violence in one form or another is directed at movement agents. Then I follow movement actions post-violence encounter. I call this "episode sequence analysis," which highlights a specific segment of a campaign interaction sequence.

Tactical adaptation is a type of performance, one with potential power. Making claims about power is linked to making claims about impact. Here I gauge the performative power of tactical adaptation to violence in two ways. The first is by asking if the adaptation contributes to maintaining movement momentum; in other words, did the tactical adaptation keep the violent assault from stopping the movement? The second and more stringent indicator is evidence that the tactical adaptation likely contributed to local campaign success.

All episode sequence cases are drawn from major campaigns during the 1960–1965 period, the "heyday" of the southern civil rights movement (McAdam 1982). By limiting case selection to this period, I produce approximate controls for several movement and context conditions, including important nonviolent strategic development that took place during the 1940s, 1950s, and early 1960s (discussed previously); political party of the presidency; the impact of Cold War context on federal government actions (McAdam 1998); and phase of movement development (McAdam 1982). The five episode cases include (1) the Nashville business desegregation movement during spring 1960; (2) the initial CORE Freedom Ride launched in May 1961; (3) the continuation or second Freedom Ride from Montgomery to Jackson, Mississippi, in May 1961; (4) the Birmingham campaign in spring 1963; and (5) the Selma-to-Montgomery march in spring 1965.

For each case, I describe the campaign setting, the violent assault on the movement, nonviolent tactical adaptation, impact of the adaptation, and the general lesson for nonviolent praxis that might be drawn from each case. These features are summarized in advance for each case in Table 2.2.

Table 2.2 Tactical adaptation to violence: cases from civil rights movement campaigns

Case 1: Nashville Business Desegregation Movement, April 1960

Violent event:	bombing of black civil rights movement lawyer's house
Tactical adaptation:	mass march culminating in public confrontation with mayor
Impact:	contributed to local desegregation success and to wider movement momentum
Lesson:	harness violent events for moral suasion to produce local "backfire"

Case 2: Initial CORE Freedom Ride, May 1961

Violent events:	bombing of bus and mob attacks on riders
Tactical adaptation:	new wave of riders (from Nashville cadre) rescued the halted campaign
Impact:	kept the Freedom Ride campaign alive and fed movement momentum
Lesson:	violence cannot be allowed to triumph over a nonviolent campaign; when the baton is dropped, someone must pick it up

Case 3: Continuation Freedom Ride to Jackson, MS., May 1961

Violent event:	Freedom Riders imprisoned upon arrival in Jackson
Tactical adaptation:	used prison as movement school, and upon release planted local movement seeds
Impact:	contributed to movement by tutoring others and inspiring many other riders to follow
Lesson:	when given lemons, make lemonade

Case 4: Birmingham Campaign, Spring 1963

Violent events:	multiple, including many attacks on children and teenage protesters
Tactical adaptation:	Birmingham campaign was a tactical adaptation to defeat in the prior Albany campaign; in Birmingham tactical adaptation took the form of solid preparation, training, and organizing; the "Children's Crusade" was especially significant
Impact:	contributed to local desegregation success; chaos and violence backfired moving Pres. Kennedy forward with civil rights bill to Congress; contributed to overall movement momentum
Lesson:	enhance planning, training, organizing and find someone to play *your* game

Case 5: Voter Registration Campaigns to Selma March, 1965

Violent events:	multiple attacks and deaths
Tactical adaptation:	after little voter registration progress in AL and MS due to heavy violent repression, tactical change to concentration venue and highly visible mass march; march plan was a direct adaptation to the murder of a young Black protester (Jimmy Lee Jackson); other brutal mass attacks and murders (Rev. James Reeb and Viola Liuzzo) occurred but did not halt the movement
Impact:	contributed to passage of Voting Rights Act; and waning support for nonviolent strategy
Lesson:	change venue, tactics, and produce drama with media coverage

Episodes of tactical adaptation to violence in the movement heyday

Case 1: Nashville business desegregation movement, spring 1960:[9] harnessing a violent event to produce local backfire

Early phases of the Nashville movement began with infrastructure development in 1958 when James Lawson moved to Nashville, coming south at the behest of Martin Luther King. Working closely with Reverend Kelly Miller Smith, Lawson built a model local movement infrastructure consisting of (1) the Nashville Christian Leadership Conference (NCLC) Action Committee connected to Smith's church and linked into the black community, (2) Lawson's own underground workshops on nonviolent philosophy, strategy, and tactics (Isaac et al. 2012, 2016), and eventually (3) the Student Central Committee (with student leader representatives from the numerous Nashville institutions of higher education). In 1959, Lawson began deliberately recruiting and training students, launching their first sequence of "test" sit-ins at local stores that fall.

The first full-fledged sit-ins began on February 13, 1960, with mobilization of more than 100 protesters. Although Lawson was a Vanderbilt Divinity student, most student insurgents came from Nashville's black institutions, especially Fisk

University, Meharry Medical School, Tennessee A&I, and American Baptist Theological Seminary. After much organizing, planning, and training, the protesters converged on McClellan's, Woolworth's, and Kress five and dime and some department stores challenging the Jim Crow norms regarding all-white lunch counters. The protests continued from February 13 into mid-April, proliferating into multiple tactical forms, including sit-ins, jail-ins, theater stand-ins, marches, and a massive economic boycott of the downtown business district (Isaac et al. 2012).

During the sit-ins, protesters were faced with direct violence on multiple occasions facilitated by police complicity and then hauled off to jail. The students responded with new waves of sit-in protesters to take their place. Besides police-facilitated beatings, there were other forms of oppositional violence as well.

On April 19th at approximately 5:30 a.m., a powerful bomb was thrown through the front window of the residence of Z. Alexander Looby, a leading black civil rights attorney who had been working with the student protest movement. The blast was so massive it destroyed most of the Looby residence and blew out 140 windows in Meharry Medical School buildings across the street. The Student Central Committee had already planned to meet at 6:00 a.m. that morning. Shocked and angered, the core cadre trained by Lawson decided, on Lawson's recommendation, to quickly mobilize a mass march. The march was to begin at Tennessee A&I campus and follow a two-and-a-half-mile route along Jefferson Avenue to the courthouse downtown where they hoped to confront Mayor Ben West. March leaders sent an invitation to the mayor, which he accepted. The Lawson-trained cadre insisted that the march would be silent (no talking while in route) but very disciplined and determined.

At the launch, marchers numbered approximately 2,000 strong; by the time they reached the courthouse, participants had doubled (Halberstam 1998). March leaders – C.T. Vivian, Diane Nash, Bernard Lafayette, Angeline Butler, and others from the Lawson workshops – confronted the mayor. In the course of the exchange, movement leaders – C.T. Vivian and Diane Nash – effectively induced the mayor to admit publicly that segregation was immoral and that eating facilities should be desegregated (Halberstam 1998: 234). The next day, the Nashville *Tennessean* headlines announced: "INTEGRATE COUNTERS – MAYOR," which the movement and most Nashvillians saw as a change in climate, a turning point, that signaled a significant new direction for the city. Within days, a plan was sketched and segregation norms in downtown businesses began to fall. Six stores complied by summer, and by 1962 virtually the entire downtown business district had been desegregated without federal intervention a full two years prior to the Civil Rights Act of 1964 (Isaac et al. 2012).

In this case, a bombing was rapidly countered by the Lawson-trained cadre. The fact that they had a highly developed local movement infrastructure and deep nonviolent training mattered for mobilizing large numbers of marchers in rapid fashion. But the quality of disciplined performance by the cadre and other marchers generated an event-based performative power. The size, discipline, and respectful yet stern exchange between movement leaders and the mayor – nonviolent tactical adaptation to a violent event – were definite features of their performative power, a power that was cultivated through previous months of training for the cadre in Lawson's workshops (Isaac et al. 2012, 2016, 2017). The insurgent's tactical adaptation produced a classic case of a movement harnessing a violent event for purposes of advancing the cause; a case where violence designed to intimidate and suppress movement actions actually had the opposite effect – "backfire" (Chalmers 2005; Hess and Martin 2006). Backfire is one form of impact due to performative power of effectively executed nonviolent action.

Case 2: Launching the Freedom Rides, 1961:[10] when the baton is dropped, someone must pick it up

The Freedom Rides, as collective action tactic, were designed to test the Supreme Court ban on segregated bus and train terminals for interstate transit handed down in the 1960 *Boynton vs. Virginia* decision. Despite the decision regarding terminals, blacks were still required to ride in the back of the bus.

The initial ride was organized by CORE, modeled after an earlier action in 1947. The tactic called for interracial groups traveling by commercial interstate carriers through the South, seating blacks in the front and whites in the back or mixed together throughout. At each scheduled bus stop, blacks would enter the "whites only" waiting room and washrooms, while whites would move to the "colored" sections. If instructed to follow segregation norms, they would refuse. James Farmer, head of CORE, explained the rest of the logic: "We felt we could then count upon the racists of the South to create a crisis, so that the federal government would be compelled to enforce federal law."

The tactical logic also played to the international Cold War context and the fault line between federal and southern state governments. The Soviets used racial injustice in the US as a key plank in their global strategy to convince, especially Third World countries, of the superiority of the Soviet line (McAdam 1998). Civil rights protests confronted by white violence captured by TV cameras produced a crisis for the administration and intensified pressure on President Kennedy to intervene on the side of racial justice. CORE planned to launch the two-bus, thirteen-rider assault from Washington, DC, on May 4th, hoping the crisis would be produced prior to Kennedy's summit with Soviet Premier Khrushchev scheduled for June 3rd. The buses – one Greyhound and one Trailways – would travel through the South to New Orleans.

Early days in the upper South were relatively uneventful. The first violence appeared at the Rock Hill, SC, stop where two Riders – John Lewis and Albert Bigelow – were beaten by whites. Georgia was surprisingly quiet. The Riders stopped for dinner with Martin Luther King in Atlanta where King warned of likely violence in Alabama, an expectation based on intelligence from Birmingham civil rights leader Reverend Fred Shuttlesworth (Halberstam 1998: 259, 264).

Moving into Alabama would prove to be a very different experience. The heart of Ku Klux Klan (KKK) territory within the Klan state (Halberstam 1998: 260) sat within the spatial territory defined by the Anniston-Birmingham-Tuscaloosa-Montgomery corridor (Chalmers 2005: 28–29), through which the buses would pass. The Greyhound bus arrived in Anniston first, where a white mob attacked and firebombed the bus. Southern Christian Leadership Conference (SCLC) leader Fred Shuttlesworth dispatched a convoy from Birmingham to rescue the Freedom Riders because police refused to assist. KKK infiltrators had boarded the Trailways bus as "regular riders" in Atlanta and attacked the Freedom Riders in route to Anniston and Birmingham. When the bus arrived in Birmingham, a massive white mob was waiting to finish the job. Riders from both buses had suffered severe beatings and/or smoke inhalation.

After their release from a local hospital reluctant to treat them, the Riders prepared to leave on the continuation journey to Montgomery. Now the bus companies could not provide drivers for the Freedom Riders, since Alabama state and law enforcement authorities had shown themselves unwilling to provide protection from white mobs, and Riders were uncertain what the federal government was going to do. With the deck heavily stacked against them, CORE abandoned the Freedom Ride and flew, with the help of Justice Department Special Assistant John Seigenthaler, to New Orleans for a scheduled rally on May 17th. John Lewis (1998: 149) would later write,

> I couldn't believe it. I understood the thinking behind the decision, but it defied one of the most basic tenets of nonviolent action – that is, there can be no surrender in the face of brute force or any form of violent oppression.

The white supremacist counteroffensives could not have had such a damaging impact on the Freedom Ride if it had not been for the major role played by the racialized Jim Crow apparatus and officials, at both state and local levels. The violent Alabama attacks were the product of multiple levels of state complicity and weeks of careful planning and organizing (Arsenault 2006: 158). Law enforcement authorities with the responsibility to protect and investigate attacks on citizens were deeply involved in the counteroffensive. Aided by police and FBI information on the Freedom Rider's itinerary, the KKK and friends[11] planned and executed the violent attacks at the bus terminals in Anniston, Birmingham, and Montgomery. Local police, state troopers, and FBI were all involved, to varying degrees, in facilitating the bloody assaults designed to stop the Freedom Riders as they moved into Alabama (Arsenault 2006: 135–160). Moreover, none of this could have happened without neglect by federal authorities.

A week after the first CORE Freedom Ride was aborted, twenty-one students from the Nashville core cadre prepared to pick up the baton. Despite pleas from parents, threats from their universities, warnings from civil rights leaders in Alabama (i.e., Rev. Fred Shuttlesworth), and commands from the Kennedy administration, the young Nashville insurgents were determined to continue the rides. Diane Nash, one of Lawson's mentees, played the role of operations manager and logistic coordinator. As Nash put it: "If they stop us with violence, the movement is dead."[12] In other words, the power of nonviolence would be lost.

The Birmingham authorities, including "Bull" Connor, attempted to foil the Nashville replacements by jailing and then driving some to the Tennessee state line and dumping them in the countryside. The Nash operation responded by sending a second wave of replacements, some by car and some by train. Nash also put Attorney General Robert Kennedy on notice. When the attorney general realized he could not persuade her to call it off, he began working to persuade Governor Patterson to provide state protection for the Riders.

On May 20th, the Freedom Riders traveled from Birmingham to Montgomery under police escort. As they approached the city, the state troopers dropped away and there was no police presence as they pulled into the bus station. The welcoming committee, a white mob, commenced beating the Riders. Among those most seriously injured were Jim Zwerg (white exchange student at Fisk), William Barbee (Tennessee A&I), and John Lewis (American Baptist Theological Seminary), all part of the Lawson-trained Nashville group. Robert Kennedy's special aid, John Seigenthaler (a Nashville native), was also badly beaten and knocked unconscious by the mob.

Under assault all night, the Riders held up in a church, along with local civil rights supporters and Martin Luther King, who came in for support. The next morning, Attorney General Kennedy ordered in federal troops and the governor declared martial law, dispersing the mob with state troopers. The Nashville Freedom Riders had forced the federal and state governments to protect constitutional rights. Two days later, they left on Greyhound and Trailways buses bound for Jackson, Mississippi.[13] They had no way of knowing what would await them in the Magnolia State, nor did they know of the deal that Attorney General Kennedy had cut with Mississippi authorities.

At this point, it was clear that the Nashville students picked up the baton and kept the movement moving. The Nashville cadre, trained under James Lawson, had stepped into an extraordinarily dangerous situation after the initial CORE Riders disbanded under violent assault in Alabama. As Bob Moses, the Student Nonviolent Coordinating Committee (SNCC) architect of the Freedom Summer campaign, would later comment, "Only the Nashville student movement had the fire to match that of the burning bus" (quoted in Arsenault 2006: 179).

The well-planned attacks by Klansmen and mobs, with police support, generated more violence than the CORE Freedom Riders had anticipated. There was no backfire to the violence, but instead a temporary halt of the movement campaign. The fact that the halt was only temporary was due to the tactical adaptation by a different set of movement agents – the Nashville core cadre – who rescued the campaign and not only kept the Freedom Rides operating, but expanded them, this in the face of heavy repression and a White House pleading to stop the rides. The Nashville group was appalled that CORE called off the ride, which in their judgment was a fundamental violation of the nonviolent praxis they had been taught in Lawson's workshops. So here the tactical adaptation came from other quarters in the movement as a new wave of young and well-trained agents mobilized to rescue the campaign. Again, this is a case of high-quality insurgents utilizing the performative power of nonviolence.

Case 3: Freedom Ride to the Gulag, 1961:[14] *when given lemons,* *make lemonade*

On May 24, two buses of Freedom Riders, reporters, and Alabama National Guardsmen, with helicopter escort, moved across the state in route to Jackson,

Mississippi. The escorted passage across Alabama was negotiated by the Kennedy administration. When the convoy arrived at the state line, Guardsmen and helicopters retreated. Unknown to the Freedom Riders, their reception in Mississippi would also be part of the negotiations with Attorney General Robert Kennedy (Carson 1981), who desperately wanted Mississippi authorities to avoid public violence for reasons of Cold War optics.

More than half of the twenty-seven Riders on the two buses were from the Nashville cadre.[15] When the Freedom Riders arrived at the Jackson station, they followed their standard practice of violating the Jim Crow racial code. Police immediately arrested and transported them to the Hinds County Jail. The local jails were quickly filled with "jail, no bail" Freedom Riders and became important scenes of "political education for student activists" (Carson 1981: 38).

On June 15, guards herded forty-five male prisoners from the cells into windowless truck trailers for transport to notorious Parchman Penitentiary. At Parchman, they were filed into the maximum security wing by armed guards, stripped naked, taunted and humiliated, run through a shower and shaved, given prison shorts and undershirts (no shoes), and put into small, primitive cells. During the intake process, several Riders were beaten by guards for failure to address them as "sir."

The built environment of Parchman was designed to minimize community among prisoners. To maintain connection and sustain energy and hope, the protesters sang. But they also sang because it infuriated their captors, who punished their singing by confiscating their mattresses and spraying them with fire hoses. After more than six weeks behind bars, the first Riders were released feeling triumphant. John Lewis felt that they had truly accomplished something important; they had gone into the belly of the beast and survived. They were now more committed to the cause than ever (Halberstam 1998). Over ensuring months, forty-three (of a total of sixty) Freedom Ride buses and trains would assault Jackson alone, and more than three hundred Riders would be arrested (Arsenault 2006: Appendix; Carson 1981: 36).

Brave Riders from all over the country were flocking to the violent Mississippi jails like moths to the flame. In the process, they were not only challenging segregation on interstate public transportation lines, they were transforming the character of the movement as well. The struggle was now going beyond specific locales to challenge a whole region; it was now directly challenging not just Jim Crow but the Kennedy administration; it was now involving protesters from all across the country; and it was now sharpening and spreading militancy fueled from within Mississippi jails.

The fact that the Freedom Riders were received differently in Mississippi than in Alabama was largely the product of state actions. Without the negotiations between the Kennedy administration and Mississippi authorities, it is quite likely that the Riders would have been greeted with much more open violence in Mississippi rather than immediate incarceration. In the one case, the violence was open and public; in the other case, it was concealed behind prison walls. The latter strategy would also be employed against the movement in Albany, Georgia.

This case consisted of the continuation Freedom Ride from Montgomery to Jackson, MS. Instead of a public violent greeting from white supremacists in Mississippi, as in Alabama, the Freedom Riders from Nashville were immediately placed in prison. Although the movement agents' freedom to mobilize in public protest was taken away, they resorted to other tactics. The highly trained cadre from Nashville helped facilitate the use of their prison time as a movement school. Agents like Jim Lawson, C.T. Vivian, William Barbee, John Lewis, Jim Bevel, Bernard Lafayette, and others held discussions about nonviolent praxis within the prison interstices. They also worked to maintain the spirits of others by singing freedom songs. The second adaptation was to plant local movement seeds (community-organizing cells) in Mississippi when they were released from prison, a payoff for the shift to dispersion tactics offered by Freedom Rides to multiple locations.

Case 4: The Birmingham campaign, 1963:[16] improve planning, training, and organizing

Hot off the Freedom Rides in mid-1961, SNCC organizers launched a broad community desegregation challenge in Albany, Georgia. Running deep into the following year, the movement generated no tangible results. Activists at the time (including King) and subsequent scholarly assessment have found a variety of factors that contributed to the campaign's failure. First, the movement encountered difficulties at all levels of government. Police Chief Laurie Pritchett followed a strategy of "legalistic control" (Barkan 2006), employing mass arrests without public shows of excessive force and violence against demonstrators. However, substantial police brutality occurred behind prison walls out of view of the national news media. As long as the local police could maintain control, the Kennedy administration followed a position of neutrality that left the movement at a disadvantage. A federal district judge (Robert Elliott) hampered the movement by issuing restraining orders against the protesters at crucial moments. FBI agents were present to monitor the action, but did nothing to protect nonviolent demonstrators (Lawson and Payne 2006).

Second, the movement contributed to the failure as well. It initially faced infighting with the local NAACP, and overall did a rather poor job of planning the campaign. If the movement was going to be in position to force federal intervention on its behalf, a crisis-level clash would have to occur between movement and white supremacist forces, one of the conclusions Dr. King reached by spring 1963 (King 1963).

King and other movement leaders knew they needed a "victory" (Lewis 1998: 195). Massive disorder brought to crisis proportions would be necessary; not an event that could be quietly managed by authorities, as in Albany. As King wrote in his *Why We Can't Wait* (1963: 34), it is important to

> move and stir the social conscience of [the] community and nation. Instead of submitting to surreptitious cruelty in thousands of dark jails cells and on

countless shadowed street corners, he [the Negro] would force his oppressor to commit his brutality openly – in the light of day – with the rest of the world looking on.

A variety of conditions made Birmingham the ideal location. First, Birmingham was the most important industrial city in the South, with ownership of steel and iron companies in the North. Second, the city had a long history of extremely violent race relations, which earned it the "Bombingham" nickname. Between the end of World War II and 1963, more than sixty bombs were directed at African American homes, churches, and businesses (Lewis 1998: 195). Third, the city's police chief, "Bull" Connor, was known to be a vicious racist with little self-control. King, Abernathy, and Shuttlesworth "all knew that Bull Connor did not have the restraint or savvy of a Laurie Pritchett" (Lewis 1998: 195). Fourth, coming into 1963, a fracture in the local capitalist class had opened between the iron aristocracy – which stoked Jim Crow segregation for the work it could do in undermining unionism and keeping wages low (Connor was muscle for this faction) – and the service-sector business community who sought economic growth and maximization of real estate values (Bloom 1987; Luders 2010). The rise of mass disorder driven by a protest campaign would likely widen the division among economic elites (Luders 2010). Fifth, the city already had a substantial local movement infrastructure in place headed by Rev. Fred Shuttlesworth (Morris 1993), who well understood the local political terrain, confiding in King, "I assure you if you come to Birmingham, the movement will not only gain prestige but it will really shake the country (quoted in Lewis 1998: 195)."

The campaign – code name "Project C" (for confrontation) – was launched during the first week of April. The SCLC organizers brought in movement leaders from all over, including members of the Nashville cadre. Leading up to the campaign, James Lawson make periodic trips to Birmingham to conduct nonviolent workshops; his job "was to train the foot soldiers for Project C" (Branch 1988: 703). Diane Nash-Bevel and James Bevel were charged with organizing the youth contingents (Lewis 1998: 195). The overall plan for the campaign called for a multifaceted approach modeled after the Nashville campaign, but on a more massive scale (Branch 1988: 752; Lewis 1998: 196), including economic boycott of downtown businesses, sit-ins, kneel-ins, jail-ins, and mass marches. The idea was to increasingly intensify the disruption and disorder until a general crisis was achieved. The primary target was the downtown business district, with the hope that businessmen would feel the economic squeeze and bring pressure on political elites (Morris 1993).

Violence by Bull Connor and his forces was expected, so there was no need for a plan to provoke it (Morris 1993). In preparation for the campaign, King said, "if it [violence] comes, we will surface it for the world to see" (quoted in Branch 1988). Leaders were concerned about the level of violence that would likely be encountered in Birmingham. Organizer Wyatt Walker, for one, did not think he would see his family again when he left his Atlanta home for Birmingham (Morris 1993: 626). During one of the last planning meetings, King told the group,

> There are eleven people here assessing the type of enemy we're going to face . . . I have to tell you that in my judgment, some of the people sitting here today will not come back alive from this campaign. And I want you to think about it.
>
> (quoted in Branch 1988: 691–692)

A major concern was how to handle or tactically adapt to violence given the high probability of its occurrence. The big question for movement leaders was – could the campaign withstand systematic violent repression long enough to put sufficient economic pressure on the downtown business district?

In the early weeks of the campaign, Bull Connor showed unexpected restraint, using arrests to control the movement's actions as much as possible. By early May, there were still no signs that white resistance would break. Movement leaders responded by intensifying the struggle to create widespread social disorder so that the local economy would cease to function. On May 1 and 2 ("D-Day" designed by James Bevel), they began the systematic release of thousands of elementary, high school, and college students whose task it was to disrupt the business district in a nonviolent manner and court mass arrest. By May 3, the jails exceeded capacity with more than 1,000 protesters, mostly young students, some as young as six years of age. When Bull Connor could no longer weaken the movement with arrests, he unleashed violence to break up the demonstrators. Water cannons, K-9 units, and clubs were turned on the young protesters. Movement keys to "handling" the violence were rooted in training and a massive nonviolent army with troop size greater than the carrying capacity of Connor's jails. Wave after wave of young students were willing to confront Connor's violence, all the while bringing economic pain to the downtown businesses and an appalling media image of white-on-black mass violence to the American people, including the president.

By May 10, business leaders agreed to movement demands. Violence continued. Participants at a Klan rally proclaimed, "Martin Luther King's epigraph can be written here in Birmingham" (Lewis 1998: 198). That night the motel where King was staying was bombed along with his brother's (Rev. A.D. King) home, triggering some rioting against police by residents not trained in nonviolence (Branch 1988: 763). A month later, President Kennedy gave his famous TV address, announcing that he would send a powerful civil rights bill to Congress.

The 1963 Birmingham campaign contains two distinct layers of tactical adaptation. First, the campaign itself was a tactical adaptation to the Albany campaign of 1961–1962 that failed to produce any concrete desegregation success in the city. That outcome was due to several factors, including moves on both the side of the authorities and miscues on the side of the movement. The conclusion drawn by movement leaders, including Dr. King, was that they would need to pick another site, one where they would do extensive planning, training, and organizing to focus their energies on vulnerable business targets to produce maximum chaos. They also looked to select a location where local law enforcement would be most likely to help produce a backfire effect for a national audience. Bull Connor's Birmingham was the answer.

The second form of tactical adaptation was actually part of the advance planning the leaders did in preparation for the violence they fully expected to receive in Birmingham. Adaptation took the form of careful preparation and training in nonviolent strategy designed to be executed through multiple protest tactics and repeatedly in multiple waves of especially young children who would first fill the jails and serve as highly visible and vulnerable nonviolent shock troops for the nation to witness. Early waves of protesters who would be arrested in large numbers, sufficiently high to exceed the carrying capacity of the city's jails, were crucial because it was at that point Connor resorted to using violent attacks as an attempt to disperse the protests. Connor's violence only contributed to the local chaos and helped spawn a spectacle and national-level backfire. The key tactical adaptation to violence in this case was to expect it, prepare for it, and mobilize a sufficiently large nonviolent army capable of withstanding the mass arrests and to absorb the violent assaults. The size of the nonviolent army, released in multiple waves, made possible by the mass recruiting and training of school children, generated sustained disruption of economic activity (bringing business leaders to the bargaining table) while demonstrating "brutality openly in the light of day" for the whole world to see (King 1963: 34).

Case 5: The Selma-to-Montgomery march, 1965:[17] *shift from spatially dispersed, low-visibility tactics to concentrated, high-visibility tactics*

There was a substantial prior history of voter registration struggle leading to the Selma campaign in 1965. Campaigns had been operating in parts of Alabama, Mississippi, and other Deep South states as early as 1961, driven by several forces. From the movement side, SNCC operatives, including Bob Moses, entered McComb, Mississippi, in 1961 pursuing voter registration because direct action was too dangerous in this environment and the tactic was also consistent with the SNCC strategy of building a long-term grassroots community base. Other streams of activists, incarcerated for Freedom Rider offenses, came into the area after release from prison, including a number from the Nashville movement (e.g., John Hardy into McComb; Jim Bevel and Diane Nash Bevel into Jackson; Bernard Lafayette into Selma). From the side of the federal government, the Kennedy administration had been pushing voter registration over other movement tactics, launching the Voter Education Project in 1962.

The SNCC workers encountered vicious repression in McComb and surrounding areas in the form of arrests, police harassment, escorted removal, and murder (e.g., Herbert Lee, Louis Allen). In fact, Lee's killing followed by high school student sit-ins brought local voter registration attempts to a halt. SNCC leader Bob Moses vacated McComb and moved operations upstate (Carson 1981; Andrews 2004: 50).

Voter registration also faced heavy resistance in Alabama, especially in the central – Birmingham, Montgomery, Tuscaloosa, Selma – region. Bernard Lafayette had been directing the voter registration project out of Selma since 1962, with little success, as in Mississippi. The major trigger for the Selma-to-Montgomery march occurred in small neighboring Marion, Alabama, where voter registration was facing fierce resistance. A SCLC activist – James Orange – was arrested, and word spread that the local Klan planned to abduct and lynch Orange. Local movement agents quickly organized a nighttime march as a buffer and deflection for Orange. During the march, Jimmy Lee Jackson was murdered by a state trooper, sending a wave of outrage through the black community (Lafayette and Johnson 2013: 120). Jackson's murder was the stimulus for renewed mass protests and the SCLC plan for the Selma-to-Montgomery march for voting rights (Carson 1981: 158). The tactic was, again, the creation of James Bevel who understood that a nonviolent mass march at that moment was critical because (1) it was important to show that nonviolence could still work, since many were talking violent retaliation for Lee's murder, and (2) it was necessary to bring national attention to the big issue of voting rights (again) and put pressure on the federal government (Lafayette and Johnson 2013: 121; Halberstam 1998: 499–505).

SNCC field workers were initially against the SCLC plan for a march with King at the helm. But some SNCC vets were planning to participate no matter what (e.g., John Lewis) and eventually Alabama SNCC agreed too. With the brutal assault on marchers during the first attempt to cross the Edmund Pettus Bridge leading out of Selma ("Bloody Sunday"), previous reservations among many SNCC workers were dispelled. Dozens of Mississippi SNCC cadre left immediately for Selma. Shortly after the second abortive march led by King, local whites attacked three white ministers who had come to Selma to participate in the march. Reverend James Reeb, a white man, died from beating injuries a few days later (Carson 1981: 160).

The Selma campaign is credited with providing "the spark for a crucial confrontation between Alabama blacks and obstinate state officials," which in turn contributed to a favorable climate of public opinion outside the South and to subsequent passage of Johnson's voting rights proposals (Carson 1981: 161). On the other hand, the campaign further deepened the belief among some blacks that the appeal and effectiveness of nonviolent strategy was evaporating. As John Lewis put it, "Black capacity to believe [that a white person] would really open his heart, open his life to nonviolent appeal was running out" (quoted in Carson 1981: 1161). It also helped diffuse seeds for the Black Panther Party out of rural Lowndes County, Alabama (Carson 1981: 161; Jeffries 2009).

As in the Birmingham case, two key layers of tactical adaptation occurred in the Selma-to-Montgomery march. First, after little progress in voter registration campaigns in Mississippi and Alabama, venue and tactics were changed. Much of the most dangerous and heroic work on voter registration was done by SNCC operatives following a grassroots, community-organizing approach across mostly small towns and rural areas. The ease with which white repression and violence permeated rural black residents' everyday life was largely responsible for the lack of actual registration progress. So the Selma-to-Montgomery march shifted the dispersed tactics of SNCC to the more concentrated and visible approach of a mass march with a host of clergy and celebrities (black and white) to enhance public attention.

There was a second layer of tactical adaptation to violence internal to the campaign itself. In fact, violence was the proximate trigger for the overall campaign shift. The march plan was the direct adaptation to the murder of a black protester, Jimmy Lee Jackson, amidst growing local black sentiment to respond in kind with armed force. The plan was the brainchild of Jim Bevel of the Nashville cadre, also the architect of the Children's Crusade in the Birmingham campaign. So violence in the form of a black life taken was the trigger for this tactical shift shaped by a highly trained nonviolent insurgent.

There would be two more murders by white supremacist opposition by the time the Selma-to-Montgomery march was completed, deaths of white marchers – Rev. James Reeb and Viola Liuzzo. While the black murder helped mobilize the tactical adaptation and give it urgency, the white deaths carried a wider appeal for a national white audience and the White House, adding weight to the importance of moving forward with a voting rights bill.

Violence played two distinct roles in the context of the voter registration campaigns. On the one hand, violence (and other forms of heavy repression) was responsible for keeping voter registration rates abysmally low (often in the 1%–2% range in many counties) in much of Mississippi and Alabama, this despite the heroic efforts of the SNCC operatives. On the other hand, violence, indeed violence against blacks, stimulated the Selma plan and mobilization as a direct tactical adaptation. In the context of the Selma march attempts, violence toward white participants (especially the murders of James Reeb and Viola Liuzzo) stimulated national outrage and action on voting rights bill from President Johnson. The sequential unfolding and impact clearly indicated the racialized significance of murder and its potential for backfire in movement context. White lives mattered for backfire in a way that black lives did not.

Discussion: performative power in tactical adaptation to violence

Civil rights movement agents' tactical adaptation to violent assaults took a variety of creative and effective forms during the movement's heyday that illustrate how performative power can be created through nonviolent direct action. Achieving performative power was due in no small measure to the level of strategic development of nonviolent praxis and the making of high-quality insurgents prior to 1960. Previously, most activists and observers were uncertain about the ways to deploy and prospects for using nonviolent action in the Jim Crow South. The only real prior standout success was the Montgomery bus boycott. Success in the Nashville desegregation campaign in spring-summer of 1960 and the rescue/ continuation by the Nashville cadre of the first violence-halted Freedom Ride were crucial in maintaining movement energy and momentum.

Violent attacks did work in some cases, if only by producing temporary halts, postponements, or containments of movement actions. However, they typically did not undermine complete campaigns, much less stop the entire movement. In cases examined here, this happened in the temporary halt of the first CORE Freedom Ride due to violent attacks and the temporary partial containment of Freedom Riders when they arrived in Jackson, Mississippi.

The key to breaking the potential power of violent counterassaults in these cases turned on both quality and quantity dimensions: well-trained, high-quality insurgents deploying *waves* of participants in creative ways. In the Nashville movement, the quality of insurgent workshop training was key, as was their use of multiple tactics and multiple waves of insurgents in the sit-ins and marches. Consider, too, the Freedom Rides. This tactical form was ideal for testing the new federal desegregation regulations on interstate commercial vehicles, but it also came with its own tactical vulnerabilities: a small group concentrated in a bus moving through areas where attacks would be relatively easy and media coverage unlikely. The solution again was the use of *waves* of Riders. In the Freedom Ride rescue, the Nashville cadre employed multiple waves of their best insurgents to accomplish the task. Once Freedom Riders were incarcerated in Mississippi, multiple waves of Riders flocked to Jackson. One major reason Birmingham was a desegregation success story but Albany was not is the advanced preparation that trained and organized waves of children greater in number than the carrying capacity of Bull Connor's jails. This numerical consideration was an explicit part of tactical planning and training executed by some Nashville cadre, SCLC leaders, and Shuttlesworth's forces. In the Selma march, again high-quality insurgents were integral – designing and leading actions – coupled with persistence in the use of multiple (three in this case) march mobilizations before the tactic was successful.

Violent repression exercised against a nonviolent movement can backfire. Cases of backfire have been documented by a variety of scholars (e.g., Sharp 1973; Chalmers 2005; Hess and Martin 2006; Chenoweth and Stephan 2011; Nepstad 2015), and some form of backfire occurred in three of my cases (see Table 2.2). The backfiring of repression happens when a nonviolent movement is attacked with heavy repression by its opposition and the fallout turns counterproductive for the opposition. Nepstad (2015: 100) puts it this way, "Violence perpetrated against unarmed resisters can have an unanticipated effect: instead of stopping the movement, civil resisters may experience enhanced participation and support while the opponent, having revealed its brutality, loses support." When backfire occurs it can change the balance of power between the nonviolent movement and its opposition (Sharp 1973), but the scale of backfire can vary. Backfire was local in Nashville but national in impact from the Birmingham and Selma campaigns.

Yet backfire is by no means a guaranteed result of nonviolent direct action; sometimes violent repression does what its users intend – it brings the nonviolent movement to a halt. Scholars have identified two important conditions for the occurrence of repression backfire: (1) information about the repressive event must reach the relevant audiences; and (2) these wider audiences must perceive the attack against the nonviolent movement as unwarranted and/or excessive (Hess and Martin 2006). But there is another key condition necessary for backfire – successful exercise of high-quality performance by nonviolent agents, an important part of which is the maintenance of nonviolent discipline in the face of violent repression; nonviolent tactical adaptation to violence (issuing from sound strategic development of high-quality insurgents) is a key and often overlooked part of this process.

Downstream outcomes following violent repression against nonviolent agents can assume forms other than failure or backfire, the two most commonly discussed results in the literature (Chenoweth and Stephan 2011; Nepstad 2015). There was no backfire in the classic sense in the Freedom Ride rescue or the imprisonment of Freedom Riders in Parchman Penitentiary, but there were, in both instances, highly significant contributions to the movement. For backfire and other positive contributions to movement as a result of tactical adaptation to violence, high-quality insurgent practice is required. In each of these five cases, members of the Nashville cadre who received unusually lengthy and intense training before moving into nonviolent combat played crucial roles. If real performative power that is possible from nonviolent practice is to be obtained, high-quality insurgents are necessary.

Conclusions

Scholars and activists alike have made claims about the power of nonviolent collective action (e.g., Lawson 1961; Sharp 2005; Schock 2005; Collyer and Zepp 2006; Nepstad 2015). Power in such claims is typically equated with impact. But too often we are not shown what *kind* of power is operating. I have argued that the form of power that typically gives nonviolent praxis its impact is performative power. It is also the case that to get this kind of power from nonviolent direct action – one form of which is the very important tactical adaptation to violence analyzed here – requires highly skilled nonviolent practitioners, something that does not show up readymade, but rather requires cultivation, training, and experience for effective execution.

My illustration of performative power in these cases of tactical adaptation to violence contributes to power theory in general and power theory within social movement studies. Among the key questions in the analysis of performative power is whether we have grounds for taking it seriously over and above other dimensions of power (e.g., relational or discursive). To what extent, when and how, does situated collective action itself produce an "outsized" impact on the movement and its goals? My assessment is that all five of the campaign tactical adaptations produced performative power that had effects on the civil rights movement and its goals, effects that cannot be reduced to relational or discursive dimensions of power. In addition to finding important performative power in the ways in which nonviolent insurgents adapted to violent assault, this suggests that it is valuable to be explicit about the dimensions of power operating in our theories and empirical studies of movement actions.

These cases also add to our knowledge about nonviolent movement tactical interactions with violent adversaries. Doug McAdam (1983) taught us that tactical innovation – changing forms of offensive tactics – could accelerate the pace of movement actions by fueling movement excitement and by keeping the opposition off-balance. But that's only part of the story. Evidence presented here shows that defensive tactical adaptation to violent assault is another way to keep violent adversaries off-balance and a source of movement momentum and persistence. Tactical adaptation to violence can also be a source of collective action repertoire augmentation (e.g., mass marches to amplify violent attacks – Nashville and Selma; multiple waves of insurgents – Freedom Rides and Children's Crusade in Birmingham; use of prison time as insurgency school – Freedom Riders in Parchman Penitentiary). By illuminating the performative power of effective tactical adaptation in key campaigns, this study also contributes to the historical sociology of the southern civil rights movement.

Insurgent quantity or movement size notwithstanding, I am highlighting the role of insurgent quality. Social movement scholars (as well as other observers) frequently take the quantity of movement participation as the gold standard by which to judge movements; movements need to grow their numbers for impact, and nonviolence has an inherent "participation advantage" that can help with that objective (Chenoweth and Stephan 2011). But the present cases, as well as other evidence (Isaac et al. 2016), indicate the importance of insurgent quality as well as sheer numbers. It is important to appreciate that the quality of a warrior is just as consequential in nonviolent struggle as it is in armed struggle.

Notes

1 It is important, however, to recognize that the threat of violent repression (from both state and civil society agents) was always working to suppress the quantity of movement participation, although this varied in form and intensity across the region.

2 I intend this contribution as one of conceptual development with empirical illustration, not one designed to "test" causal conditions.

3 Chenoweth and Stephan (2011) find that movements across the twentieth and twenty-first centuries disproportionately (88% of the cases) faced violent repression from adversaries.

4 In addition to McAdam (1983), other conceptualizations are related to the one I propose to examine here. For instance, McCammon (2012) employs "strategic adaptation" defined as "proactive, self-conscious decision making and tactical revision" carried out by women's jury movement participants. Here I opt for "tactical adaptation" because tactics better describe the processes of interest here and the interaction emphasis in McAdam's (1983) original article is preserved.

5 The reference to the "long civil rights movement" (a strand of the African American Freedom struggle) is employed by some scholars (e.g., Hall 2005; Isaac 2008) to expand the temporal scope of the movement both back before and after the conventional periodization (c. 1955–1968) of the movement.

6 Isaac (2009: 942, 2012) refers to those activists and sympathizers who are "artistic producers – writers, musicians, poets, and actors – who play a role in *aesthetic activism* by producing and circulating movement-relevant culture in creative and entertaining ways," and who are not necessarily engaged in direct action tactics.

7   The Americanized version of "*satyagraha*" – the Gandhian neologism for "truth force" or "firmness in truth" (Scalmer 2011: 70–73) – was established by CORE as consisting of four basic steps: investigation, negotiation, publicity, and direct action.
8   This second effect has also been identified by Alexander (2011: 150–152).
9   Major sources for this case include Halberstam (1998), Hogan (2007), Isaac et al. (2012), and Houston (2012).
10 Major sources for this case include Halberstam (1998), Lawson and Payne (2006), Arsenault (2006), and Hogan (2007).
11 The KKK was joined by the ultra-conservative National States Rights Party (NSRP), which was known for its "virulent strain of white supremacist and anti-Semitic extremism" (Arsenault 2006: 153).
12 Later Nash would reflect, "I strongly felt that the future of the movement was going to be cut short if the Freedom Rides had been stopped as a result of violence." [It would have signaled] "That whenever a movement starts, all that has to be done is that you attack it with massive violence, and the blacks will stop" (quoted in Hogan 2007: 47).
13 The Freedom Ride from Montgomery to Jackson departed on May 24th. The Greyhound bus contained fifteen Riders, seven from the Nashville cadre; the Trailways bus carried twelve Riders, seven from the Nashville cadre (Arsenault 2006: Appendix).
14 Major sources for this case include Carson (1981), Halberstam (1998), Arsenault (2006), and Hogan (2007).
15 Participants from the Nashville cadre included Lucretia Collins (TSU), John Lewis (ABTS), Ernest "Rip" Patton (TSU), LeRoy Wright (Fisk), Clarence Thomas (ABTS), John Copeland (Nashville minister), Grady Donald (minister, NCLC), Alexander Anderson (AME minister), James Bevel (ABTS), Joseph Carter (ABTS), Bernard Lafayette (ABTS), James Lawson (FOR, SNCC, NCLC activist), C.T. Vivian (ABTS, NCLC), and Matthew Walker (Fisk) (Arsenault 2006: Appendix).
16 Major sources for this case include King (1963), Bloom (1987), Branch (1988), Halberstam (1998), Lewis (1998), Morris (1993), Lawson and Payne (2006), and Luders (2010).
17 Major sources for this case include Garrow (1978), Carson (1981), Halberstam (1998), Andrews (2004), and Lafayette and Johnson (2013).

References

Alexander, Jeffrey C. 2011. *Performance and Power*. Malden, MA: Polity Press.
Andrews, Kenneth T. 2004. *Freedom Is a Constant Struggle: The Mississippi Civil Rights Movement and Its Legacy*. Chicago: University of Chicago Press.
Arsenault, Raymond. 2006. *Freedom Rides: 1961 and the Struggle for Racial Justice*. Oxford: Oxford University Press.
Barkan, Steven E. 2006. "Criminal Prosecution and the Legal Control of Protest." *Mobilization* 11(1): 1181–1195.
Bloom, Jack M. 1987. *Class, Race, & the Civil Rights Movement*. Bloomington, IN: Indiana University Press.
Branch, Taylor. 1988. *Parting the Waters: America in the King Years, 1954–63*. New York, NY: Simon and Schuster.
Carson, Clayborne. 1981. *In Struggle: SNCC and the Black Awakening of the 1960s*. Cambridge, MA: Harvard University Press.
Carson, Clayborne. 2010. "Introduction." Pp. ix–xxvii in *Stride toward Freedom: The Montgomery Story*, edited by Martin Luther King, Jr. Boston, MA: Beacon Press.
Chabot, Sean. 2010. "Dialogue Matters: Beyond the Transmission Model of Transnational Diffusion between Social Movements." Pp. 99–124 in *The Diffusion of Social*

Movements, edited by Rebecca K. Givan, Rebecca Kolins, Kenneth M. Roberts, and Sarah A. Soule. Cambridge: Cambridge University Press.

Chabot, Sean. 2012. *Transnational Roots of the Civil Rights Movement*. New York, NY: Lexington Books.

Chalmers, David. 2005. *Backfire: How the Ku Klux Klan Helped the Civil Rights Movement*. New York, NY: Rowman and Littlefield.

Chenoweth, Erica, and Maria Stephan. 2011. *Why Civil Resistance Works: The Strategic Logic of Nonviolent Conflict*. New York, NY: Columbia University Press.

Cobb, Charles E., Jr. 2014. *This Nonviolent Stuff'll Get You Killed: How Guns Made the Civil Rights Movement Possible*. New York, NY: Basic Books.

Collyer, Charles E., and Ira G. Zepp, Jr. 2006. *Nonviolence: Origins and Outcomes*. Victoria, BC: Trafford.

Eyerman, Ron and Andrew Jamison. 1991. *Social Movements: A Cognitive Approach*. University Park, PA: Pennsylvania State University Press.

Fredrickson, George M. 1995. *Black Liberation: A Comparative History of Black Ideologies in the United States and South Africa*. Oxford, England: Oxford University Press.

Gilmore, Glenda Elizabeth. 2008. *Defying Dixie: The Radical Roots of Civil Rights*. New York, NY: W.W. Norton and Company.

Halberstam, David. 1998. *The Children*. New York, NY: Ballantine Books.

Hall, Jacqueline Dowd. 2005. "The Long Civil Rights Movement and the Political Uses of the Past." *Journal of American History* 91(4): 1233–1263.

Hess, David, and Brian Martin. 2006. "Repression, Backfire, and the Theory of Transformative Events." *Mobilization* 11(2): 249–267.

Hill, Lance. 2004. *The Deacons of Defense: Armed Resistance and the Civil Rights Movement*. Chapel Hill, NC: University of North Carolina Press.

Hogan, Wesley C. 2007. *Many Minds, One Heart: SNCC's Dream for a New America*. Chapel Hill, NC: University of North Carolina Press.

Houston, Benjamin. 2012. *The Nashville Way*. Athens, GA: University of Georgia Press.

Ganz, Marshall. 2000. "Resources and Resourcefulness: Strategic Capacity in the Unionization of California Agriculture, 1959–1966." *American Journal of Sociology* 105: 1003–1062.

Garrow, David J. 1978. *Protest at Selma: Martin Luther King, Jr. and the Voting Rights Act of 1965*. New Haven, CT: Yale University Press.

Isaac, Larry W. 2008. "Movement of Movements: Culture Moves in the Long Civil Rights Movement." *Social Forces* 87(1): 33–63.

Isaac, Larry W. 2009. "Movements, Aesthetics, and Markets in Literary Change: Making the American Labor Problem Novel." *American Sociological Review* 74(5): 938–965.

Isaac, Larry. 2012. "Literary Activists and Battling Books: The Labor Problem Novel as Contentious Movement Medium." *Research in Social Movements, Conflicts, and Change* 33: 17–49.

Isaac, Larry W., Jonathan S. Coley, Daniel B. Cornfield, and Dennis C. Dickerson. 2016. "Preparation Pathways and Movement Participation: Insurgent Schooling and Nonviolent Direct Action in the Nashville Civil Rights Movement." *Mobilization* 21(2): 155–176.

Isaac, Larry W., Daniel B. Cornfield, Dennis C. Dickerson, James M. Lawson, Jr., and Jonathan S. Coley. 2012. "Movement Schools and Dialogical Diffusion of Nonviolent Praxis: Nashville Workshops in the Southern Civil Rights Movement." *Research in Social Movements, Conflicts, and Change* 34: 155–184.

Isaac, Larry W., Anna W. Jacobs, Jaime Kucinskas, and Allison McGrath. 2017. "Social Movement Schools: Sites for Consciousness Transformation, Training, and Future

Social Development." Presented at International Sociological Association Meetings, Vienna, Austria.

Jeffries, Hasan Kwame. 2009. *Bloody Lowndes: Civil Rights and Black Power in Alabama's Black Belt*. New York, NY: New York University Press.

King, Martin Luther, Jr. 1963. *Why We Can't Wait*. Boston, MA: Beacon Press.

Lafayette, Bernard, Jr., and Kathryn Lee Johnson. 2013. *In Peace and Freedom: My Journey in Selma*. Lexington, KY: University of Kentucky Press.

Lawson, James M., Jr. 1961. "Eve of Nonviolent Revolution?" *The Southern Patriot* 19(9): 2–3.

Lawson, Steven F., and Charles Payne. 2006. *Debating the Civil Rights Movement, 1945–1968*. Lanham, MY: Rowman and Littlefield.

Lewis, John. 1998. *Walking with the Wind: A Memoir of the Movement*. New York, NY: Harcourt Brace & Company.

Luders, Joseph E. 2010. *The Civil Rights Movement and the Logic of Social Change*. Cambridge: Cambridge University Press.

Maney, Gregory. 2012. "The Paradox of Reform: The Civil Rights Movement in Northern Ireland." *Research in Social Movements, Conflicts, and Change* 34: 3–26.

McAdam, Doug. 1982. *Political Process and the Development of Black Insurgency, 1930–1970*. Chicago: University of Chicago Press.

McAdam, Doug. 1983. "Tactical Innovation and the Pace of Insurgency." *American Sociological Review* 48: 735–754.

McAdam, Doug. 1988. *Freedom Summer*. Oxford: Oxford University Press.

McAdam, Doug. 1998. "On the International Origins of Domestic Political Opportunities." Pp. 251–267 in *Social Movements and American Political Institutions*, edited by Anne N. Costain and Andrew S. McFarland. Lanham, MY: Rowman and Littlefield.

McCammon, Holly J. 2012. *The U.S. Women's Jury Movements and Strategic Adaptation*. Cambridge: Cambridge University Press.

Meier, August, and Elliott Rudwick. 2007. "The Origins of Nonviolent Direct Action in Afro-American Protest." Pp. 307–404 in *Along the Color Line*, edited by A. Meier and E. Rudwick. Urbana, IL: Illinois University Press.

Morris, Aldon D. 1984. *The Origins of the Civil Rights Movement*. New York, NY: Free Press.

Morris, Aldon D. 1993. "Birmingham Confrontation Reconsidered: An Analysis of the Dynamics and Tactics of Mobilization." *American Sociological Review* 58(5): 621–636.

Nepstad, Sharon Erickson. 2015. *Nonviolent Struggle: Theories, Strategies, & Dynamics*. Oxford: Oxford University Press.

Nepstad, Sharon Erickson, and Lester R. Kurtz. 2012. "Introduction in Nonviolent Conflict and Civil Resistance." Special Issue of *Research in Social Movements, Conflicts, and Change* 34: xi–xxvii.

Reed, Isaac A. 2013. "Power: Relational, Discursive, and Performative Dimensions." *Sociological Theory* 31(September): 193–218.

Rochon, Thomas R. 1998. Culture Moves: Ideas, Activism, and Changing Values. Princeton, NJ: Princeton University Press.

Santaro, Wayne, and Max Fitzpatrick. 2015. "The Ballot or the Bullet: The Crisis of Victory and Radicalization of the Civil Rights Movement." *Mobilization* 20(2): 207–229.

Scalmer, Sean. 2011. *Gandhi in the West: The Mahatma and the Rise of Radical Protest*. Cambridge: Cambridge University Press.

Schock, Kurt. 2005. *Unarmed Insurrections*. Minneapolis: University of Minnesota Press.

Sewell, William H., Jr. 2005. *Logics of History*. Chicago: University of Chicago Press.

Sharp, Gene. 1973. *The Politics of Nonviolent Action. Part 3: The Dynamics of Nonviolent Action*. Boston, MA: Porter Sargent Publishers.

Sharp, Gene. 2005. *Waging Nonviolent Struggle*. Boston: Porter Sargent Publishers Inc.

Siracusa, Anthony. 2017. "From Pacifism to Resistance: The Evolution of Nonviolence in Wartime America." *Journal of Civil and Human Rights* 3(1): 59–79.

Strain, Christopher B. 2005. *Pure Fire: Self-Defense as Activism in the Civil Rights Era*. Athens, GA: University of Georgia Press.

Tilly, Charles. 2006. *Regimes and Repertoires*. Chicago: University of Chicago Press.

Tyson, Timothy B. 1998. "Robert F. Williams, 'Black Power,' and the Roots of the African American Freedom Struggle." *Journal of American History* (September): 540–570.

3 Asserting land rights

Rural land struggles in India and Brazil

Kurt Schock

For much of the twentieth century, especially during the era of national devel-opmentalism from the 1910s to 1970s, challenges to rural land inequality and dispossession frequently adopted *strategies of agrarian revolution* that sought revolutionary change through armed resistance (Bernstein 2002; Wolf 1969). Major agrarian revolutions leading to significant redistributions of land include the Mexican and Russian Revolutions in the 1910s, the Chinese Revolution in 1949, and revolutionary struggles in Bolivia, Cuba, Algeria, Kenya, and Vietnam in the 1950s and 1960s and in Ethiopia and Nicaragua in the 1970s. Since the 1970s, however, there has been a pronounced decline in the frequency and effectiveness of agrarian revolution strategies, due in part to the end of the Cold War, democ-ratization, and the global diffusion of a human rights regime. Struggles adopting agrarian-revolutionary strategies in the post-1970s altered landscape have failed to gain widespread support or topple the state, such as the Sendero Luminoso in Peru, the Communist New People's Army in the Philippines, and the Naxalites in India.

With the ascendance of neoliberalism in the 1980s, many policymakers and academics declared that "land reform is dead" (Lipton 2009). Nevertheless, from the 1980s onward grassroots social movements sprung up around the world call-ing for redistributive land reform. One strategy adopted in certain contexts is a *land rights strategy* that promotes land reform through a combination of cam-paigns of nonviolent resistance and institutional legal action. Rather than pursuing their goals through political parties, and rather than viewing the state and its laws solely as instruments of the powerful elite, challengers implementing rights-based strategies recognize that the state and its laws, as well as international law, may provide opportunities for counterhegemonic resistance and radical reform (Hirsch and Lazarus-Black 1994; Hunt 1990; Rajagopopal 2005; Santos and Rodríguez-Garavito 2005). Land rights challenges struggle for socioeconomic rights, such as the "right" to land, and draw on national laws as well as an international "rights" discourse that has diffused throughout the world. Scholars have identified various manifestations of this strategy implemented by land reform movements, such as the "bibingka strategy" in the Philippines (Borras 1998; Franco 2008), "rightful radical resistance" in Brazil and India (Schock 2015a), and rights-based struggles for land reform in relatively democratic polities throughout the global South (Kapoor 2017; Moyo and Yeros 2005).[1]

Although particular manifestations differ, the common denominator of land rights strategies is that, rather than struggling for complete autonomy from the state or struggling to overthrow the state, challengers adopt an integrated political-legal strategy involving mass mobilization of extrainstitutional acts of nonviolent resistance – which may be legal or illegal – in an effort to compel the state to implement existing land rights codified in law or to compel the state to implement new land reform legislation.[2] The form that grassroots mobilization takes and the specific methods of resistance implemented vary across countries depending on contextual factors such as politics, geography, demography, history, and cultures of protest, and the practical experience and innovation of activists.

Land rights strategies are not only a marked change from agrarian revolution strategies, but also a clear rejection of acquiescence or subordination to the status quo, in which the state and its laws are used solely to benefit and provide legitimacy for the elite. Of course, there are substantial obstacles to rural mass mobilization. Poor rural people are often geographically dispersed and difficult to organize due to poverty, illiteracy, and traditional deference to authority (Schock 2015b). These obstacles may be diminished through leveraging existing civil society organizations and through strong grassroots organizing by a committed cadre of militant activists. There are also constraints to promoting counterhegemonic reform through legal channels, which are typically biased toward the interests of the elite due to their inordinate resources and influence. These constraints may be loosened if support is cultivated among broader elements of civil society and reform-minded state officials. Thus, land rights strategies may promote land reform if mass mobilization is sustained in the face of legal and extralegal maneuvers of the elite and state actors are compelled to implement the rule of law.[3] Not an easy task, however; under certain conditions barriers to land redistribution may be attenuated.

In this study, I explain why land rights strategies have been adopted by two land reform movements and analyze their dynamics of contention. The Ekta Parishad (Unity Forum) in India and the Movimento dos Trabalhadores Rurais sem Terra (Landless Rural Workers Movement or MST hereafter) in Brazil are motivated by counterhegemonic visions of rural development and a more equitable distribution of land. Despite increasing land inequality in recent decades, both countries have constitutional principles and laws that support more equitable distributions of land, and both social movement organizations have forged broadly comparable strategies that are designed to compel state agents to intervene in land conflicts. I argue that the adoption of comparable strategies is due to similarities in theoretically relevant aspects of the national political context, especially democracy and the rule of law. I also argue that the struggles are characterized by similar dynamics, despite differences in specific methods of collective action and ideology. I draw from theoretical perspectives from three literatures to explain the adoption and dynamics of land rights strategies: regimes and repertoires, law and social movements, and civil resistance.

Theory

The *theory of regimes and repertoires* assumes that the organization of national political regimes strongly affects contentious repertoires, and in a given type of regime some repertoires of contention will be more frequent and effective than others (Tilly 2005, 2006). According to Tilly (2006: 19), a regime refers to "repeated, strong interactions among major political actors including a government." He differentiates between four rough regime types based on two dimensions: democracy and government capacity. Democracy refers to the "extent to which persons subject to the government's authority have broad, equal rights to influence governmental affairs and to receive protection from arbitrary governmental action" (21). Government capacity refers to the "degree to which governmental actions affect distributions of populations, activities, and resources within the government's jurisdiction, relative to some standard of quality and efficiency" (21). A cross-classification of the two dimensions provides four regime types: high-capacity nondemocratic, low-capacity nondemocratic, high-capacity democratic, and low-capacity democratic (27).

Repertoires of contention refer to clumps of claim-making routines that apply to the same claimant-object pairs, such as employers and workers, peasants and landlords, or rival nationalist factions. Repertoires vary from place to place, time to time, and pair to pair (Tilly 2008). According to Tilly, modal repertoires of contention vary across regime types, with rival armed groups competing for power in low-capacity nondemocratic regimes, and occasional short outbursts of protest met with military repression in high-capacity nondemocratic regimes. In low- and high-capacity democracies, protest is more tolerated and less likely to be met with military repression (2006).

A problem with Tilly's conception of regimes is that rule of law is built into his definition of democracy. However, many formal democracies exclude segments of the population from political influence – not through laws that explicitly exclude some categories of people – but rather due to a lack of the rule of law. Here I use a slightly different conceptual map of regimes than does Tilly, drawing on the work of Alexander and Welzel (2011) who disaggregate popular rights and rule of law and identify regime types based on a cross-classification of these two dimensions. They conceptualize democracy as varying by the degree to which popular rights (civil liberties and political rights) are granted to citizens. The most democratic regimes grant full popular rights, whereas the most autocratic regimes do not grant any popular rights. They define rule of law as government (whether democratic or autocratic) bound to legal norms. Thus, rule of law does *not* differentiate democratic from autocratic governments; it differentiates rational governments from despotic governments and protects people from arbitrary power in both democracies and autocracies. A cross-classification of popular rights with rule of law yields four rough regime types: (1) *rational autocracy*, when rule of law is strong and popular rights are limited; (2) *despotic autocracy*, when rule of law is weak and popular rights are limited; (3) *effective democracy*, when rule of law is strong and popular rights are extensive; and (4) *ineffective democracy*, when rule of law is weak and popular rights are extensive. The four regime types and the placement of 188 countries are mapped out across the two dimensions in Figure 3.1.

Although Alexander and Welzel (2011) do not search for variations in contentious repertoires across their regime types, their conceptual map is useful for shedding light on variations in modal repertoires of contention in land struggles. A notable feature of Figure 3.1 is that contemporary struggles over arable land occur primarily in despotic autocratic and ineffective democratic regimes, i.e., in regimes where rule of law is relatively low. In rational autocracies and effective democracies, where the rule of law is relatively high, contemporary struggles over arable land are less frequent. This is due in part to the fact that in more economically developed countries, a much lower proportion of the population depends on

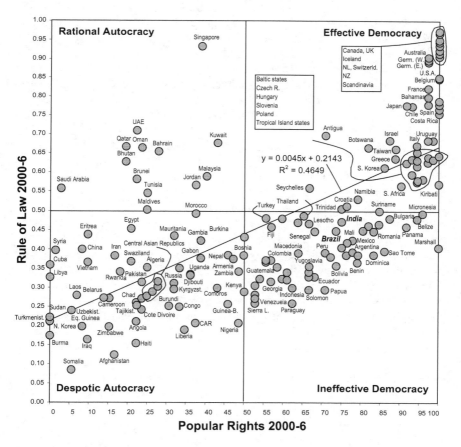

Figure 3.1 Rule of law by popular rights

Note: Dataset with variable description downloadable at www.worldvaluessurvey.org/publications

Source: Alexander, Amy C., and Christian Welzel. 2011. "Measuring Effective Democracy: The Human Empowerment Approach." *Comparative Politics* 43: 271–289. Reprinted with permission.

access to land for a dignified livelihood. But it is also because in countries where the rule of law is high, land conflicts are more likely to be adequately resolved within institutional channels without the necessity of resorting to nonroutine collective action. Thus, the most theoretically relevant variation in strategies of land struggles occurs across despotic autocracies and ineffective democracies, where significant proportions of people depend on access to land for a dignified livelihood and levels of democracy and/or rule of law are low.

Land struggles in *despotic autocracies* tend to be characterized by sporadic outbursts of violence that are met with state repression. In despotic autocracies with lower-than-expected levels of the rule of law (situated below the regression line in Figure 3.1), as in Afghanistan, the Democratic Republic of Congo, and Somalia, armed conflict between rival warlords for land and resources should not be uncommon. In despotic autocracies with higher-than-expected levels of the rule of law (situated above the regression line in Figure 3.1), violent resistance should be more sporadic and limited, due in part to higher repressive capacities of the state and in part to the state's ability to resolve conflicts based on institutionalized (yet undemocratic) procedures. In these countries, unarmed protest and appeals to authorities occur that highlight contradictions between official central government policies and land dispossession occurring at the local level, as in forms of rightful resistance implemented in China and Vietnam (e.g., O'Brien and Li 2006; Kerkvliet 2014).

By contrast, I expect land struggles in *ineffective democracies* to be characterized by unarmed mass mobilization much more frequently than violence. Of course, violent or armed resistance may occur in these contexts; however, they are likely to occur in isolated pockets and are unlikely to draw widespread support or succeed in regimes that are formally democratic (Tilly 2006; Martin 2006).

Virtually all ineffective democracies are characterized by lower-than-expected levels of the rule of law (situated below the regression line in Figure 3.1), and this is precisely the issue with regard to unenforced land reform legislation and rural elites who act with impunity in using violence against those who struggle for land rights (Hammond 2009; Heil 2010; Human Rights Watch 1992). A key factor differentiating effective democracies from ineffective democracies is state failure in the enforcement of the rule of law. The codification of popular rights establishes nominal democracy, but rule of law is necessary to translate nominal democracy into effective democracy (Alexander and Welzel 2011). Therefore, unarmed challenges that promote the implementation of existing laws or the passage and implementation of new land reform laws are likely to occur in these contexts.

> *Hypothesis 1*: Land rights strategies are more likely to be adopted in ineffective democracies, where the rule of law is lower than expected given the relatively high degree of democracy, than in other types of regimes.[4]

Literature on *law and social movements* addresses issues such as whether law can be used by oppressed groups to attain or expand rights or promote counter-hegemonic social change. From functionalist and liberal legalistic perspectives, law is typically viewed as a neutral instrument for regulating social conflict. From Marxist and other critical perspectives, the state and its laws are viewed as instruments of the bourgeois elite used to perpetuate class domination, and it is assumed that counterhegemonic change cannot be attained through institutional legal channels. Situated between these two perspectives are a range of views that call attention to the possibilities and limits of rights-based strategies for challenging inequality. Although recognizing that legal orders embody asymmetrical power relations, these views suggest that law should not be viewed simply and always as an instrument of domination. In fact, the relationship between law and power is paradoxical. Certainly, law is implicated in the production and maintenance of hegemony, but it can also facilitate resistance by becoming a vehicle through which hegemonic relations are challenged and subjected to open contestation (Hirsch and Lazarus-Black 1994; Hunt 1990). Certainly, law is implicated in skewing the distribution of resources, but it may also play a role in struggles to make the distribution of resources more just. In fact, some maintain that struggles to realize the universality of the rule of law offer the best possibility for constraining arbitrary actions of dominant groups and enabling popular struggles (Thompson 1975; Cole 2001).

The use of the legal sphere and rights-based strategies may be a *significant, but not exclusive*, method for attaining goals of counterhegemonic movements (e.g., Hunt 1990; Bartholomew and Hunt 1991; Santos 2002). When organized grassroots mobilization exposes the gap between "rights in law" and "rights in reality," and the gap between "arbitrary power" and "the rule of law," then opportunities for leveraging legal channels may arise. Specifically, land rights movements attempt to expose and leverage *land rights gaps* between land laws and their non-implementation, as well as broader *human rights gaps* between human rights laws or norms and their violation. These gaps may provide fulcra and mass mobilizations may provide levers that compel the state to intervene in land conflicts and perhaps even implement laws that facilitate land redistribution.

> *Hypothesis 2*: Rights-based strategies may be necessary but not sufficient for extending land rights to marginalized groups in democracies. In addition, extrainstitutional campaigns of sustained mass mobilization may be necessary to compel state actors to intervene in land conflicts.

Literature on *civil resistance* suggests that oppressed groups may have some strategic advantages using nonviolent resistance rather than violent resistance, especially armed resistance, in contexts where institutional political channels are blocked or ineffective and authorities are not averse to using violent repression in addition to the law to defend their interests (e.g., Chenoweth and Stephan 2011; Nepstad 2011; Schock 2005).[5] Physical, moral, and informational barriers to participation tend to be lower for campaigns waged through nonviolent resistance compared to violent or armed campaigns, thus participation may be higher and campaigns may be more widespread when they rely on unarmed action (Chenoweth and Stephan 2011). Similarly, oppressed groups engaged in nonviolent struggle are more likely to receive support from civil society groups and gain broader public support than are oppressed groups that engage in violent, especially armed, resistance. Moreover, repression of nonviolent resistance may be more difficult for authorities to justify compared to repression of violent or armed resistance. Thus, the backfire dynamic, whereby state repression leads to increased mobilization and support for the challengers, may be more likely to occur. Moreover, backfire is more likely to occur in democratic contexts, where information about acts of violent repression is more likely to be disseminated to the general public (Martin 2007).

A problem with the literature on civil resistance, however, is that it has over-whelmingly focused on prodemocracy struggles in authoritarian regimes and much less on struggles against structural inequalities and oppression, or using Galtung's term (1969), structural violence, in more democratic contexts. To make an analogy in terms of Gramsci's (1971) theory, the preponderance of recent civil resistance literature has focused on *wars of maneuver*, in which nonviolent resis-tance (and some unarmed violence) is mobilized in frontal assaults to topple a regime, with much less focus on *wars of position* in which civil society groups struggle through campaigns of civil resistance to gain positions of influence while forging counterhegemonic projects.

For example, the Color Revolutions and the Arab Spring uprisings might be considered *wars of maneuver* against dictatorships. The problem with these peo-ple power movements, however, from a Gramscian perspective, is that the multi-class blocs did not formulate a clear counterhegemonic program. Therefore, once the dictatorship was toppled, a vacuum emerged that was filled by neoliberalism and representative democracy in the case of the Color Revolutions, or by the military in the case of Egypt (Chabot and Sharifi 2013). By contrast, land rights struggles in democratic contexts are analogous to wars of position, whereby the landless struggle to gain positions of influence through attaining land and exercis-ing citizenship rights, while simultaneously forging a counterhegemonic project of agrarian reform and participatory democracy.

Moreover, critics suggest that while nonviolent resistance may be an effective strategy in contexts where there is a clear dichotomy between oppressor and oppressed and vast segments of society have been alienated by the regime – as in an autocracy – it is more problematic in challenging economic exploitation and structured inequalities in contexts legitimated by a hegemonic ideology (Chabot and Vinthagen 2015). Indeed, Gene Sharp (1973), an influential theorist of non-violent resistance, focused almost exclusively on challenges to authoritarian regimes, leaving challenges to structural violence for other scholars to address. In this study, I address the gap by analyzing cases where civil resistance is mobi-lized in wars of position against the state to challenge the structural violence of land inequality and dispossession in democratic contexts where neoliberalism is hegemonic.

Hypothesis 3: Challengers to structural violence and systemic oppression who adopt nonviolent resistance – even coercive and illegal nonviolent resistance – are more likely to generate widespread participation and external support than are challengers relying on violent or armed resistance.

Thus, I draw on three literatures, but extend them in innovative directions. I apply the regimes and repertoires framework to the analysis of land reform struggles; I apply the legal mobilization framework to struggles outside the US and to struggles for socioeconomic rights rather than political or civil rights; and I apply insights from the civil resistance approach to war of position struggles against structural violence in democratic regimes.

Cases and research methods

The Ekta Parishad and the MST are selected for comparison to illustrate the dynamics of contemporary rural challenges adopting land rights strategies. Both have engaged in sustained nonviolent campaigns over decades to promote land redistribution and prevent land alienation. The case selection may seem odd to those who view the MST as a revolutionary Marxist movement that engages in illegal land occupations and "violence" as a prelude to the alleged next stage of armed struggle. This perception is cultivated by large landowners and the corporate mass media to justify repression (Hammond 2004). As others have argued, however, the MST is better understood as a social movement that promotes political and socioeconomic rights primarily through nonviolent action, despite its militancy and attempts by opponents and the media to brand it as armed, violent, and anti-democratic (Carter 2011, 2015; Mészáros 2007, 2013; Robles 2000).

The case selection may also seem odd to area studies scholars who reserve for comparison political dynamics in countries bound by common history, culture, and geographic proximity. India and Brazil, of course, diverge in terms of history, culture, geographic proximity, and countless other factors, including religion, ethnolinguistic fractionalization, and GNP per capita. Nevertheless, the contexts in which the movements occur are markedly similar across a few key theoretically relevant variables. Both have capitalist economies and significant rural populations that depend on access to land for dignified livelihoods (although the rural population in India is much larger than in Brazil). Governments in both countries have been implementing neoliberal policies since the 1990s. Most significantly, both India and Brazil have relatively high degrees of democracy (through 2017) and constitutions and laws that support land reform and social justice, although the laws have not been effectively implemented due to corruption and disregard of the rule of law.

By their placement in Figure 3.1, India and Brazil are shown to be very similar in terms of popular rights (democracy) and the rule of law. The specific measures used by Alexander and Welzel (2011) for popular rights is a combination of Freedom House's civil liberties and political rights indicators. Civil liberties measure personal freedoms and political rights measure political freedoms. The two scores are averaged and transformed into a 0–100 range so that a score of 0 indicates no popular rights and 100 indicates complete popular rights. For the rule of law,

Table 3.1 Contextual factors: India and Brazil

Variable	India	Brazil	Range	Source
Democracy	9	8	−10 to 10	Polity IV
Rule of law	.51	.55	0 to 1.0	World Justice Project
Corruption	38	38	0 to 100	Transparency International

Alexander and Welzel (2011) average two World Bank indicators: (1) the rule of law index, which measures how strictly government officials abide by laws, based on the perceptions of country experts and citizens, and (2) the control of corruption index, which measures the extent to which exploitive power practices violate laws. The combined scores are transformed to a 0–1.0 range.

Moreover, as indicated in Table 3.1, the similarity of the Indian and Brazilian contexts regarding level of democracy and rule of law is not an artifact of the specific measures used by Alexander and Welzel (2011). Table 3.1 shows strikingly similar scores for Brazil and India using three alternative measures of democracy and the rule of law (and corruption). These three measures are:

1   The *Polity IV Dataset* measures democracy on a scale from negative 10 to positive 10, with 10 representing the highest degree of democracy (Marshall, Gurr, and Jaggers 2015). The scale is based on an evaluation of the competitiveness and openness of a state's elections, the nature of political participation, and the extent of checks on executive authority. For 2015, India's score was 9 while Brazil's score was 8. Both countries are above the world mean and fall into the ordinal category of "Democracy," which is less democratic than countries that are in the "Full Democracy" category, but more democratic than countries that fall into the categories of "Open Anocracy," "Closed Anocracy," and "Autocracy." These scores are consistent over time as Brazil received a score of 8 annually from 1988 to 2015, while India received a score of 9 annually from 1995 to 2015.

2   The *World Justice Project* measures the rule of law on a scale from 0 to 1, with 0 indicating the highest level of corruption and 1 indicating the lowest level. The index is based on eight factors, including constraints on government powers, absence of corruption, open government, fundamental rights, order and security, regulatory enforcement, civil justice, and criminal justice. For 2016, India's score was .51 and Brazil's score was .55. Both countries fall in the middle-third of the index and below the world mean. Brazil's global rank is 52 out of 113 and India's global rank is 66 out of 113 (where a ranking of 1 indicates the lowest level of corruption and a ranking of 113 indicates the highest level).

3   *Transparency International* measures corruption on a scale from 0 to 100, with 0 indicating the highest degree of corruption and 100 indicating an absence of corruption (Transparency International 2015). Their Corruption Perception Index ranks countries based on how corrupt a country's public

sector is perceived to be. It is a composite index, drawing on corruption-related data from expert and business surveys carried out by a variety of independent and reputable institutions. India and Brazil have the exact same score of 38 and rank of 76 out of 168 countries. Both countries fall in the middle-third of the index and below the world mean.

Using these additional measures of democracy, rule of law, and corruption confirms that India and Brazil are extremely similar in these dimensions. The lack of rule of law (and corruption) is significant, especially in rural areas, in that it reflects barriers to the implementation of land reform as exemplified by unenforced land laws. Similarly, it reflects the impunity of large landowners (as well as government officials influenced by them) who use illegal actions and violence against the landless to maintain or increase landholdings. The relatively democratic context is significant in two ways. First, it affords opportunities for sustained mass mobilization. Second, it is possible that existing land laws and constitutional provisions can be leveraged through mass mobilization to compel state actors to intervene in land conflicts. In some cases, state actors may come down on the side of the landless. Moreover, the post–Cold War international context characterized by a greater emphasis on human rights and greater transnational linkages among social movements facilitates a land rights strategy of resistance. Paradoxically, the "rule of law," an alleged principle of neoliberalism, is also invoked in these counterhegemonic struggles.

Rather than formally testing the hypotheses with the analysis of quantitative data, I use comparative-historical analysis and incorporate a synchronic paired comparison to identify and explain similarities in strategies and dynamics of contention across the two movements. A systematic comparison of matched cases facilitates the identification of causal factors that account for similarities. The first hypothesis concerning regimes and repertoires is assessed incorporating the logic of Mill's method of agreement (Ragin 2014: 36–42). An argument is made that despite the vast and innumerable differences across the two countries, the similar regime structures are causally related to the form in which effective resistance has assumed. The second and third hypotheses concerning nonviolent rights-based mobilization and its impact are assessed through an identification of likely causal mechanisms (Beach and Pedersen 2013; George and Bennett 2005).

Political context in India

The Indian Constitution, enacted in 1950, includes principles of socioeconomic justice. Article 39(b) of the Constitution specifies that states should direct their policy toward securing (1) that the citizens, men and women equally, have the right to an adequate means to livelihood; (2) that the ownership and control of the material resources of the community are so distributed as best to serve the common good; and (3) that the operation of the economic system does not result in the concentration of wealth and means of production to the common detriment (Government of India 2015). Specifically, with regard to land reform, upon independence the Indian National Congress Party addressed land inequalities through the J. C. Kumarappa Committee, which outlined broad principles. These principles were subsequently incorporated into the Indian Constitution of 1950 (Gae 1973; Merillat 1970; Saxena 2011: 174–176). The land reforms included (1) the abolition of the *Zamindari* system[6] and intermediaries, (2) tenancy reforms designed to provide secure land tenure for small farmers and ownership rights for tenants, and (3) land ceilings that imposed limitations on individual (or family) landholdings with compensation to the landowner and redistribution of the surplus to the landless.

Land is a state issue in India, and state governments were directed to enact appropriate laws consistent with the national policy and take measures to implement land reform. State-level laws were passed that eliminated intermediaries, imposed land ceilings, reformed tenancy relations, as well as prohibited the transfer of *adivasi* land to non-*adivasis*. However, there is general consensus that the state-level land reforms adopted after independence have not been adequately implemented (Vertika and Rodrigues 2015; Saxena 2011). Partial exceptions include Kerala in the late 1960s and 1970s and West Bengal in the 1970s and 1980s, where coalitions of left-wing parties took office and implemented significant land reform. Overall, however, only about 3% of India's arable land has been redistributed since independence; 2.7% as a result of the post-independence reforms (Tai 1968: 75) and 0.3% as a result of the Bhoodan land gift movement (King 1977: 285; Schock 2017).

Despite the liberal constitution and land laws, land inequalities persist. Hierarchical social structures based on inequality and exploitation have characterized land relations in rural India for centuries, inhibiting more equitable redistributions of land (Bandyopadhyay 1993); and powerful landowners have maintained or increased their landholdings and prevented reforms from being implemented largely because the landed elite comprise the Indian National Congress party's rural base (Vertika and Rodrigues 2015; Saxena 2011). In effect, there has been a lack of political will in overcoming the interests of the landed elite in order to implement constitutionally mandated land reform (Bandyopadhyay 1986; Radhakrishnan 1990). Moreover, in recent years the Bharatia Janata Party (BJP, hereafter) has promoted neoliberal policies that have transformed the Indian state into a "land broker state" that facilitates the dispossession of land from peasants and indigenous people and its transfer to capitalist and rentier classes (Levien 2011, 2013).

Political context in Brazil

In the twentieth century, Brazilian governments began implementing a series of liberal land laws. A strong legal presumption in favor of the *social function of property* dates back to its establishment as a principle in the Brazilian Constitution of 1934. The 1934 constitution states, "the right of property is protected, provided it is not exerted against any social or collective interests, in the forms determined by law." "Any social or collective interest" encompasses the concept of the social function of property (dos Santos Cunha 2011: 1175). All subsequent constitutions (1937, 1946, 1967, and 1988) have included a "social function of property" clause (dos Santos Cunha 2011: 1175 fn 21). Even the Land Statute of 1964, passed at the beginning of the military dictatorship, authorized the government to expropriate large landholdings if the land was unproductive and the expropriation served the public interest (Dalton 2012: 178–179). Most recently, Article 184 of the 1988 Brazilian constitution, adopted in the aftermath of the twenty-one-year military dictatorship, states, "It is within the power of the Union to expropriate on account of social interest . . . rural property which is not performing its social function" (Dalton 2012: 179). Subsequently, social function was defined by statute that (1) at least 80% of the land is in productive use, (2) with adherence to labor and environmental standards, and (3) that the use of the land benefits landowners and workers (Ankersen and Ruppert 2006: 102).

Nevertheless, despite liberal land laws, Brazil never implemented a serious land reform program and has one of the highest levels of land inequality in the world. As in India, there is a sharp contrast between "land rights in law" and "land rights in reality." Large landowners and capitalists in Brazil have been able to increase their concentration of landholdings through manipulating land laws, bureaucratic intransigence, as well as fraud, intimidation, and violence (Hammond 2009; Wright and Wolford 2003: 19–27). Large landowners and capitalists engage in violence with near impunity to maintain or expand their landholdings. The overwhelming preponderance of violence in rural areas is carried out against marginalized people who struggle for land. According to data collected by the *Comissão Pastoral da Terra* (Pastoral Commission on Land, or CPT hereafter) between 1985 and 2014, 1,566 landless peasants, small farmers, and their sympathizers were murdered (*Comissão Pastoral da Terra 2015*). According to Mészáros,

> The only consistent feature of Brazil's justice system is its inconsistency, namely its capacity to deviate from many of the basic premises advanced by a range of Rule of Law advocates. The system is notoriously unjust, bureaucratic, cripplingly slow, and saturated with class bias.
>
> (2007: 6)

Asserting land rights in India

Recognizing that land conflicts could not be adequately resolved solely through conventional political channels and that isolated villagers and tribals were more prone to violence and dispossession, the Ekta Parishad was founded in 1989 by Gandhian activist Rajagopal P. V.[7] He had been an activist in the state of Madhya Pradesh since the 1970s, working with Gandhians on the problem of armed banditry in the Chambal region. Their efforts contributed to the mass surrender and rehabilitation of *dacoits* (bandits). Rajagopal P. V. subsequently turned his attention to the displacement of *adivasis* from forestland and then broader issues of land dispossession and reform.

In Madhya Pradesh, *adivasis* continue to be forced off their land despite the state's Land Revenue Code of 1959 that banned the transfer of land from *adivasis* to non-*adivasis* without the permission of the government and the more stringent 1976 code that banned all such transfers. Similarly, the 1960 Madhya Pradesh Land Ceiling Act, which limits the amount of land a family can hold, has not been adequately enforced (Ramagundam 2001). In response, between 1994 and 1998 the Ekta Parishad mobilized pressure against the state government of Madhya Pradesh through several nonviolent tactics: marches, political rallies, *chakkajams* (road blockages), *gheraos* (surrounding a building), and *dharnas* (sit-ins). By 1999, a defining method of the Ekta Parishad became the extended foot march, or *padayatra*. The template for the *padayatra* is Gandhi's 1930 Salt March, a 26-day march to the Arabian Sea punctuated by stops in villages to mobilize people into the independence struggle. Since 1999, the Ekta Parishad has organized scores of *padayatra* campaigns. Statewide *padayatras* lasted from weeks to many months. *Padayatra* campaigns require substantial planning and preparation and are carried out in a highly organized and disciplined manner. Activists based in the countryside arrange logistics concerning the route of the *padayatra* and accommodations for marchers.

The first and longest statewide *padayatra* occurred in Madhya Pradesh from December 10, 1999, to June 18, 2000. The campaign was the first mass-based effort to promote the land rights of marginalized populations in Madhya Pradesh. Over 190 days, the campaign covered 3,800 kilometers and passed through approximately 1,500 villages. The campaign generated press coverage and educated the public about land conflicts. During the course of the campaign, over 19,000 landless and near landless submitted land-related grievances to *jan adalats* (public courts) in the villages (Pai 2007: 11; Ramagundam 2001).

As a result of the campaign, the state government agreed to form a task force to examine the problem of landlessness and to specify mechanisms to redress the issue. The task force formulated a program to provide land titles to *dalits* and *adivasis* who had been cultivating government land, provide land titles to *adivasis* who lived on forestland prior to 1980, and redistribute land from illegal encroachers to the landless. The implementation of the program, however, was highly uneven with the distribution of land to the landless occurring in some districts, but not in others. Moreover, when the BJP took control of the state assembly in 2003, the program ended. Thus, the Ekta Parishad realized that it was necessary to scale up pressure on the central government to implement land reform policies (Pai 2007: 11–12).

Since 2007 the Ekta Parishad, in coalition with numerous NGOs and SMOs, has organized two national *padayatra* campaigns, and planning for a third is underway (see Table 3.2). The *Janadesh* (Peoples' Verdict) *Satyāgraha* in 2007 was the Ekta Parishad's first national campaign. From October 2 to October 28, 2007, approximately 25,000 landless people along with their supporters, including activists from over fifteen states and advocates from nineteen countries, marched nearly 350 kilometers along the national highway from Gwalior, Madhya Pradesh, to Delhi (Pai 2007: 10). Political rallies and press conferences were

Table 3.2 Long marches organized by Ekta Parishad

	Date	Outcomes
Janadesh Satyāgraha, Gwalior to Delhi	October 2 to October 28, 2007	*Report of the Committee on State Agrarian Relations and the Unfinished Task in Land Reforms*
Jan Satyāgraha, Gwalior to Agra	October 2 to October 11, 2012	*Ten Point Agreement on Land Reforms* *Draft National Land Reforms Policy*
Jai Jagat	October 2018	

held along the way to publicize the issues for which the landless were marching, resulting in national and international media attention. Upon reaching Delhi, the landless set up an encampment at a fairground and threatened to march to the parliament building and engage in a *dharna* until the government agreed to their demands for a new land reform policy.

As a result of the pressure, the government agreed to organize a National Council on Land Reforms headed by the Minister of Rural Development, with 50% of its members selected by grassroots organizations. The committee was charged with drawing up a National Land Policy and empowered to direct state governments to enact appropriate land reform legislation. The committee issued a *Report of the Committee on State Agrarian Relations and the Unfinished Task in Land Reforms* by the Ministry of Rural Development (Government of India 2009). The document was the result of a thorough analysis of agrarian relations and is significant in that it is a comprehensive demand repository for social movements struggling for land redistribution. Its recommendations could form the basis of a national land reform policy (Vertika and Rodrigues 2015: 30–31).

Due to lack of government action in addressing the recommendations of the report, the Ekta Parishad followed the *Janadesh Satyāgraha* in 2007 with the *Jan Satyāgraha* in 2012. This too was a campaign organized to march 350 kilometers from Gwalior to Delhi, this time with 60,000 landless people and their supporters. However, nine days into the march, in the town of Agra, the minister for rural development, Jairam Ramesh, met with the marchers, agreed to the demands of the *satyāgrahis* and signed a ten-point agreement with Rajagopal P. V. that specified a roadmap for land reform (see Table 3.3). The crux of the agreement involved effective implementation of existing laws at the local level. The Ekta Parishad agreed to call off the remainder of the march, but threatened to reorganize the march at some time in the future if concrete progress concerning the implementation of the rule of law did not occur.

As a result of pressure by and input from the Ekta Parishad and other people's organizations, the *Draft National Land Reforms Policy* was written and published by the central government of India in 2013 for public discussion (Government of India 2013). The *Draft National Land Reforms Policy* is another step forward by the government toward fulfilling the demands of the Ekta Parishad and other

Table 3.3 Ten-point agreement on land reforms between the Ministry of Rural Development and Jan Satyāgraha (October 11, 2012)

1 Construction of a National Land Reform Policy by the Ministry for Rural Development.
2 Ministry of Rural Development works with states to develop programs to distribute agricultural land to the landless in "backward" districts and homestead land to homeless in rural areas.
3 Doubling the budget for the "Indira Awas Yojana" program for providing homestead land to the homeless.
4 Effective implementation of existing laws that protect land rights and access to land by poor communities.
5 Establish fast track land tribunals to deal with pending cases on land conflict.
6 Effective implementation of Panchayats Extension to Scheduled Areas Act of 1996.
7 Effective implementation of the Forest Rights Act.
8 Resolve land disputes between the Forest Department and the Revenue Department.
9 Survey and update records of common property resources.
10 Establish a Task Force on Land Reforms by the Ministry of Rural Development to implement the preceding points.

SMOs. To keep pressure on the government, the *Jai Jagat* campaign, a third long march, is being organized for October 2018.

Asserting land rights in Brazil

In the late 1970s, increasing levels of land inequality and the failure of the Brazilian government to adequately address land reform led to a large and growing population of aggrieved landless people. In an effort to attain land, poor rural people in southern Brazil began taking over unproductively used land through unarmed land occupations in the late 1970s and early 1980s. Progressive Catholic and Lutheran clergy affiliated with the CPT and Marxist activists concerned with land inequality and rural violence subsequently began working with the landless to organize land occupations. Activists realized that they could not depend solely on institutional politics to promote change and recognized the potential power of land occupations in forcing the government to redistribute land if they were implemented in an organized, disciplined, and strategic manner. They also realized that sustained mass mobilization was necessary to generate pressure from outside the system and that a national movement would be in a stronger position to resist repression and confront landowners and the state. Their efforts led to the founding of the *Movimento dos Trabalhadores Rurais sem Terra* (MST) in 1984. Since its founding, the MST has grown into the largest social movement in Latin America (Carter 2011, 2015; Hammond 1999, 2009; Robles 2000; Stédile and Fernandes 1999; Wolford 2010; Wright and Wolford 2003).

Before a land occupation is organized, the MST identifies land that fulfills two characteristics. First, the land must be expropriable, i.e., considered not in productive use and/or not serving its social function and thus eligible for redistribution under Brazilian law; and second, the land must be cultivable; i.e., suitable for supporting an agricultural settlement. To a lesser extent, the MST also targets land in which there is doubt over rightful ownership and unused state-owned land. After suitable land is identified and a sufficient number of landless people have been mobilized, an occupation is carried out. Occasionally armed agents of land-owners or the state meet the occupiers to prevent the occupation or evict them from the land. Although defensive violence by the MST has sometimes occurred, especially in earlier years of the movement, the *modus operandi* of the MST is to retreat and organize a new occupation rather than to challenge landowners and the state with armed violence – a strategy with which it would be at a decided disadvantage. Once land has been occupied, lawyers working with the MST initi-ate legal proceedings to challenge eviction notices and to have the land officially expropriated and redistributed by the government (a process that may take years). If the legal battle is won, then activists attempt to build a permanent agricultural settlement. If not, then an encampment is set up on the side of a road or on other public land and preparation for a new land occupation begins. Although the MST mobilizes pressure against the state, it also relies on the state's agrarian reform agencies to implement the rule of law by legitimizing its possession of occu-pied land and providing agricultural credit and technical assistance once land is attained.

In an attempt to deter land occupations, the Fernando Henrique Cardoso gov-ernment issued an executive order in August 2001 stating that land occupied by the landless would not be eligible for redistribution. This initially served as a deterrent to land occupations (as indicated in the steep decline in land occupations in 2001, see Figure 3.2). However, the MST responded with tactical innovation by occupying land *near to where* land was eligible for redistribution. Thus, the tar-geted land remained eligible for redistribution and the land occupations continued to pressure the government.

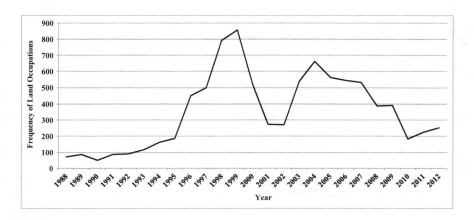

Figure 3.2 Land occupations in Brazil, 1988–2012

Source: from Gráfico 1 – Brasil – Número de Ocupações – 1988–2012. DATALUTA: Banco de Dados da Luta pela Terra. 2013. *Relatório Brasil 2012.*

From the mid-1980s to the early 2000s, land occupations forced the government to redistribute over 20 million acres of land to over 350,000 formerly landless families (Wright and Wolford 2003: xiii). Today the MST still organizes and implements land occupations to attain land for the landless, but as a result of their success in attaining land, their emphasis has shifted to promoting the interests of small-scale cooperative farmers and opposing industrial export-oriented agriculture. In other words, there has been a shift in the movement from a "struggle for land" to the "struggle on land" (Carter 2015; Lundström 2017).

Analysis

The first hypothesis states that land rights strategies are more likely to be adopted in ineffective democracies, where the rule of law is lower than expected given the relatively high degree of democracy, than in other types of regimes. Of course, without cross-national data on regime type and contentious repertoires implemented in land struggles, we cannot definitively assess this hypothesis. Nevertheless, evidence from India and Brazil suggests that the adoption of broadly similar land rights strategies is related to similarities in the political context with regard to levels of democracy and the (un)rule of law. In both countries, the logic of the struggle reflects the political context: (1) laws exist that embody land redistribution and social justice; (2) the un-rule of law, as manifested in the traditional political force of rural elites and their arbitrary use of power and violent repression, has inhibited land reform; and (3) sustained grassroots mobilization of nonviolent resistance, which takes advantage of democratic space and emphasizes land rights gaps, is necessary to compel state actors to intervene. In some cases state actors come down on the side of the landless. The land rights strategy adopted by the Ekta Parishad and the MST rejects both electoral politics and violent resistance, while embracing the mobilization of grassroots campaigns of civil resistance outside of conventional political channels to gain leverage in promoting change through institutional legal channels.

From its inception, the Ekta Parishad viewed the legal system as a means for struggling for land redistribution along with mass mobilization. In collaboration with progressive lawyers, they have brought lawsuits against landowners, corporations, and the Forestry Department in order to prevent land alienation or to attain compensation for the dispossessed. In addition to pressuring the government to implement existing land legislation, such as land ceilings, they have pressured the government to enact new legislation concerning land distribution and use. An important law that was implemented as a result of pressure mobilized by the Ekta Parishad and numerous other grassroots organizations was the Forest Rights Act of 2006. The Act addressed "historical injustice to the forest dwelling Scheduled Tribes and other traditional forest dwellers" by providing tenure rights to *adivasis* and preventing further land alienation (Government of India 2014: 1).

In contrast to the Ekta Parishad, when the MST emerged in the 1980s it was very skeptical of the legal system, maintaining the critical position that law works solely for the benefit of the capitalist elite and not for the poor and oppressed.

However, the MST was drawn into the legal sphere through criminal charges brought against its members who occupied land. Through the work and insight of progressive lawyers who donated time and effort to defend members of the MST, the MST gradually began to realize the potential of rights-based legal mobilization in promoting counterhegemonic change (Mészáros 2013).

Since the 1990s, the MST has remained autonomous from, but has worked closely with, the National Network of Peoples' Lawyers (*Rede Nacional de Advogados e Advogadas Populares*, or RENAP) in their efforts to promote land reform. Significantly, although land occupations are illegal, in 1996 the *Superior Tribunal de Justiça* ruled that land occupations with the intent to hasten land reform were substantially distinct from criminal acts against property (Carter 2011: 206; Mészáros 2007). This was a significant ruling that would not have likely occurred without the support of a network of progressive lawyers. Moreover, Santos and Carlet (2010) conclude that the creative combination of nonviolent direct action *and* legal practices by the MST has enabled hegemonic institutions such as judicial courts to be used to promote counterhegemonic claims and interests.

The disjuncture between the law and its nonimplementation and the reality of land inequality and dispossession provide a fulcrum for change; but in order to generate leverage within institutional political and legal spheres, sustained mass mobilization and the related dynamic of territorialization are necessary.

The second hypothesis states that rights-based strategies may be necessary but not sufficient for extending land rights to marginalized groups. Extrainstitutional campaigns of sustained mass mobilization may be necessary to compel state actors to intervene. Mobilizing relatively large numbers of committed people is probably necessary for winning new collective benefits for those underrepresented in politics (Amenta et al. 2005), and higher levels of participation in campaigns of civil resistance increase their likelihood of success (Chenoweth and Stephan 2011). First, however, constraints on mobilization must be overcome, of which geographical challenges are especially significant.

An advantage of large landowners is that rural populations tend to be geographically dispersed and difficult to mobilize. In order to overcome the disadvantage of geographic isolation, rural movements must territorialize; i.e., organize actions beyond their original territorial base. According to Fernandes (2005: 326), "Territorialized movements are those that are organized and act in different places at the same time, made possible by their form of organization, which permits spatialization of the struggle for land. The MST is an example of this." From its emergence in the far south of Brazil in the early 1980s, the MST gradually expanded north. This occurred through activists, who had already attained land through a land occupation, traveling north to work with landless people to organize additional land occupations. Territorialization provides challengers with the ability to more effectively confront landowners, security forces, and the state. By contrast, isolated rural struggles are more easily suppressed through violence (Fernandes 2005).

Similarly, the impetus driving the formation of the Ekta Parishad was the realization that isolated rural struggles were more prone to repression, whereas territorialization would protect and empower marginalized rural people. In the 1990s the Ekta Parishad increasingly took the form of a decentralized umbrella organization facilitating the coordination of previously unconnected Gandhian organizations dealing with rural development issues, as well with SMOs concerned with sustainable development, indigenous peoples, and human rights. Beginning in the state of Madhya Pradesh, it territorialized eastward to Chhattisgarh, Bihar, Jharkhand, and Odisha, some of the poorest states in India, on its way toward developing a national presence. The coordinated action of many peoples' organizations in a number of states under the umbrella of the Ekta Parishad enabled the movement to territorialize.

Like the land occupations in Brazil that forced the government to act, the long marches organized by the Ekta Parishad that mobilized tens of thousands of people along the national highway to Delhi were too big for the government to simply ignore. The series of *padayatras* compelled the government to take action with regard to land conflicts.

The third hypothesis states that challengers to structural violence adopting non-violent resistance – even coercive and illegal nonviolent resistance – are more likely to generate widespread participation and outside support than are challengers relying on violent or armed resistance. In addition to sustained participation, the nonviolent methods of resistance implemented by the Ekta Parishad have facilitated its ability to cultivate support from and engage in coalitions with numerous civil society organizations.

A comparison of the Ekta Parishad with Maoist Naxalites, who also struggle against land dispossession and promote a more equitable distribution of land, seems appropriate. Naxalites are active in a number of states along the "Red Corridor" with large *adivasi* populations, most notably Jharkhand, Chhattisgarh, and Andhra Pradesh. According to data compiled by the Indian Ministry of Home Affairs, Naxal-related violence caused 20,012 deaths between 1980 and 2015, with a majority of them civilian deaths (12,146 civilian deaths, 4,761 Naxalite deaths, and 3,105 state security personnel deaths) (Anand and Singh 2015). In contrast to the Ekta Parishad, it is unlikely that the Naxalite challenge in India will gain widespread support, due to its armed resistance and extensive killing of innocent civilians. By contrast, the Ekta Parishad has been able to mobilize large numbers of people under its umbrella and cultivate broad support through campaigns of nonviolent resistance.

In Brazil, armed resistance is not a feasible option given the capacity of the Brazilian state and the coherence of the military. The last violent peasant rebellion of note, in northern Paraná by peasants affiliated with the *Partido Comunista Brasileiro* (Brazilian Communist Party), was suppressed by the military in 1951. Moreover, it is unlikely that an armed struggle would be able to mobilize the vast numbers of people that the MST has mobilized through land occupations. Land occupations have occurred on a continuous basis in Brazil since the 1980s, with 8,789 reported for the 25 years between 1988 and 2012, involving 1,221,658 families, with peaks in 1999 (856 occupations) and 2004 (662 occupations) (DATALUTA: Banco de Dados da Luta Pela Terra 2013; Gráfico 1, Tabela 1). The MST has not organized all of the land occupations in Brazil, as numerous other groups have emulated the land occupation method, but the MST was instrumental in demonstrating the viability of land occupations and has implemented more occupations than any other organization.

Moreover, the MST recognizes that support from the public would decline if they were to engage in violent land occupations. According to a public opinion poll by the Brazilian Institute of Public Opinion and Statistics, "85% approved of land occupations *as long as they were not violent*" (as reported in Hammond 1999: 475; emphasis added). Moreover, it is unlikely that church organizations such as the CPT would support the MST if it were an armed, rather than an unarmed, struggle. Thus, through civil resistance the Ekta Parishad and the MST have mobilized relatively large numbers of people and cultivated the support of segments of the public and allies within officialdom that they otherwise would have not been able to do if their challenges were violent or armed.

Conclusion

In contrast to armed strategies of agrarian revolution that characterized many land struggles in the twentieth century, contemporary land reform movements implement a variety of strategies. In despotic autocracies where the rule of law is low, armed conflict between rival warlords is not uncommon. In despotic autocracies where the rule of law is higher, rightful resistance may occur in which peasants engage in sporadic unarmed protest and appeals to authorities that highlight contradictions between official central government policies and land dispossession occurring at the local level. In ineffective democracies, some movements, such as the Zapatistas in Mexico or the Naxalites in India, opt for complete autonomy from the state and are willing to take up arms to do so. However, other movements in ineffective democracies, such as the Ekta Parishad in India and the MST in Brazil, have forged a land rights strategy that uses a combination of mass-based nonviolent resistance and the legal system to compel states to implement new or existing laws that promote counterhegemonic reform.

The land rights strategy of the Ekta Parishad and the MST draws upon existing land rights discourse as embodied in constitutional laws in order to expose its unfulfilled implementation. They have illustrated that the innovative implementation of nonviolent protest and sustained mass mobilization, under certain conditions, can raise public awareness of problems of land inequality and dispossession and compel authorities to implement land policies that promote a more equitable distribution of land. Both movements have also illustrated that under certain conditions rights can be a significant component of counterhegemonic strategies, and bringing the struggle into the legal sphere can provide a potentially fruitful approach to the prosecution of transformative political practice.

Notes

1 "Rightful" or "rule-based" resistance is a comparable strategy implemented in more closed polities, such as by peasants in China who expose gaps in central policy directives

and their nonimplementation or violation at the local level; see O'Brien and Li (2006), Li (2010), and So (2007).
2 Beyond this, land rights movements may engage in nonviolent construction to promote local autonomy. This important issue is not addressed in this study.
3 The term "rule of law" means different things to different people. For example, neoliberals support a conservative and minimalist "rule of law" that facilitates market-based transactions, and authoritarians often invoke "rule of law" rhetoric to justify their repression. However, I use the term to refer to limitations on the arbitrary use of power and constraints on corruption (see Thompson 1975).
4 Hypotheses are used in this study to organize arguments and evidence. They are not formally tested through quantitative analysis.
5 For overviews of the literature, see Hallward and Norman (2015), Nepstad (2015), and Schock (2015c).
6 In the *Zamindari* system, *zamindars* ruled over areas like feudal lords. They were responsible for maintaining order and collecting taxes from peasants for the state.
7 His full name is Rajagopal Puthan Veetil. He prefers to use only his first name in public to avoid caste-related stereotyping that might be associated with his full name.

References

Agreement on Land Reforms between the Ministry of Rural Development and Jan Satyāgraha. October 11, 2012. www.ektaparishad.com/Portals/0/Documents/JanSatyagraha-Agreement-on-Land-Reforms.pdf (Accessed November 16, 2016).
Alexander, Amy C., and Christian Welzel. 2011. "Measuring Effective Democracy: The Human Empowerment Approach." *Comparative Politics* 43: 271–289.
Amenta, Edwin, Neal Caren, and Sheera Joy Olasky. 2005. "Age for Leisure? Political Mediation and the Impact of the Pension Movement on U.S. Old-Age Policy." *American Sociological Review* 70(3): 516–538.
Anand, Jatin, and Mahim Pratap Singh. 2015. "Civilians Biggest Casualty of Naxal Violence." *The Hindu*, 19 April.
Ankersen, Thomas T., and Thomas Ruppert. 2006. "*Tierra y Libertad*: The Social Function Doctrine and Land Reform in Latin America." *Tulane Environmental Law Journal* 19: 69–120.
Bandyopadhyay, D. 1986. "Land Reforms in India: An Analysis." *Economic and Political Weekly* 21(25/26): A50–A56.
Bandyopadhyay, Rekha. 1993. "Land System in India: A Historical Review." *Economic and Political Weekly* 28(52): A149–A155.
Bartholomew, Amy, and Alan Hunt. 1991. "What's Wrong with Rights?" *Law and Inequality* 9: 1–58.
Beach, Derek, and Rasmus Brun Pedersen. 2013. *Process-Tracing Methods: Foundations & Guidelines.* Ann Arbor: University of Michigan Press.
Bernstein, Henry. 2002. "Land Reform: Taking a Long(er) View." *Journal of Agrarian Change* 2(4): 433–463.
Borras, Saturnino M. 1998. *The Bibingka Strategy in Land Reform Implementation: Autonomous Peasant Movements and State Reformists in the Philippines.* Quezon City, the Philippines: Institute for Popular Democracy.
Carter, Miguel. 2011. "The Landless Rural Workers Movement and Democracy in Brazil." *Latin American Research Review* 45: 186–217.
Carter, Miguel, ed. 2015. *Challenging Social Inequality: The Landless Rural Workers Movement and Agrarian Reform in Brazil.* Durham, NC: Duke University Press.

Chabot, Sean, and Majif Sharifi. 2013. "The Violence of Nonviolence: Problematizing Nonviolent Resistance in Iran and Egypt." *Societies without Borders* 8: 205–232.

Chabot, Sean, and Stellan Vinthagen. 2015. "Decolonizing Civil Resistance." *Mobilization* 20(4): 517–532.

Chenoweth, Erica, and Maria J. Stephan. 2011. *Why Civil Resistance Works: The Strategic Logic of Nonviolent Conflict*. New York: Columbia University Press.

Cole, Daniel H. 2001. "An Unqualified Human Good: E. P. Thompson and the Rule of Law." *Journal of Law and Society* 28: 177–203.

Comissão Pastoral da Terra. 2015. *Conflitos no Campo Brasil 2014*. Goiânia: Comissão Pastoral da Terra.

Dalton, Taylor Reeves. 2012. "Rights for the Landless: Comparing Approaches to Historical Injustice in Brazil and South Africa." *Columbia Human Rights Law Review* 44: 171–198.

DATALUTA: Banco de Dados da Luta pela Terra. 2013. *Relatório Brasil 2012*. Presidente Prudente, São Paulo: Núcleo de Estudos, Pesquisas e Projetos de Reforma Agrária, UNESP.

Fernandes, Bernardo Mançano. 2005. "The Occupation as a Form of Access to Land in Brazil: A Theoretical and Methodological Contribution." Pp. 317–340 in *Reclaiming the Land: The Resurgence of Rural Movements in Africa, Asia, and Latin America*, edited by Sam Moyo and Paris Yeros. London: Zed Books.

Franco, Jennifer C. 2008. "Making Land Rights Accessible: Social Movements and Political-Legal Innovation in the Rural Philippines." *Journal of Development Studies* 44(7): 991–1022.

Gae, R.S. 1973. "Land Law in India: With Special Reference to the Constitution." *International and Comparative Law Quarterly* 22(2): 312–328.

Galtung, Johan. 1969. "Violence, Peace, and Peace Research." *Journal of Peace Research* 6(3): 167–191.

George, Alexander L., and Andrew Bennett. 2005. *Case Studies and Theory Development in the Social Sciences*. Cambridge, MA: MIT Press.

Government of India. 2009. "Report of the Committee on State Agrarian Relations and the Unfinished Task in Land Reforms." Ministry of Rural Development, Government of India, New Delhi.

Government of India. 2013. "Draft National Land Reform Policy." Ministry of Rural Development, Government of India, New Delhi.

Government of India. 2014. "Forest Rights Act, 2006: Act, Rules and Guidelines." Ministry of Tribal Affairs, Government of India, New Delhi.

Government of India. 2015. "Constitution of India." Ministry of Law and Justice, Government of India, New Delhi.

Gramsci, Antonio. 1971. *Selections from the Prison Notebooks*. New York: International Publishers.

Hallward, Maia Carter, and Julie M. Norman, eds. 2015. *Understanding Nonviolence: Contours and Contexts*. Cambridge: Polity.

Hammond, John L. 1999. "Law and Disorder: The Brazilian Landless Farmworkers' Movement." *Bulletin of Latin American Research* 18(4): 469–489.

Hammond, John L. 2004. "The MST and the Media: Competing Images of the Brazilian Landless Farmworkers' Movement." *Latin American Politics & Society* 46(4): 61–90.

Hammond, John L. 2009. "Land Occupations, Violence, and the Politics of Agrarian Reform in Brazil." *Latin American Perspectives* 36(4): 156–177.

Heil, Erin C. 2010. "The Brazilian Landless Movement, Resistance and Violence." *Critical Criminology* 18: 77–93.

Hirsch, Susan F., and Mindie Lazarus-Black. 1994. "Performance and Paradox: Exploring Law's Role in Hegemony and Resistance." Pp. 1–31 in *Contested States: Law, Hegemony and Resistance*, edited by S. F. Hirsch and M. Lazarus Black. London: Routledge.

Human Rights Watch. 1992. *The Struggle for Land in Brazil: Rural Violence Continues.* New York: Human Rights Watch.

Hunt, Alan. 1990. "Rights and Social Movements: Counter-Hegemonic Strategies." *Journal of Law and Society* 17: 309–328.

Kapoor, Dip, ed. 2017. *Against Colonization and Rural Dispossession: Local Resistance in South and East Asia, the Pacific and Africa*. London: Zed Books.

Kerkvliet, Benedict J. Tria. 2014. "Protests over Land in Vietnam: Rightful Resistance and More." *Journal of Vietnamese Study* 9: 19–54.

King, Russell. 1977. *Land Reform: A World Survey*. Boulder, CO: Westview Press.

Levien, Michael. 2011. "Special Economic Zones and Accumulation by Dispossession in India." *Journal of Agrarian Change* 11(4): 454–483.

Levien, Michael. 2013. "The Politics of Dispossession: Theorizing India's 'Land Wars'." *Politics & Society* 41(3): 351–394.

Li, Lianjing. 2010. "Rights Consciousness and Rules Conscious in Contemporary China." *The China Journal* 64: 47–68.

Lipton, Michael. 2009. *Land Reform in Developing Countries: Property Rights and Property Wrongs*. New York: Routledge.

Lundström, Markus. 2017. *The Making of Resistance: Brazil's Landless Movement and Narrative Enactment*. New York: Springer.

Marshall, Monty G., Ted Robert Gurr, and Keith Jaggers. 2015. *Polity IV: Political Regime Characteristics and Transitions*. Vienna, VA: Center for Systemic Peace.

Martin, Brian. 2006. "Paths to Social Change: Conventional Politics, Violence and Nonviolence." Chapter in *Nonviolent Alternatives for Social Change*, edited by Ralph Summy, in *Encyclopedia of Life Support Systems*. Oxford: Eolss Publishers.

Martin, Brian. 2007. *Justice Ignited: The Dynamics of Backfire*. Lanham, MD: Rowman and Littlefield.

Merillat, H.C.L. 1970. *Land and the Constitution in India*. New York: Columbia University Press.

Mészáros, George. 2007. "The MST and the Rule of Law in Brazil." *Law, Social Justice & Global Development* 1: 1–24.

Mészáros, George. 2013. *Social Movements, Law and the Politics of Land Reform: Lessons from Brazil*. New York: Routledge.

Moyo, Sam, and Paris Yeros, eds. 2005. *Reclaiming the Land: The Resurgence of Rural Movements in Africa, Asia, and Latin America*. London: Zed Books.

Nepstad, Sharon Erickson. 2011. *Nonviolent Revolutions: Civil Resistance in the Late 20th Century*. New York: Oxford University Press.

Nepstad, Sharon Erickson. 2015. *Nonviolent Struggle: Theories, Strategies, and Dynamics*. Oxford: Oxford University Press.

O'Brien, Kevin, and Lianjiang Li. 2006. *Rightful Resistance in Rural China*. Cambridge: Cambridge University Press.

Pai, Sudha. 2007. "Janadesh 2007: The Land Question." *Economic and Political Weekly* 42(45/46): 10–12.

Radhakrishnan, P. 1990. "Land Reforms: Rhetoric and Reality." *Economic and Political Weekly* 25(47): 2617–2621.

Ragin, Charles C. 2014. *The Comparative Method: Moving Beyond Qualitative and Quantitative Strategies*. Berkeley: University of California Press.

Rajagopopal, Balakrishnan. 2005. "The Role of Law in Counter-Hegemonic Globalization and Global Legal Pluralism: Lessons from the Narmada Valley Struggle." *Leiden Journal of International Law* 18: 345–387.

Ramagundam, Rahul. 2001. *Defeated Innocence: Adivasi Assertion, Land Rights and the Ekta Parishad Movement*. New Delhi: Grassroots India Publishers.

Robles, Wilder. 2000. "Beyond the Politics of Protest: The Landless Rural Workers Movement of Brazil." *Canadian Journal of Development Studies* 21(3): 657–691.

Santos, Boaventura de Sousa. 2002. *Toward a New Legal Common Sense: Law, Globalization, and Emancipation*. Cambridge: Cambridge University Press.

Santos, Boaventura de Sousa, and Flávia Carlet. 2010. "The Movement of Landless Rural Workers in Brazil and Their Struggles for Access to Law and Justice." Pp. 60–82 in *Marginalized Communities and Access to Justice*, edited by Yash Ghai and Jill Cottrell. New York: Routledge.

Santos, Boaventura de Sousa, and César A. Rodríguez-Garavito. 2005. "Law, Politics and the Subaltern Counter-Hegemonic Globalization." Pp. 1–26 in *Law and Globalization from Below: Towards a Cosmopolitan Legality*, edited by Boaventura De Sousa Santos. Cambridge: Cambridge University Press.

Santos Cunha, Alexandre dos. 2011. "The Social Function of Property in Brazilian Law." *Fordham Law Review* 80(3): 1171–1181.

Saxena, K.B. 2011. "Land Reforms: Unfinished Agenda or Reversal of Policy." Pp. 173–193 in *India Social Development Report 2010: The Land Question and the Marginalized*, edited by Manoranjan Mohanty. New Delhi: Oxford University Press.

Schock, Kurt. 2005. *Unarmed Insurrections: People Power Movements in Nondemocracies*. Minneapolis: University of Minnesota Press.

Schock, Kurt. 2015a. "Rightful Radical Resistance: Mass Mobilization and Land Struggles in India and Brazil." *Mobilization* 20(4): 493–515.

Schock, Kurt. 2015b. "Rural Movements and Economic Policy." Pp. 171–186 in *Understanding Nonviolence: Contours and Contexts*, edited by Maia Carter Hallward and Julie M. Norman. Cambridge: Polity.

Schock, Kurt. 2015c. *Civil Resistance Today*. Cambridge: Polity.

Schock, Kurt. 2017. "Gandhian Struggles for Land in India: The Bhoodan and Ekta Parishad Movements." Pp. 208–229 in *Nonviolence in Modern Indian History*, edited by David Hardiman. New Delhi: Orient Blackswan.

Sharp, Gene. 1973. *The Politics of Nonviolent Action*. Boston: Porter Sargent Publishers Inc.

So, Alvin Y. 2007. "Peasant Conflict and the Local Predatory State in the Chinese Countryside." *Journal of Peasant Studies* 34(3 & 4): 560–4581.

Stédile, João Pedro, and Bernardo Mançano Fernandes. 1999. *Brava Gente: A Trajetória do MST e a Luta pela Terra no Brasil*. São Paulo: Fundação Perseu Abramo.

Tai, Hung-chao. 1968. "The Political Process of Land Reform: A Comparative Study." *Civilisations* 18: 61–79.

Thompson, E.P. 1975. *Whigs and Hunters: The Origins of the Black Act*. New York: Pantheon.

Tilly, Charles. 2005. "Regimes and Contention." Pp. 423–440 in *The Handbook of Political Sociology: States, Civil Societies, and Globalization*, edited by Thomas Janoski, Robert R. Alford, Alexander M. Hicks, and Mildred A. Schwartz. Cambridge: Cambridge University Press.

Tilly, Charles. 2006. *Regimes and Repertoires*. Chicago: University of Chicago Press.

Tilly, Charles. 2008. *Contentious Performances*. Cambridge: Cambridge University Press.

Transparency International. 2015. *Corruption Perception Index*. Berlin, Germany: Transparency International.

Vertika, and Valerian Rodrigues. 2015. "The Indian State and the Unfinished Task of Land Reforms: A Critical Analysis." Pp. 29–47 in *Land and Disaster Management Strategies in Asia*, edited by Huong Ha. New Delhi: Springer.

Wolf, Eric. 1969. *Peasant Wars of the Twentieth Century*. New York: Harper and Row.

Wolford, Wendy. 2010. *This Land Is Ours Now: Social Mobilization and the Meanings of Land in Brazil*. Durham, NC: Duke University Press.

World Justice Project. 2015. *Rule of Law Index*. Washington, DC: World Justice Project.

Wright, Angus, and Wendy Wolford. 2003. *To Inherit the Earth: The Landless Movement and the Struggle for a New Brazil*. Oakland, CA: Food First Books.

4 Defections or disobedience?

Assessing the consequences of security force collaboration or disengagement in nonviolent movements

Sharon Erickson Nepstad

In studies of nonviolent regime transformation, researchers have found that security force defections can powerfully influence the outcome of so-called people power struggles. In fact, Chenoweth and Stephan's (2011) study found that a civil resistance movement was forty-six times more likely to succeed when security forces defected. Due to the predictive power of this factor, various researchers have sought to explain why defections occur. These studies document how, on the one hand, regimes promote loyalty by giving security forces economic or political incentives for supporting the state; on the other hand, they also document how civil resisters attempt to erode troop loyalty by increasing the costs of obedience in moral, political, and historical spheres while decreasing the personal costs of defection (Binnendijk and Marovic 2006; Makara 2013; Nepstad 2013; Seymour 2014). Others have emphasized the role of international relations. If an allied nation is willing to intervene in a conflict to support a regime, then that state will appear more durable, thereby diminishing the likelihood of defections (McLauchlin 2010). In addition, Lee (2014) argues that regime type matters. Personalistic authoritarian governments are more likely to create divisions and dissatisfaction within the armed forces, increasing the chance of defection. In contrast, authoritarian regimes that share power with elites and have mechanisms to curtail a dictator's discretionary behavior are more likely to keep security forces loyal.

Yet in this growing body of literature, the value of security force defections is almost never questioned (one notable exception is Chenoweth 2013). We must ask: are there any negative consequences of defections for civil resistance movements? Moreover, other possible security force responses have not been thoroughly explored even though members of the armed forces have multiple options when ordered to repress a civilian uprising. In this article, I examine some of the problems associated with military defections. I also examine how new democracies are threatened if civil resisters do not reconfigure and transform the military during the uprising as well as in the post-conflict transition phase. Using four case studies – Tunisia's revolution (2011), Serbia's electoral revolution (2000), the Philippines People Power movement (1986), and the Egyptian uprising (2011) – I explore alternatives to defection, arguing that civil resisters should promote outright disobedience, exiting, or compromised service.

The role of the security forces in civil resistance movements

In authoritarian regimes, the loyalty of security forces is fundamental to state survival. Removing this loyalty is critical for the success of nonviolent civilian revolts (Chenoweth and Stephan 2011; Katz 2004; Nepstad 2011). Time and time again, we have seen how rapidly regimes fall when armed forces withhold their support. This was evident in the 1986 "People Power" movement in the Philippines, in the 1997 Indonesia's revolt against President Suharto, in the 2000 "Bulldozer Revolution" in Serbia, the 2004 "Orange Revolution" in Ukraine, and Tunisia and Egypt during the Arab Spring of 2011 – to name but a few. Yet removing an authoritarian ruler does not automatically mean that a civil resistance movement will successfully implement and consolidate democracy. In fact, in some cases, security force defections have helped civil resisters oust an incumbent ruler but then created new problems that thwarted a nation's ability to genuinely democratize.

What problems can result from defections? One of the main concerns is that defectors may take their weapons, regroup, and mount an armed struggle against the state – as recently happened in Syria. This scenario transforms a nonviolent conflict into a violent one, shifting the struggle from civil resistance to civil war. Once civil war erupts, the chances of achieving a durable democracy decrease while the extent of human, infrastructural, and environmental devastation expands (Chenoweth and Stephan 2011; Johnstad 2010). A second problem that can result from security force defections is that the military may seize more political power once it cuts ties from the state. When security forces side with the opposition, officers may usurp the movement's momentum and impose their own agenda, which may not be consistent with the opposition's goals. Finally, if the armed forces side with the opposition and help remove a ruler, that same military may feel free to continue exerting its force with future political leaders – including those who are democratically elected. This was the case in the Philippines, where there were a series of attempted coups in the years following the People Power revolution (Katz 2004).

Since security force defections can pose challenges for a nonviolent democracy movement, civil resisters ought to be aware of the other responses that troops can choose. As depicted in Figure 4.1, there are five potential responses. First, security forces can remain *loyal* to the state, defending and reinforcing the regime against oppositional challenges. Second, security forces can intentionally *compromise their service* through shirking and selective compliance. Shirking is a form of everyday resistance whereby troops intentionally do a poor job or pretend to misunderstand orders, or covertly disobey in order to maintain plausible

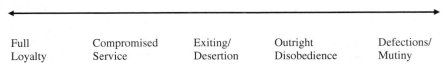

| Full | Compromised | Exiting/ | Outright | Defections/ |
| Loyalty | Service | Desertion | Disobedience | Mutiny |

Figure 4.1 Spectrum of security force responses to civil resistance movements

deniability. As one Serbian civil resister noted, "[Direct] insubordination is easy to punish, but incompetence is not" (quoted in Chenoweth 2013). Another way to compromise service is through selective compliance – that is, choosing to carry out some orders while ignoring or refusing others. With shirking and selective compliance, security forces are not fully supporting the state, but they also give no outward sign that they are supporting the movement. Third, security forces can *exit*. This means that they may desert (leaving their military post without permission and without the intention of returning), go into exile, or simply remain in the barracks when they are called up to mobilize (Albrecht and Ohl 2016). Fourth, security forces can engage in *outright disobedience*. This refers to a situation whereby troops refuse orders to suppress civil resisters. They do not flee but rather publicly withdraw from the conflict. In other words, they cut ties to the regime and refuse to cooperate with it, but they do not side with the movement. Fifth and finally, security forces can engage in *defections and mutiny*. Defections entail a shift of allegiance from one side to another; troops cut ties to the state and cast their support with civil resisters. Mutiny entails an open challenge to authorities whereby security forces now actively try to overthrow the state.

Which of these security force responses is most beneficial for a nonviolent uprising? To answer this question, I examine four cases to illustrate the different dynamics that can arise when the military simply refuses to interfere (Tunisia in 2011) and when the security forces became unpredictable through selective obedience (Serbia in 2000) versus the military's decision to defect and side with civil resisters (the Philippines in 1986 and Egypt in 2011). I argue that civil resisters should, first and foremost, encourage troops to engage in outright disobedience, which neutralizes the sanctioning power of the regime and consequently strengthens the movement. Secondarily, they should encourage exiting, which can raise questions about the regime's legitimacy and leaves fewer people to carry out orders, thus compromising the state's ability to repress. If these are not viable options, then civil resisters should encourage compromised service, which diminishes the chance that repressive orders will be carried out.

Yet in addition to neutralizing security forces, civil resisters *must* also simultaneously work to transform the military as an institution. In other words, they must engage in what Gandhi called the constructive program. Gandhi coined this term to denote that lasting change can only be created through the dual processes of the "obstructive program," which entails civil resistance to oppressive and unjust structures, and the "constructive program," which refers to building alternative practices or institutions or transforming existing ones to be compatible with and supportive of the movement's long-term goals. In other words, it is not enough to resist oppression; one must also simultaneously build an alternative society. In Gandhi's India, the constructive program entailed implementing educational programs, promoting village sanitation, establishing local businesses and promoting economic development, advancing equality for women and the "untouchables," and furthering basic health care. To truly establish Indian independence, Gandhi argued that they needed political independence but also the economic and cultural independence that such institutions can create (Bondurant 1958).

Precisely what does the constructive program look like vis-à-vis the military? I propose that civil resisters must encourage security forces to (re)define their mission to be defenders of democratic principles, civil liberties, and national borders – not defenders of a particular political leader or party. This is one reason why encouraging security forces to engage in outright disobedience is the best option, since it reinforces the expectation that militaries defend political principles. It also inculcates the belief that the military is a professional institution subordinated to civilian rule rather than a political institution that has the capacity to rule itself. Removing an incumbent authoritarian ruler without transforming the military can lead to some of the problems discussed previously, which can derail a democratic transition.

Methods

To examine the effects of various security force responses to civilian uprisings, I use comparative-historical analysis and the technique of process tracing. This technique involves dissecting causation by looking for links between independent variables and particular outcomes in an historical case (George 2005; Tansey 2007). Specifically, in each case study I trace the links between security forces' choices to defect (Philippines and Egypt), to refuse orders (Tunisia), or compromise their service (Serbia) to the extent of regime transformation after the revolution. I show how these decisions shaped the viability of civil resistance movements' longer-term goals.

Cases

Disobedience in the Tunisian revolution

The Arab Spring erupted in Tunisia in late 2010. Tunisians had many reasons to protest: the country suffered from an ailing economy, a corrupt regime, and lack of political freedoms. Yet up until 2010, there had had been little organized resistance to the 23-year-long rule of President Zine el-Abidine Ben Ali. What galvanized popular dissent was the atrocity that occurred on December 17, 2010. On this date, a young vegetable vendor had his cart confiscated by police, who stated that he had violated the law by not having a vending license. When he unsuccessfully appealed to officials to return his cart, he became desperate. In protest, he set himself on fire. A few days later, a few other Tunisians followed his example. These immolations led to an outburst of demonstrations in several cities. By January 2011, tens of thousands of Tunisians participated in protests and strikes throughout the nation.

Tunisia's police units were overwhelmed and unable to bring the situation under control. Consequently, President Ben Ali declared a curfew and deployed the army to the capital city of Tunis. By some accounts, Ben Ali ordered the military to use force against the civil resisters, opening fire if necessary. To the president's surprise, Army Chief of Staff General Rachid Ammar reportedly refused to comply with orders. Instead, the army withdrew from Tunis.

Knowing the tide had turned against him, Ben Ali attempted to assuage civil resisters with promises of reform, including the creation of 300,000 new jobs, reduction of food prices, the release of imprisoned protesters, and a pledge to not run for re-election. It was too little, too late. Tunisians wanted his resignation and the implementation of full democracy. With the police unable to stop the movement and the military withdrawing from the conflict, Ben Ali capitulated and fled to Saudi Arabia on January 14, 2011 (Bayat 2017; Gelvin 2012).

There is evidence that Ben Ali never actually ordered the military to open fire on protesters. General Ammar himself has denied that he ever received such orders (Bou Nassif 2015). Nonetheless, there is strong evidence that the military would not have been willing to carry out a crackdown, if one had been ordered. Tunisia's retired Navy chief of staff claimed,

> The officers would not have opened fire on the protesters. By officers I do not mean mid-ranking and junior officers alone, but the officer corps as a whole, including senior officers. The overwhelming majority in the officer corps was unhappy with the regime. . . . Had the orders been given to shoot, the officer corps in its entirety would have turned against Ammar.
>
> (Bou Nassif 2015: 79–80)

Tunisia's retired Air Force chief of staff also underscored this point: "I don't believe that Ben Ali would have ordered Ammar to open fire on the protesters. Had he done so, the armed forces would not have followed orders. I don't have a single doubt about that" (Bou Nassif 2015: 80).

This unwillingness to carry out orders is not the equivalent of defections or mutiny. While some members of the army did take action to protect the protesters, the military did not officially side with the opposition movement or help to oust the Tunisian president (Brooks 2013: 215). As one political analyst put it,

> The neutrality of the army was one of the key elements that led the revolution to overturn the Ben Ali regime. . . . It wasn't the role of the army to overthrow Ben Ali, but they didn't intervene, and this was a chance for the people to do it for themselves.
>
> (quoted in Parker 2013)

Bou Nassif concurs, arguing that, "In order to bring the regime to its end, the military had only to decline to uphold the status quo, which is precisely what it did" (2015: 80). In other words, the military refused to play a central role in helping either side win; rather, it simply removed the sanctioning power of the state, thereby weakening the regime and emboldening the protesters.

After Ben Ali fled, Tunisia began its transition to democracy. The head of the military, General Rashad Ammar, announced that he supported the revolution's goals and that the armed forces would maintain order and guarantee stability so that elections could be held. General Ammar made clear that the military would hold no political role in the transition; it was completely up to civil society groups to create and implement a new political system (Hanlon 2012). This was consistent with the Tunisian military's history, which had for some time promoted itself as a professional, depoliticized institution that was independent of the regime's interests (Signé and Smida 2014).

While the democratization process had its share of challenges, Tunisia is largely seen as a success story. In October 2011, the country held free and fair elections for the National Constitutional Assembly. A new governing coalition was put in power, headed by the Islamist movement Ennahdha, in conjunction with two secularist parties – the Congress for the Republic and Ettakatol. In November 2011, the assembly passed laws expanding freedom of the press. By April 2013, the assembly had agreed upon a political structure that combined a presidential and parliamentary system. In June 2013, the assembly passed a new constitution that provided the foundation for elections and political negotiations (Bellin 2013).

Naturally, there are many contributing factors to this outcome, including the presence of various structural factors deemed essential for democratization, including a well-educated population, a large middle class, and an ethnically homogeneous citizenry. Yet part of this equation is, in fact, the role that the military took during the revolutionary uprising. Although they were not happy with Ben Ali's favoritism toward the police and secret service, military leaders did not exploit the opportunity to impose their own agenda. Rather, they left the political space open for civil society groups and newly forming political organizations to take the lead in transforming the nation into a democracy.

It didn't take long for Tunisia's new democracy to face its first serious challenge. In the summer of 2013, after the assassination of two political figures, the civilian opposition became worried that the leading Ennahdha party was creating a dictatorship. Civilian leaders abandoned the work of drafting a new constitution and instead returned to the streets to protest. They called for the ouster of the Ennahdha government and the dissolution of the national assembly. While the military could have sided with protesters or staged a coup, it did not. It was committed to the ideals of citizen-led governance through democratic processes. It once again remained neutral, refusing to side with either the state or the movement. As a result, political leaders pulled together and produced the new constitution with near complete consensus. This enabled new elections to be held and a peaceful transition of power (Grewall 2016).

As civil resisters assert, one cannot state that the means are justified by the ends. During a democratic transition, the military must act as a professional institution that defends borders and protects citizens – not an institution that takes a political role in protecting or overthrowing a regime. If the military had sided with the civil resistance movement, then it would have accepted a political role. It was the military's neutrality that paved the way for democracy in the post-revolutionary stage.

Serbian security forces and selective compliance

A second case, the Serbian movement that ousted President Slobodan Milošević, shows how a military that is unreliable can also be useful to civil resisters. Starting in the 1990s, a growing number of Serbs were frustrated with Milošević, whose brutal wars with Croatia, Kosovo, and Bosnia earned him the title of "Butcher of the Balkans." These conflicts led to international condemnation and isolation, causing Serbia's economy to decline. Opposition groups had mobilized unsuccessfully in the early 1990s. In 1998, a group of students decided to launch a new movement, which they named Otpor ("Resistance"), using the techniques of civil resistance. They quickly established eighty chapters throughout the country to make it difficult for the state to isolate and repress the movement. Then, Otpor leaders introduced their strategy: they would pressure the state to hold elections and then organize citizens to vote Milošević out of office. They anticipated that he would try to steal the election; in that event, they would launch a variety of nonviolent campaigns to expose the fraud and force the courts to establish new elections that would be monitored by international observers (Vejvoda 2009).

To create a sense of electoral urgency, Otpor conducted a variety of actions and aired news stories with details of Milošević's corrupt practices. The government quickly responded, arresting Otpor activists and censoring independent media stations. Yet such actions only highlighted the grievances that the movement articulated, thereby expanding Otpor's popularity and support. In June 2000, Milošević passed legislation allowing him to run for another term. In July that year, he announced the elections would be held in two months, on September 24. By not allowing much time for the opposition to organize, Milošević thought that he could quickly clinch the election, granting him the appearance of democratic legitimacy.

Otpor, however, was ready. The activists mobilized rapidly, registering voters and helping unite the eighteen opposition parties into the coalition known as the Democratic Opposition of Serbia, which backed the candidacy of Vojislav Kostunica. On election day, independent polls indicated that Kostunica received 50.2% of the vote compared to Milošević's 37.2%. However, state polls gave a less favorable outcome to the opposition coalition. Using the state results, which many believed to be fraudulent, the Federal Election Commission argued that Kostunica had not received a majority and thus a run-off election was scheduled for October (Vejvoda 2009).

In response, Otpor launched campaigns of civil resistance. Within three days of the Federal Election Commission's announcement, hundreds of thousands of Serbians poured into the streets. Otpor also called for strikes, and the Kolubara coal miners heeded the call. This strike had an immediate effect, since the mine supplied roughly half of the country's electricity. Next, the mayor of Belgrade called for a general strike. Cities throughout Serbia follow suit, shutting down major urban centers. Milošević responded by sending the secret police to take over the mines and restart coal production. However, when 20,000 peaceful civil resisters showed up at the mines to demonstrate their support for the strikers, the police left (Nikolayenko 2011).

The culminating action was held on October 5, 2000. Otpor and other opposition organizers asked civil resisters to convene in Belgrade to nonviolently occupy the federal parliament building until Milošević resigned. Yet Otpor recognized that this could also elicit a crackdown, and thus they discussed ways of discouraging the military and the police from carrying out repressive orders. They did this in two ways. First, they implemented measures to ensure that nonviolent discipline was kept within their ranks. They recalled a previous protest in 1991, where police used tear gas and water cannons to disperse the crowd. Protesters fought back violently and found themselves quickly defeated and the movement crushed. Otpor knew that violence would only push security forces to protect the state. Second, they invited troops to support the goal of democracy and to see themselves as allies of the opposition movement rather than enemies. They did this by appealing to the military to serve the Serbian people, not the ruling party. They also invited army reservists to speak at their rallies and they emphasized that two retired generals were involved in the opposition coalition leadership. All of this was designed to help them identify with the movement rather than seeing civil resisters as a threat (Binnendijk and Marovic 2006).

Otpor did not encourage security forces to defect and side with the opposition. They merely wanted the military and the police to remain neutral. Yet they had no guarantees of how the security forces would respond during the Belgrade protest. Some police commanders had openly stated that they would not crack down on protesters, but those individuals were quickly fired. Other police leaders subtly implied that they would not intervene. Yet there was little sense of what the military would do. As opposition political leader Zoran Djindjic stated, "We hadn't managed to find out what was the real mood in the Army, not even a few days before October 5th" (Binnendijk and Marovic 2006: 418, f. 14, 423).

When October 5 arrived, hundreds of thousands of Serbians gathered in Belgrade. Some protesters borrowed a local farmer's bulldozer so that they could break down any barricades that would keep people from congregating and calling for Milošević's resignation. The military did mobilize troops on the outskirts of the city, but they made no serious effort to stop those headed to the protest. As people gathered in front of parliament, the police did not stop the civil resisters, who quickly occupied the federal building. The next day, October 6, 2000, the Constitutional Court reversed the election ruling and declared the opposition coalition candidate the legitimate winner. By December, national parliamentary elections were held, in which the Democratic Opposition of Serbia won a majority of seats. The old Milošević regime was officially over.

Serbians were filled with hope in the months following the "Bulldozer Revolution," yet the nation struggled to consolidate its new democracy. Shortly after the 2000 elections, deep and destructive conflicts emerged between the main political parties, culminating in failed elections and the assassination of Serbian Prime Minister Zoran Djindjic. One of the main issues that generated these contentious dynamics is that the new political leaders of Serbia did not sufficiently dismantle and restructure the military and the secret police that operated during the Milošević era. Although security forces had remained neutral during the uprising, there was no concerted "constructive program" effort to transform the armed forces' mission to be protectors of civilians rather than political power brokers in the new state. In fact, the situation worsened when Prime Minister Djindjic put himself in charge of the secret police instead of having them under parliamentary control, which left many citizens skeptical of Djindjic's promise to purge the secret police from politics. In response, Kostunica, head of the other major party in Serbia, postponed talks to reform the military. Thus, many of the Milošević-era military leaders remained in office. This led one politician to claim,

> We made the mistake to not replace most prominent persons from the police, secret police, army secret police and army general headquarters. They continued to knit their net and after some time we came to the stage where everything is the same, only he [Milošević] is missing.
>
> (Pribicevic 2004: 109–110)

After years of failed elections and a highly vulnerable government, the democratization process in Serbia has not followed a smooth path. Much of this is due to ongoing problems in the Serbian economy and culture. Part of the uncertainty, however, stemmed from the ongoing power and influence of the security forces. This illustrates the importance of not having security forces take on political roles during nonviolent revolutions *and* the importance of reconstructing the security forces in the post-revolutionary era to be under civilian control and to have a professional purpose and mission.

How security force defections create long-term challenges for democracy

Defections in the Philippines People Power movement

In 1986, the "People Power" movement overthrew the long-standing dictatorship of Philippine President Ferdinand Marcos. Marcos had originally been elected to the presidency in 1965 through free and fair elections. However, as he was nearing the completion of his second term, he pushed through a constitutional amendment in 1971 that would allow him to run for office again. This provoked massive demonstrations, as a growing segment of the population was outraged by Marcos's nepotism and his use of office to enhance his personal fortune. Marcos used the demonstrations as a reason to declare martial law, suspend the presidential election, and imprison his opponents, including his primary rival Senator Benigno "Ninoy" Aquino (Thompson 1995).

Opposition to Marcos expanded further in the late 1970s, as the economy declined, imposing financial hardship on many Filipinos, while the president grew wealthier due to corrupt practices. To keep a lid on protest, Marcos expanded the military and implemented more repressive techniques, including torture. Yet the situation changed when Ninoy Aquino returned to the Philippines. After his arrest in 1971, Aquino had spent roughly eight years on death row in Philippine prisons. In 1980, he developed a heart condition and was allowed to travel to the United States to receive medical treatment. He stayed there until 1983, when he heard that his homeland would hold legislative elections. He decided to return to lead the fledgling opposition movement and to nonviolently oust Marcos from office (Schock 2005).

Aquino flew back to the Philippines in August 1983. After landing in Manila, he exited the plane and was shot on the tarmac. He died instantly. Although the assassination was designed to end opposition to Marcos's rule, it had the opposite effect: it galvanized resistance, with nearly two million people joining in the funeral procession. The murder was also a turning point for economic elites, who had previously felt immune to the violence but were now outraged to see one of their own killed under government orders (Nepstad 2011).

After Aquino's death, the opposition quickly organized. To ensure that the planned revolution would occur nonviolently, opposition leaders appealed to the head of the Philippine Catholic Church, Cardinal Jaime Sin, who invited trainers to lead nonviolent action workshops in parishes through the country. Soon thereafter, these newly trained activists began organizing demonstrations, which brought greater international scrutiny to Philippine politics. Consequently, Marcos announced that he would hold legislative elections in 1984; he hoped that this would grant him legitimacy in the public eye. However, when elections occurred, they were marred by irregularities and fraud. When challenged on this matter, Marcos declared that these were "childish claims" and that he would settle concerns by holding presidential elections in February 1986 (Burton 1989; Thompson 1995).

The opposition selected Aquino's widow, Corey, to run against Marcos. Then they invited international election observers to be present during the vote. When election day came, those observers pointed out widespread fraud and declared the state results to be invalid. Not surprisingly, Marcos ignored these accusations and declared himself the victor. In response, the movement announced a series of civil resistance campaigns, including boycotts, tax resistance, and general strikes.

Yet before the campaigns were fully implemented, a key event occurred: soldiers began defecting. This started when the defense minister and the deputy chief of staff for the armed forces made a televised announcement that they could no longer support an illegitimate regime and they were resigning. Cardinal Sin knew that these defectors were in jeopardy, so he made an announcement on the Catholic Radio station, calling citizens to go to Camp Aguinaldo to protect the defectors. Within 24 hours, one million people gathered, forming a human barricade. Religious orders organized food brigades to feed the crowds. When Marcos's troops arrived at Camp Aguinaldo in tanks, the commander warned the civil resisters that they had 30 minutes to disperse. When the allotted time passed, the people refused to move. Nuns kneeled in prayer in front of the tanks. Unwilling to harm the nuns and other unarmed citizens, a few soldiers climbed out of the tanks and joined the crowd. Soon, more defected. And more. Within four days, an estimated 80–90% of the troops had joined the opposition. On February 25, 1986, inauguration day, Marcos knew that he had no ability to rule. He fled to Hawaii, and civil resisters stormed the presidential palace. People power had defeated the Marcos dictatorship (Lee 2009).

This case has been considered a successful instance of nonviolent revolution (Chenoweth and Stephan 2011; Nepstad 2011; Schock 2005). Indeed, many of the hallmarks of democracy were evident in the months and years following the people power revolt. For instance, in February 1987, the nation overwhelmingly approved a new constitution that spelled out democratic principles, procedures, and civil liberties. In May 1987, congressional elections were held, followed by local elections in January 1988 (Thompson 1996). Yet the consolidation of democracy in the Philippines was precarious, largely because of challenges from the armed forces. In the first few years after Marcos fled, Aquino and her successors faced eight coup d'état attempts (Thompson 1996).

Why did the military that helped promote democratization subsequently attempt to undermine it? Undoubtedly, many factors contributed to the precarious nature of the Philippines' political system – including ongoing economic difficulties and the presence of an armed insurgent group. Yet one cannot overlook the role of the military in the transition phase. In fact, one political analyst argued, "The most serious challenge faced by Aquino came from her erstwhile revolutionary partners, the military rebels" (Thompson 1996: 187). These defectors had helped civil resisters oust Marcos – not by remaining neutral and refusing orders to repress – but rather by actively assisting in the overthrow. In short, the military was not acting as a professional institution committed to the protection of its citizens; it was acting as a political player. Since this was true during the overthrow, it is not surprising that a military who found it appropriate to use its force to overturn Marcos would continue trying to use force to overthrow newly elected leaders who did not sufficiently address the interests of the armed forces. Indeed, Juan Ponce Enrile, Marcos's defense minister who started the defections, proclaimed that he and his fellow military defectors were the rightful victors of the people power revolution. And similar to the Serbian situation, the old military leaders continued to hold their posts in the new democratic state. A new military with a new professional mission was not instituted.

What this case demonstrates are the dangers of having the military take on the role of being a political force rather than an institution that serves civilian interests and political initiatives. It also underscores the importance of asking the armed forces to serve a neutral role during a nonviolent revolution to begin creating the new institution that is not political in orientation. Civil resisters' work is not over once the authoritarian ruler has been ousted. Rather, the rebuilding of new institutions (which ideally should begin before the overthrow) must continue, ensuring that the military is defined in a manner that will support rather than threaten democracy.

The Egyptian military defecting and siding with civil resisters

Inspired by the success of the 2011 nonviolent uprising in Tunisia, Egyptians began demanding change since they, too, suffered from various social problems. Many citizens experienced economic hardship. At the time of the Arab Spring movement, there was a 60% unemployment rate for people under the age of 30. In addition, nearly 25% of the population was living in poverty. A small number of people however, had become quite wealthy: approximately 90% of Egypt's private sector wealth was owned by just 200 families (Bassouini 2016: 55). Egyptians were also angered by police abuses. Thousands of citizens had been arrested and tortured during Mubarak's 30-year-long rule. One of the movement's social media sites was named after Khaled Said, a young man who died from injuries incurred by the Egyptian police. In addition, Egyptians were indignant about the country's political corruption, as the parliamentary elections of 2010 were blatantly fraudulent. As a result of these grievances, tens of thousands of Egyptians responded when civil resisters called for a major demonstration in Cairo's Tahrir Square on January 25, 2011. To sustain the momentum, organizers scheduled another event three days later, known as the "Day of Rage." Hundreds of thousands participated in this protest, which led to a continuous occupation of the square throughout the duration of the uprising.

President Hosni Mubarak could not ignore the protests. He took a variety of approaches to stop the movement. He promised various government reforms. He also imposed a curfew, cut internet and cell phone services, and ordered the police to crack down on protesters. The police did not hesitate, using tear gas, rubber bullets, and, in some cases, live ammunition. Still, given the sheer number of protesters, the police were unable to subdue the uprising. At that point, Mubarak ordered his military units to disperse the crowds by any means necessary. The military did not comply with his orders. Instead, they often protected civil resisters from the aggressive actions of the Egyptian police. Then, on January 31, the military leadership, headed by General Tantawi, publicly announced that they would not shoot at demonstrators. Instead, they joined in the call for Mubarak's resignation, siding with the opposition movement (Bassouini 2016: 59).

There was another attempt to scare civil resisters away through repressive measures. On February 2, pro-Mubarak thugs came into Tahrir Square on camels and horseback, armed with whips, clubs, rocks, and knives. They attacked protesters, causing hundreds of injuries and nearly a dozen deaths, and thus the event was dubbed "The Battle of the Camel" (Hellyer 2016: 17). It is widely believed that many of these thugs were hired by the regime to quash the demonstrations. After this event, US President Barack Obama stated that it was time for President Mubarak to step down (Ritter 2015).

The Battle of the Camel and other repressive acts brought international condemnation of Mubarak's regime, which emboldened civil resisters, who were determined that they would not relent until Mubarak relinquished power. By early February, well over a million Egyptians were in the streets. On February 7, President Mubarak fled and civil resisters began the task of constructing a state that would embody the ideals of democracy (Gelvin 2012).

The military's decision to withhold support from Mubarak and its refusal to repress protesters was an essential factor in the movement's victory. Yet why would the military cut ties to the state – especially one that had endowed it with such lucrative benefits? Numerous scholars have argued that the Egyptian military was on the verge of losing significant financial assets if Hosni Mubarak stayed in power and handed the presidential office over to his son, Gamal, upon retirement. Over several decades of Mubarak's rule, the military had developed strong "crony capitalist links" to the regime (Bellin 2012: 134). By some accounts, the military controlled an estimated 40% of the country's industries, operating businesses that made everything from flat screen televisions to automobiles to pasta and refrigerators (Gelvin 2012; Nepstad 2013). Mubarak had intentionally allowed the military to develop such wealth as a way to maintain their loyalty: keeping the president in office would ensure ongoing access to these profitable businesses. Yet all of this was threatened by the prospect of Gamal Mubarak taking over, since he planned to privatize these industries. In addition, as Obama encouraged Mubarak to resign, the military did not want to strain its relationship with United States, who sent $1.3 billion in military aid to Egypt annually (Hashim 2011). For all these reasons, the military sided with the protesters, helping them to oust Mubarak (Nepstad 2013).

As the nation faced the task of building a new government, the military again played a critical role. Until elections could be held, the Supreme Council of the Armed Forces (SCAF) retained political control, giving itself the power to make constitutional declarations. SCAF was comprised of fifteen top military commanders and headed by General Tantawi, who had been the defense minister since 1991. The pro-democracy movement was concerned about the dominant role of the military and thus they began organizing once more, calling for a "second Friday of Anger" on May 27, 2011. Hundreds of thousands demonstrated in Cairo, Alexandria, and Suez; these numbers indicate that many Egyptians were resisting SCAF's dominance and power (Bassouini 2016) Yet the democracy movement's numbers had dwindled, and the military cracked down on the anti-SCAF protests (Hellyer 2016). Eventually, however, the military bowed to pressure to hold elections. In June 2012, the Muslim Brotherhood's candidate, Mohamed Morsi, was elected president and the military relinquished political control.

It did not take long for Egyptians to grow disillusioned with the Muslim Brotherhood and Morsi's leadership. Within months of the election, Morsi began to overreach the limits of his power. For instance, he required all civil society groups to register with the state, which gave the government greater capacity to control or repress these organizations. Morsi additionally passed legislation that exempted his decrees from judicial review and made criticism of the president a crime. His administration also acquitted the police officers who were responsible for attacks on protesters, which greatly angered civil resisters. The economy continued to deteriorate and Morsi, who had promised economic reforms, did not effectively address these problems. Moreover, many citizens were deeply concerned that Morsi was moving the nation toward a theocracy – something that the majority of Egyptians rejected (Bassouini 2016).

In response, a group of dissatisfied citizens launched the "Tamarod" ("revolt") campaign in April 2013. The goal was to collect signatures for a no confidence vote on Morsi's leadership and to demand early presidential elections. Within approximately two months, the Tamarod campaign had collected 22 million signatures and called upon Morsi to step down. Campaign organizers also demanded the dissolution of the 2012 constitution and the drafting of a new constitution that would be put to a referendum. On June 30, 2013, the movement had ten trucks deliver the signed petitions to the palace. Millions of civil resisters poured into the streets, calling for Morsi's resignation. That evening, campaign organizers appealed to the army, the police, and the judiciary to side with the movement and support their efforts to nonviolently oust Morsi. The security forces responded, deposing Morsi on July 3 (Brown 2013). The head of the military, Sisi, assumed power. Civil resisters chanted victoriously, "The people and the army are one!" (Chenoweth 2013).

Since Morsi's ousting, Egypt has been embroiled in conflict. In 2014, the nation elected Abdel Fattah al-Sisi as their president. Yet genuine democracy still eludes the nation. New protests have erupted, emphasizing the government's economic mismanagement, restrictions on political liberties (such as a ban on protests), and security force abuses. Tens of thousands of Egyptian citizens have been detained and imprisoned for holding oppositional views. Human rights abuses have increased. Moreover, Sisi, a former army general and commander in chief, has given more power and economic advantages to the military, indicating that the armed forces still retain significant influence.

The Egyptian army's support of the opposition movement did contribute to the successful ousting of Mubarak, and thus many civil resisters considered this a victory. Many protesters felt that the military's backing of the Tamarod campaign was also useful, since it helped them depose Morsi. Yet this collusion between the army and the movement has not led to genuine democratization or political stability. Some political analysts argue that the military may have used the movement for its own purposes, regaining political power with the appearance of civilian support. That is indeed what has happened: the army is once again a major power broker and political player, which has demonstrated its willingness to use its force to remove heads of state – a situation that makes any democracy fragile and precarious.

Discussion

Democratization – the end goal of these civil resistance movements – does not naturally or easily develop once an authoritarian ruler has been deposed. While many factors contribute to the derailing of democratization processes, I argue that part of the problem is that civil resisters (and the academics who study them) have too often restricted their sights to the removal of the person or party that they do not want. To use Gandhi's terms, they have focused almost exclusively on the "obstructive program" of resistance and largely ignored the "constructive program" of rebuilding institutions that can carry and sustain revolutionary ideals. Hence, civil resistance models have focused too heavily on neutralizing the military as a "pillar of state support" and not placed enough emphasis on transforming that institution so it supports a new democracy. Failure to include a constructive program in a nonviolent struggle will weaken the chances of achieving long-term success (Chabot and Sharifi 2013).

So what would a constructive program look like vis-à-vis the military? I argue that nation states in the process of democratization after a nonviolent revolution must first redefine the mission of the armed forces. This mission must be strictly limited to the defense of national borders and projects that protect and aid civilians, such as humanitarian relief endeavors. Second, the military must be refashioned as a strictly professional institution, not a political one. To move in that direction, members of the armed forces must be trained so that their purpose and oath is to uphold the constitution and its principles, not a particular political leader or party. This is no easy task as the concept of a nonpoliticized, professional military is often seen as a foreign one – both in theory and in practice. Third, the military must be placed unambiguously under civilian control. Fourth, key leadership positions within the armed forces should be changed to ensure that old practices and expectations are removed.

This conceptualization of the armed forces explains why Tunisia successfully consolidated its democracy, even as it faced a similar situation to Egypt. Before the revolution, Tunisia's military already embodied these principles and thus they remained neutral and apolitical during and after the revolution (Brooks 2016). In contrast, the military in Serbia, the Philippines, and Egypt were not transformed and thus the path to democratization was far rockier and, in the case of Egypt, failed.

Yet civil resisters should not wait until the revolution wins to start this process of transforming the armed forces. True to the Gandhian method of prefigurative politics, these expectations should be built into the uprising itself. That means that civil resisters should not encourage collaboration or ask the military to share their political goals. Instead, pro-democracy activists should encourage the armed forces to refuse orders to repress (outright obedience) or encourage selective compliance in terms of upholding laws that support civil and human rights but refusing orders that are intended to preserve a particular party's power.

If rebuilding the military is essential for long-term success, why have both civil resisters and academics paid so little attention to this? One plausible explanation is that many people have an aversion to Gandhian principled nonviolence. In the decades of debates between advocates of pragmatic nonviolence (in the tradition of Gene Sharp) and advocates of principled nonviolence (in the tradition of Gandhi), many have dismissed Gandhi's approach as unrealistic. Gandhi's emphasis on *satyagraha* (truth force) and the conversion of one's opponents (instead of nonviolently coercing them) seems impractical to many (Nepstad 2015). Yet in dismissing Gandhian nonviolence, some civil resisters have lost sight of the very pragmatic aspects of Gandhi, including his call to combine resistance with the building of alternative institutions. We need to synthesize the best of both models to construct a method of nonviolent action that enables civil resisters to reject the system that they oppose while creating the system they want.

A second explanation is that redesigning the mission and structure of the armed forces may seem a daunting task. Indeed, it is no easy goal to shift security forces, who have held political power, toward an apolitical institution where actors understand their purpose as serving and protecting civilians. Yet revolutionary change is always difficult, and I argue that revolutionaries must set their sights on transforming the political system as well as the security forces.

Conclusion

In this chapter, I have conducted four case studies and concluded that civil resistance movements seeking democratization will only secure this goal in the long-run if they encourage security forces to remain neutral during the nonviolent uprising by taking a position of outright disobedience, selective compliance, or exiting. As Chenoweth (2013) argued in her analysis of the failure of the Egyptian revolution:

> For those seeking greater civilian control over the outcome of civil resistance, outright disobedience is almost always the most promising form of defection, since it means that security forces are fully prepared to submit to popular will. In the meantime, civil resistance campaigns should avoid the belief that the people and the military are always "one hand," as has been chanted so often in Egypt. Instead, they should see that security forces have their own interests, and they can easily manipulate the movement to suit their own purposes in ways that undermine the movement's own agenda. Movements with massive and diverse participation, nonviolent discipline, and the ability to withstand repression have been historically capable of forcing those in power to change. But only when a campaign pressures elites to suspend or reevaluate their own interests will they step out of the way of genuine transformation.

In short, civil resisters should encourage security forces to simply withhold their support from the state.

Yet neutralizing security forces through outright disobedience or selective compliance will only help in ousting the incumbent regime. To ensure that the newly created democracies stabilize and endure, there must simultaneously be a reconfiguration and re-visioning of the security forces. Failure to do so can lead to attempted coups and a return to authoritarianism. Hence, this study calls on civil resisters to move beyond the Sharp model of strategic nonviolence to a new model that combines civil resistance and the constructive program of rebuilding the military. It also requires us, as activists and academics, to move beyond the overly simplistic dichotomies of strategic and principled nonviolence. New activist models should include both, and new academic studies should measure the effects of constructive program efforts or the lack thereof.

As more civil resistance movements take seriously the need to neutralize and redesign the military, future researchers should pay attention to the fact that the military is not the only type of security force that operates in authoritarian states. Although no attention has been devoted to this matter in this chapter, the reality is that authoritarian rulers typically have multiple components to their security apparatus, including the military, the police, secret police, and paramilitary groups. These various branches of the security forces do not always share the same interests or take the same sides, which complicates the scenario of encouraging neutralization. As in the case in Egypt, a movement might find that it has won over the military but not the police. This can pose both challenges as well as opportunities. As Hank Johnston (2017: 13) has noted, "social control is, in reality, riven with competition, lapses, administrative turf wars, redundancies, and complex commitments among state actors." More research is needed to theorize and empirically explore how these competing interests among security forces may change the dynamics of nonviolent revolutionary movements.

Finally, how do these findings have any relevance to the field of social movements, which is largely focused on collective action in democratic settings such as North America and Western Europe? US movements have much to learn from civil resistance studies in terms of encouraging outright disobedience or selective compliance among the police. The most obvious contemporary case is that of the Sanctuary Movement, which has encouraged campus police and city police throughout the country to not enforce immigration policies that would lead to the arrest and deportation of undocumented immigrants. Today we see entire police departments refusing to comply with federal policies, even under threats from the Trump administration of losing federal funds. Moreover, the notion of a constructive program for security forces could also inspire new strategies in the Black Lives Matter movement, as it re-envisions the purpose and practices of police departments. Serious dialogue between social movement scholars and civil resistance researchers can cross-pollinate ideas, bringing new insights to both of these fields.

References

Albrecht, Holger, and Dorothy Ohl. 2016. "Exit, Resistance, Loyalty: Military Behavior during Unrest in Authoritarian Regimes." *Perspectives on Politics* 14(1): 38–52.

Bassouini, M. Cherif. 2016. "Egypt's Unfinished Revolution." Pp. 53–87 in *Civil Resistance in the Arab Spring: Triumphs and Disasters*, edited by Adam Roberts, Michael J. Willis, Rory McCarthy, and Timothy Garton Ash. Oxford, UK: Oxford University Press.

Bayat, Asef. 2017. *Revolution without Revolutionaries: Making Sense of the Arab Spring*. Stanford: Stanford University Press.

Bellin, Eva. 2012. "Reconsidering the Robustness of Authoritarianism in the Middle East: Lessons from the Arab Spring." *Comparative Politics* 44(2): 127–149.

Bellin, Eva. 2013. "Drivers of Democracy: Lessons from Tunisia." *Middle East Brief* 75: 1–10.

Bellin, Eva. 2014. "Explaining Democratic Divergence: Why Tunisia Has Succeeded and Egypt Failed." *Project on Middle East Political Science*. https://pomeps.org/2014/12/10/explaining-democratic-divergence/

Binnendijk, Anika Locke, and Ivan Marovic. 2006. "Power and Persuasion: Nonviolent Strategies to Influence State Security Forces in Serbia (2000) and Ukraine (2004)." *Communist and Post-Communist Studies* 39: 411–429.

Bondurant, Joan V. 1988 [1958]. *Conquest of Violence: The Gandhian Philosophy of Conflict*. Princeton, NJ: Princeton University Press.

Bou Nassif, Hachim. 2015. "A Military Besieged: The Armed Forces, the Police, and the Party in Bin Ali's Tunisia, 1987–2011." *International Journal of Middle East Studies* 47(1): 65–87.

Brooks, Risa. 2013. "Abandoned at the Palace: Why the Tunisian Military Defected from the Ben Ali Regime in January 2011." *The Journal of Strategic Studies* 26(2): 205–220.

Brooks, Risa. 2016. "Subjecting the Military to the Rule of Law: The Tunisian Model." Pp. 109–130 in *Building the Rule of Law in the Arab World: Tunisia, Egypt, and Beyond*, edited by Eva Bellin and Heidi E. Lane. Boulder, CO: Lynne Rienner Publishers.

Brown, Nathan J. 2013. "Egypt's Failed Transition." *Journal of Democracy* 24(4): 45–58.

Burton, Sandra. 1989. *Impossible Dream: The Marcoses, the Aquinos, and the Unfinished Revolution*. New York: Warner.

Chabot, Sean, and Majid Sharifi. 2013. "The Violence of Nonviolence: Problematizing Nonviolent Resistance in Iran and Egypt." *Societies without Borders* 8(2): 205–232.

Chenoweth, Erica. 2013. "Changing Sides Doesn't Always Make for Transformation: Just Look at Egypt." *Open Democracy*. July 31. https://www.opendemocracy.net/transforma tion/erica-chenoweth/changing-sides-doesnt-always-make-for-transformation-%E2% 80%94-just-look-at-e

Chenoweth, Erica, and Maria Stephan. 2011. *Why Civil Resistance Works: Strategic Logic of Nonviolent Conflicts*. New York: Columbia University Press.

Gelvin, James L. 2012. *The Arab Uprisings: What Everyone Needs to Know*. New York: Oxford University Press.

George, Alexander L. 2005. *Case Studies and Theory Development in the Social Sciences*. Cambridge, MA: MIT Press.

Grewall, Sharan. 2016. "A Quiet Revolution: The Tunisian Military after Ben Ali." Carnegie Middle East Center Report. February 24.

Hanlon, Querine. 2012. "Security Sector Reform in Tunisia: A Year after the Jasmine Revolution." USIP Special Report #304. March.

Hashim, Ahmed. 2011. "The Egyptian Military, Part II: From Mubarak Onward." *Middle East Policy* 18(4): 106–128.

Hellyer, H.A. 2016. *A Revolution Undone: Egypt's Road Beyond Revolt*. Oxford, UK: Oxford University Press.

Johnstad, Petter Grahl. 2010. "Nonviolent Democratization: A Sensitivity Analysis of How Transition Mode and Violence Impact the Durability of Democracy." *Peace and Change* 35(3): 464–482.

Johnston, Hank. 2017. "Repertoires of Resistance and Repression: The Authoritarian Governance Arena." Paper prepared for delivery at the American Sociological Association Annual Meeting, Montreal, Canada, August 12–15.

Katz, Mark N. 2004. "Democratic Revolutions: Why Some Succeed, Why Others Fail." *World Affairs* 166(3): 163–170.

Lee, Terrence. 2009. "The Armed Forces and Transitions from Authoritarian Rule: Explaining the Role of the Military in 1986 Philippines and 1998 Indonesia." *Comparative Political Studies* 42: 640–669.

Lee, Terrence. 2014. *Defect or Defend: Military Responses to Popular Protest in Authoritarian Asia*. Baltimore: The Johns Hopkins University Press.

Makara, Michael. 2013. "Coup-Proofing, Military Defection, and the Arab Spring." *Democracy and Security* 9(4): 334–359.

McLauchlin, Theodore. 2010. "Loyalty Strategies and Military Defection in Rebellion." *Comparative Politics* 42(3): 333–350.

Nepstad, Sharon Erickson. 2011. *Nonviolent Revolutions: Civil Resistance in the Late 20th Century*. New York: Oxford University Press.

Nepstad, Sharon Erickson. 2013. "Mutiny and Nonviolence in the Arab Spring: Exploring Military Defections and Loyalty in Egypt, Bahrain, and Syria." *Journal of Peace Research* 50(3): 337–349.

Nepstad, Sharon Erickson. 2015. *Nonviolent Struggle: Theories, Strategies, and Dynamics*. New York: Oxford University Press.

Nikolayenko, Olena. 2011. *Citizens in the Making of Post-Soviet States*. New York: Routledge.

Parker, Emily. 2013. "Tunisia's Military: Striving to Sidestep Politics and Challenges Mount." *Tunisia Live*. June 25.

Pribicevic, Ognjen. 2004. "Serbia after Milosevic." *Southeast European and Black Sea Studies* 4(1): 107–118.

Ritter, Daniel. 2015. *The Iron Cage of Liberalism: International Politics and Unarmed Revolutions in the Middle East and North Africa*. Oxford, UK: Oxford University Press.

Schock, Kurt. 2005. *Unarmed Insurrections: People Power Movements in Nondemocracies*. Minneapolis: University of Minnesota Press.

Seymour, Lee J.M. 2014. "Why Factions Switch Sides in Civil Wars: Rivalry, Patronage and Realignment in Sudan." *International Security* 39(2): 92–131.

Signé, Landry, and Remy Smida. 2014. "The Army's Decision to Repress: A Turning Point in Tunisia's Regime Change." Working Paper, Volume 151, Center for Democracy, Development, and the Rule of Law (CDDRL), April 24.

Tansey, Oisin. 2007. "Process Tracing and Elite Interviews: A Case for Non-Probability Sampling." *PS: Political Science and Politics* 40(4): 765–772.

Thompson, Mark R. 1995. *The Anti-Marcos Struggle: Personalistic Rule and Democratic Transition in the Philippines*. New Haven, CT: Yale University Press.

Thompson, Mark R. 1996. "Off the Endangered List: Philippine Democratization in Comparative Perspective." *Comparative Politics* 28(2): 179–205.

Vejvoda, Ivan. 2009. "Civil Society Versus Slobodan Milošević: Serbia, 1991–2000." Pp. 295–316 in *Civil Resistance and Power Politics: The Experience of Nonviolent Action from Gandhi to the Present*, edited by Adam Roberts and Timothy Garton Ash. Oxford: Oxford University Press.

5 Protest waves and authoritarian regimes

Repression and protest outcomes

James Franklin

Some of the most dramatic political events of recent times have involved protests against authoritarian regimes. Such protests showcase both the power and danger of nonviolent strategies, as protests can lead to the downfall of the authoritarian regime or to violent repression of the opposition. My research here focuses on protest waves under authoritarian regimes to assess outcomes. Along with the rising frequency of protest waves has come increasing scholarly attention to civil resistance. This literature has focused on outcomes and nonviolent tactics, and it has provided evidence for the superior efficacy of nonviolent resistance relative to violence, even in repressive, authoritarian regimes. This is perhaps most prominently argued in Chenoweth and Stephan's *Why Civil Resistance Works* (2011). However, this and other works have also come under criticism for case selection, overly simple conceptualizations, and failure to fully consider contextual factors that may also explain protest outcomes. This chapter reports the first steps in a project that examines protest tactics and outcomes while considering these criticisms.

To choose a representative sample, I use a relatively new events-data source (the Global Data on Events, Location, and Tone dataset description follows) to catalog all protest waves that occurred around the world from 1979 to 2011. The sampling process, described next, identified 302 protest waves in authoritarian regimes during this period. As shown in Franklin (2014), these protest waves coincide with nearly all recognized "democratic revolutions," yet they include many more cases that did not have such spectacular results or that simply have not been studied. The second phase of research, still ongoing, is the validation of these protest waves using secondary and news sources and gathering specific data on major protests and government responses. To analyze protest wave outcomes, this chapter focuses on ten of these protest waves that have been validated. They occur across three periods for three regions: South America in the 1980s, Northeast Asia in 1989–1990, and Eastern Europe in the late 1990s–2000s.

In line with the suggestions that David Meyer makes in chapter seven, I consider important contextual factors from the literatures on authoritarian regimes and democratization. I also provide a more detailed and nuanced analysis of government repression and its effects. Importantly, I move beyond a simple binary treatment of outcomes as successes versus failures to consider how long the wave extends and the process that political change takes – reform or revolution.

One interesting finding from these cases is the prevalence of democracy and human rights demands in the protests studied. Democratization was the leading demand in eight of the ten countries studied here and was the second-leading demand in the other two, behind human rights. Comparison of these cases allows an initial analysis of the outcomes of protest waves with consideration of the impact of political repression along with protest tactics, strength of the opposition, and strength of the authoritarian state. Overall, the cases studied here support the importance of considering both state-centered and challenger-centered factors. Successful democratization here was more likely when the opposition was able to mobilize larger numbers and could draw from a relatively urbanized population. These factors indicate the strength of opposition. Furthermore, the strength and unity of the authoritarian state was an important factor in protest wave outcomes. Authoritarian governments that are internally divided or that exercise power through semidemocratic institutions were largely less repressive in response to protests and were more vulnerable to democratization. My comparisons indicate that the level of repression is not a critical factor in outcomes. Rather, a worsening *trend* in repression is associated with demobilized protest waves. Preemptive repression against opposition organizations is more effective than reactive repression against protests. Finally, the protest waves examined show two distinct strategies. Both democratic revolution and demobilization tend to result from protests that follow a centralized confrontation strategy of extended occupations in a strategic location. Democratic reform tends to result from a pattern of serial protest, in which individual protests are of short duration but the wave as a whole lasts longer.

What are we studying?

There are many recent episodes of large-scale protests challenging authoritarian regimes. The Arab Spring uprisings of 2011 especially captured the popular imagination, but there have been many similar episodes before and after. How can we best draw generalizations about the causes and consequences of such protests? What should we call these episodes? Some use the term *democratic revolutions* (Beissinger 2007; Thompson 2004), which Thompson (2004) defined as "spontaneous popular uprisings – peaceful, urban-based, and cross-class in composition – which topple unyielding dictators and begin a transition process which leads to the consolidation of democracy" (1). However, if we study only protests that succeed in toppling dictators, then we cannot analyze the different outcomes of protests. A growing literature on civil resistance, developing from theory and practice of nonviolent action, has focused on explaining these episodes of protest (Nepstad 2015; Schock 2015; Vinthagen 2015). Schock (2005) called these episodes *unarmed insurrections*, while Nepstad (2011) used the term *nonviolent revolts*. Chenoweth and Stephan (2011) used the term *nonviolent campaigns*, which they contrast with violent campaigns. Earlier works on civil resistance were aimed more for practitioners than social scientists (Schock 2015), and therefore the selection of cases served a goal of showing that nonviolence *can* work (e.g., Ackerman and Duvall 2000), rather than offering a rigorous empirical test of the effectiveness of civil resistance. Bringing social scientific rigor to this field, Schock (2005) and Nepstad (2011) offered comparisons of successful and unsuccessful campaigns, Franklin (2009) examined government responses to over 800 contentious challenges, and Chenoweth and Stephan (2011) offered an analysis of 323 campaigns that occurred between 1900 and 2006. In the latter study, nonviolent campaigns were chosen from a review of the literature on nonviolent conflict and social movements, encyclopedias, a comprehensive bibliography on nonviolent civil resistance, and consultation with experts in the field. Violent campaigns were chosen from databases on civil wars and insurgencies. Despite these efforts to achieve a representative sample, this study was criticized by Lehoucq (2016), who argued that the list of campaigns is incomplete. Focusing on Central America, Lehoucq listed a few violent campaigns and several nonviolent campaigns that were not in Chenoweth and Stephan's list. Once these cases are added, Lehoucq argued, there is virtually no difference in success between nonviolent and violent campaigns. Discrepancies in one region do not necessarily undermine Chenoweth and Stephan's larger conclusions, and the additional cases included by Lehoucq may not meet all of the inclusion criteria specified by Chenoweth and Stephan. However, this does highlight an inherent problem studying contentious campaigns – there is no master list of such campaigns. Any listing now depends on which campaigns scholars have chosen to study, and it is entirely possible that successful campaigns are more likely to be chosen by scholars and media sources and thus find their way into databases. Furthermore, a *campaign* is quite an inclusive term, even if, following Chenoweth and Stephan (2011), we limit our attention to antiregime, antioccupation, and secession campaigns. It is quite plausible that a careful search of news accounts would yield additional sets of events that would fit the definition of campaign.

To some extent this is the nature of research in the field of contentious politics, and it may be impossible to completely satisfy the skeptics. However, I argue here that a focus on protest waves reduces some of these concerns. *Protest* here refers to an event in which inhabitants of a country gather in a common location or collectively refuse to cooperate in some routine activity for the purpose of publicly expressing opposition to something or to advocate change in the status quo within that country. Tarrow (2011) argued that protests, along with social movements, rebellions, riots, strikes, and revolutions, are encompassed by the term *contentious collective action*. Tarrow (1989) further asserted that contentious actions rise and fall over time in a cyclical nature and that

> what needs to be explained is not why people periodically petition, strike, demonstrate, riot, loot, and burn, but rather why so many of them do so at particular times in their history, and if there is a logical sequence to their actions.
> (13)

He defined a cycle of contention most basically as "a phase of heightened conflict across the social system" (Tarrow 2011: 199). Following Koopmans (1993) and

Almeida (2003), I use the term *protest wave*, which captures periods of higher-than-normal protest in a country. The focus here on protest waves allows me to use recently available events data to create a master list of protest waves.

This list of protest waves, described in the next section, corresponds with most of the prominent civil resistance campaigns or democratic revolutions identified by experts, yet includes many more that have not received as much attention.

Identifying protest waves

As a starting point, then, we need to identify when and where protest waves occurred. Prior research has been hampered by a lack of data on protest for a large sample of cases. One advance of this project is the inclusion of a worldwide sample of countries covering the period 1979–2011. This is possible by use of the new Global Data on Events, Location, and Tone (GDELT) dataset, which uses machine coding methods to identify and describe a wide variety of political events from multiple international news sources (Leetaru and Schrodt 2013). One class of events coded by GDELT is protest, which includes demonstrations, strikes, boycotts, hunger strikes, obstructing passage, and violent protests. Automated coding allows a range of coverage that is simply impossible with human coders, and Leetaru and Schrodt (2013) cite studies that find that the accuracy of automated coding is comparable to human coding. GDELT was used to create a protest variable that measures the number of protests in each of 194 countries for each year from 1979 to 2011.

Specification of protest waves requires the identification of periods within a country in which protest is at a heightened level. Previous studies of protest waves have used an indicator of the rate of protests in their country of study, gathered with media sources. A simple graph of protest incidence over time was sufficient to identify heightened periods of protest in previous studies (Almeida 2003, 2008; Brockett 2005; Inclán 2009; Koopmans 1993; Tarrow 1989), but what is satisfactory for a study of one or two countries gives us insufficient guidance for a study of nearly 200 countries for over 30 years. Here it is crucial to operationally define an *elevated incidence of protest*. To deal with widely divergent rates of protest across countries and remarkable increases in the reported rate of protests over time across the world, the incidence of protest in each year was compared to the median number of protests for three time periods for each country. As detailed and justified further in the appendix, I identified all country-years in which the incidence of protest was at least 1.8 times the median rate of protest for the country and time period, in which there were at least twenty protests, and in which the regime was identified as authoritarian. Finally, multiple years of elevated protest may combine into a single protest wave, so the final step is to define the delineation of protest waves, which is also discussed in the appendix. After applying the coding rules to the entire sample, 302 separate protest waves were identified under authoritarian regimes in 133 countries. The maximum duration of protest waves was ten years, though the vast majority were much shorter-lived, as over 60% only occurred within a single year. The global distribution of authoritarian protest waves is displayed in Figure 5.1.

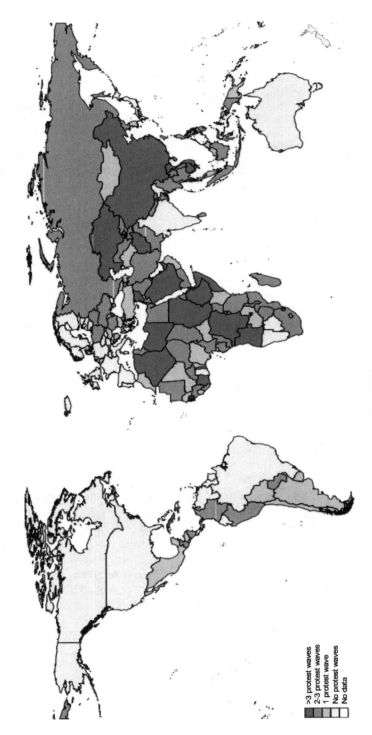

Figure 5.1 Incidence of protest waves in authoritarian regimes, 1979–2011

Source: Generated by author using Stata and original data.

Comparison of the distribution of protest waves as identified here does correspond well with other datasets that identify major protest campaigns. Twenty-nine (91%) of the 32 democratic revolutions (or attempts at democratic revolution) identified by Thompson (2004) and Beissinger (2013) coincide with protest waves as identified here. Schock (2005) identified thirty-one major unarmed insurrections, and twenty-five of these correspond with protest waves as identified here. One refers to a country that cannot be included here,[1] and in two cases, a protest wave was identified in the year following the one identified by Schock. Chenoweth and Stephan (2011) identified 323 prominent nonviolent and violent campaigns that occurred between 1900 and 2006. Fifty-eight of these campaigns *could* correspond with protest waves in my dataset, in that they were nonviolent and took place in authoritarian regimes in countries and years that correspond with my study, and forty-eight (83%) of these actually coincide with protest waves as identified here. These remaining ten campaigns have incidences of protest that are too low to be counted as a protest wave according to my definition, which is to be expected since campaigns do not necessarily occur during nationwide protest waves. On the other hand, my method identifies 254 additional protest waves during this time period. Therefore, the pattern of protest waves identified using GDELT covers the vast majority of major protest campaigns identified by other authors, while also including hundreds of other possible protest waves not identified in these studies.

This provides a satisfactory starting point in identifying protest waves, but further validation is necessary. As mentioned earlier, the GDELT dataset is based on computer coding of events. These events could involve actions that do not fit the definition of protest used here, such as diplomatic protests by a foreign government or protests by citizens of a country against a foreign government. Thus, it is possible that some of these protest waves could be false positives. Second, the dynamics of aggregate protest frequencies may not fit with the timing of distinct protest waves as identified by country experts. For example, the procedures used here identified a long protest wave from 1988 to 1997 in Yugoslavia/Serbia, but accounts by country experts identified four distinct protest waves during this period (Bunce and Wolchik 2011; Cvejic 1999; Popadic 1999; Vujovic 1999). Therefore, the protest waves identified using the procedures described previously will be validated using secondary sources on protest waves and by perusing news sources on protests. The news sources also allow more specific coding of protest characteristics such as demands, tactics, participation, and government responses that are not available in the basic events coding in GDELT.

A pilot study

This full validation process will be time consuming, but for the purpose of this research, ten countries were chosen for in-depth study, and validations were completed for these cases. I chose a few cases that were from the same region and roughly the same time period but in which some experienced improvement in democracy and some did not. These cases are listed in Table 5.1, along with the

Table 5.1 Cases studied

Country	Protest wave year(s)	Improvement in political rights[a]	Protest demands	
			Democracy	Human rights
Bolivia	1980	−4	100.0%	25.0%
Argentina	1982–1983	+4	27.6%	58.6%
Chile	1983–1988	+2	68.9%	36.5%
China	1989	−1	78.6%	28.6%
Mongolia	1989–1990	+5	60.0%	70.0%
Taiwan	1990–1991	+1	63.6%	21.2%
Serbia	1996–1997	0	100%	0%
Serbia	2000	+3	100%	0%
Ukraine	2004–2005	+1	100%	0%
Belarus	2006	0	100%	0%

a Measured by subtracting the reversed Freedom House political rights indicator for the year before the wave began from the level for the year after the end of the wave; positive scores indicate increasing respect for political rights

primary demands expressed in protests and the change in the reversed Freedom House political rights ratings from the year before the wave began to the year after the end of the wave. First, from Latin America I examine protest waves in Bolivia, Argentina, and Chile. Within Northeast Asia, China, Mongolia, and Taiwan will be examined. Finally in postcommunist Eastern Europe, two protest waves from Serbia as well as Ukraine and Belarus are studied. For these cases, I examined news accounts of all demonstrations with at least 100 participants and all occupations, sit-ins, blockades, boycotts, and hunger strikes that had some basic information on participants and/or demands. I also gathered data on strikes that made political demands. The examination of news sources allows a review of the types of grievances expressed and demands made by protesters. While some of these cases were chosen because they experienced democratic improvement, it is still striking how often democracy and human rights were the central demands of protests. This could be due to the case selection or due to Western media interest in struggles for regime change in authoritarian regimes, but alternatively it could indicate that grievances under authoritarian rule quickly turn to regime change, since leaders and policies are insulated from public participation.[2] We should also keep in mind the findings by Beissinger (2013) that the stated demands or grievances expressed by elites are not the same as the actual motivations of participants, yet a "negative coalition" of people who oppose a dictator can still have a democratizing effect, even if the participants do not agree on specific reforms.

Which outcomes?

Prior studies of nonviolent campaigns often took a dichotomous view of outcomes – success or failure. This is a natural starting point, but here I will consider a wider range of possibilities. Since this initial analysis finds that democracy is a widespread goal of protests under authoritarian rule, we should consider democratic effects. One type of democratizing effect is *democratic reform*: reforming electoral or other political procedures in ways that make them more democratic. This could be a dramatic change, such as holding multiparty elections in place of single-party elections or no elections at all. This could alternatively be more subtle, such as reforming the electoral authority so that it is not controlled by the governing party, which occurred, for example, in Mexico in the 1990s (Preston and Dillon 2004). Another type of democratizing effect is the *irregular removal of incumbent*. This goes beyond the incumbent agreeing to hold an election and then handing over power to the winner. Removal involves an irregular process, such as an incumbent resigning, being arrested, or fleeing the country. It could also include an incumbent who initially refused to recognize an electoral loss later being pressured to admit defeat. A *democratic revolution* would include both irregular removal of the incumbent and democratic reform. Some protest waves may result in democratic reform without forcing the removal of the incumbent, and here the outcome is *democratic reform*. It is possible that the incumbent could be removed in the name of democracy but the resulting regime is not actually democratic. This would be called a *stolen revolution*.

In cases in which protest waves do not lead to either democratic reform or the removal of the incumbent, there are various possibilities. First, if protesters do not seek democratic reform, this typology would not apply. However, as mentioned earlier, all of the protest waves in this pilot study do seek democratic reform. Second, protest could experience *demobilization*, either through repression or from internal collapse due to exhaustion or conflict within the opposition. A third possibility is that protests continue but the government refuses to make any substantial democratic concessions. Here we can say that the protest wave is in *stalemate*. Here we must also consider the duration of the wave. Every protest wave experiences at least some period of stalemate before reaching one of the other outcomes. To be usefully treated as a separate outcome, we should limit the stalemate category to protest waves that have been in stalemate for a longer than a typical period. Over 78% of the protest waves studied here lasted one or two years, but this still leaves sixty-four protest waves that lasted at least three years, and two of them lasted ten years. For this pilot study, protest waves that continue longer than two full years (730 days) without major democratic reforms will be considered to be in stalemate. These different outcomes are summarized in Figure 5.2.

Irregular Removal of Incumbent?	Democratic Reform?		
	No		Yes
No	Demobilization	Stalemate	Democratic Reform
Yes	Stolen Revolution		Democratic Revolution

Figure 5.2 Potential outcomes for protest waves with democratic demands

Literature review and theory

The rest of this chapter will examine outcomes of the ten selected protest waves. A theoretically grounded analysis must consider the literature on protest, social movements, and nonviolent action. Since democratization was such a prevalent demand, it is important to also consider the literature on democratization. A full review of these literatures is not possible here, but for the purposes of developing a theoretical framework, I will focus on actions by challengers and political authorities as well as the underlying strength of opposition and the state.

Actions by challengers

As mentioned previously, a growing literature on nonviolent action or civil resistance has developed to explain prominent protest waves. As Schock (2005) points out, the literature on nonviolent action (see e.g., Sharp 1973) pays most attention to contentious tactics, and the most basic argument and finding, established most prominently by Chenoweth and Stephan (2011), is that nonviolent action is more effective than violence. Other tactical considerations are important. Bunce and Wolchik (2011) emphasized the importance of a unified opposition in defeating authoritarian leaders, though Schedler (2013) did not find support for this. DeNardo (1985) argued that there is power in numbers (i.e., larger protests are more effective) and Chenoweth and Stephan (2011) found support for this. Schock (2005) argued that having clear and limited goals, having a decentralized yet coordinated organization, and using multiple tactics, including methods of dispersed protests (e.g., strike or boycott) as well as large, concentrated methods of protest (e.g., demonstration), are important in achieving success in struggles against authoritarian regimes. In Franklin (2009), I presented a model that proposed that government responses (repression, concessions, or toleration) depend in part on the tactics of challengers. In particular, I proposed that nonviolent disruption (rather than symbolic protests or political violence) was more likely to lead to concessions, and I did indeed find that occupations and hunger strikes were more likely to result in governmental concessions. This study also showed that increasing the duration of contentious challenges increased the likelihood of concessions. Therefore, these works suggest the outcomes of protest waves depend at least in part on the size of protests, the types of protest tactics used, and the duration of protest events.

Actions by authorities

However, Lehoucq (2016) citing findings from Trejo (2012) argues that opponents do not actually choose which strategy to pursue, as it is instead determined by the level of repression used by authorities. While I am quite skeptical of this claim, this does call for the consideration of how authorities respond to protests. Political repression has received the most scholarly attention, dating back over 40 years. However, the impact of repression is complex, and scholars have proposed a wide variety of hypotheses. Logically, we might expect repression to quell or at least reduce protest, since that is its intended effect. Snyder and Tilly (1972) and Hibbs (1973) found that repression reduces contention, and the bloody military crackdown on the Chinese student movement in 1989, studied next, is a famous case in which repression crushed a protest wave. On the other hand, repression can backfire, leading to even larger protests. Gurr (1970) argued that this is likely in the long run due to the relative deprivation created by repression.

These divergent effects of repression on contentious action have fueled a great deal of theorizing and research. Gurr (1970) and DeNardo (1985) asserted that the relationship is curvilinear, as repression incites more contention at median levels and discourages it at high and low levels. Lichbach and Gurr (1981) theorize basically the opposite, that median levels of repression discourage protest. Opp and Roehl (1990) and Rasler (1996) distinguished between long-term and short-term effects, with repression discouraging protest in the short run and inciting it in the long run. Lichbach (1987) proposed that the divergent effects of repression are caused by opposition groups shifting tactics. Finally, Brockett (2005) argued that the differential impact of repression depends on whether it occurs during a wave of contention. This literature suggests that repression during a protest wave is an important factor to consider when analyzing outcomes.

In a recent article (Franklin 2015), I examined the impact of repression by observing the persistence of contentious campaigns in seven Latin American countries. I did not find a consistent, robust effect of repression on challenger persistence. Instead, persistence was greater when challengers included organized groups, when they staged previous contentious challenges, when they sought regime change, when they opposed authoritarian regimes, and when they mobilized a larger number of protesters. In explaining these patterns, I argued for a filter theory of repression that posits that harsh repression can deter contention for some time, as it filters out opposition members who are not committed enough to risk likely repression. However, over time, protests may emerge, and here the participants are likely to expect repression and thus they are more persistent in the face of subsequent repression. According to these previous findings, all of the protest waves studied here would be expected to be persistent since they took place in authoritarian regimes and sought regime change. The logic of the filter theory also suggests that we consider the intensity of repression before a protest wave. If repression has already been the norm, then protesters may be more persistent if repression continues at similar levels. Changes in levels of repression from before to during a protest wave may be especially important.

Strength of the state

Many works on social movements, revolutions, and democratization have taken a structural approach that contrasts with the civil resistance literature. Skocpol (1979), in her influential study of social revolutions, argued, "the fact is that historically no successful social revolution has ever been 'made' by a mass-mobilizing, avowedly revolutionary movement" (17). She focused on severe weaknesses in the state as a crucial factor in revolutions. Goodwin (2001) extended this state-centered perspective to Cold War–era revolutions. Several works from the social movement literature (e.g., Eisinger 1973; McAdam 1982; Tarrow 2011) also examined the importance of the political opportunity structure in the emergence of social movements or protests. Tarrow (2011), in particular, considers increasing access to the political system, shifting political alignments, divisions among elites, and influential allies as important opportunities for contentious action. Works on authoritarian regimes and democratization also focus on strength and unity within authoritarian regimes as crucial factors. O'Donnell and Schmitter (1986) saw divisions within authoritarian regimes as the critical factor that start regime transitions that may result in democratization. Thompson (2004) argued that personalistic authoritarian regimes are especially vulnerable to democratic revolutions. In a similar vein, Geddes (1999) argued that military regimes are more likely to experience splits and negotiate an exit, whereas personalist regimes are least likely to split but also more likely to end in being overthrown. Likewise, Goodwin (2001) argued that patrimonial states are especially vulnerable to revolutionary movements. Levitsky and Way (2010) discussed competitive authoritarian regimes that allow semicompetitive elections that, while biased, still provide the opposition an opportunity to remove them from power. They argued that such regimes are especially likely to fall when they are closely linked to the West, when their political and economic weakness make them vulnerable to pressure from Western states, and when they lack coercive capacity, a strong ruling political party, and state economic control.

Two works in particular defend structural approaches against the strategic challenger-centered approach in the nonviolent action literature. Way (2008) criticized the growing emphasis on strategy and diffusion in analyses of the "color revolutions" in postcommunist Eurasia, arguing that the outcomes of such events depend on the degree of state and party capacity as well as the strength or weakness of links to the West. Lehoucq (2016), similarly, argued that works on nonviolent protest need to pay more attention to regime characteristics. Therefore, to truly test the efficacy of nonviolent tactics and protest in general, it is crucial to control for important structural factors. In terms of strength of the state, I will consider divisions within the authoritarian regime and whether the regime is full authoritarian or competitive authoritarian.

Strength of opposition

The literature on democratization also considers structural factors that can strengthen the opposition. Most famously, modernization theory proposes that socioeconomic development results in democratization (Lipset 1959). This effect may be due to mobilization of new social groups that demand democracy (Moore 1966; Fukuyama 2014; Rueschemeyer et al. 1992). In a complementary way, Inglehart and Welzel (2005) showed that postindustrial development of a country leads to the rise of self-expression values among citizens. Citizens with these values desire greater freedom and take a more activist stance to politics. Thus, this suggests that more socioeconomically developed countries have a greater potential for protests against authoritarian regimes.[3] Urbanization may be an especially relevant factor, as an indicator of development and because urban protests are such a major factor in democratic revolutions (Beissinger 2013; Thompson 2004).[4] Therefore, urbanization will be considered in the analysis that follows.

Comparing cases

Considering important aspects of authoritarian regimes, socioeconomic context, and opposition, I will examine the ten protest waves chosen for study. In this section, protest outcomes will be compared to possible factors identified earlier. I will proceed region by region, starting with Latin America.

Latin America

Three protest waves from 1980s South America were chosen for comparison: Bolivia 1980, Argentina 1982–1983, and Chile 1983–1988. The Chilean case is well-known, emphasized by scholars of nonviolence (Ackerman and DuVall 2000), and seen as an influence on subsequent antiauthoritarian movements (Bunce and Wolchik 2011). On the other hand, the Bolivian protest wave was short-lived, and I have found no scholarly literature on it. The protest wave in Bolivia was a reaction to a military coup on July 17, 1980, that occurred a few weeks after a presidential election in which no candidate won a majority. A similar military coup in 1979 was reversed following popular protest, and protesters in 1980 hoped to repeat their earlier success. Tin miners occupied their mines, a short general strike was held, and protests were held in La Paz, but only 200 took part in one of the main events reported. Protests fizzled out in less than three weeks.

Authoritarian regimes had already been in place ten years in Chile and six years in Argentina when the protest waves began. Both began in the context of economic recessions, and Argentina's military was also deeply divided and then launched the disastrous invasion of the Falklands/Malvinas islands in April 1982. After Argentine forces surrendered, the president resigned and a new military president announced the return to civilian rule. Human rights groups staged protests demanding an investigation into human rights abuses. A coalition of political parties demanded a swift return to real democracy and also backed the human rights demands. Democratic elections in Argentina were held in October 1983, and the winning candidate, Raúl Alfonsin, refused to grant an amnesty to the military for human rights abuses.

The opposition in Chile held huge monthly protests through 1983 and 1984. President Pinochet responded with easing of repression and talks with the opposition, but he was unwilling to consider stepping down or calling an early election. The constitution approved under military rule, however, called for a plebiscite in 1988 on whether Pinochet would get another eight-year term as president. Several opposition parties that banded together for protests ran a campaign for a "no" vote on the plebiscite and were successful. This instigated presidential elections and democratization. Using the outcomes proposed in Figure 5.2, Argentina is considered a case of democratic reform. Chile's protest wave was much longer than the rest considered here (1,975 days), and thus the stalemate outcome applies for 1983–1987 and democratic reform for 1988–1989. The outcome in Bolivia is demobilization.

These three cases are compared across several variables in Table 5.2. *Duration* refers to the duration in days of the protest wave, starting with the first protest reported in news reports during the protest wave period and continuing until the end of the final reported protest of the wave. *Protest rate* here refers to the number of protests per day during the protest wave. It measures the number of protests identified in perusal of news media, adjusted for the duration in days of each protest, divided by the number of days of the protest wave. *Median size* is the median size of protests for which estimates are available. Because of the frequent use of vague term like "thousands" when estimating protest size, participation is measured using an ordinal system with ranges of participants. Therefore, the range of the median category is shown in Table 5.2. The percentage of protest events that involved noncooperation (i.e., boycotts or labor strikes) is displayed under *% noncooperation*, and *% NV intervention* refers to the percentage of protest events that involved nonviolent intervention, including occupations, sit-ins, blockades, and

Table 5.2 South American protest waves

Variable	Argentina 1982	Chile 1983–1988	Bolivia 1980
Outcome	Democratic reform movement: Democratic elections held; military regime unable to impose amnesty	Stalemate followed by democratic reform movement: Pinochet refuses to step down or call early elections, but opposition wins plebiscite	Demobilization; protests fizzle out
Duration in days	631	1971	16
Protest rate	0.07	0.14	1.5
Median size	10,000–99,999	5,000–9,999	1,000–4,999
% noncooperation	13.0	14.7	50.0
% NV intervention	8.7	26.5	50.0
Political Terror Scale	5 → 3	4.3 → 3.8	2.7 → 3
Political repression of protests	Most protests tolerated	Repression used in response to most protest events, but not overwhelming	Crackdown on opposition organizations on eve of protest wave
Urbanization	83.3%	82.2%	44.4
Authoritarian divisions	Severe	Low	Divisions reported
Type of regime	Full authoritarian	Full authoritarian	Full authoritarian

hunger strikes. Repression is measured, first, by the *Political Terror Scale*, which varies from 1 (low incidence of disappearances, torture, political imprisonment, and political killings) to 5 (high levels of these abuses). The table reports, at the left, the average PTS level for the three years before the wave and, at the right, the average PTS level during the protest wave. Political repression is also described qualitatively, based on news accounts of the protests. *Urbanization* is measured for the year before the protest wave began using data from the World Bank. While admittedly difficult to measure, *authoritarian divisions* are described based on accounts from country experts and news accounts. *Type of regime* uses Levitsky and Way's (2010) typology of competitive authoritarian regimes and full authoritarian regimes. Levitsky and Way identify many of these cases, particularly for Eastern Europe, and I assign the rest using their criteria.

Several of the attributes and tactics of protest do not explain the differences in these three cases. Bolivia actually had the highest rate of protest and also had higher rates of noncooperation and intervention. However, it was smallest in terms of protest size, especially regarding urban protests. This may be related to the much lower rate of urbanization in Bolivia, but it probably also reflects the low institutionalization of political parties in Bolivia relative to Argentina and Chile (Mainwaring and Scully 1995). Chile's parties had been especially institutionalized, but they were divided into separate coalitions that disagreed over the role of violence in the resistance. Argentine parties united in the *Multipartidaria*, and while political parties, unions, and human rights organizations organized separate events, their goals were complementary. The level of repression during the protest wave, measured by the Political Terror Scale, does not explain the different outcomes, since Bolivia was no more repressive than Argentina and actually less repressive than Chile. Repression may have been a factor in two other ways, however. First, the PTS scores show that repression worsened during the protest wave year in Bolivia, while it lessened in Argentina and Chile. Perhaps protesters in Argentina and Chile, having experienced harsher repression, were better prepared for the severity of repression they faced. Furthermore, a closer examination shows that Bolivia experienced a crackdown right as protest was beginning that targeted the main opposition organizations – unions and political parties. Authoritarian divisions are not sufficient for protest wave success, as shown by Bolivia and its chronically divided military, which was nonetheless able to suppress protests. On the other hand, the relatively rapid success in Argentina versus the long drawn out process in Chile owes a lot to the severe divisions in the Argentine military regime (Munck 1998), whereas Pinochet had established a dominant position in Chile (Constable and Valenzuela 1991).

Asia

Three protest waves in Northeast Asia are compared – China 1989, Mongolia 1989–1990, and Taiwan 1990–1991. The Tiananmen Square protests of 1989 are one of the best-known cases in which brutal repression quashed a massive protest wave led by students. Hence, the outcome is demobilization. The protests began in mourning the death of Communist Party member Hu Yaobang, who was seen as a political reformer. Student demands quickly turned to freedom, democracy, and government transparency. Mongolia experienced a less publicized yet surprisingly successful wave of protests led by a newly declared opposition party. In response to these protests, the country's Communist Party agreed to end its monopoly on political power and hold multiparty elections. The Communist Party won the 1990 election, but the opposition won elections in 1996. This is considered a case of democratic reform. The White Lily Movement of Taiwanese students in March 1990 is recognized as an exemplary case of nonviolent action in the Global Nonviolent Action Database, but the protest wave identified here for Taiwan also includes actions by the opposition Democratic Progressive Party (DPP) and extends through 1991. At this point, Taiwan was making slow political reforms under President Lee Teng-Hui of the ruling Kuomintang Party (KMT). The opposition DPP, supported by students, called for immediate removal of certain measures that cemented the influence of legislators elected in mainland China in 1947. Their demands were not immediately met, but the reforms they demanded were largely met in subsequent months (Chen 2011). Therefore, this is also considered a democratic reform outcome. A comparison of these cases is summarized in Table 5.3.

Table 5.3 Northeast Asian protest waves

Variable	Mongolia 1989–1990	Taiwan 1990–1991	China 1989
Outcome	Democratic reform movement: Communist Party holds multiparty elections with later turnover of power	Democratic reform movement: Opposition demands are not granted at first, but reforms are made later in the year	Demobilization: Protests repressed
Duration in days	148	657	50
Protest rate	0.13	0.15	1.06
Median size	1,000–4,999	500–999	10,000–99,999
% noncooperation	0	6.9	7.1
% NV intervention	33.3	34.5	21.4
Political Terror Scale	Data not available	$2 \rightarrow 2$	$3 \rightarrow 5$
Political repression of protests	Opposition allowed to organize and protest	Repression light considering aggressiveness of protests	Protests end after severe repression
Urbanization	57.1	75.0	25.7
Authoritarian divisions	Divided between reformers and hardliners, with former ascendant	Divided between reformers and hardliners, with former ascendant	Some signs of divisions, but hardliners said to reassert control
Type of regime	Full authoritarian	Competitive authoritarian	Full authoritarian

Protest size and rate do not help explain outcomes for these three cases, as China's protesters had the largest and most frequent protests. Protest tactics do not appear to be closely related to outcomes, although an extended hunger strike in Mongolia immediately preceded the Communist Party's announcement of an end to their monopoly on power. Like in South America, the unsuccessful protest wave was in the least urbanized country (China). The Political Terror Scale was not available for Mongolia for this period, but China experienced a hardening of repression to the maximum level, whereas repression remained the same in Taiwan. Similar to South America, the trend on this scale is related to outcomes. The communist government in Mongolia was largely tolerant of protests, and opposition activists were able to form a political party. Repression in Taiwan was light considering the disruptiveness and aggressiveness of protests, including smashing windows of cars, attempting to block access to the legislature, and throwing tea at the speaker of the National Assembly. Repression in China, of course, was brutal, inflicted on a massive scale. An earlier attempt to repress protests in Tiananmen Square was blocked by Beijing citizens on May 20–22, but authorities called in military forces a second time on June 4, and despite confusion and some dissent they cleared the square with estimates of over 2,500 killed (Lim 2014). Authoritarian divisions also help explain outcomes, as Mongolia and Taiwan were led by reformers (Fish 1998; Chen 2011), whereas hardliners were seen as regaining control just before the crackdown in China (Schock 2005).

Eastern Europe

Protest waves in postcommunist countries have been the subject of comparative analysis, often under the rubric of "color revolutions" (see Beissinger 2007; Bunce and Wolchik 2011; Tucker 2007; Way 2008). The "Bulldozer Revolution" of Serbia in 2000 and the "Orange Revolution" of Ukraine in 2004–2005 are well-known examples of "color revolutions" in which attempts at rigging presidential elections were reversed under popular pressure. They fit the definition of democratic revolution. In Serbia, the long-standing president Slobodan Milosevic was running for re-election. The opposition-led election tally gave a majority to opposition candidate Vojislav Kostunica, but the official announcement gave him just under 50%, necessitating a runoff. Protests over a four-month period forced Milosevic to acknowledge defeat. Protests in Ukraine also began with a disputed presidential election. The official results of the runoff in 2004 gave Viktor Yanukovych, the government-backed candidate, a slim victory. However, an independent exit poll showed Viktor Yushchenko, the candidate of the opposition Orange Coalition, with a clear majority. This sparked a month of protest and occupation of the central Maidan square in Kiev, which helped force a revote that confirmed Yushchenko's victory. The protests in Belarus in 2006 followed the same script as Serbia and Ukraine, starting with disputed election results followed by demonstrations and occupation of a central square in the capital, but here protests were stopped by moderate repression and incumbent President Lukashenka maintained power. The Serbian protests of 1996–1997 also started with disputed election results, though here they were local elections. Protests did not lead to fundamental regime change, but they did force President Milosevic to recognize opposition gains in local elections. This is considered a case of democratic reform. A comparison of variables is shown in Table 5.4.

In this case, the rate of protest does correspond with protest wave outcomes, as Belarus had a lower rate than the other cases. The median size of protests does not correspond with outcomes, though, since Ukraine had the smallest median level of participation. However, the maximum protest size correlates more with outcomes,

Table 5.4 Protest waves in Eastern Europe

Variable	Serbia 2000	Ukraine 2004–2005	Serbia 1996–1997	Belarus 2006
Outcome	Democratic revolution: President Milosevic acknowledges electoral defeat	Democratic revolution: Fraudulent runoff results dismissed, opposition candidate Yuschenko wins revote	Democratic reform movement: Milosevic acknowledges opposition victories in local elections	Demobilization: Protests end after moderate repression
Duration in days	9	92	122	24
Protest rate	1.67	.72	1.68	.29
Median size	>100,000	1,000–4,999	10,000–99,999	10,000–99,999
% noncooperation	50.0	0	33.3	0
% NV intervention	83.3	50.0	33.3	50.0
Political Terror Scale	4.7 → 4	2.7 → 3	4 → 3	2.7 → 3
Political repression of protests	Most protests tolerated; government tries to discredit opposition	Protests tolerated; military reportedly refused to carry out repression	Most protests tolerated; government tries to discredit opposition	After period of toleration, protesters forced out. Much more prior organizational repression.
Urbanization	52.9	67.4	51.8	72.4
Authoritarian divisions	Defections reported after protests begin	Split between Kuchma and Yanukovych; military refused to repress protest	None reported	None reported
Type of regime	Competitive authoritarian	Competitive authoritarian	Competitive authoritarian	Full authoritarian

as the largest protest in Belarus had roughly 20,000 participants, whereas Serbia in 2000 had a protest estimated between 500,000 and 1 million and Ukraine also had participation of around 1 million. The largest protest in the Serbian protests of 1996–1997 had around 150,000 participants. The use of disruptive tactics surely played a role in success in Serbia in 2000, including the combination of a sit-in strike at a critical coal mine, blockades of streets in Belgrade, and eventually the occupation of the parliamentary and state television buildings by protesters after bulldozers cleared barriers put in place by authorities. Similar to the other regions, falling PTS scores are associated with positive outcomes in the Serbian cases and rising PTS scores are associated with demobilization in Belarus, but Ukraine does not fit the pattern. A closer look at repression of protests better fits the outcomes. Opposition protests and occupation of a central square in Belarus were tolerated for five days, but then troops cleared out the square early in the morning of the sixth day, arresting the few hundred who had camped out. Belarus gave less space to opposition organizations and arrested leaders of opposition NGOs just before the 2006 elections. The Milosevic government's approach to protests in Serbia was generally to discredit the opposition rather than defeat them directly with repression. Protests were also generally tolerated in Ukraine. There was reportedly an attempt for a Tiananmen-style crackdown there that was canceled due to military opposition (Wilson 2005). This episode reveals divisions within the government in Ukraine that were exacerbated by the fact that the incumbent president, Leonid Kuchma, was not running for re-election and was reportedly not willing to take high risks to ensure the victory of Yanukovych (Wilson 2005: 136). Levitsky and Way's (2010) distinction between competitive authoritarian and full authoritarian regimes also helps shed light on these factors. As competitive authoritarian regimes, Serbia and Ukraine allowed opposition parties, which held elective offices. Belarus, as a full authoritarian regime, was less tolerant of real opposition (Bunce and Wolchik 2011). In contrast to South America and Asia, levels of urbanization do not correlate with protest outcomes.

Conclusions

Protest may be the only option for citizens frustrated by the barriers to participation and influence that are the defining feature of authoritarian regimes. As detailed previously, using global events data, I have identified 302 protest waves that occurred in authoritarian regimes around the world between 1979 and 2011. One long-term goal of this project is to understand the outcomes of global protest waves. This chapter, situated in an early phase of this project, sets a more modest goal. I provide a focused study of ten protest waves from three separate regions and time periods – Argentina, Bolivia, and Chile in the 1980s; China, Mongolia, and Taiwan in 1989–1991; and Serbia (two separate waves), Ukraine, and Belarus from 1996 to 2006. One notable initial finding regards the prevalence of democratic reform or outright democratic regime change as the most prominent opposition demand.

These protest waves are compared to assess whether the outcomes were consistent with challengers' demands. Analysis of these ten protest waves suggest that success in reaching challenger outcomes depended on the presence of broad opposition organizations that work together, the ability to mobilize larger numbers, and the presence of a relatively urbanized population. Authoritarian governments that were internally divided or limited by semidemocratic institutions were more vulnerable. Concerning repression, the comparison here indicates that reactive repression (i.e., in response to a contentious challenge) often does not work in stopping a protest wave, unless the opposition has a relatively weak organizational base and/or repression is taken to extreme levels. On the other hand, preemptive repression against opposition organizations is more effective, but this effect wears off over time as shown by Argentina and Chile.

Overall, the cases studied here support the importance of considering both state-centered and challenger-centered factors. The Chinese student movement in 1989 engaged in massive demonstrations and also took part in extended occupations and a hunger strike, but the state was strong and unified enough to carry out a massive crackdown that ended the protest wave. However, a strong authoritarian state will not automatically defeat a protest wave. In Chile, the authoritarian government was strong and resolute, yet the opposition was as well, resulting in stalemate from 1983 to 1987. The opposition here faced consistent repression, yet they persisted and after six years saw their struggle reach success with the defeat of the dictator Pinochet in a plebiscite.

Most of the successful cases, such as Argentina 1982–1983, Mongolia 1989–1990, Serbia 1996–1997, Serbia 2000, and Ukraine 2004, had an opposition working in a complementary way to organize large protests with varied tactics. Governmental divisions seemed to prevent a heavy-handed repressive response. When repression did occur, it tended to be reactive to particular protests and ineffective. On the other hand, in Bolivia, there were historic and contemporary signs of divisions within the military, but the political opposition was not capable of organizing a large-scale show of opposition in the capital.

All this suggests that we pay greater attention in the future to the variety of protest outcomes, as the variety is certainly more complex than successful versus unsuccessful. Some cases resemble the term democratic revolution, while others achieved democratic reform without actually removing the chief executive. Some protest waves were repressed, but the protest wave in Chile persisted for several years without any certain outcome. A final logical possibility is a protest wave that leads to removal of the chief executive but without democratic reform. None of the ten cases analyzed here fit this category, but Kyrgyzstan may be an example. This country's "Tulip Revolution" of 2005 seems to fit the pattern of other postcommunist "color revolutions" in which authoritarian leaders were ousted following election-related protests (Beissinger 2007). However, according to Freedom House, there was no discernable improvement in democracy. The outcomes of the ten protest waves studied here are displayed in Figure 5.3.

Irregular Removal of Incumbent?	Democratic Reform?		
	No		Yes
No	Demobilization □　Bolivia 1980 (16) □　China 1989 (50) □　Belarus 2006 (24)	Stalemate □　Chile 1983– 　　1987 (1696)	Democratic Reform Movement □　Chile 1988–89 (275) □　Argentina 1982–83 (631) □　Mongolia 1989–90 (148) □　Taiwan 1990–91(657) □　Serbia 1996–97 (122)
Yes	Stolen Revolution □　*Kyrgystan*		Democratic Revolution □　Serbia 2000 (9) □　Ukraine 2004 (92)

Figure 5.3 Potential protest wave outcomes and examples

Note: number in parentheses is the duration in days.

These data show a clear difference in duration for protest waves that resulted in demobilization or democratic revolution, on the one hand, and waves that resulted in stalemate or democratic reform, on the other. This is at least in part related to two different protest strategies. One is what we can call a *centralized confrontation* in which the opposition occupies a strategic space (often a central square in the capital city) and refuses to leave until the government gives in to its demands. This resulted in democratic revolution in Ukraine (2004), but occupations in China and Belarus were dispersed, effectively ending these waves. In Serbia (2000), the first occupation was at a strategic coal mine, and then opposition supporters occupied the parliamentary building a few days later; Milosevic admitted defeat the following day. In Bolivia, an occupation occurred in a tin mine, but protests and attempts to occupy zones in La Paz seemed to be poorly attended and were unsuccessful. In all of these cases, the duration of the wave was less than 100 days, with most of them far less. This centralized confrontation strategy appears to be a high-risk/high-reward strategy as it puts intense pressure on the government, but dispersing the occupation can quash the entire protest wave. Much depends here on the determination of political leaders to order repression and the willingness of security forces to carry out the order. This centralized confrontation strategy is similar to the "method of concentration" discussed by Burrowes (1996) and Schock (2005).

The other protest waves were longer than 100 days in duration, most of them far more. Here, the basic strategy can be described as *serial protest*, in which opposition groups organize a series of protests. Here, each event is much shorter (typically less than one day), but the wave as a whole is longer. This characterizes the protest waves in Argentina, Chile, Mongolia, Taiwan, and Serbia (1996–1997). This strategy applies less pressure during each protest event, but it is more difficult to repress once and for all. Here, the opposition cannot cause a revolution but demonstrates endurance, and each of these cases resulted in democratic reform. This relates somewhat to the "methods of dispersion" discussed by Burrowes (1996) and Schock (2005), but their term focuses on strikes and boycotts, and most of the events in serial protest are demonstrations.

It is important to keep in mind that this is a pilot study. The ten cases chosen here offer diverse contexts and outcomes, but they may not be representative of the larger sample of protest waves. Still, this research has found interesting and novel tentative findings about protest waves and their outcomes. Future research will expand the analysis to the other protest waves identified using global events data. These tentative conclusions will thus be tested in other cases.

Appendix
Identifying protest waves

The identification of protest waves began with defining an *elevated incidence of protest*. One could simply specify a minimum number of protests, but numbers vary tremendously from country to country. For instance, GDELT identified 267 protests that occurred in the Philippines in 1986 (the year of the "People Power" protests), which certainly stands out for that period in that country, but is far less than recent years in Iran and China in which over 1,000 protests per year are the norm. It is likely that there is some form of reporting bias, in that events from some countries systematically gain more media coverage than others. Thus, there is reason to measure protest relative to an average level of protest for that country. GDELT events also show period effects, as events have been far more numerous in recent years. This is likely due in large part to increased electronic news media availability and not wholly to an actual increase in events. If we were to examine protests relative to the median for a country over the entire period, we would find that very few years in the 1980s and 1990s pass the bar, whereas nearly every year from 2007 and beyond registers as having an elevated incidence of protest.

Due to these complications, the incidence of protest in each year was compared to the median number of protests for three time periods for each country. Since the mean is more sensitive to outliers (and the study of historic protest waves, by definition, involves outliers), the median is a more useful basis for comparison. The time periods are based on the distribution of all GDELT events, displayed by Leetaru and Schrodt (2013), which shows that the frequency of events across all countries was relatively low from 1979 to 1995, noticeably reaches a higher plateau from 1996 to 2006, and then rises dramatically from 2007 to 2011. An important question is, where exactly do we set the bar? For example, should we count countries at any point above the median or twice the median? Setting the bar too high may miss important protest waves, but setting it too low could overwhelm future analyses with cases that would be better characterized as normal years of protest, rather than exceptional protest waves. Since one long-range goal of this research is to identify protest waves that might become democratic revolutions, it is desirable that the protest waves identified here include past democratic revolutions identified by experts. Therefore, I referred back to cases identified by Thompson (2004) as democratic revolutions (or repressed attempts) and by Beissinger (2013) as urban civic revolutions. Rather than just setting an arbitrary number, then, I determined that 29 of the 32 expert-identified democratic revolutions occurred when protest was at least 1.8 times the median, and the three cases that fall below this point are rather questionable as democratic revolutions.[5] Therefore, I identified all country-years in which the incidence of protest was at least 1.8 times the median rate of protest for the country and time period. One additional problem is that protest is rare in some countries, such that the median level of protest could be one or zero. In this case, a year with three protests is far above the median, but it seems a stretch to call this a protest wave. Therefore, the second criterion for being considered an elevated incidence of protest is that a country must have at least twenty protests in a year. This minimum, again, was set with reference to past democratic revolutions, as all thirty-two cases satisfy this stipulation. The analysis here focuses on authoritarian regimes, which are defined here as country-years that score less than four on the reversed Freedom House political rights indicator.[6] Thirty of the thirty-two democratic revolutions identified by Thompson and Beissinger satisfied this condition.[7] I also tested Cheibub et al.'s (2010) dichotomous indicator of democracy, but there were several cases in which protests over democratic grievances occurred in countries that were coded as democracies in this indicator, yet in which the level of competition was questionable. An example of this is Ukraine's Orange Revolution of 2004. The Freedom House political rights indicator better accounts for these hybrid regimes that have multiparty but largely unfair elections. Furthermore, Freedom House indicators are available over the entire period of this study, whereas the dichotomous democracy indicator was not at the time of this analysis.

Many of the years of elevated incidence of protest happen consecutively within the same country, so it is helpful to consider them part of the same protest wave. Furthermore, there may be other years before and after such waves that may not pass the bar as elevated, but may still be close enough to the peak to be considered part of the wave. Indeed, Tarrow (2011) sees a demobilization phase as a crucial part of a cycle of contention. Furthermore, extending years of elevated protests into broader waves helps to correct for quirks associated with the calculation of protest medians for different periods. This begins with the country-years identified as having elevated levels of protest. If these are consecutive in the same country, they are considered part of the same protest wave. Then, the task is to extend the protest wave out to earlier and later years until there is a significant drop-off. Operationally, each wave is extended to earlier or later years if the number of protests is at least 75% of the adjacent year within a wave.

Notes

1 The geographical identification system in GDELT is based on a unified Germany, so earlier events in East Germany cannot be separated.
2 Democracy here includes demands for election or reforms that would increase the scope for democracy, as well as protests against dictatorship and against rigged elections. Human rights includes denouncing the arrest of people for political reasons, protesting violence used against protesters, demanding information and justice for past abuses, and demanding greater civil liberties.

3 In contrast to these theories, however, Przeworski et al. (2000) found that socioeconomic development sustains democracy but does not cause it.

4 Surveys conducted in Latin America show that city dwellers are more likely to report taking part in protests than are individuals living in rural areas (Booth and Seligson 2009). It is not clear why this is the case, but it may be that individuals with self-expression values prefer to live in cities. Cities should also provide more of a critical mass of participants, which encourages further mobilization according to threshold models such as Granovetter (1978).

5 Philippines 2001 had 279 protests, which is 1.5 times the median, but this case is questionable since it occurred in what was already considered a democracy by standard indicators (Freedom House and Cheibub et al. 2010) and was associated with no democratic improvement. Iran 2002 and Pakistan 1988, identified by Thompson, are questionable because their levels of protest are equal to or below the median. Furthermore, Thompson did not see them as "full" democratic revolutions, as Iran is identified as repressed and Pakistan is identified as not resulting in consolidated democracy. Beissinger (2013) does not recognize any of these three cases as urban civic revolutions.

6 The reversed political rights indicator ranges from 0 (least democratic) to 6 (most democratic). Both current and previous years are included because a country that experienced a transition from an authoritarian to a democratic regime in a particular year would sometimes be coded as democratic for the entire year. In these cases, consideration of the previous year would identify cases that may have been authoritarian when protests took place.

7 The exceptions were Philippines 2001 and Madagascar 2002.

References

Ackerman, Peter, and Jack DuVall. 2000. *A Force More Powerful: A Century of Nonviolent Conflict*. New York: Palgrave.

Almeida, Paul D. 2003. "Opportunity Organizations and Threat-Induced Contention: Protest Waves in Authoritarian Settings." *American Journal of Sociology* 109: 345–400.

Almeida, Paul D. 2008. *Waves of Protest: Popular Struggle in El Salvador, 1925–2005*. Minneapolis: University of Minnesota Press.

Beissinger, Mark. 2007. "Structure and Example in Modular Political Phenomena: The Diffusion of Bulldozer/Orange/Tulip Revolutions." *Perspectives on Politics* (June): 259–276.

Beissinger, Mark. 2013. "The Semblance of Democratic Revolution: Coalitions in Ukraine's Orange Revolution." *American Political Science Review* 107(3): 574–592.

Booth, John A., and Mitchell A. Seligson. 2009. *The Legitimacy Puzzle in Latin America: Political Support in Eight Nations*. Cambridge, UK: Cambridge University Press.

Brockett, Charles D. 2005. *Political Movements and Violence in Central America*. Cambridge, UK: Cambridge University Press.

Bunce, Valerie J., and Sharon L. Wolchik. 2011. *Defeating Authoritarian Leaders in Postcommunist Countries*. Cambridge, UK: Cambridge University Press.

Burrowes, Robert J. 1996. *The Strategy of Nonviolent Defense: A Gandhian Approach*. Albany: State University of New York Press.

Chen, Chien-Kai. 2011. "The State-Society Interaction in the Process of Taiwan's Democratization from 1990 to 1992." *East Asia* 28: 115–134.

Cheibub, José Antonio, Jennifer Ganghi, and James Raymond Vreeland. 2010. "Democracy and dictatorship revisited." *Public Choice* 143: 67–101.

Chenoweth, Erica, and Maria J. Stephan. 2011. *Why Civil Resistance Works: The Strategic Logic of Nonviolent Conflict*. New York: Columbia University Press.

Constable, Pamela, and Arturo Valenzuela. 1991. *A Nation of Enemies: Chile under Pinochet*. New York: W. W. Norton.

Cvejic, Slobodan. 1999. "General Character of the Protest and Prospects for Democratization in Serbia." In *Protest in Belgrade: Winter of Discontent*, edited by Mladen Lazic. Budapest: Central European University Press.

DeNardo, James. 1985. *Power in Numbers: The Political Strategy of Protest and Rebellion*. Princeton, NJ: Princeton University Press.

Eisinger, Peter K. 1973. "The Conditions of Protest Behavior in American Cities." *American Political Science Review* 67: 11–28.

Fish, M. Steven. 1998. "Mongolia: Democracy Without Prerequisites." *Journal of Democracy* 9(3): 127–141.

Franklin, James C. 2009. "Contentious Challenges and Government Responses in Latin America." *Political Research Quarterly* 62(4): 700–714.

Franklin, James C. 2014. "Democratic Revolutions and Those That Might Have Been: Comparing the Outcomes of Protest Waves under Authoritarian Rule." Paper prepared for delivery at the 2014 Annual Meeting of the American Political Science Association, Washington, DC, August 28–31.

Franklin, James C. 2015. "Persistent Challengers: Repression, Concessions, Challenger Strength, and Commitment in Latin America." *Mobilization: An International Quarterly* 20(1): 61–80.

Fukuyama, Francis. 2014. *Political Order and Political Decay: From the Industrial Revolution to the Globalization of Democracy*. New York: Farrar, Straus, and Giroux.

Geddes, Barbara. 1999. "What Do We Know about Democratization after Twenty Years?" *Annual Review of Political Science* 2: 115–144.

Goodwin, Jeff. 2001. *No Other Way Out: States and Revolutionary Movements, 1945–1991*. Cambridge, UK: Cambridge University Press.

Granovetter, Mark. 1978. "Threshold Models of Collective Behavior." *American Journal of Sociology* 83(6): 1420–1443.

Gurr, Ted Robert. 1970. *Why Men Rebel*. Princeton, NJ: Princeton University Press.

Hibbs, Douglas A. 1973. *Mass Political Violence: A Cross-National Causal Analysis*. New York: John Wiley.

Inclán, María de la Luz. 2009. "Repressive Threats, Procedural Concessions, and the Zapatista Cycle of Protests, 1994–2003." *Journal of Conflict Resolution* 53: 794–819.

Inglehart, Ronald, and Christian Welzel. 2005. *Modernization, Cultural Change, and Democracy: The Human Development Sequence*. Cambridge, UK: Cambridge University Press.

Koopmans, Ruud. 1993. "The Dynamics of Protest Waves: West Germany, 1965 to 1989." *American Sociological Review* 58(October): 637–658.

Leetaru, Kalev, and Philip A. Schrodt. 2013. "GDELT: Global Data on Events, Location and Tone, 1979–2012." Paper presented at the International Studies Association meetings, San Francisco, CA.

Lehoucq, Fabrice. 2016. "Does Nonviolence Work?" *Comparative Politics* 48(January): 269–287.

Levitsky, Steven, and Lucan A. Way. 2010. *Competitive Authoritarianism: Hybrid Regimes after the Cold War*. Cambridge, UK: Cambridge University Press.

Lichbach, Mark Irving. 1987. "Deterrence of Escalation? The Puzzle of Aggregate Studies of Repression and Dissent." *Journal of Conflict Resolution* 31(2): 266–297.

Lichbach, Mark Irving, and Ted Robert Gurr. 1981. "The Conflict Process: A Formal Model." *Journal of Conflict Resolution* 25: 3–29.

Lim, Louisa. 2014. *The People's Republic of Amnesia: Tiananmen Revisited*. New York: Oxford University Press.

Lipset, Seymour Martin. 1959. "Some Social Requisites of Democracy: Economic Development and Legitimacy." *American Political Science Review* 53: 69–105.

Mainwaring, Scott, and Timothy R. Scully. 1995. "Introduction: Party Systems in Latin America." In *Building Democratic Institutions: Party Systems in Latin America*, edited by Scott Mainwaring and Timothy R. Scully. Stanford, CA: Stanford University Press.

McAdam, Doug. 1982. *The Political Process and the Development of Black Insurgency, 1930–1970*. Chicago: University of Chicago Press.

Moore, Barrington. 1966. *Social Origins of Dictatorship and Democracy: Lord and Peasant in the Making of the Modern World*. Boston: Beacon Press.

Munck, Gerardo. 1998. *Authoritarianism and Democratization: Soldiers and Workers in Argentina, 1976–1983*. University Park, PA: Pennsylvania State University Press.

Nepstad, Sharon Erickson. 2011. *Nonviolent Revolutions: Civil Resistance in the Late 20th Century*. New York: Oxford University Press.

Nepstad, Sharon Erickson. 2015. *Nonviolent Struggle: Theories, Strategies, and Dynamics*. New York: Oxford University Press.

O'Donnell, Guillermo, and Philippe C. Schmitter. 1986. *Transitions from Authoritarian Rule: Tentative Conclusions about Uncertain Democracies*. Baltimore: The Johns Hopkins University Press.

Opp, Karl-Dieter, and Wolfgang Roehl. 1990. "Repression, Micromobilization, and Political Protest." *Social Forces* 69(2): 521–547.

Popadic, Dragan. 1999. "Student Protests: Comparative Analysis of the 1992 and 1996–97 Protests." In *Protest in Belgrade: Winter of Discontent*, edited by Mladen Lazic. Budapest: Central European University Press.

Preston, Julia, and Samuel Dillon. 2004. *Opening Mexico: The Making of a Democracy*. New York: Farrar, Straus, and Giroux.

Przeworski, Adam, Michael Alvarez, José Antonio Cheibub, and Fernando Limongi. 2000. *Democracy and Development: Political Institutions and Well-Being in the World, 1950–1990*. Cambridge: Cambridge University Press.

Rasler, Karen. 1996. "Concessions, Repression, and Political Protest in the Iranian Revolution." *American Sociological Review* 61(February): 132–152.

Rueschemeyer, Dietrich, Evelyne Huber Stephens and John D. Stephens. 1992. *Capitalist Development & Democracy*. Chicago: University of Chicago Press.

Schedler, Andreas. 2013. *The Politics of Uncertainty: Sustaining and Subverting Electoral Authoritarianism*. Oxford: Oxford University Press.

Schock, Kurt. 2005. *Unarmed Insurrections: People Power Movements in Nondemocracies*. Minneapolis: University of Minnesota Press.

Schock, Kurt. 2015. *Civil Resistance Today*. Cambridge, UK: Polity.

Sharp, Gene. 1973. *The Politics of Nonviolent Action*. Boston: Porter Sargent Publishers Inc.

Skocpol, Theda. 1979. *States and Social Revolutions: A Comparative Analysis of France, Russia, and China*. Cambridge: Cambridge University Press.

Snyder, David, and Charles Tilly. 1972. "Hardship and Collective Violence in France, 1830–1960." *American Sociological Review* 37: 520–532.

Tarrow, Sidney. 1989. *Democracy and Disorder: Protest and Politics in Italy, 1965–1975*. Oxford: Oxford University Press.

Tarrow, Sidney. 2011. *Power in Movement: Social Movements and Contentious Politics*, 3rd edition. Cambridge, UK: Cambridge University Press.

Thompson, Mark R. 2004. *Democratic Revolutions: Asia and Eastern Europe*. London: Routledge.

Trejo, Guillermo. 2012. *Popular Movements in Autocracies: Religion, Repression, and Indigenous Collective Action in Mexico*. New York: Cambridge University Press.

Tucker, Joshua A. 2007. "Enough! Electoral Fraud, Collective Action Problems, and Post-Communist Colored Revolutions." *Perspectives on Politics* 5(3): 535–551.

Vinthagen, Stellen. 2015. *A Theory of Nonviolent Action: How Civil Resistance Works*. London: Zed Books.

Vujovic, Sreten. 1999. "Protest as an Urban Phenomenon." In *Protest in Belgrade: Winter of Discontent*, edited by Mladen Lazic. Budapest: Central European University Press.

Way, Lucan. 2008. "The Real Causes of the Color Revolutions." *Journal of Democracy* 19(3): 55–69.

Wilson, Andrew. 2005. *Ukraine's Orange Revolution*. New Haven, CN: Yale University Press.

6 Bound by the red lines?

The perils and promises of moderate mobilization under authoritarianism

Dana M. Moss

Social movements that erupt to protest against dictatorships have long captivated the imaginations of social scientists by heralding new hope for liberal change and democratization. As witnessed during the 2011 Arab Spring protest wave, movements chanting the refrain "the people want the fall of the regime!" challenged entrenched views of the masses as apathetic and regimes as enduring. But while scholars frequently turn their attention to mobilization in authoritarian states only after the "unthinkable" occurs (Kurzman 2004), activism in these contexts is often far less exceptional and disruptive than assumed (Bayat 2013[2010]). In recent decades, pressures from above and below have compelled regimes to implement liberalizing reforms and permit the formation of oppositional political parties, nongovernmental organizations (NGOs), and social movements that tread a middle path between subversive "talk" and the "walk" of mass insurgency (Johnston 2004).

The rise of liberalized authoritarianism as a predominant regime type has spurred debate as to how meaningful moderate mobilization is in these contexts. On the one hand, activists operating in regime-delimited civic zones must abide by an unfair set of rules (Schlumberger 2007), espouse "loyalist intentions" (O'Brien and Li 2006; Scott 1990), and work within heavily policed limits (Khalili and Schwedler 2010). Because liberalization has not wrought democratization in the Middle East, China, Russia, and elsewhere to date, many scholars have concluded that moderate mobilization is antithetical to meaningful change (Langohr 2004; Lust-Okar 2005, 2007; Posusney 2004; Wiktorowicz 2001). On the other hand, a growing body of scholarship on collective action in nondemocracies submits that state-society relations are far more complex than that of top-down cooptation (Chen 2012; Fu and Cullen 2008; Lee and Zhang 2013; Mertha 2008; O'Brien and Li 2006; Perry 2002; Stern and Hassid 2012; Straughn 2005). Researchers have instead illustrated that legalized mobilization is highly contentious and challenges regime neglect, corruption, and injustice. As a result, a growing body of work on contention under authoritarianism argues that moderate mobilizers are also change-makers, albeit in incremental and localized ways.

In order to contribute to this debate, this paper takes up the case of aboveground activism in the Kingdom of Jordan and asks: what are the perils and promises of moderate mobilization under liberalized authoritarianism? In the sections that follow, I argue that activists mobilizing within regime-controlled civic spaces are not simply treading a narrow path bound by the state. Instead, the rules governing the civic sphere are opaque and unpredictable, and activists are embroiled in a dynamic process of uncertainty, risk, and discovery about what is and is not permissible at any given time. But because moderate mobilizers also view themselves as loyal, lawful, and rightful regime constituents, they routinely challenge regimes to live up to elites' promises of liberalization. In so doing, moderate mobilization may not expand formal political rights or portend democratization, but it can transform sociopolitical norms and expand the practice of citizenship under nondemocracies. Because this dynamic parallels the findings of other studies examining protest events and civic advocacy in China and elsewhere (e.g., O'Brien and Li 2006; Spires 2011), I propose that moderate mobilization can be a vehicle for change across liberalized authoritarian states. This chapter concludes with implications for the study of contention, authoritarianism, and social change more generally.

Theorizing contentious engagement with the liberalized authoritarianism state

In the contemporary era, the majority of nondemocratic states are not governed by totalitarian dictatorships that wield absolutist control through corporatism and an iron fist. Since the fall of the Soviet Union, regimes have increasingly adopted the trappings of democracy. Described as semi-authoritarian, electoral, competitive, and hybrid, among other variants, regimes operating in this "gray zone" (Carothers 2002) permit some degree of political and civic participation (Diamond 2002; Geddes 1999; Levitsky and Way 2010; Linz 2000; Schedler 2002, 2013). By legalizing party politics and elections, permitting international and local nongovernmental organizations to conduct relief and advocacy work, and tolerating limited forms of protest (Chen and Moss, forthcoming), these changes have signified long-awaited "political opportunities" for mobilization (McAdam 1999[1982], 1996; Meyer 2004; Tarrow 2011; Tilly 1978).

However, the failure of liberalization to transform into democratization in many cases has cast doubts on how meaningful these opportunities are in a tightly controlled environment. Instead of heralding democratization, scholars have instead found that moderate mobilization contributes to authoritarian power in a variety of ways (Langohr 2004; Lust-Okar 2005, 2007; Posusney 2004; Robertson 2010; Wiktorowicz 2000, 2001; cf. Brownlee 2009). Dictators have infamously legitimated their reigns by manipulating election outcomes and channeling their opponents into state-controlled party politics that are unfree and unfair (Albrecht 2005; Albrecht and Wegner 2006; Wegner 2004; Wickham 2004). The work of civic organizations and NGOs bolster regimes by placating the populace and allowing the regime to take credit for their efforts (Pioppi 2007; Spires 2011). Even protests have been shown to buttress regimes by providing a mechanism to let the masses blow off steam and to resolve disputes amongst elites themselves (Lorentzen 2013; McAdam et al. 2001: 208). Regimes also more easily infiltrate and monitor dissenters who operate openly on the streets and online (Gunitsky

2015). Researchers have therefore shown that rather than clearing a pathway to democracy, liberalizing measures instead bolster authoritarian legitimacy and longevity (Chen and Moss, forthcoming; Lucas 2003; Yom 2009).

On the other hand, other research demonstrates that viewing moderate mobilization as a futile or counterproductive mode of change neglects the reality of state-society relations in these contexts, which are more complex than that of top-down cooptation for several reasons (Cai 2010; Chen 2012; Fu and Cullen 2008; Lee 2007; Lee and Zhang 2013; Mertha 2008; Perry 2002; Stern and Hassid 2012; Su and He 2010). First, regimes are subject to "liberalizations and deliberalizations as the balance of competitive and authoritarian elements changes over time" (Robertson 2010: 6). This means that regime-instigated opportunities for mobilization in authoritarian states do not produce stable civic arenas governed according to clearly articulated rules and procedures (Stern and O'Brien 2012). Instead, the actual limits of dissent are often opaquely decoupled from regimes' formal claims about their degree of permissiveness and subject to change in unstated ways. This means that the "nature of political sensitivity and risk" is vastly less apparent to insiders than outsider researchers often surmise (Spires 2011: 20). Because the limits of regime-approved mobilization are likely to fluctuate in accordance with shifting elite agendas and perceptions of threat, activists may not know how or in what direction state agents will react until they make their next move.

Second, authoritarian regimes are not monoliths (Arendt 1968; Shi and Cai 2006). Instead, they are comprised of varied sets of actors, including national elites, local authorities, and security agencies that act according to different priorities, competing ideologies, and varied interests, both within and between different levels of authority. As a result, the boundaries delimiting what actions and discourses are "safe" or low-risk are often contested within regime circles. While some regime agents may ignore or permit mobilization, for example, others may react in ways that violate top-down mandates for stability out of frustration, confusion, and enmity (Barkan 1984; Snow and Moss 2014). "Beyond some well-patrolled forbidden zones," as Stern and O'Brien (2012: 178) explain, "the state speaks with many, contradictory voices. On different days and on different issues, the politically engaged encounter a multifaceted state that may endorse, tolerate, or suppress their activities." Regimes are also not as omnipotent or omnipresent within society as is often assumed. Instead, their members often lack the foresight, capacity, and coordination to systematically regulate actors in the civic sector in all times and places due to limited resources, the discretion of street-level enforcers (Lipsky 2010[1980]; Su and He 2010), and human error (Stern and O'Brien 2012).

The cumulative effect of this complex and often befuddling context is that even when activists attempt to abide by regime-imposed limits, they do not and cannot always have perfect information as to what the "safe" words or actions are in reality. As such, activists constantly risk overstepping "a fuzzy and frequently shifting political line" (Spires 2011: 12) because even moderate forms of activism condoned in law may breach invisible minefields. This is not to say that activists work within a field characterized by anomie; through experience and observation, these actors ascertain patterns about regime behaviors and adapt accordingly

(McAdam 1983; Moss 2014). Nevertheless, even relatively mundane legalized actions such as distributing humanitarian aid, publishing fact-finding reports, holding conferences, forming political parties, and holding peaceful demonstrations may warrant punishment in the eyes of regime members at certain times and places. No matter how savvy or calculating these activists may be, walking the middle path in these contexts is likely to be a perilous undertaking.

Furthermore, because moderate mobilization can be perilous, recent research into grassroots mobilization suggests that it also holds promises for liberal change (Chen 2012; Fu, forthcoming; Lee and Zhang 2013; O'Brien and Li 2006; Stern and O'Brien 2012; Su and He 2010). This is due in part to the paradox inherent to liberalized authoritarianism. When regimes liberalize in order to quell international criticisms and domestic pressures, they cannot then repress rightful, lawful mobilizers without risking a destabilizing backlash and international condemnation (Hess and Martin 2006). Advocates' claims are therefore difficult for regimes to dismiss or repress outright because they demand "scrupulous enforcement of existing commitments" (O'Brien 2003: 53) regardless of whether those commitments were enacted in good faith. Research on the relative toleration of oppositional mobilization therefore suggests that regimes seeking to maintain a liberalized façade are likely to tolerate some degree of meaningful challenge from below so long as activists do not call for systemic or revolutionary change (Moss 2014).

Accordingly, many studies also demonstrate that activists seeking to walk this middle path are surprisingly confrontational in their claims and actions. Studies of pensioners and protesters in China in the post-1989 context, for example, demonstrate that activists have the potential to challenge regime practices and use "troublemaking" tactics to pressure the state to live up to its promises (Cai 2010; Chen 2012; O'Brien and Stern 2008). In so doing, activists challenge the limits of what regime consider "rightful" and permissible in peaceful and symbolic ways (O'Brien and Li 2006), thereby prompting regimes to tolerate their activities (Spires 2011) and even grant concessions (Chen 2012; Su and He 2010). As a result, even the most modest mobilizers are embroiled in contentious relations with regimes and launch claims and tactics that straddle the border between strictly contained and transgressive (O'Brien 2003). Rather than being tightly bound by the red lines, which refer to sociopolitical and cultural taboos restricting protest, scholars of mobilization "from below" instead suggest that mobilization under liberalized authoritarianism has the potential to expand the limits of the permissible. As O'Brien (2003: 58) argues, citizenship practices in these contexts are often "preceding the appearance of citizenship as a secure, universally recognized status. In fact, practice may be creating status." Taking up the call of researchers to investigate the paradox of permissible resistance under authoritarianism (O'Brien and Li 2006), I investigate these dynamics in the Kingdom in Jordan.

The Kingdom of Jordan

The Kingdom of Jordan was enshrined as a constitutional monarchy in 1952, but democracy was deferred after a series of destabilizing crises led King Hussein to impose martial law in 1967. This continued until the 1989 global economic crisis led to "bread riots" among traditional tribal constituencies; in response, the king instituted a number of liberalizing measures by permitting candidates to compete for seats in the lower house of the bicameral National Assembly and by lifting strict bans on media reporting. In the 1990s, political parties, nongovernmental organizations, and journalists gradually moved to fill this civic space. However, King Hussein did not fully restore the rights that had been rescinded since 1952, and Jordan's system of political inclusion and competition remain deeply flawed today.[1] The Kingdom has been consistently ranked as "unfree" by Freedom House since King Abdullah II inherited the throne from his father in 1999. The king retains broad powers to appoint the National Assembly's upper house, the prime minister, the cabinet, and governors,[2] and he has periodically dissolved the government and governed for extended periods by decree. The one-man, one-vote electoral system for the lower house is also unfair; districting is skewed in favor of the largely rural Transjordanian population in order to disadvantage the Islamic Action Front party, Jordan's Muslim Brotherhood, and voters of Palestinian origin who are largely concentrated in the capital city of 'Amman.

Numerous other problems contribute to Jordan's democracy deficit. The General Intelligence Directorate (*al-Mukhabarat*, referred to in the following as the Intelligence) retains the power to interfere in politics and civil society and is the primary enforcer of "red lines" in Jordan, which is a common phrase denoting taboo topics and banned means of expression. The country's massive refugee population of Palestinians, Iraqis, and Syrians outnumber Transjordanians but face widespread discrimination and disenfranchisement. Corruption is pervasive at all levels, though the regime launched an Anticorruption Commission in 2007 and brought several high-profile cases to court in 2010. Neoliberal reforms have resulted in the selling off of public land and assets to private corporations and regime members, creating widespread discontent. Media freedoms are also poor; journalists are subjected to a restrictive Press and Publications Law and are required register with the government. State agents regularly refer journalists and activists to the State Security Court for crimes of treason or on trumped-up charges of criminality.

Protests have emerged intermittently in the Kingdom against the 1994 Wadi Araba Treaty with Israel and the 2003 invasion of Iraq (see Schwedler 1998, 2003, 2005). However, any gathering had to be approved by the relevant governor in advance under a restrictive assembly's law until it was overturned in 2011. Some unions and union-like associations are legal and engage in economic and political campaigns, and the engineers' association has taken a leading a role in "anti-normalization" campaigns with Israel. Though NGOs are permitted to operate, they require regime permission to enact their programs and are subject to oversight by the Intelligence. Even regime-sponsored organizations are forced to censor their positions, as when the National Center for Human Rights "changed its official position on both the election law and the new information law after first announcing critical opinions" in 2010 (Freedom House 2011). So, despite the existence of political parties, associations, international and local NGOs, and social movement groups, activists in the civic sphere faced numerous challenges and risks in their work under Jordan's "liberalized" authoritarian system (Moss 2014).

Moderate mobilization in a time of revolution

In order to understand the "quotidian world of resistance and response" (O'Brien and Stern 2008) under liberalized authoritarianism, I conducted fieldwork in Jordan in the second half of 2011. The very fact that I could travel across the country to interview activists was itself a product of Jordan's liberalization; I interviewed fifty-seven activists, all of whom agreed to be recorded, who were involved in international nongovernmental organizations (INGOs), a range of independent and government-founded NGOs, and social movement groups (SMOs) (see Table 6.1). Most had had contact from Western-based researchers and welcomed the opportunity to air their grievances and experiences to me in their homes, coffee shops, and offices. I arrived with a simple motivating question: how was it that these activists were able to survive and persist in their advocacy work in an authoritarian state?

On the surface, the answer appeared to be that activists who operated openly abided by the rules of liberalization and were dedicated to regime-supported and regime-supporting advocacy. Though this research took place during the tumultuous first year of the Arab Spring, even interviewees supportive of revolts in nearby countries viewed revolutionary change in Jordan as undesirable because it could have destabilizing effects on security, discredit activists in the eyes of the wider public, and lead to a takeover by Jordan's Muslim Brotherhood. Activists also viewed their position as favorable to those mobilizing in neighboring states. As one anti-normalization activist described,

> because it's not bloody regime like in Syria and Libya . . . the people here agree that the King should stay the King and not [ask for] a radical toppling of the regime. Here, we're talking about reform, not the fall [of the regime], so it's more of a dialogue process and it's not as confrontational.

Table 6.1 Organizational affiliations of interviewees[a]

SMOs	
Popular pro-reform movements	36
Labor movements (teachers, daily laborers, veterans)	6
The Anti-Normalization Coalition	6
Local NGOs	16
Government-founded NGOs	8
International NGOs (INGOs)	4
Political parties	4

a Numbers do not add to 57 because some interviews have multiple affiliations

Many activists also described their work as nonpolitical, even when advocating for the right to form a labor association or for changes to institutional policies regarding refugee inclusion. Because the term "political" was suggestive of being subversive or ideological, activists instead described themselves as driven by professional, social, and economic goals, working to address what they perceived as legitimate and lawful. For example, an NGO representative working on human rights emphasized, "we are not an ideological organization. We are a professional organization, a human rights foundation. But we are not a *political* organization." These self-characterizations signaled that they were not seeking to challenge or overturn the political system, but instead intended to work within that system to implement reform-oriented policies and programs.

Moderate mobilizers in Jordan's civic sector also described having a more complex relationship with the state than one of straightforward opposition or animosity. All interviewees instead viewed maintaining working relations with specific officials in various ministries and in the Intelligence as desirable and necessary (see also Moss 2014: 271–273). As an NGO director elaborated:

> Working with the government is not an easy thing in the Arab countries because the government is targeting any independent organization in order to contain these NGOs. But we are serious to be independent, and to have the bridge between us and the government . . . Without dialogue with the government there is no access to information. You need to develop your relations with the government to go in with solid ideas [about] how to change the laws . . . you cannot work regionally, for example, without having this relation with the government to allow to you to [establish yourself] and to invite [outside] people to the workshops.

In addition to requiring government support to carry out their campaigns and missions, many interviewees also expressed sympathy with Intelligence agents sent to observe and question them. As a representative of a social movement group recalled,

> We try not to have any friction [with the Intelligence agents] . . . We welcome them . . . This is very important, to be fair with the Intelligence. I'm sure that [for] most of the Intelligence officers, the feeling of these officers is with the movement because they know that there is corruption.

Another INGO activist expressed her dismay with the Intelligence as a system designed to "keep the powers that be in place," but she also acknowledged that "as a system it's one thing, but individually [Intelligence officials] are just poor guys who make 300 Jordanian dinars [about 420 US dollars] a month." Recognizing that the regime's rank-and-file were often comprised of the very people whose rights they were advocating for, activists expressed nuanced and surprisingly sympathetic orientations toward the individuals sent to monitor them.

The perils of the middle path

While moderate mobilization appeared to be contained, nontransgressive, and generally accommodating of the "hegemony" (Scott 1990), its very existence pointed to a paradox at the heart of liberalized authoritarianism: while respondents sought to work within the boundaries set by the state, their rhetoric and actions constantly crossed the "red lines." They did so by addressing a range of social problems that touched upon Jordan's most sensitive issues, including the discrimination of persons of Palestinian descent; human rights' abuses and the status of women and refugees; the unfair electoral system and media censorship; Jordan's normalized relations with Israel and political interference by the US; the Intelligence's extensive power and use of torture and illegal detention; the privatization of state-owned property and industry; and even the royal family's political, social, and economic practices, among others. So rather than express loyalty by backing the regime and the current status quo, each activist challenged regime policies by calling attention to, and working to correct, widespread social problems and injustices.

In addition to breaching red-line issues as part and parcel of their everyday work, the pursuit of their missions also frequently spanned the boundaries between lawful and transgressive due to the regime's inherent sensitivity to public shaming and disruption (O'Brien 2003: 53; see also O'Brien 1996; O'Brien and Li 2006). NGO leaders, for example, commonly conducted trainings on international human rights law in universities and with state agencies and published research reports on the status of rights and liberties in the Kingdom. While both of these tactics might appear as mundane or innocuous forms of "talk" (Johnston 2004), respondents described the latter as perilous. As one NGO head described, "sometimes, you feel that your relation [with the government] is good. But if you have a harsh press release against the government, the government will change its mechanism to deal with you." The head of another government-founded NGO described that although their organization was "protected" by the monarchy, they faced backlash from elites and the Intelligence for publishing damning reports. Doing training on international human rights law behind closed doors was more acceptable, this respondent explained, than holding conferences or publishing reports:

> We have a lot of training workshops [and] no one, even the Intelligence, refuses training . . . The government said that there should be no interference with our training [because] it's peaceful way – it's *not* a kind of advocacy – to talk in a scientific way without media, it's fine . . . [The government and the Intelligence] take what they like from the trainers and NGOs and discard what they don't like.
>
> But if we talk about working another way – let's say, *reporting* – that's different. I can give you an example . . . For more than five or six years, we trained the government about the international protection laws for refugees . . . After that, we published a big research report about this, more than 150 pages. And we try to make a national discussion about it . . . [but] it was

a catastrophe. They attacked us by a tough and aggressive way . . . But what the researcher who authored this report wrote, it's the *same* as what he *said* in the training! But because this is a *report* . . . they considered it more sensitive.

Other NGO members also described experiencing reprisals for reporting on illiberal state practices. An activist who opened a research center in 1998 had his NGO forcibly closed by the Interior Ministry and the Intelligence in 2002, for example, for drawing too much publicity to the regime's discriminatory practices:

> The was a lot of abuses . . . [and] we started to work on some topics which they considered it as a red line. We crossed the red lines in doing that. Specifically at that time, we worked because there is thousands of Jordanians who we call them "compulsory in exile" . . . They are outside Jordan, [and] they [are not allowed to] renew their passports. [The regime] doesn't allow them to come even with an emergency certificate to return back to Jordan . . . We received 400 names they have dropped their nationality . . . we give it in other annual report, and this of course was in the media at that time.

As a result, this respondent explained that officials justified closing his organization by claiming, "we work for the Palestinians, we go [against] the authority of the King," denoting thinly veiled language for treason.

Moderate mobilization was also risky because activists received conflicting signals about what types of actions were permissible. This was because their advocacy efforts often required the permission of multiple entities occupying overlapping spheres of control. Even approval from the king did not preclude disapproval from other state entities who might be acting as the "bad cop" on behalf of the king, thus allowing him to save face, or in direct contradiction of royal imperatives. For example, the Movement of Retired Army Generals began lobbying in 2002 for expanded benefits for retired military persons and to regain what they perceived to be a loss in their social status. While forming dozens of social clubs across the country appeared to be permissible, they later crossed a red line by requesting to form a political party. One of the founders explained that this party was intended specifically to give "power to the state or the regime" and to counterbalance the Islamic Action Front, whom he claimed worked solely on behalf of Palestinians and "have their own agendas . . . not for the benefit of the country. There should be a political party that really cares for the state and the regime and is on the side of the regime – a supportive party." However,

> After the King gave his agreement . . . we started to have meetings to write the by-laws and the basic things. And one week after, I was invited to the "house of my auntie on my mother's side" – this is a joke name for the Intelligence. They told me . . . the King may have another point of view, but it's not possible to approve it. I said frankly that this party is to be established in the face of the Muslim Brotherhood. The Intelligence officer said back to me, the Muslim brothers, we know how to control them. But *you* we do not

know how to control. They were right! [Laughs.] The guy told me that "for you, if you have a membership of 50,000, and after some time you think that the government is not the one that what you want, you will say to the King you have to change it. And because you are all known persons in your tribes, you can control a lot of people in your local societies. So you will be really dangerous, in such a case. What are we going to do with you every time you want a change?"

Accordingly, the proposal by the generals to form a political party was denied because the Intelligence viewed this as a potential vehicle for a coup d'état. As such, even the most explicit forms of loyalist mobilization could be perceived by state agents as treading on the red lines, likely because from "the state's perspective, a large domestic or international constituency can give even the most innocuous service provider a threatening cast" (Stern and O'Brien 2012: 6). For these reasons, loyalist reform-oriented activism was sometimes perceived as having revolutionary implications and warranted a crackdown by the state, which in this case led to the organizers of the generals' movement to be summoned to the State Security Court on trumped-up criminal charges.[3]

Activists also reported that the degree of censorship and repression they faced was at times surprising and seemingly arbitrary. Despite their best efforts to work within state-sanctioned limits, red lines comprised "a hazy, shifting boundary" (Stern and O'Brien 2012: 177) that could widen or shrink in unpredictable ways. For example, despite a proliferation of NGOs and INGOs in Jordan with the term "rights" (*huquq*) in their organizational titles, one interviewee faced problems in securing permission to form a human rights organization. He recalled:

We faced, even [from] the ministries, obstacles in putting the objectives of the center. And we had a problem even in the name! . . . At that time [in 2007], they didn't agree to put the human rights in the objectives . . . And I told them I want women's rights, and they said no. Children's rights, they said no. I told them, let us say that we want to work *against* human rights! [Laughs.] They didn't laugh. . . . This really surprised me. *Why everything is no?*

Activists who worked as journalists also reported experiencing crackdowns that appeared arbitrary and sudden. This signified that rather

than prepublication censorship, the norm is unpleasant consequences after a sensitive story angers political or economic elites . . . Shifting forbidden zones and the absence of detailed rules mean that even experienced journalists or editors can get in trouble over stories they thought were unexceptional.
(Stern and O'Brien 2012: 182–183)

As one SMO participant and journalist described, after publishing an article about the existence of a Facebook page calling for the "changing of the crown prince in Jordan," he was imprisoned and referred to the State Security Court for treason. He described that this incident was "very strange and made people very angry":

I didn't say my *opinion*. I just said that there *exists* a page on Facebook calling for changing the crown prince . . . Two days later I was called for the State Security Court, and they issued that I should be jailed for fifteen days . . . I was charged on working on changing the Constitution in an illegal way. The astonishing thing in the case is that the only penalty for this charge is execution. That was astonishing for everybody. No one could understand that. It really was very strange and very shocking.

When I asked this journalist why this was strange, he replied that writing such an article was "normal, it's nothing," and that he had been writing potentially sensitive articles for some time.[4] Being subjected to harsh enforcement after lulls in repression meant that "even the most alert are sometimes surprised by who lands in trouble" (Stern and O'Brien 2012: 177).

Other activists expressed puzzlement for the opposite reason – that the regime was exhibiting more leniency in response to the Arab Spring revolutions in neighboring countries than they had anticipated, even when individuals surpassed the highest "red line" by criticizing the royal family directly. This leniency was not universal; some activists and students were imprisoned during this period for defaming the king in protest events and online in 2010 and beyond (Freedom House 2011). Even so, social movement participants described that the Intelligence's perceived tolerance appeared to have widened in an ad hoc fashion. For example, one SMO leader recalled that in the past, he received calls from Intelligence officers who would exclaim "why are you writing this? You are Jordanian, you should be with the King." But as of 2011,

The strange thing, at this time, is that in of the fact that I am writing very, *very* clear articles against the King and the Queen, they are not calling me . . . I'm very sure that the Intelligence of these days is not the same Intelligence of 10 years ago . . . [but] to be honest, I can't understand the way the Intelligence is now acting on the earth. It is very very strange for me. I feel sometimes that they are happy with [our work], because they want to say to the King: "Look! There are some problems." If there is nothing happening on the sidelines, the King would say that the people are happy and that they accept everything.

Forecasting the degree of risk involved in mobilization was tricky, therefore, because on the one hand, the regime viewed reform-oriented activism as treasonous and punished dissenters in a range of ways (Moss 2014). On the other hand, the Intelligence sometimes backed off, appearing to give activists a green light. For these reasons, activists' anticipations about repression often produced conflicting accounts. One interviewee working on behalf of women's rights and the environment mused,

I think that they will let me go without any abuse, simply because I'm not being active in something dangerous for the monarchy itself, like [criticizing] the constitutional monarchy, limiting the monarchy, or accusing the monarchy of corruption itself. I don't do that.

On the other hand, because his recent campaigns challenged one of the king's stated economic develop policies, he mused,

> Now, I'm basically fighting the King, I'm fighting the big boss. I'm expecting that any point that I'll get shit. I'm really expecting that, you know? Anything, yeah . . . I could expect that they could put drugs in my car . . . fake money . . . We'll see.

This contradiction reflected the broader tensions inherent in the liberalized authoritarian system and the reality that everyday activist work is unpredictable in its consequences.

In sum, because Jordan's civic sphere occupied an ever-shifting ground patrolled by shadowy elites who gave off mixed signals as to what was permitted and which regime entity was actually in charge, moderate activism took on a degree of risk and confrontation with authorities in challenging the status quo.

The promise of moderate mobilization

As activists across Jordan bumped up against the red lines, this dynamic produced contentious confrontation between moderate mobilizers and regime representatives. Despite being nonrevolutionary, respondents contributed to sociopolitical change in two ways: first, they prodded the regime to relinquish specific concessions, and second, they refuted illiberal sociopolitical norms, particularly the red lines encircling the royal family as an off-limit object of criticism. As a result, by mid-2011, activists reported that the boundaries of the acceptable had been expanded to an unthinkable degree.

Activists cited numerous examples in which they challenged the regime to uphold its liberalizing promises. An NGO involved in monitoring elections, for example, exploited the "embarrassment" caused by corruption in the 2007 election to challenge the regime's handling of elections in 2010:

> In 2010 the general atmosphere was different because in 2007 they cheated the election, and it was a big embarrassment . . . So when we issued our report, we put them in a very bad state. In 2010, when we started, we said we don't *need* your permission as a government. You can arrest us, you can do whatever you want, but we will work, and we start working from the registration for the voters, six months before the election.

By prodding the regime to respond, activists discovered where the limits of repression lay and became further emboldened as "rightful" resistors (O'Brien 1996). And when the regime refrained from using harsh tactics such as imprisonment and violence, this fortified their positions and emboldened them to challenge the red lines. As a participant in the social movement to form a teacher's association described,

When [the Intelligence] started calling us, I was first concerned because you would hear about how brutal or how violent they are, but surprisingly things have changed . . . They would use things like appealing, and also threatening. So [saying] things like "oh, you want to be with your family? You want to keep your job? [Then] you should decrease your demands." And so there would be threats also, like you will lose your job, you will be thrown in prison, you're demanding an association which is a red line, you are overreaching, saying things out of line about the leadership [of the government].

Recognizing that the regime also sought to avoid mass disruptions, respondents came to discover the fuller extent of their bargaining power over the course of their campaigns and to wield the threat of potential of mass mobilization as a "negative inducement to bargaining" (Lipsky 1968; McAdam 1983; Moss 2014). As another teacher's movement organizer explained, by 2010,

Having an association became a crucial demand, and we were not going to retreat. [The Intelligence] were saying that it's unconstitutional . . . so we were saying why not amend the constitution so that it would allow having a teacher's association? It's a red line? We can make it *not* a red line! And the teachers were among the very first to call for constitutional amendments. And we stopped fearing. There wasn't anything that we wouldn't talk about in our meetings with the Intelligence . . . We said you guys need to go fight corruption! Why you are just stuck being against the teacher's association?

Recognizing that the regime wanted to avoid having its "dirty laundry" aired by the media and on the streets, as one NGO head put it, activists described a willingness to take the risk of exploiting regime sensitivities to gain attention and concessions. For instance, an INGO director explained in describing his relationship with the Intelligence,

[I say to them] "I have complaints, I have problems. I can talk with you, I don't want to go to the media or advocate against you. Please try to solve this problem." If they have respect for what we say or discuss, this is good, and that's it – we have accomplished what we need to do . . . That's how we start off, by the soft way. Discussing our issues. But if they don't discuss with us, we use the hard way using the media, making statements.

By 2011, one of the most notable ways that activists were expanding the regime's zone of tolerance was to push back on the red lines by criticizing the royal family. So though activists mobilizing during the Arab Spring period relied on moderate tactics to pursue their aims, such as writing opinion-editorials in newspapers and on websites and holding peaceful demonstrations, their grievances and claims increasingly came to breach the highest red line of royal family. According to Freedom House's 2011 country report, "those who violate redlines regarding the royal family and certain societal taboos face arrest, causing widespread self-censorship." Yet, despite the risks, it had become increasingly common for activists to chip at the walls of the royal palace. As one NGO leader declared,

> Now, the people are talking about a lot of things they cannot talk about before six months ago or ten months ago, before Tunisia. They are criticizing the government openly. They are sometimes mentioning the royal families. Before that, before the Spring of the Arab, [nobody] can do it. Now, in the content of the newspaper, the content of the website, there is less of the self-censorship now.

Activists also stretched the red lines by linking grievances about corruption – a relatively safe gripe given the regime's crackdown on corrupt officials in 2010 – and economic inequality with individual members of the royal family. As one 'Amman-based activist recalled, despite the fact that "there is a red line about the head of the majority, the King," the "ceiling" of their demands had been raised to new heights:

> When an activist from Irbid came to our meeting and told us . . . "We will not say anything about the regime, only corruption." Now he is talking *way* above [this] . . . how is the corruption is *in* the palace, *around* the palace, everywhere.

A further sign of their emboldened attitudes was that respondents felt empowered to voice strong grievances about the royal family to a relatively unknown American researcher. As the head of an SMO (who was also a retired regime elite) explained with exasperation, the king had recently blamed "dinosaurs" in the Intelligence for stalling his reform efforts, but this "cannot be believed":

> RESPONDENT: The King now says that you have unlimited free speech, and then when he met with young protesters he is complaining about the Intelligence, as if he doesn't *know* about the whole thing. This – it cannot be understood . . . In *one minute*, he can change the head of the intelligence. *He!* Not the Prime Minister! He is able to change it easily, without any problems! So how can you live with this contradiction?
>
> AUTHOR: So there wouldn't be any people in the Intelligence who would make problems for him if he did so?
>
> RESPONDENT: This is very impossible, no. This is kind of political hypocrisy. Call it what you want, but this cannot be believed.

Other activists aired their grievances about King Abdullah exuberantly in semi-public places (of the interviewees' choosing, in accordance with Internal Review Board mandated procedures) where any person might be listening, and interviewees appeared to be unconcerned about who might overhear her or his admonishments. The head of a human rights NGO described on the patio of a coffee shop, for example, that the central problem facing Jordan was the King himself:

If you insult the King or any Prince, they can put you in jail from one year to three years, according to the law. So these points, they make the people to be quiet . . . But in the in future, I think it will be changed. Because the people here, all the problems, what we face, *is from the regime*! The *King*! If he is the King, and he wants democratic reform, political reform, and . . . the government doesn't want, [or is] very slow [to implement reforms], ok, kick them out! You [the King] have the power! If you say the *mudeer al-mukhabarat* [director of the General Intelligence Directorate] is wrong, ok, kick him out! This means two things. Either [the King] is *able*, and he doesn't want to make these changes, or he is *unable*, and it means that he is *not* the King! And this makes the people think if he is unable, it means that he is not the ruler! So why do we have to keep him?!

After I asked this activist what the hypothetical consequences would be if I published these criticisms using his name, he replied:

RESPONDENT: About the King, it depends which point. No, on the King, if you said regarding that the people, that they are not with him, I don't mind, say it . . . The King, he is losing support from the Eastern [Jordanians] . . . This means that he is about to lose all of this legitimacy. *Let* them put me in trouble again, I don't mind . . . But I don't say that I want to make a coup d'état against him. [Laughs.]

AUTHOR: But even if you don't say you want a coup, they can still claim that you are speaking against the King and that can get you in trouble, right?

RESPONDENT: Ok, you will visit me in jail then. [Laughs.]

His response indicated a fine distinction between criticizing the king in the spirit of *revolution*, which was illegitimate, from criticizing of the king in the spirit of *strengthening* the monarchy, which was legitimate, though it could still land the interviewee in trouble.

Others also criticized the king in the same spirit of loyalism. As one SMO activist decried, Jordan required "real," rather than symbolic, political change. He exclaimed,

I'm wondering why the King is not taking actions? I mean we are not calling *against* him, and we want him to stay the King. However, we want to be ruled by *civilized rules and laws* . . . And he should send [corrupt officials] to the court, because otherwise, his reputation is, you know, *under discussion* with the Jordanian people.

The head of a social movement for political reform echoed this grievance:

In order to *protect* the King and *preserve* the system, the King's powers need to be reduced . . . But the problem is that the King is acting like the Prime Minister and interfering with the executive . . . The right thing is that the King should not be involved with this . . . The government should be responsible but practically now the King is blamed if there is some interference, [because] he is not far above this whole process. He should be far above it, but he's not. How can we trust the authority of the government, the legislative, if they are elected through interference [fraud] . . . and the King himself is also not far from this? That's why it's very dangerous.

In all, respondents attested that the ways in which activists and everyday people were referring to the monarchy in protests and on social media was undergoing a transformation. As an NGO head described,

In the street [and in] many general meetings, you hear that they are talking about the King and about the Queen in ways that cross all the red lines . . . They said the Constitution of "the 2nd Abdullah," but this kind of language is not common. Before they are supposed to say "the Constitution Coming by Decree of His Royal Majesty King Abdullah the Second."

Others affirmed this observation, describing how in demonstrations in front of various government buildings in 'Amman, activists challenged the normative practice of the king bestowing gifts (*hibba*) on his constituents, rather than rights (*huquq*). "We have started to be more accurate and more clear on our callings," one such SMO organizer explained. "In Jordan they used to say *Long Live the King*! Now the saying is different, now, it's *Long Live the Jordanian People*! And that health, education, is one of our *rights*. They are not a *gift* from anyone." This activist gleefully described how she had distributed bumper stickers proclaiming that universal education and health care are "our human rights" across the country and slapped one on the table where we were sitting for me to take home.

Another prominent topic of criticism was also Queen Rania and her family, whom activists perceived as benefitting from corruption and privatization. As a young protest participant from Irbid decried,

We are with the constitutional monarchy, and we want the King to have limited authority, not unlimited authority. But the family of the King are not a part of the state! They are just relatives. And they should not have any privilege in the country.

Other activists were more explicit in their targeted grievances about Queen Rania, and they framed their complaints as lawful because the "Queen does not have any official status in the Constitution." As one SMO leader explained:

Queen Rania – and I will say this in the street. She was *nothing* before she became the – I'm not calling her the Queen, by the way, in my writings – I'm saying that she is the King's *wife*. Because in the constitution there is nothing called "the Queen." The constitution is talking about the King, and she [should have] nothing to do in the political life. However, she is controlling everything in Jordan in a very, very tragic way.

Others also mentioned the broaching of red lines during protest events in which participants would "play" on the popular Arab Spring slogan "the people demand the fall of the regime." As one interviewee described, violence against protesters in the small city of Kerak in August 2011 led to an escalation in which riotous crowds began to purposefully breach the red lines using this popular slogan:

> When we got to Kerak . . . we saw [thousands of] people gathered and they were throwing tomatoes at the mayor's office . . . There was a much higher ceiling [to their slogans] than we had accepted [before]. They chanted "prices are higher than fire!" "Abdullah is gambling!" and they played on the slogan [of the Arab Spring], "the people demand reform, or we will finish the slogan" [with "the fall of the regime"]! They chanted about Queen Rania, talked about her and her brother who is a multi-billionaire now, and also telling the King: "look at [Hosni] Mubarak where he is now [in prison]!"

Moderate mobilization held promise for social change, therefore, because activists pushed back against the red lines by pressuring the regime to expand its zone of tolerance or else face embarrassment and a potentially destabilizing backlash. This practice reshaped the boundaries denoting legitimate and rightful resistance over the course of 2011, such that activists noticed a sharp change from general grievances about corruption and privatization to open criticism on the street by activists and ordinary persons about the monarchy itself. It was through their participation in a relatively "safe" zone of activism and civic engagement that they discovered where regime sensitivities and vulnerabilities lay, became emboldened to challenge authorities, and challenged red lines by enacting Jordan's liberalized promise. While these changes were incremental in comparison to the dramatic victories of the early Arab Spring period in Tunisia and Egypt, the efforts of moderate mobilizers nevertheless widened the civic sphere under entrenched authoritarianism.

Conclusion and discussion

In the contemporary era, regimes increasingly exhibit liberalized characteristics, permitting some degree of modest oppositional mobilization. Many studies suggest that moderate mobilization is bound by red lines that denote taboo topics and tactics. Thus, the failure of liberalization to induce democratization has castigated regime-permitted mobilization as ineffective at best and harmful at worst. In line with a growing body of researching telling a different story, however, this chapter demonstrates that moderate mobilization in the Kingdom of Jordan is far from coopted. On the contrary, collective actors working conscientiously within a regime-delimited middle ground walk a perilous path. Even when activists try to work within the red lines, they often stray into no-go areas, continuously testing and confronting the state at the borders of the permissible. Rather than occupying a safe zone, the Jordanian case illustrates how even seemingly mundane forms of advocacy can strike at the regime's nerve centers by calling attention to regime failures, shortcomings, and illiberal practices. Furthermore, because the boundaries denoting the permissible are opaque and ever changing, activists often do not know what will be allowed until they act. As Stern and O'Brien (2012: 177) describe, while there are some clear off-limit topics, "conflicting signals are equally (if not more) common."

The case of Jordan also points to another promise of liberalization: if regimes are unwilling to repress at all costs, activists have the potential to gain new ground and incrementally fulfill the promise of the liberalized authoritarian state. In justifying their actions as loyal and rebuking repression as unlawful and arbitrary, activists pushed back against regime-imposed limits and became increasingly emboldened in word and deed. They also sometimes won concessions from regime members. By the summer of 2011, this dynamic had manifested in the relative routinization of public criticisms of the royal family, which had been considered as a hardline taboo just a few years prior. Moderate mobilization in Jordan, therefore, was doing more than gaining concessions in a piecemeal fashion. Taken collectively, these activists were engaged in a dynamic process of reshaping normative citizenship practices in an authoritarian state.

This study has several implications for the study of mobilization and social change. First and most fundamentally, movements that are less than revolutionary in authoritarian states deserve as much scholarly attention as their radical counterparts. It is certainly the case that social movement groups and nongovernmental organizations working within regime-delimited spaces can reproduce hegemonic social structures and norms in problematic ways. On the other hand, by challenging state actors to live up to their promises, these actors take risks in a heavily but inconsistently policed environment to enact the regime's promises of welfare provision, political reform, and liberal social change. Moderate mobilizers are therefore engaged in a constant dynamic of tactical innovation (McAdam 1983; Moss 2014) and undertake significant risks to push for what they perceive as rightful and just (Chen 2012; O'Brien 1996).

Second, because scholars of contention in China, such as Kevin O'Brien, Rachel Stern, and Xi Chen (who are cited throughout this paper), have uncovered many of the same dynamics as I have found in the Jordanian case, I suggest that moderate mobilizers across liberalized authoritarian states face similar perils and possibilities for change. This suggests the need for more collaborative research dedicated to comparing mobilization dynamics across world regions. Such comparisons may uncover further parallels, but also discern key differences. For example, while local protests in China sometimes go unnoticed in rural or otherwise isolated contexts due to the sheer vastness of the state (O'Brien and Li 2006), demonstrations in small countries with relatively high media and internet penetration like Jordan may prove comparatively harder for regimes to censor or ignore. Cross-country comparisons will help to further illuminate how regime repression and mobilization varies by state-level characteristics and other factors, such as activists' identities, both real and ascribed (Thornton 2007; Wiktorowicz 2001).

This begs a further theoretical question: does liberalization simply signify a "political opportunity" for change-oriented mobilization, as scholars of social movements have argued (McAdam 1999[1982]; Meyer 2004; Tarrow 2011; Tilly 1978)? In a broad sense, yes. The relative relaxation of the most extreme forms of repression and the establishment of "indigenous structures" for activism can give rise to protests that test the waters by submitting moderate demands (McAdam 1999[1982]; Shultziner 2013). However, the political opportunity perspective is insufficient for understanding the dynamics of mobilization in these contexts. First, mobilization does not emerge automatically or consistently in response to broad-based liberalization measures. So-called opportunities in this context are highly unstable and vary by group, place, and the social control entity at play (Armstrong and Bernstein 2008; Barkan 1984; Bloom 2015). Furthermore, opportunities may rescind or expand under liberalization without formal changes to the political structure (Robertson 2010), and it is only *after* activists take the risk of coming out in the open that these changes become apparent. To argue that mobilization is likely to emerge after liberalization also does not explain how activists evaluate the risks involved, what kinds of risks they undertake, or how they induce social change.

Rather than arguing that liberalization is an opportunity that predicts mobilization, I instead claim that after the initial emergence of activism following liberalization, it is the continuous process of mobilization that signifies and creates a subsequent "opportunity structure" for collective action. This is because after regimes make declarations about freedom and liberty, it is only through the act of populating the civic sphere that activists discover whether these opportunities exist in reality. If the door quickly slams shut, as it did after Syria's "Damascus Spring" under Bashar al-Assad ended in a devastating crackdown in the early 2000s, for example, it is the act of mobilization that signals whether the opportunity is real. It is through the high-risk process of mobilization, therefore, that activists test and fulfill state commitments to liberalization, gain information about the limits of what will be tolerated, and signal to others what is permissible. This is not to say that macro- and meso-level changes to formal institutions are irrelevant; only that scholars neglect the fact that everyday collective actions are what signify what opportunities exist where and how.

At the same time, this does not mean that moderate mobilization will lead to increasing liberalization in a linear fashion over time. This argument would be making the same mistake of earlier works forecasting liberalization as portending democratization. As we have seen, states are likely to shrink and expand the civic action field in accordance with a range of factors outside of activists' direct control. When the field expands, as in the case of Jordan during the Arab Spring, moderate mobilization can set new sociopolitical and cultural precedents of what is rightful and lawful. These gains may fall well short of radical liberal change, but nevertheless signify the enactment of citizenship without democratization. In other times and places, however, the field may shrink, as is the case in Russia, China, and The Philippines at the time of this writing. Yet, moderate mobilization still matters, because it is these activists who occupy the front lines to defend the civic action zone. And even when their mobilizations switch to defensive modes of action, it is these groups who fight to retain what territory they have gained and keep liberalization a meaningful reality.

Overall, investigating the paradoxes, perils, and promises of moderate mobilization enables researchers to trace how political systems change over time, even when states forestall formal democratization. For these reasons, movements in the middle warrant the same degree of enthusiasm and attention as the revolutions that unfold alongside them.

Notes

1 I have dubbed Jordan a "liberalized authoritarian regime" because the Kingdom does not fit into dominant definitions of hybrid or competitive authoritarian categories due to the king's vast powers and the lack of elections for Jordan's leading positions.
2 For more information, see Freedom House's yearly reports on the Kingdom, such as the 2011 report published around the time that this research was conducted, available at https://freedomhouse.org/report/freedom-world/2011/jordan.
3 The interviewee explained that he and the other leaders would have been tried for treason if not for the fact that the revolution in Tunisia prompted the regime to back down in order to defuse the potential for mass revolt.
4 This activist attested that he was released after five days in prison because protests erupted over his imprisonment and international media covered his case.

References

Albrecht, Holger. 2005. "How Can Opposition Support Authoritarianism? Lessons from Egypt." *Democratization* 12(3): 378–397.
Albrecht, Holger, and Eva Wegner. 2006. "Autocrats and Islamists: Contenders and Containment in Egypt and Morocco." *The Journal of North African Studies* 11(2): 123–141.
Arendt, Hannah. 1968. *The Origins of Totalitarianism*. Orlando: Harcourt, Inc.
Armstrong, Elizabeth A., and Mary Bernstein. 2008. "Culture, Power, and Institutions: A Multi-Institutional Politics Approach to Social Movements." *Sociological Theory* 26(1): 74–99.
Barkan, Steven E. 1984. "Legal Control of the Southern Civil Rights Movement." *American Sociological Review* 49(4): 552–565.
Bayat, Asef. 2013 [2010]. *Life as Politics: How Ordinary People Change the Middle East*, 2nd edition. Stanford: Stanford University Press.
Bloom, Joshua. 2015. "The Dynamics of Opportunity and Insurgent Practice: How Black Anti-Colonialists Compelled Truman to Advocate Civil Rights." *American Sociological Review* 80(2): 391–415.
Brownlee, Jason. 2009. "Portents of Pluralism: How Hybrid Regimes Affect Democratic Transitions." *American Journal of Political Science* 53(3): 515–532.
Cai, Yongshun. 2010. *Collective Resistance in China: Why Popular Protests Succeed or Fail*. Stanford: Stanford University Press.
Carothers, Thomas. 2002. "The End of the Transition Paradigm." *Journal of Democracy* 13(1): 5–21.
Chen, Xi. 2012. *Social Protest and Contentious Authoritarianism in China*. New York: Cambridge University Press.
Chen, Xi, and Dana M. Moss. Forthcoming. "Social Movements and Authoritarian Regimes." In *The Blackwell Companion to Social Movements*, 2nd edition, edited by David Snow, Sarah Soule, Hanspeter Kriesi, and Holly McCammon.
Diamond, Larry Jay. 2002. "Thinking about Hybrid Regimes." *Journal of Democracy* 13: 21–35.

Freedom House. 2011. "Jordan: Freedom in the World 2011." https://freedomhouse.org/report/freedom-world/2011/jordan (Accessed October 28, 2018).

Fu, Diana. Forthcoming. "Fragmented Control: Governing Contentious Civil Society in China." *Governance: An International Journal.*

Fu, Hualing, and Richard Cullen. 2008. "Weiquan (Rights Protection) Lawyering in an Authoritarian State: Building a Culture of Public-Interest Lawyering." *China Journal* 59: 11–27.

Geddes, Barbara. 1999. "What Do We Know about Democratization after Twenty Years?" *Annual Review of Political Science* 2: 115–144.

Gunitsky, Seva. 2015. "Corrupting the Cyber-Commons: Social Media as a Tool of Autocratic Stability." *Perspectives on Politics* 13(1): 42–54.

Hess, David, and Brian Martin. 2006. "Repression, Backfire, and the Theory of Transformative Events." *Mobilization: An International Journal* 11(2): 249–267.

Johnston, Hank. 2004. "Talking the Walk: Speech Acts and Resistance in Authoritarian Regimes." Pp. 108–137 in *Repression and Mobilization*, edited by Christian Davenport, Hank Johnston, and Carol Mueller. Minneapolis: University of Minnesota Press.

Khalili, Laleh, and Jillian Schwedler, eds. 2010. *Policing and Prisons in the Middle East: Formations of Coercion.* New York: Columbia University Press.

Kurzman, Charles. 2004. *The Unthinkable Revolution in Iran.* Cambridge, MA: Harvard University Press.

Langohr, Vickie. 2004. "Too Much Civil Society, Too Little Politics: Egypt and Liberalizing Arab Regimes." *Comparative Politics* 36(2): 181–204.

Lee, Ching Kwan. 2007. *Against the Law: Labor Protests in China's Rustbelt and Sunbelt.* Berkeley: University of California Press.

Lee, Ching Kwan, and Yonghong Zhang. 2013. "The Power of Instability: Unraveling the Microfoundations of Bargained Authoritarianism in China." *American Journal of Sociology* 118(6): 1475–1508.

Levitsky, Steven, and Lucan A. Way. 2010. *Competitive Authoritarianism: Hybrid Regimes after the Cold War.* New York: Cambridge University Press.

Linz, Juan J. 2000. *Totalitarian and Authoritarian Regimes.* Boulder, CO: Lynne Rienner Publishers.

Lipsky, Michael. 1968. "Protest as a Political Resource." *The American Political Science Review* 62(4): 1144–1158.

Lipsky, Michael. 2010 [1980]. *Street-Level Bureaucracy: Dilemmas of the Individual in Public Services.* New York: Russell Sage Foundation.

Lorentzen, Peter L. 2013. "Regularizing Rioting: Permitting Public Protest in an Authoritarian Regime." *Quarterly Journal of Political Science* 8: 127–158.

Lucas, Russell E. 2003. "Deliberalization in Jordan." *Journal of Democracy* 14(1): 137–144.

Lust-Okar, Ellen. 2005. *Structuring Conflict in the Arab World: Incumbents, Opponents, and Institutions.* New York: Cambridge University Press.

Lust-Okar, Ellen. 2007. "The Management of Opposition: Formal Structures of Contestation and Informal Political Manipulation in Egypt, Jordan, and Morocco." Pp. 21–58 in *Debating Arab Authoritarianism.* See entry for Schlumberger, 2007.

McAdam, Doug. 1983. "Tactical Innovation and the Pace of Insurgency." *American Sociological Review* 48(6): 735–754.

McAdam, Doug. 1996. "Political Opportunities: Conceptual Origins, Current Problems, Future Directions." Pp. 23–40 in *Comparative Perspectives on Social Movements*, edited by Doug McAdam, John D. McCarthy, and Mayer N. Zald. New York: Cambridge University Press.

McAdam, Doug. 1999 [1982]. *Political Process and the Development of Black Insurgency, 1930–1970*, 2nd edition. Chicago: University of Chicago Press.

McAdam, Doug, Sidney Tarrow, and Charles Tilly. 2001. *Dynamics of Contention*. New York: Cambridge University Press.

Mertha, Andrew C. 2008. *China's Water Warriors: Citizen Action and Policy Change*. Ithaca: Cornell University Press.

Meyer, David S. 2004. "Protest and Political Opportunities." *Annual Review of Sociology* 30: 125–145.

Moss, Dana M. 2014. "Repression, Response, and Contained Escalation under 'Liberalized' Authoritarianism in Jordan." *Mobilization: An International Quarterly* 19: 489–514.

O'Brien, Kevin J. 1996. "Rightful Resistance." *World Politics* 49(1): 31–55.

O'Brien, Kevin J. 2003. "Neither Transgressive nor Contained: Boundary-Spanning Contention in China." *Mobilization: An International Quarterly* 8(1): 51–64.

O'Brien, Kevin J., and Lianjiang Li. 2006. *Rightful Resistance in Rural China*. New York: Cambridge University Press. 8(1): 51–64.

O'Brien, Kevin J., and Rachel E. Stern. 2008. "Introduction: Studying Contention in Contemporary China." Pp. 11–25 in *Popular Protest in China*, edited by Kevin J. O'Brien. Cambridge: Harvard University Press.

Perry, Elizabeth J. 2002. *Challenging the Mandate of Heaven: Social Protest and State Power in China*. New York: M. E. Sharpe.

Pioppi, Daniela. 2007. "Privatization of Social Services as Regime Strategy: The Revival of Islamic Endowments (*Awqaf*) in Egypt." Pp. 129–142 in *Debating Arab Authoritarianism*. See entry for Schlumberger, 2007.

Posusney, Marsha Pripstein. 2004. "Enduring Authoritarianism: Middle East Lessons for Comparative Theory." *Comparative Politics* 36(2): 127–138.

Robertson, Graeme B. 2010. *The Politics of Protest in Hybrid Regimes: Managing Dissent in Post-Communist Russia*. New York: Cambridge University Press.

Schedler, Andreas. 2002. "The Menu of Manipulation." *Journal of Democracy* 13(2): 36–50.

Schedler, Andreas. 2013. *The Politics of Uncertainty: Sustaining and Subverting Electoral Authoritarianism*. New York: Oxford University Press.

Schlumberger, Oliver, ed. 2007. *Debating Arab Authoritarianism: Dynamics and Durability in Nondemocratic Regimes*. Stanford: Stanford University Press.

Schwedler, Jillian. 1998. "Protesting Sanctions against Iraq: A View from Jordan." *Middle East Report* 28. www.merip.org/mer/mer208/protesting-sanctions-against-iraq (Accessed September 15, 2011).

Schwedler, Jillian. 2003. "More Than a Mob: The Dynamics of Political Demonstrations in Jordan." *Middle East Report* 226: 18–23.

Schwedler, Jillian. 2005. "Cop Rock: Protest, Identity, and Dancing Riot Police in Jordan." *Social Movement Studies: Journal of Social, Cultural and Political Protest* 4(2): 155–175.

Scott, James C. 1990. *Domination and the Arts of Resistance: Hidden Transcripts*. New Haven, CT: Yale University Press.

Shi, Fayong, and Yongshun Cai. 2006. "Disaggregating the State: Networks and Collective Resistance in Shanghai." *The China Quarterly* 186: 314–332.

Shultziner, Doron. 2013. "The Social-Psychological Origins of the Montgomery Bus Boycott: Social Interaction and Humiliation in the Emergence of Social Movements." *Mobilization: An International Quarterly* 18(2): 117–142.

Snow, David A., and Dana M. Moss. 2014. "Protest on the Fly: Toward a Theory of Spontaneity in the Dynamics of Protest and Social Movements." *American Sociological Review* 79(6): 1122–1143.

Spires, Anthony J. 2011. "Contingent Symbiosis and Civil Society in an Authoritarian State: Understanding the Survival of China's Grassroots NGOs." *American Journal of Sociology* 117(1): 1–45.

Stern, Rachel E., and Jonathan Hassid. 2012. "Amplifying Silence: Uncertainty and Control Parables in China." *Comparative Political Studies* 45(10): 1230–1254.

Stern, Rachel E., and Kevin J. O'Brien. 2012. "Politics at the Boundary: Mixed Signals and the Chinese State." *Modern China* 38(2): 174–198.

Straughn, Jeremy Brooke. 2005. "'Taking the State at Its Word': The Arts of Consentful Contention in the German Democratic Republic." *American Journal of Sociology* 110(6): 1598–1650.

Su, Yang, and Xin He. 2010. "Street as Courtroom: State Accommodation of Labor Protest in South China." *Law & Society Review* 44(1): 157–184.

Tarrow, Sidney. 2011. *Power in Movement: Social Movements and Contentious Politics*, 3rd edition. New York: Cambridge University Press.

Thornton, Patricia M. 2007. "Manufacturing Sectarian Divides: The Chinese State, Identities, and Collective Violence." Pp. 171–189 in *Identity Matters: Ethnic and Sectarian Conflict*, edited by James L. Peacock, Patricia M. Thornton, and Patrick B. Inman. New York: Berghahn Books.

Tilly, Charles. 1978. *From Mobilization to Revolution*. Reading, MA: Addison-Wesley.

Wegner, Eva. 2004. "Islamist Inclusion and Regime Persistence: The Moroccan Win-Win Situation." Pp. 75–89 in *Debating Arab Authoritarianism*. See entry for Schlumberger, 2007.

Wickham, Carrie Rosefsky. 2004. "The Path to Moderation: Strategy and Learning in the Formation of Egypt's Wasat Party." *Comparative Politics* 36(2): 205–228.

Wiktorowicz, Quintan. 2000. "Civil Society as Social Control: State Power in Jordan." *Comparative Politics* 33(1): 43–61.

Wiktorowicz, Quintan. 2001. *The Management of Islamic Activism: Salafis, the Muslim Brotherhood, and State Power in Jordan*. Albany: State University of New York Press.

Yom, Sean L. 2009. "Jordan: Ten More Years of Autocracy." *Journal of Democracy* 20(4): 151–166.

Part II

Nonviolence and social movements

Engagements

7 How the effectiveness of nonviolent action is the wrong question for activists, academics, and everyone else

David S. Meyer

As alarmed as we might be about the election of Donald Trump, the flowering of diverse activism against the new administration and its policies has been both heartening and fascinating. The spread of issues and constituencies engaging a wide variety of overwhelmingly nonviolent efforts at resistance can provide provocation for us as scholars and inspiration as citizens. Although many of the demonstrations and campaigns have been the work of long-established organizations, new groups have also sprung up with the express intent of staging effective action.

One of the many new groups calls itself White Rose Resistance (http://whiteroseresistance.org/), a name that explicitly evokes a religious and spiritual resistance campaign against Hitler Nazi Germany over about 6 months in 1942. (More about that to follow.) The contemporary White Rose strategy is based on three components: activism directed at influencing Congress, including letter writing, phone calls, town meetings, and electoral participation; public demonstrations; and activating a new "underground railroad," intended to help threatened individuals find safe places, sometimes in other countries. Most of this is pretty much what scores of other organizations are now doing, some of which developed in the moments after Trump was elected and others that had been engaged in politics for decades. There's a great deal of visible anti-Trump activism, including large demonstrations by women, for science, and on behalf of the climate, citizen strikes on behalf of women and immigrants, litigation launched by both interest groups and elected officials, campaigns to coordinate letters, phone calls, and emails to elected officials, organized questioning at town hall meetings, and directed efforts in elections. This is only a partial list, of course. And there have been a few scattered antifa or black bloc efforts directed at showing resistance by demonstrating, damaging property, and confronting police. It's not hard to find resistance.

The original White Rose, however, presents a very different picture, appearing at a time when domestic resistance to Hitler was very difficult to find. Starting in June of 1942, Hans and Sophie Scholl, along with a handful of other students at the University of Munich inspired by philosophy professor, Kurt Huber, drafted and distributed a series of six leaflets, sometimes through the mail to other universities, sometimes by hand delivery to select individuals. The White Rose activists also left their leaflets anonymously in the pages of telephone books, where they thought sympathetic people might pick them up, read them, and duplicate them in accord with the only explicit appeal for action in each of the leaflets. The papers criticized Hitler and the Nazis for the distortion of the German people and the disrespect for Christian values, international accords, and basic civil liberties and democracy. They called for "passive resistance" in ways that were not really defined, save to acknowledge that individuals find their own way to stage the opposition. In a risky act of escalation, several of the students went on graffiti campaigns, painting slogans on house walls near the university on a few nights in February 1943 (Nuborn and Dumbach 2007).

One day in February 1943, a custodian at the university saw the leaflets in the possession of the Scholls and reported them to the police. In short order, they and other members of the collective were arrested, interrogated, summarily tried, and executed (www.holocaustresearchproject.org/revolt/whiterose.html). Although the Nazis didn't execute everyone involved, the first arrests marked the end of the movement. Like the overwhelming majority of the contemporary resistance, the White Rose was determinedly nonviolent and strongly committed. Similarities end there: the twentieth century White Rose activists operated largely alone and clandestinely.

Although the White Rose offers some amount of moral inspiration to contemporary activists, it is not really a very encouraging example. It's hard to find a measure by which we can call the small student movement a political success: White Rose activists were unable to spread their ideas very far; they didn't bring down Hitler and the Nazi regime; they didn't temper offensive policies; and, mostly, they didn't survive. The leafletters were courageous and committed, but the example they offer contemporary activists seems disheartening. At one level, their efforts provided an inspirational tale of moral commitment that recirculates periodically, but it's hardly a model for effective collective action. Of course, it's not a lack of fortitude or strategic vision that doomed the White Rose – and it's not as if other German efforts directed against the regime were notably more successful. Rather, by 1942, the Nazis had long since consolidated control of the state and its repressive capacity. The key to understanding the extremely limited influence of the White Rose campaign lay not in its integrity or its strategies, tactics, or ideas, but in the larger political context.

This is a bit of a long introduction to my argument: a focus on the effect or lack of effect of nonviolent action, per se, is a mistaken emphasis for activists, academics, and virtually everyone else. Fixating on a particular portion of the spectrum of collective action leads to a number of analytical missteps, and thus, a misunderstanding of what's possible, as well as a devaluing and dishonest reinterpretation of the range of goals behind those staging a collective action.

In this chapter, I outline inherent difficulties in answering the question of the effectiveness of nonviolent tactics and advance the argument that the effectiveness of nonviolence – or indeed, of any particular tactic, is the wrong question. I'll suggest other questions and approaches. I begin by acknowledging just how difficult honest inquiry into the effectiveness of nonviolence is, largely because of the appeal of obviating the difficulty of making moral choices. I then address the attractions and the analytical difficulties of finding a cookbook approach to activism, in which the independent effects of particular tactical choices can be identified, calibrated, and evaluated apart from context. Particularly, I contend that it's important to understand a constellation of tactics and approaches to social change. It's necessary to consider the range of actors operating in a collective action challenge and the difficulties of ascribing causal influence to one particular actor or strategy. Focusing on liberal democracies in general and the United States in particular, I look at the unexpected influence of violent actions taken by actors on the left and the right. I then argue for a fuller but more difficult evaluation of collective action that focuses on a broader historical and analytical frame.

Search for recipes

We want to know, as both scholars and citizens, what consequences follow from strategic social movement action. In this context, the search for the impact of non-violent tactics on a campaign's prospects for success is understandable and attractive. But in the real world, the process of social change doesn't work as much like a recipe as we'd like to imagine. Like would-be chefs scanning a cookbook, activists and analysts like to imagine a process of making social change that's accessible and, relatively, unconflicted. Scholarship that inventories the varieties of nonviolent action (e.g., Schock 2005, 2015; Sharp 1973; Sibley 1963; Vinthagen 2015) has always found an attentive audience, eager to imagine other settings in which those recipes could work. But the focus on the tactic belies the larger truth that the context in which contentious politics takes places is generally more consequential than the particular recipe of tactics. No matter how good the recipe, the basic ingredients, tools, and settings dramatically affect what the effort will produce. Chance, contingency, and context all end diminished in an analysis that focuses on tactics. The focus on isolating one set of tactics, albeit an attractive one, produces analytical errors that merit direct attention.

Censoring the repertoire of contention

Although we can imagine a spectrum of contention that is extraordinarily broad, in which numbers, commitment, unity, and worthiness are displayed, in actual practice activists in a particular setting rely on a relatively narrow list of approaches. The larger political world makes some tactics extraordinarily difficult in some contexts but not others (Tilly 2006). Take, for example, the mass demonstration, which has become a staple in contemporary American politics. Negotiated management systems with authorities reduce the uncertainty and risk attendant to social movement campaigns, such that it is safe to demonstrate. Surely, this makes it easier for people to demonstrate by marching in Washington, DC, or in many other places. Police accustomed to largely routinized performances can, with appropriate training and effort, allow a dramatic demonstration while simultaneously minimizing the risk of injury or serious disruption for all involved (McPhail et al. 1998). At the same time, by reducing the risks and costs of a particular tactic, that tactic no longer demonstrates the same degree of commitment. Compare, for example, the spate of large American demonstrations to the much smaller, much riskier, recent demonstrations in Russia, where counts of participants numbered in the hundreds. The size of the demonstration is a poor diagnostic for the amount of organization and commitment required to stage it. It is also an unsteady indicator of the degree of disruption that it will cause, as well as the extent of directed action that will follow.

Logically, working from a more limited list of ingredients or approaches can't be intrinsically more effective than having a full repertoire of actions at disposal. A limited set of ingredients can spur creativity, but it's always preferable to enjoy additional options. To be sure, embracing particular tactics, like putting cyanide in the black bean soup, could be destructive, but then the appropriate question isn't about the effectiveness of nonviolence so much as the negative consequences of particular violent actions. And this is also contextual, as I will discuss later.

Although it's tempting to think of activists choosing from a broad spectrum from tactics, groups more commonly pick approaches from the much smaller menu (or playlist) that they've employed in the past. Theoretically, potential tactics are censored by available resources, including experience, authorities' tolerance, and the values of those who engage in them. Although it's entirely appropriate, even admirable, for activists to foreswear particular tactics that violate their moral sensibilities, it's irresponsible for academics to make the same choices in their analyses.

Episodes versus longer stories

The focus on nonviolent action as the predictor of any kind of outcome can lead to a kind of myopic attention to episodes. But the contentious events or episodes only take on meaning in the context of a larger story about politics and contention. The impact of the event itself is largely dependent upon the context in which it is embedded, and the stream of less visible actions that support it. Vaclav Havel (1985) once wrote that events represent the 1/10th of an iceberg visible above the water. Focus on the event neglects the 9/10ths submerged, but that portion is likely more consequential.

Additionally, there is a temporal dimension, in which a long stream of action leads up to the contentious event that marks the beginning of a story. Stories about the American civil rights movement, for example, often focus on dramatic events divorced from a larger historical context affecting both individuals and organizations. As with the success story of an entertainer, overnight success often comes only after decades of effort. Decontextualizing the event risks a severe misunderstanding of what actually matters.

Censoring actors

The definite article is something that scholars deploy more than activists do. Movements are comprised of diverse individuals and – at least in liberal polities – organizations, cooperating to some extent on particular campaigns. Even events, portrayed monolithically in histories, are comprised of organized groups and committed individuals who may agree broadly on some things but often disagree vigorously on both ultimate goals and/or short-term tactics. The demonstration that is portrayed as a singular effort features a diversity of actors doing different things more or less simultaneously (McPhail 2017 [1992]). It's no surprise then that broader campaigns include a range of tactics, some of them violent and some of them explicitly disowned by particular actors. The easy story of the civil rights movement, for example, emphasizes the purposeful nonviolence of collective action during the 1950s and early 1960s, disrupted and derailed by a few groups willing to use violence later. In reality, however, the dramatic nonviolent actions valorized historically were often surrounded by less visible and sometimes violent actions (see Cobb 2015). And violent or destructive acts by one set of actors can have differential effects on the likelihood of success of others (Haines 1988).

Particularly in liberal polities, it's a mistake to credit any particular actor within a larger campaign with the influence that led to a favorable outcome. In this regard, the nonviolent actors who demonstrate against war can be augmented or diminished by others who are lobbying elected officials and still others who are conducting selected acts of violence. Thoughtfully studying influence means acknowledging and assessing interactions and combined impact.

Temporal censoring

Comprehensive stories about social movement campaigns are always longer than the attention span of most audiences. The frequently told tale of Rosa Parks's successful effort to initiate a buy boycott edits out not only Mrs. Parks's long history of political activism, but also a large number of similar actions by others that did not generate the same response. Mrs. Parks's emergence as a visible activist in 1955 followed more than a dozen years of civil rights work, including a visit to the Highlander Folk School where she studied both civil disobedience and the *Brown v. Board of Education* decision. (Here, the recipe for success includes secret ingredients not found in the action.) It also edits out the committed and long-term efforts of other organizations directed to both promoting collective action and offering other ways to challenge segregation. The success of the bus boycott in Montgomery was affected by the organized efforts of the NAACP, which worked with local church communities and benefited from training and education from the labor movement. All was enabled by a reasonably new openness from national political figures to act on civil rights with the intent of engaging in a propaganda war with the Soviet Union (Dudziak 2002). The point is that a tunnel vision fixation on a courageous act leads to a distorted emphasis on the act itself, rather than the context in which it takes place.

Thus, when we look at successful collective action campaigns, we often neglect the long investments that produce successful action.

Professional ethics and motivated reasoning

The human costs of even the most nobly motivated social change efforts can be so extensive that we understandably always search for ways to reduce the moral tension and unfortunate trade-offs involved in making social change. We blanch, for example, when we hear about the Bible-toting crusader against slavery, John Brown, executed his opponents with broadswords. Although the notion that harsh conflict, including violence, may play a critical role in redressing injustice and undermining oppression and is surely not difficult to accept in the abstract, it leaves us to find ways to balance, excuse, or justify costly, destructive, and violent actions in which innocents are always hurt. Legitimating the idea of moral trade-offs risks countenancing destructive acts aimed at redressing someone's vision of injustice. This is hard.

In contrast, tales of heroic and consequential nonviolent actions, Gandhi's Salt March, Rosa Parks's resistance on a bus, Lech Walesa's strike in Gdansk, or the mass assembly in Tahrir Square, make the moral accounting much simpler. Individual acts of courage inspire larger numbers to join in collective action aimed at convincing oppressors to cede power or abandon onerous policies. Challengers take on personal difficulties, to be sure, but do so without moral compromise, such that the fault always lies with those in power. The theories of nonviolent action that emphasize the relationship between ends and means and the ideal of prefigurative politics promise a less destructive path to social change, where those struggling for justice don't themselves perpetrate injustice. Authors, sometimes activists, like Martin Luther King, Vaclav Havel, and Henry Thoreau, emphasize both the moral virtue and political efficacy of living in truth, that is, withdrawing cooperation from an oppressive government so that it is forced to concede, while simultaneously building, in embryo, the more just society that will replace it.

It's hard not to want this political strategy to work; given the carnage often accompanying other strategies for change, most scholars – and certainly those scholars who choose to address such topics – have a rooting interest in how the analysis comes out. The danger here is the drive for "motivated reasoning," that is, rigorous analytical work that's directed to support a particular finding (Lodge and Taber 2013). Much as an attorney will aggressively, but honestly, look for evidence and arguments that support the position of her client, the committed scholar is likely to work hard to find a desired outcome, rather than an undisclosed answer.

And there is much in the analysis of collective action that is necessarily ad hoc, providing many opportunities for distortion. Take, for example, the largely nonviolent mass actions in Tahrir Square in 2011. A simple story recounts the massive mobilization over days, featuring large numbers of determined citizens turning out and taking risks, including suffering the violence of recruited thugs. Over a period of nearly three weeks of mostly peaceful protests, longtime president Hosni Mubarak left office. At this level, it's easy to code as a win for nonviolent action. If we expand the scope of the story just a little bit, we will see that the Egyptian Army, a powerful and autonomous institution, took the side of the protesters and forced Mubarak to leave. Army pleas were convincing at least partly because it was the army, not the state, that enjoyed a monopoly on the exercise of legitimate violence, and Mubarak surrendered to the army – not to the protesters in the street. The win for nonviolent civil action is not quite so clear. Expand the time frame a little further, and we see that Mubarak's ouster was followed by the effective rule of the army for more than a year and an administration that was at least as repressive as Mubarak's regime, particularly in dealing with protest. Muhammed Morsi took office in June of 2012, representing the popular, but surely not democratic, Islamic brotherhood. Morsi himself faced large demonstrations and calls for his resignation, and was deposed by the army after slightly more than a year in office. Within a year, Abdel Fattah el-Sisi, head of the Egyptian Armed forces, left the army, stood for election, and gained power, as the new representative of the army. The win for nonviolence and democracy is much less clear.

The point is that there are different factual ways to tell the story of the Egyptian revolution of 2011. Depending upon the length of the story and the scope of vision employed, we get very different answers about the effectiveness of nonviolent action. And a focus on nonviolence can lead us to overstate the possibilities of effective collective action in some contexts and to hyperinflate the consequences of an action.

More generally, motivated reasoning understandably leans to a diversity of potential outcome measures, such that opinion change, moral victories, or later mobilization can be selectively deployed as wins. Although entirely appropriate for advocates, this is a disturbing turn to the pursuit of social science.

Beyond the accumulation of stories, some scholars have worked to advance systematic research comparing nonviolent and violent campaigns for change. Most impressively is the large-data comparisons provided by Chenoweth and Stephan (2008, 2011). The authors found that nonviolent campaigns were significantly more likely to achieve reforms than violent campaigns. This is a serious study, and the authors recognize the methodological challenge of sorting out causes from effects: simply, the relative freedom that allows a nonviolent campaign to be sustained and the internal organization necessary to mount some campaigns (see particularly Nepstad 2008) are likely to be associated with a range of other factors that correlate with political influence. A sustained nonviolent challenge requires an unusual combination of some degree of tolerance and restraint from the dominant regime (recall the fate of Germany's White Rose campaign) and internal organization and discipline. Unlike an armed insurrection, nonviolent activists cannot control distinct regions in the face of armed opposition, administer governance, and extract resources to expand their administration and influence. It's hard to develop rigorous statistical methods to deal with context in a meaningful ways (but see Chenoweth and Ulfelder 2017).

Assessing the correlates of policy reform in democracies or regime change in authoritarian governments is a more useful analytic strategy than isolating nonviolence as a potentially critical factor. What I have in mind is a research program that addresses these critical issues:

1   We want recipes for effectiveness, but the context changes what works and what doesn't.
2   We want to understand collective action, but focusing on nonviolence just censors the spectrum of possibilities.

3   We want to see the downsides of destructive efforts, but this leads us to ignore the potential effects, positive and negative, of collective action that doesn't censor violent acts.

Reassessing the impact of violence

I raise these issues to suggest that rather than finding ways to valorize a set of tactics most of us find attractive, it may make more sense, at least in a liberal polity, to look at the impact of less appealing approaches in events that transgress by employing violence. Two examples stand as contrast at this moment, a contrast that should enlighten some kind of meaningful comparison. I start with the recent antifa protests, which have been mostly, but not exclusively, confined to the San Francisco Bay area. Related efforts appeared in protesting against Donald Trump's inauguration on January 20, 2017, and in staging a counterdemonstration to a racist right demonstration in Charlottesville, Virginia. These activists are understandably outraged by the election of Donald Trump. In Berkeley, the protesters have turned out in numbers with enthusiasm in response to planned lectures by very conservative speakers, including Milo Yiannopoulos and Ann Coulter (e.g., BAMN 2017; Sheffield 2017).

The direct unfiltered action approach calls for challenging expressions of racism and fascism where they emerge and particularly making it unacceptable to espouse such ideas in public. Toward that end, the confrontations over such speeches have led to volatile demonstrations, destruction of property, and some arrests. It's also made for national coverage.

In the context of contemporary American politics, the disruptive response has made for bumps in attention to speakers who might otherwise be marginal and the transformation of provocateurs into martyrs. Berkeley is fast becoming the indispensable spot on any conservative's book tour. What's more, the willingness to embrace violent street action has been used by the far right as legitimation for its own violence, creating heroes out of street fighters like the stick man, who achieved acclaim within the radical right for brutally attacking antifa marchers (Chang 2017). In total, to date it appears that violent action against racism or Trump has done much more to build the racist right than to discredit it, while simultaneously becoming a burden for other opponents of the Trump presidency.

At the same time, battle-ready demonstrators turned up in large numbers to counter the UNITE THE RIGHT rally in Charlottesville in August of 2017. The counterdemonstrators outnumbered the racist right by large numbers. Rather quickly, demonstrators on each side were confronting each other forcefully and physically; the planned racist rally was disrupted, but at great cost. Later in the day, a disgruntled right-wing protester drove a car through the crowd, killing one peaceful demonstrator (Democracy Now 2017). At first glance, it seems like the presence of the antifascist antiracist demonstrators did little to advance their cause and brought the racist right additional attention. At the same time, a group of clergy committed to nonviolence credited those willing to fight with saving their lives.

So, what are we to make of violence?

To start, we should not generalize to see the range of all these consequences as a function of the use of violence. It's not about the violence, per se, but the context in which it takes place. It's useful to consider the antiabortion movement and the relatively rare successful attacks on property or persons that have erupted around the edges of the movement over the past four decades. In addition to lobbying, rallies, electoral politics, and clinic-based demonstrations, sometimes including civil disobedience, some antiabortion partisans have bombed clinics while a few have attacked and killed doctors who perform abortions.

Selected acts of violence have ultimately been helpful to the antiabortion movement. Operating aggressively, and mostly nonviolently, in the United States episodes of violence directed against doctors and clinics have erupted on occasion since the 1980s. Although clinic bombings and physician assassination mark a clear contrast with the rhetoric of protecting life, they've also had the impact of making abortion more expensive and the practice less attractive to physicians. The threat to life has had unfortunate consequences of making physicians who perform abortions more careful about their public profiles and dissuaded medical students and residents from learning the procedure. All of this contributes to an ongoing stigmatization of abortion. It's made it easier for legislators who would never think of shooting a physician to pass bills limiting funding and restricting medical practice, all within a rhetoric of safety for all concerned (Joffee 2010). Although most of us, including opponents of abortion, might find the tactics of property destruction and assassination morally reprehensible, we must honestly consider their impact in the context of a broader movement and a changing political environment.

What is to be done

I've argued that focusing primarily on a category of tactics at the expense of context leads us to make misjudgments and to miss larger effects. This is particularly true when the researcher has some inherent sympathy or antipathy with the tactic. It's understandable that we might want to vindicate those with discipline and noble motives and that we would be reluctant to validate morally reprehensible actions with claims of efficacy. At the same time, responsible social science, particularly for those who might have activist commitments in addition, requires looking beyond the visceral reaction to a moment to look at larger movements or campaigns.

If the efficacy of nonviolence is the wrong question, what is the right one? I would submit that we would do well to expand the frame of analysis to include a broader range of actors involved in any movement campaign, including those on the fringes of the main action and those engaged in more institutional politics, sometimes in tacit sympathy with protesters. I'd suggest that it's critical to work to extend the historical frame of analysis beyond the scope of any individual event, to assess the long run-up and longer outcomes of collective action.

The distinctions between disruptive and less disruptive actions and among various forms of coercive confrontation are well worth examination, but better questions would consider the sources of those actions. It's worthwhile to understand when nonviolent forms of expression emerge, and when more vigorously coercive actions, including sabotage, armed marches, and confrontation with police, appear, as well as how they are managed, by both activists and authorities.

On one level, this is far less likely to produce the simple recipes that can be downloaded into action for any given campaign at any given time. This is inherently frustrating, because we still want to know what works and when. Perhaps an alternative, however, that emerges from careful and honest study, is a set of principles that can guide us in understanding and, perhaps, choreographing collective action mindful of its interaction with a changing context and an eye toward its ultimate influence.

References

Chang, Clio. 2017. "The Unlikely Rise of an Alt-Right Hero." *The New Republic.* March 31. https://newrepublic.com/article/141766/unlikely-rise-alt-right-hero

Chenoweth, Erica, and Maria J. Stephan. 2008. "Why Civil Resistance Works: The Strategic Logic of Nonviolent Conflict." *International Security* 33: 7–44.

Chenoweth, Erica, and Maria J. Stephan. 2011. *Why Civil Resistance Works: The Strategic Logic of Nonviolent Conflict.* New York: Columbia University Press.

Chenoweth, Erica, and Jay Ulfelder. 2017. "Can Structural Conditions Explain the Onset of Nonviolent Uprisings?" *Journal of Conflict Resolution* 61(2): 298–324.

Cobb, Charles E., Jr. 2015. *This Nonviolent Stuff'll Get You Killed: How Guns Made the Civil Rights Movement Possible.* Durham, NC: Duke University Press.

Democracy Now. 2017. "Cornel West & Rev. Traci Blackmon: Clergy in Charlottesville Were Trapped by Torch-Wielding Nazis." *Transcript.* August 14. www.democracynow. org/2017/8/14/cornel_west_rev_toni_blackmon_clergy

Dudziak, Mary L. 2002. *Cold War Civil Rights.* Princeton, NJ: Princeton University Press.

Haines, Herbert H. 1988. *Black Radicals and the Civil Rights Mainstream, 1954–1970.* Knoxville: University of Tennessee Press.

Havel, Vaclav. 1985. "The Power of the Powerless." Pp. 23–96 in Havel et al. *The Power of the Powerless: Citizens against the State in Central Eastern Europe.* Oxford and New York: Taylor and Francis.

Joffee, Carole. 2010. *Dispatches from the Abortion Wars: The Costs of Fanaticism to Doctors, Patients, and the Rest of Us.* Boston: Beacon Press.

Lodge, Milton, and Charles Taber. 2013. *The Rationalizing Voter.* New York: Cambridge University Press.

McPhail, Clark. 2017 [1992]. *The Myth of the Madding Crowd.* London and New York: Routledge. [Transaction].

McPhail, Clark, David Schweingruber, and John McCarthy. 1998. *Policing Protest in the United States: 1960–1995.* Minneapolis: University of Minnesota Press.

Nepstad, Sharon Erickson. 2008. *Religion and War Resistance in the Plowshares Movement.* New York: Cambridge University Press.

Nuborn, Jud, and Annette Dumbach. 2007 [1986]. *Sophie Scholl and the White Rose,* revised and expanded edition. Oxford, UK: Oneworld Publications.

"Protest Ann Coulter." 2017. Leaflet. BAMN (By Any Means Necessary).

Schock, Kurt. 2005. *Unarmed Insurrections: People Power Movements in Nondemocracies.* Minneapolis: University of Minnesota Press.

Schock, Kurt. 2015. *Civil Resistance Today*. Cambridge, UK: Polity.

Sharp, Gene. 1973. *The Politics of Nonviolent Action*, 3 volumes. Boston: Porter-Sargent.

Sheffield, Matthew. 2017. "Trolling for a Race War: Neo-Nazis Are Trying to Bait Leftist 'Antifa' Activists into Violence – and Radicalize White People." *Salon*. April 27. www.salon.com/2017/04/27/trolling-for-a-race-war-neo-nazis-are-trying-to-bait-leftist-antifa-activists-into-violence-and-radicalize-white-people/

Sibley, Mulford Q. 1963. *The Quiet Battle: Writings on the Theory and Practice of Non-Violent Resistance*. Garden City, NY: Doubleday.

Tilly, Charles. 2006. *Regimes and Repertoires*. Chicago: University of Chicago Press.

Vinthagen, Stellan. 2015. *A Theory of Nonviolent Action: How Civil Resistance Works*. London: Zed Books.

White Rose Resistance. http://whiteroseresistance.org/

8 Three common objections to the study of nonviolent resistance

Erica Chenoweth

In this chapter, I identify three primary objections lodged by various scholars to recent empirical work on the strategic effectiveness of nonviolent resistance. I then lay out some of the theoretical, empirical, or methodological advances provoked by these challenges – most of which advance the field of civil resistance in important ways.

I want to suggest that, in fact, these ongoing debates provide fertile soil for the study of mobilization and resistance more generally, since unresolved controversies and the push for greater rigor have provoked various methodological innovations, a potentially productive normative dialogue between critical and empirically orientated scholars, and new resources and data from which to further study the causes, dynamics, and outcomes of mass mobilization. I suggest that moving forward, how we answer questions about mobilization may be as important as the questions we take on in the first place.

Nonviolent or violent? It's complicated

Objection I: Nonviolent and violent campaigns are too simply categorized as ideal types.

One of the primary challenges to the field of civil resistance concerns measurement of "nonviolent" and "violent" resistance as ideal, static categories. In particular, much of the work in the field analyzes nonviolent resistance campaigns as the units of analysis, thereby making important (and unrealistic) assumptions about tactical homogeneity or otherwise downplaying the presence of incidental acts of violence from within the campaign. Some have even argued that none of the campaigns coded as "primarily nonviolent" in the Nonviolent and Violent Campaign Outcomes (NAVCO) 1.0 dataset were nonviolent at all (Gelderloos 2016; Kadivar and Ketchley 2018). This is clearly the most important objection since, if true, it would undermine the empirical regularity of campaign success as relating to their nonviolent character (Chenoweth and Stephan 2011; Schock 2005).

Another long-standing concern among both scholars and activists is that certain categories of direct action – like sabotage, property destruction, shutdowns, and/or human barricades – are considered violent by the targets and nonviolent by the dissidents. Whether such actions are considered nonviolent or violent by third-party observers varies quite a bit from context to context, meaning that establishing empirical regularities about their generalized effects is difficult and controversial. Among activists, there is a particular concern that researchers who classify such events as violent (or not purely nonviolent) are lending legitimacy to government propaganda, allowing states to rationalize more repressive responses to such actions than they would otherwise merit.

Even if one allows that we can observe and distinguish primarily nonviolent campaigns from primarily violent ones, there remains the problem of incidents of violence in the midst of nonviolent campaigns (and incidences of nonviolent mobilization in the midst of violent ones). This is an unavoidable problem with the use of highly aggregated units of analysis like "campaigns."

Some scholars have attempted to grapple with the simultaneity of nonviolent and violent resistance by expressly incorporating the presence of violent flanks as a covariate – or even as a key explanatory variable – in studies on the effectiveness of resistance campaigns. For example, Chenoweth and Schock (2015) evaluated the impacts of violent flanks on the success rates of primarily nonviolent campaigns. They found that violent flanks were associated with a lower success rate for such campaigns because of reduced participation. Others have found that the use of violence by otherwise nonviolent movements repels potential allies, increases widespread repression (Thompkins 2015), and discourages defections from potentially sympathetic third parties (Wasow 2017). Moreover, violent flanks also tend to predispose societies to a higher risk of losing political influence (Wasow 2017), a higher risk of mass civil conflict (Chenoweth and Stephan 2011), and higher risks of mass killings in the longer term (Chenoweth and Perkoski 2018). That the reduced success rates for nonviolent movements with violent flanks has already been validated by independent studies relying on events data (Huet-Vaughn 2016; Wasow 2017) lends greater confidence to these findings.

Indeed, the perceived need to better understand gradations of nonviolent and violent resistance rather than dichotomous ideal types has resulted in the production of new events data (Chenoweth et al. 2018; Salehyan et al. 2012) meant to specifically address these questions. A possible solution to the over-aggregation problem, then, is to use events-based datasets, like SCAD (Salehyan et al. 2012), NAVCO 3.0 (Chenoweth et al. 2018), or different country-specific protest events databases (e.g., Olzak and West 1995), to estimate *proportions* or *sequences* of violent or nonviolent mobilization over different temporal periods (weeks, months, or quarters). Of course, underreporting is a hazard here – particularly if it introduces a systematic bias in underreporting nonviolent events that fail in their infancy. This is a well-documented problem that plagues most studies of social behavior (Earl 2003; Earl et al. 2004). Of course, scholars can theorize and model the sources of underreporting. Such possibilities have produced new estimation techniques like latent variable analyses, which can use variations in existing data to (1) produce estimates of the measurement error involved in observed protest and other nonviolent methods and (2) produce estimates of unobserved or latent protest and/or resistance (Chenoweth et al. 2018).

Moreover, the push to disaggregate campaigns into more granular units of analysis (armed and unarmed methods and tactics, e.g. Kadivar and Ketchley 2018) and the new availability of data resources make process-based approaches (Goldstone 2001; Lawson 2017; Nepstad 2017; Ritter 2017) within reach for quantitative scholars.

What is success?

Objection II: The outcome of interest (success) is too immediate, too narrowly defined, and overdetermined.

Some critics have argued that conceptualizing and measuring the effectiveness of nonviolent campaigns are futile exercises. It is no accident that most scholars of social movements, contentious politics, and nonviolent action have avoided the question altogether. Tarrow (2001) argues that social movement scholars have tended to focus on the origins and dynamics of social movements rather than their outcomes in part because identifying and isolating movement effects on political, social, and economic outcomes is far too theoretically and empirically complex (see Davenport 2015 for an exception).

First, there is disagreement about whether "success" ought to include the accomplishment of process goals as well as strategic goals. A persistent controversy, for instance, is whether violence is effective in achieving important political gains short of full success – like autonomy short of full self-determination (Krause 2013), a seat at the negotiating table short of military victory (Thomas 2014), the expansion of the costs of repression (Kadivar and Ketchley 2018), or extensive media coverage, notoriety, and agenda-setting power short of full overthrow of an opponent elite (Krause 2013). Therefore, some have focused on success conceptualized at different levels of analysis, such as identifying the effects of nonviolent actions on concessions to labor organizations using direct action (Huet-Vaughn 2016), concessions by corporations to civilian groups in developing countries (Chenoweth and Olsen 2016), concessions to dissidents by governments (Chenoweth et al. 2018), public opinion (Murdie and Purser 2016; Simpson et al. 2018; Wasow 2017), and electoral outcomes (Wasow 2017).

The second common objection concerns short- versus long-term effects. As an empirical matter, the establishment of causal links and mechanisms becomes more and more difficult as time progresses because of the introduction of new variables that may influence outcomes. Moreover, the decision to evaluate effects of mobilization on revolutionary outcomes during specified time periods can lead to somewhat arbitrary temporal bounds (i.e., 1-year, 5-year, or 10-year effects). This problem of arbitrariness can be addressed somewhat by the use of time-varying models like survival analysis/hazard modeling, which remain agnostic as to the length of time it may take for a given condition to affect an outcome (Celestino Rivera and Gleditsch 2013; Bayer et al. 2016).

As a practical matter, many observers wonder whether mass uprisings that disrupt existing orders cause more chaos and instability than peace and normalcy – a critique lodged against many of the Arab Awakenings as justification for their ultimate failure (Ash and Roberts 2016). Some scholars have focused on the long-term effects of different methods of resistance in response to such concerns, studying the effects of nonviolent resistance on democratization (Chenoweth and Stephan 2011, Chapter 8; Celestino and Gleditsch 2013; Bayer et al. 2016), human development (Stoddard 2013), and mass killings (Chenoweth and Perkoski 2018), reaching conclusions that generally undermine concerns that nonviolent resistance is a more destructive phenomenon than violent or hybrid resistance.

The third common objection concerns the quality of victory – or the ability to change systems and regimes rather than just regime leadership and/or governing relationships within the polity. This objection largely emerges from critical analyses, which argue that civil resistance is not an effective means of struggle if it cannot remove, replace, or transform neoliberal systems of power and oppression (Chabot and Vinthagen 2015). There is an empirical variant of this argument as well: in observational terms, there are different categories of "regime change," including "deck-shuffling" coups, popular coups, overwhelmings, and pacted transitions (Pinckney 2015; Joseph Wright n.d. [private conversation with author]). Each of these different regime transitions can have different characteristics and different long-term effects at home and abroad. As such, what appear to be short-term victories may in fact result in worsening oppression over the medium to long term.

The fourth issue concerns overdetermination. Untangling cause and effect is virtually impossible in the midst of countless omitted variables that may have contingent effects case by case or generalized effects across cases. Beck (2017) discusses two such possible examples in his identification of global economic output and human rights treaties as potential confounds in explaining the success of nonviolent resistance campaigns. Because of the limited time series available for observational data on nonviolent conflict, I often wonder whether this phenomenon and its success is a function of the liberal international order or whether it is a more stable and durable global phenomenon in spite of the presence of the liberal international order. This question is largely hypothetical at this stage, owing to the fact that the technique was widely adopted after Gandhi's popularization of the method in the 1930s and 1940s. Hence the global rise and diffusion of nonviolent resistance has occurred in the context of the postwar liberal international order; it is unclear whether that order is a necessary scope condition for the persistence and/or success of nonviolent resistance (Ritter 2015).

In response to these concerns, some scholars have begun to use more sophisticated statistical techniques to assess the effects of various confounds. One technique that has emerged in recent years, for example, is the use of cross-validation through predictive modeling to isolate the effects of potential confounds (Chenoweth and Ulfelder 2017; Chenoweth and Perkoski 2018). Such approaches use stepwise deletion and/or addition procedures to identify changes in predictive accuracy as variables are added or deleted. Rather than relying on diagnostics that focus solely on statistical significance of individual covariates, this approach provides a way to isolate both the statistical significance and the magnitude of the effect of different covariates. Moreover, such techniques allow for an inductive approach to modeling, where researchers can include numerous variables with some initial agnosticism about their likely effects and let the predictive exercise reveal which variables provide the most predictive power – and whether the models that predominated during a given time period, region, or system are identical to those that obtain in others. This can be quite productive in generating new explanations, particularly regarding changes in system effects (Bowlsby et al. 2019).

Endogeneity and reverse causality

> *Objection III: The potential for endogeneity and reverse causality, particularly with regard to repressive contexts, is too severe to ask about the effectiveness of methods.*

Perhaps the most challenging objection is the one suggesting that nonviolent campaigns only emerge in settings where they are likely to succeed in the first place. This is the difficult inferential problem of endogeneity. For instance, many scholars have argued that certain repressive contexts – or certain modes of repression – preclude the mobilization of nonviolent resistance, thereby explaining both the dissident choices to escalate to violence and the generalized tendency for violence to have a higher association with the ultimate failure of the campaign (Goodwin 2001; Foran 2005; Lehoucq 2016; Sullivan 2016; Trejo 2012; Davies 2014; Hashemi and Postel 2013; Ritter and Conrad 2016; Ash and Roberts 2016; DeMeritt 2016). Some also argue that many dissidents do not see nonviolent and violent resistance as strategic options under the harshest contexts, which either preclude nonviolent action altogether (Lehoucq 2016) or lead dissidents to improvise their activity with whatever methods are immediately available to them (Seymour 2014; DeMeritt 2016). Thurber (2015) and Wittels (2016) have argued that a lack of mobilization capacity at the outset – defined as the prospects for mass participation and defection on the basis of shared identity and/or available public spaces for mass acts – can also preclude the nonviolent resistance option, leading dissidents to conclude that the use of violence is a gamble worth taking.

These are, of course, fairly typical examples of the problem of endogeneity in social processes. Research on civil resistance (and mobilization more generally) is hardly unique in regards to the difficulty of causal identification. Here it is crucial to acknowledge that inferential techniques built to address endogeneity are still under development in social science research, in part because the typical approach to resolving this issue – the use of instrumental variables or the use of randomized controlled experiments to isolate causal effects – have been extremely difficult to undertake for both practical and ethical reasons. That said, some important advances are worth mentioning here.

First, the "gold standard" of causal inference is the randomized controlled experiment, which is often approximated in the civil resistance field as survey experiments. For instance, recent survey experiments have suggested divergent preferences based on respondent familiarity with nonviolent movements, which increases willingness to participate in or have confidence in nonviolent resistance (Dorff 2015; Simpson et al. 2018).

Second, some have developed instruments that are correlated with the selection of nonviolent, violent, or mixed resistance and are not correlated with the error term of success as the dependent variable (Chenoweth and Stephan 2011; Wasow 2017; Huet-Vaughn 2016; Wittels 2016; Cunningham 2017). Such approaches have, so far, mainly reinforced and validated the core argument that nonviolent methods are more likely to yield concessions or lead to full success than violent resistance.

Third, some validation techniques have attempted to compare the predictability of nonviolent and violent resistance campaign onset, since stochastic and/or semi-random processes explaining the onset of such campaigns would undermine the argument that their outcomes are preordained by some stable set of systemic conditions. Using predicting modeling and cross-validation techniques, Chenoweth and Ulfelder (2017) find that nonviolent resistance onset is much less predictable than violent resistance onset.

Although none of these approaches on its own provides a silver bullet to the endogeneity problem, taken together they provide powerful validation to core insights from the field.

Conclusion

I conclude with several general principles for further consideration and discussion. First, the blunt facts are these: the processes under study here are endogenous, multi-causal, context-contingent, and equifinal. Scholars of resistance, mobilization, and revolution must accept – and make explicit – some degree of uncertainty with regard to endogeneity, measurement, and estimation. I would urge scholars in this field to respond to critiques about endogeneity not by promising to run a randomized controlled experiment in the midst of several emergent revolutions, as some may be tempted to do, but instead by addressing endogeneity like a prosecuting attorney.[1] Rather than finding a smoking gun, we often have to settle for some degree of uncertainty in our inferences, while adjudicating different claims according to the most comprehensive evidence available to us. Thus, this is a call for the embrace of pluralistic approaches to methodology, availing ourselves of recent data resources as well as innovative tools for addressing the stickiest problems of measurement and causal inference. This includes, of course, rigorous qualitative case study analysis, as others also suggest (Nepstad 2017; Lawson 2017).

Second, we should identify productive research questions based upon what the real world is asking, rather than where extant scholarship has left off. Here are some of the questions I've heard activists articulate in recent months and years: (1) How many people does it take – for how long – to succeed? (2) What are the most effective sequences of methods against a repressive regime? (3) How can dissidents respond to/succeed in spite of militarized police? (4) How have people effectively built coalitions across groups – particularly across and among marginalized groups? (5) What are the realistic alternatives to current economic structures and systems? (6) How are movements sustained over time? (7) How can activists organize and communicate in the digital age without surveillance and/or sabotage from governments using digital tools for repression (see, for instance, Gohdes 2015)?

Finally, we should rethink long-standing assumptions about structure that downplay or underestimate the agency of dissidents. The research programs on mobilization and revolutions in particular have long been defined by scholarship that identifies macro structures as preordaining the behavior of different actors. What is clear in much recent work is that nonviolent dissent – and dissent more generally – often occurs and succeeds where no one would expect it to. Such episodes remind us that dissident actions and agency are not necessarily only conditioned by structural conditions – or at least by structural conditions about which we can generalize.

Acknowledgements

I thank Hank Johnston, participants in the *Mobilization* conference on Nonviolent Strategies and State Repression at San Diego State University in May 2017, and participants in a workshop on Rethinking Revolutions at the London School of Economics in May 2017 for their feedback on an earlier draft of this chapter.

Note

1   I thank Cullen Hendrix for pointing me toward this metaphor.

References

Ash, Timothy Garton, and Adam Roberts. 2016. *Civil Resistance in the Arab Spring: Triumphs and Disasters*. Oxford: Oxford University Press.

Bayer, Markus, Felix S. Bethke, and Daniel Lambach. 2016. "The Democratic Divided of Nonviolent Resistance." *Journal of Peace Research* 53(6): 758–771.

Beck, Colin. 2017. Let's Stop Citing. Typescript.

Bowlsby, Drew, Erica Chenoweth, Cullen Hendrix, and Jonathan D. Moyer. 2019. "The Future is a Moving Target: Forecasting Political Instability." *British Journal of Political Science*.

Celestino, Mauricio Rivera, and Gleditsch Kristian S. 2013. "Fresh Carnations or All Thorn, No Rose? Nonviolent Campaigns and Transitions in Autocracies." *Journal of Peace Research* 50(3): 385–400.

Chabot, Sean and Stellan Vinthagen. 2015. "Decolonizing Civil Resistance." *Mobilization: An International Quarterly* 20(4): 517–532.

Chenoweth, Erica, and Tricia Olsen. 2016. "Civil Resistance and Corporate Behavior: Mapping Trends and Assessing Impact." DRG Working Paper, United States Agency for International Development (USAID). August 12.

Chenoweth, Erica, and Evan Perkoski. 2018. How Risky Is Nonviolent Dissent? Typescript.

Chenoweth, Erica, and Kurt Schock. 2015. "Do Contemporaneous Armed Challenges Affect the Outcomes of Mass Nonviolent Campaigns?" *Mobilization* 20(4): 427–451.

Chenoweth, Erica, and Maria J. Stephan. 2011. *Why Civil Resistance Works: The Strategic Logic of Nonviolent Conflict.* New York: Columbia University Press.

Chenoweth, Erica, and Jay Ulfelder. 2017. "Can Structural Conditions Explain the Onset of Nonviolent Uprisings?" *Journal of Conflict Resolution* 61(2): 298–324.

Chenoweth, Erica, Jonathan Pinckney, and Orion A. Lewis. 2018. "Days of Rage: Introducing NAVCO 3.0." *Journal of Peace Research* 55(4): 524–534.

Chenoweth, Erica, Joseph Wright, Christopher Farriss, and Vito D'Orazio. 2017. A Latent Dimension of Protest. Typescript.

Cunningham, Kathleen. 2017. The Effectiveness of Nonviolence. Typescript.

Davenport, Christian. 2015. *How Movements Die*. New York: Cambridge University Press.

Davies, Thomas. 2014. "The Failure of Strategic Nonviolent Action in Bahrain, Egypt, Libya, and Syria." *Global Change, Peace, and Security* 26(3): 299–313.

DeMeritt, Jacqueline H.R. 2016. *The Strategic Use of State Repression and Political Violence*: Oxford Research Encyclopedia of Politics. New York: Oxford University Press. http://politics.oxfordre.com/view/10.1093/acrefore/9780190228637.001.0001/acrefore-9780190228637-e-32.

Dorff, Cassy. 2015. *Civilian Opinion and Nonviolent Resistance: Survey Evidence from Mexico*. Washington, DC: International Center on Nonviolent Conflict.

Earl, Jennifer. 2003. "Tanks, Tear Gas, and Taxes: Toward a Theory of Movement Repression." *Sociological Theory* 21(1): 44–68.

Earl, Jennifer, Andrew Martin, John D. McCarthy, and Sarah A. Soule. 2004. "The Use of Newspaper Data in the Study of Collective Action." *Annual Review of Sociology* 30: 65–80.

Foran, John. 2005. *Taking Power: On the Origins of Third World Revolutions*. New York: Cambridge University Press.

Gelderloos, Peter. 2016. *The Failure of Nonviolence*. St. Louis: Left Bank Books.

Gohdes, Anita R. 2015. "Pulling the Plug: Network Disruptions and Violence in Civil Conflict." *Journal of Peace Research* 52(3): 352–367.

Goldstone, Jack. 2001. "Towards a Fourth Generation of Revolutionary Theory." *Annual Review of Political Science* 4: 139–187.

Goodwin, Jeff. 2001. *No Other Way Out: States and Revolutionary Movements, 1945–1991*. New York: Cambridge University Press.

Hashemi, Nader, and Danny Postel, eds. 2013. *The Syria Dilemma*. Cambridge, MA: MIT Press.

Huet-Vaughn, Emiliano. 2016. Quiet Riot: Estimating a Causal Effect of Violence. Typescript.

Kadivar, Mohammad Ali and Neil Ketchley. 2018. "Sticks, Stones, and Molotov Cocktails: Unarmed Collective Violence and Democratization." *Socius* 4: 1–16.

Krause, Peter. 2013. "The Political Effectiveness of Non-State Violence: A Two-Level Framework to Transform a Deceptive Debate." *Security Studies* 22(2): 259–294.

Lawson, George. 2017. Rethinking Revolutions. Typescript.

Lehoucq, Fabrice. 2016. "Does Nonviolence Really Work?" *Comparative Politics* 48(2): 269–287.

Murdie, Amanda and Carolin Purser. 2016. "How Protest Effects Opinions of Peaceful Demonstration and Expression Rights." *Journal of Human Rights* 16(3): 351–369.

Nepstad, Sharon. 2017. The Value of a Movement-Centered, Meso-Level Approach to Revolutions. Typescript.

Olzak, Susan, and Elizabeth West. 1995. "Ethnic Collective Action in Contemporary Urban U.S. From 1954 to 1992." In *National Science Foundation, Sociology Program (SES-9196229)*. Stanford, CA: Department of Sociology, Stanford University Press.

Pinckney, Jonathan. 2015. *Winning Well: Civil Resistance, Democracy, and Civil Peace.* (Master's Thesis). Denver: University of Denver.

Ritter, Daniel. 2015. *The Iron Cage of Liberalism: International Politics and Unarmed Revolutions in the Middle East and North Africa*. Oxford: Oxford University Press.

Ritter, Daniel. 2017. Rethinking Revolutions. Typescript.

Ritter, Emily H., and Courtenay Conrad. 2016. "Preventing and Responding to Dissent: The Observational Challenges of Explaining Strategic Repression." *American Political Science Review* 110(1): 85–99.

Salehyan, Idean, Cullen S. Hendrix, Jesse Hamner, Christina Case, Christopher Linebarger, Emily Stull, and Jennifer Williams. 2012. "Social Conflict in Africa: A New Database." *International Interactions* 38(4): 503–511.

Schock, Kurt. 2005. *Unarmed Insurrections: People Power Movements in Nondemocracies*. Minneapolis: University of Minnesota Press.

Seymour, Lee. 2014. "Acting without Choosing: Strategic Choice and (Non-)violent Resistance." Paper for the Actors, Strategies and Tactics in Contentious Direct Action Workshop Peace Research Institute, May 8–9.

Simpon, Brett, Robb Willer, and Matthew Feinberg. 2018. "Does Violent Protest Backfire? Testing a Theory of Public Reactions to Activist Violence." *Socius* 4: 1–14.

Stoddard, Judith. 2013. "How Do Major Nonviolent and Violent Opposition Campaigns Impact Predicted Life Expectancy at Birth?" *Stability: International Journal of Security and Development* 2(2).

Sullivan, Christopher M. 2016. "Political Repression and the Destruction of Dissident Organizations: Evidence from the Archives of the Guatemalan National Police." *World Politics* 68(4): 645–676.

Tarrow, Sydney. 2001. *Power in Movement*. New York: Cambridge University Press.

Thomas, Jakana. 2014. "Rewarding Bad Behavior: How Governments Respond to Terrorism in Civil War." *American Journal of Political Science* 58(4): 804–818.

Thompkins, Elizabeth. 2015. "A Quantitative Reevaluation of Radical Flank Effects within Nonviolent Campaigns." *Research in Social Movements, Conflicts and Change*: 103–135.

Thurber, Richard Ches. 2015. *Strategies of Violence and Non-Violence in Revolutionary Movements*. (PhD Dissertation). Medford: Tufts University.

Trejo, Guilliermo. 2012. *Popular Movements in Autocracies: Religion, Repression, and Indigenous Collective Action in Mexico*. New York: Cambridge University Press.

Wasow, Omar. 2017. "Does Protest Matter? The Effects of the 1960s Black Protest Movements on White Voting Behavior." Typescript.

Wittels, Stephen. 2016. "Estimating the Link between Popular Participation and Successful Political Resistance." Typescript.

Wright, Joseph. n.d. Private correspondence with Erica Chenoweth.

9 The missing unarmed revolution

Why civil resistance did not work in Bahrain

Daniel P. Ritter

Since the late 1970s, unarmed revolutions against authoritarian leaders have become relatively common occurrences on the world's political stage (Goodwin 2001: 294–295; Foran 2005: 259). By relying on predominantly nonviolent methods of struggle, such as strikes, demonstrations, and boycotts, unarmed revolutionaries have forced dictators out of office on virtually every continent. Some of the most spectacular scenes in this unfolding global drama to date took place in Tunisia and Egypt in the early days of 2011 when Tunisia's Ben Ali and Egypt's Mubarak were overthrown within a month of one another. For a region that has often been depicted as fundamentally incompatible with democracy, the early days of the "Arab Spring" appeared to prove many experts wrong. Reacting to the events in Tunis and Cairo, hopeful protesters took to the streets throughout the Middle East and North Africa. However, no other country would manage to repeat Tunisia's and Egypt's predominantly nonviolent successes.[1]

A country that appeared to be on the verge of nonviolent success but where protesters eventually had to succumb to government repression was Bahrain. Unlike in Yemen, Libya, and Syria, the protests did not degenerate into civil war or large-scale violence, but rather dissipated and came to naught as the government's efforts neutralized the movement. Before that, the initial days of the Bahraini uprisings gave both activists and sympathizing supporters much cause for optimism. Like other Western allies in the region, the regime seemed torn between its natural instinct to do whatever necessary to cling to power and its desire to appear civilized in its handling of the protesters. In both Tunisia and Egypt, the reluctance to order overwhelming repression had relatively quickly forced both Ben Ali and Mubarak from power. On the other hand, in Libya and Syria, similar initial wavering had soon been replaced by iron fist strategies that put both countries on the path to civil war.

Bahrain constitutes an interesting case study since it is one of the few – if not the only – Middle Eastern countries that emerged from revolution-seeking mass protests in 2011 without either regime change or civil war. While struggles for change failed in several countries in the region, nowhere else did the regime manage to repress the movement at such minimal cost to its own domestic and international legitimacy. This exploratory chapter seeks to understand this outcome by asking, "why did civil resistance not work in Bahrain?"

Understanding civil resistance

The study of nonviolent resistance has made important gains over the past decades (Carter 2009; Nepstad 2015; Schock 2013, 2015). This development is not only the result of increasingly numerous and impressive contributions to the literature (Chenoweth and Stephan 2011; Schock 2005; Nepstad 2011), but is also due to the fact that nonviolent struggles have proliferated over the past three to four decades and have therefore become relatively popular phenomena for social scientists to examine (Lawson 2015b). Whereas scholars interested in understanding unarmed (or nonviolent/civil) forms of contention in the past had to exert substantial effort to make their uninitiated colleagues understand their topic of research – let alone recognize its importance – those of us active today have few such difficulties, as the current volume attests to. Furthermore, each time unarmed revolutionaries remove yet another autocrat from power, the wider salience of civil resistance increases.

But despite important advances in the study of unarmed resistance, or perhaps precisely because of them, some long-held but debatable "truths" about nonviolent forms of struggle persist. Foremost among them is the characterization of civil resistance popularized by Gene Sharp (1973, 2002, 2005) as little more than a battle of wits between elite incumbents and popular challengers. This Sharpian legacy has at times been challenged (Schock 2005; Nepstad 2011; Ritter 2015), but scholars have typically remained in agreement with Sharp's central thesis, namely that nonviolent action is essentially a matter of human agency and effective strategizing (Ackerman and DuVall 2000; Ackerman and Kruegler 1994; Ackerman and Rodal 2008; Chenoweth and Stephan 2011; Chenoweth and Ulfelder 2017; Clark 2009; Helvey 2004; Stephan 2009; Stephan and Chenoweth 2008; Zunes et al. 1999). In order to achieve nonviolent victory, this perspective posits that protesters must weaken the regime's "pillars of support" by forcing them to withhold cooperation and backing (Sharp 1973, 2002, 2005).

Erica Chenoweth and Maria Stephan's (2011) *Why Civil Resistance Works* (aptly subtitled *The Strategic Logic of Nonviolent Conflict*) represents the pinnacle of academic research on strategic nonviolence. In it, the authors describe their approach to the topic as "voluntaristic," finding as they do that features "related to the skills of the resistors, are often better predictors of success than structural determinants" (Chenoweth and Stephan 2011: 18). In the end, they conclude that a nonviolent campaign's ability to make "strategic adjustments to changing conditions" – rather than those conditions in themselves – is "crucial to its success" (Chenoweth and Stephan 2011: 221). They further assert that the reason why protesters employing civil resistance strategies are twice as likely as their violent counterparts to accomplish their objectives is due to civil resistance's participation advantage: since more people can partake in a nonviolent movement, it is more likely to succeed because greater numbers maximize the pressure on the regime and its allies (Chenoweth and Stephan 2011: 7–11). Inspiring as their message to would-be revolutionaries might be, some scholars have raised concerns about the uneven emphasis on actors at the expense of structures.

For instance, Sharon Nepstad (2011, 2013) has sought to nuance the Sharpian approach to nonviolent resistance by emphasizing the other side of the protester-regime divide. Most importantly, she has shown that the organization and behavior of the state's security forces is of crucial importance when it comes to determining why some nonviolent movements result in euphoric successes while others end in devastating failure. Nepstad (2011) argues that the advantage nonviolent movements have over violent ones is that the former are more likely to convince soldiers to defect. Also, Johnston (chapter one in this volume) points out that the security apparatus and ruling-party cadres, whether by wavering loyalty or inefficiency and bumbling, may create gaps where the resistance can flourish. From this point of view, nonviolent success is to a great extent facilitated by the implosion of the regime's means of repression, which may or may not be connected to the strategies embraced by the protesters.

But persuasive as this argument may be, it does not, as Nepstad (2013) herself point out, seem to hold for Bahrain, where the protesters' nonviolent tactics failed to prevent the security forces from obeying orders to repress them. To explain this outcome, Nepstad suggests that sectarian divides in a given society may alter the nature of the protester-military relationship. In countries like Egypt and Tunisia, where ethnic and religious divides are marginal (notwithstanding the fact that Egypt has a relatively large Coptic community), the military cannot be swayed by sectarian loyalties. However, in places like Syria and Bahrain, where the military leadership is drawn primarily from the ruling ethnic minority (the Alawites in Syria and the Sunnis in Bahrain), sectarianism is a powerful tool at the regime's disposal that allows it to maintain the loyalty of the security forces. Since soldiers have a vested interest in seeing their religious or ethnic group remain in power, they will be more reliable when it comes to carrying out orders to repress unarmed protesters (Nepstad 2013: 344; see also Bellin 2012 and Gause 2011).

In what follows, I seek to build on Nepstad's insight that understanding the fortunes of a movement necessitates an understanding of the behavior of the security forces. However, expanding on my previous work and following Meyer's call for contextualizing the study of nonviolent movements (chapter seven in this volume), I propose that we put the crucial Bahraini factors identified by Nepstad (2013), Bellin (2012), and Gause (2011) – the armed forces' behavior and sectarianism – in their relevant international context. Doing so, I suggest, will help us more fully understand why sectarian conflicts and government repression interacted to contribute to civil resistance failure in Bahrain. Unlike strategy-centered arguments, which would argue that if sectarian divides lead to repression, such divides should be bridged through careful strategizing by activists, I propose that there are times when sectarianism, again, placed within its proper international context, becomes a nearly impossible strategic puzzle for the activists to solve.

To be clear, it is not my intention to dismiss the role of human actors in unarmed revolutionary episodes. Rather, my objective here is to show how strategic and structural explanations necessarily work in tandem (Ritter 2015: chapter seven). After all, any good strategy is per definition a response to a certain context. In other words, it is not that strategic explanations of civil resistance are incorrect, but simply that they are partial explanations at best. Furthermore, and consistent with this line of reasoning, it seems probable that there exist contexts in which civil resistance strategies are unlikely to be effective, just as there exist contexts in which such strategies are highly likely to result in a successful movement. Instead of spending all of our intellectual efforts on understanding *why* civil resistance works, we might also want to explore *when* and *where* it does so.

Elsewhere I have sought to do precisely this, arguing that in order to understand why unarmed revolutionaries have at times been able to defeat seemingly invincible strongmen we must historicize and contextualize strategic choices in such episodes of mobilization (Ritter 2015: chapter one). Examining the Iranian Revolution of 1979 and the 2011 revolutions in Tunisia and Egypt, I posited that the success of these three revolutions could be explained by each regime's relationships with foreign patrons. All three leaders (Mohammad Reza Shah, Zine el-Abidine Ben Ali, and Hosni Mubarak) and their governments enjoyed close and friendly relations with the West, and while this afforded them plenty of advantages in the short term – economic, political, and military – the relationships also came at a relatively high price in the long term. As high-profile Western clients, each regime was implicitly (and sometimes explicitly) expected to behave in a manner befitting its standing as an ally of the democratic world. While clearly uninterested in both "real" democracy and the protection of human rights, all three regimes were therefore forced to behave *as if* they were, which meant publicly endorsing and appropriating the West's language of liberal democracy. This rhetorical commitment, I propose, provided regime critics with opportunities to challenge the state and made each of the three regimes vulnerable to the effects of nonviolent mobilization. Discursively committed to democracy and human rights, all three leaders – and their domestic allies – hesitated to openly repress nonviolent mass protests that before international audiences demanded precisely these universal goods. Trapped in what I call the "iron cage of liberalism," the fates of the shah, Ben Ali, and Mubarak were thus sealed (Ritter 2015). On the other hand, leaders in Iran (2009) and Libya and Syria (2011) faced few constraints on their repressive capabilities, courtesy of the absence of curtailing relations with the West. Instead, the clerics in Iran, Muammar Gaddafi, and Bashar al-Assad could rely on continued support from allies such as Russia and China, as well as one another, regardless of their active and deadly disrespect for protesters' human rights and democratic principles (Ritter 2015: 209).

The Bahraini case challenges the iron cage of liberalism argument. Like the shah's Iran, Tunisia and Egypt, Bahrain was, and remains, a close US ally. As a consequence, we would expect Bahrain's leaders to face the same constrains that the shah, Ben Ali, and Mubarak did, which should then have led the regime to refrain from employing the security forces to overtly suppress the uprising. But this is not what happened in those early months of 2011. As will become clear, the Khalifa government brutalized the protesters, thereby defeating the challenge posed against its hold on power. In an effort to present a non-voluntaristic explanation of the outcome of the uprising, this chapter examines the international contexts in which Bahrain's attempt at an unarmed revolution played out in order to understand why the country's rulers did not find themselves constrained by their relationship with the United States (and the West more generally). The chapter begins with a short discussion of existing scholarship on the international dimensions of contentious politics. Thereafter I summarize the key events of Bahrain's uprising before examining the international contexts in which the government's repression played out and the ways in which it justified its brutal response. Finally, a brief conclusion summarizes the findings and articulates a revised version of the iron cage of liberalism argument.

Contentious politics and international contexts

Although international conditions have not received the attention they deserve in civil resistance research, they have also not been altogether absent from the discussion. As Schock (2015: 140–157) has shown, international (or transnational) factors have featured in the nonviolent resistance literature as "diffusion," "external third-party assistance," and "internationalization." Diffusion refers to the process by which would-be nonviolent actors (and their opponents) in one country learn – directly or indirectly – from veteran activists in other countries (Beissinger 2007). For instance, prior to commencing their own movement, American civil rights activists traveled to India to learn from Gandhi and the nonviolent independence movement. Similarly, many potential twenty-first century revolutionaries from around the world have been trained by Serbian Otpor activists (Schock 2015: 145–146, 151–152), and Egyptian protesters in January and February of 2011 received advice from their Tunisian counterparts. External third-party assistance refers to actions taken by actors not party to a particular conflict, usually foreign individuals and institutions, that either pressure oppressors from afar, what Dudouet (2011: 248–249) refers to as "off-site nonviolent campaigns," or physically place themselves at the heart of the conflict in order to de-escalate tensions or provide safe haven for activists (Dudouet 2011: 249; Nepstad 2004). Finally, internationalization, as conceptualized by Maria Stephan (2009), refers to the process by which activists deliberately seek to involve external actors in their struggle by encouraging them to abandon or pressure the movement's adversary.

While each concept does emphasize international aspects of civil resistance, diffusion, external third-party assistance, and internationalization primarily turn international structures into transnational interactions between strategic agents. In other words, international factors are reduced to an array of strategic opportunities and threats to be managed, rather than as structural conditions that are preexisting and sometimes nearly impossible to manipulate. This minimization of what George Lawson (2015a) calls "the international" is not unique to civil resistance scholarship. Unfortunately, however, it results in a skewed understanding of how international factors impact contentious politics. As Lawson explains in the case of revolution studies, international factors have often been added to explanations as little more than the backdrop against which revolutions occur. Instead, he argues, the international is a crucial dependent variable that holds explanatory power in itself. A few scholars have begun to problematize this strictly strategic approach to international factors. For instance, Schock (2005) argued that human rights norms can impact a movement's chances of success, regardless of protesters' abilities or efforts to exploit this opportunity. As noted earlier, Ritter (2012, 2015) has expanded on this notion by showing that liberal international norms become serious obstacles for those autocratic governments and regimes that voluntarily appropriate Western values as part of their broader foreign and domestic policies.

Despite these attempts to conceptualize the international, civil resistance studies have as a whole not placed enough emphasis and attention on this critical aspect of nonviolent social change. Fortunately, related research areas, especially those focusing on social movements (della Porta and Diani 2006; Johnston 2011; Smith and Wiest 2012; Tarrow 1998, 2005) and revolutions (Calvert 1996; Halliday 1999, 2001; Katz 2001; Lawson 2005; Snyder 2001; Walt 2001), have made greater progress in their understanding of how international conditions affect domestic politics. Arguably, the most influential conceptualization of the international dynamics surrounding social movements is Keck and Sikkink's (1998) seminal work on transnational activist networks. They argue that such networks impact movement outcomes by helping activists in one place invoke salient international norms and values elsewhere, thus giving rise to new forms of transnational collaborations and opportunities. Although Keck and Sikkink's work emphasizes the role of strategizing activists, their theory never loses sight of the structural realities in which mobilization occurs. The key point here is that structural contexts do not nullify the importance of activists' strategies. Rather, it is a matter of acknowledging the iterative relationship between the two. Unlike the strategic actors of much of the civil resistance literature, for Keck and Sikkink international contexts constitute both possibilities and constraints for activists, neither of which can be ignored in accounts of episodes of mobilization.

In a similar vein, recent work in the field of revolution studies has sought to bring international factors to the forefront (Beck 2014; Foran 2005; Lawson 2005, 2015a, 2015b; Ritter 2015). Beck, Lawson, and Ritter have all questioned the notion that international factors simply serve as the backdrop against which revolutions play out and have instead suggested that "the international" is the lens through which we should examine all aspects – causes, processes, and outcomes – of revolutions. Following this line of internationalizing reasoning, the remainder of this chapter explores the Bahraini uprising from a perspective that emphasizes both the "real" and the rhetorical international dimensions of the uprising. By doing so, I hope to show that the failure of civil resistance campaigns can be reasonably explained without pointing to the lack of strategic ingenuity within the ranks of the civil resisters.

It is worth noting that this perspective differs from more established theories of how international factors impact on revolutions. For instance, Skocpol (1979) famously argued that military and/or economic competition between a state and its foreign rivals could cause the former to face a revolutionary situation if that competition pushed the state to the brink of its capacities, thus affecting its abilities to fulfill domestic obligation. The argument proposed here, however, departs from a messier view of the international aspects of revolutionary uprisings. Rather than bitter rivalries, it is contradictory friendships and alliances that contribute to revolutionary success by exposing the hypocrisy resulting from such relationships.

Bahrain: the pearl revolution that wasn't

Just days after Hosni Mubarak had announced via proxy that he was surrendering his office, protesters in Bahrain stepped up the pressure on their own government. The days preceding these protests had been marked by some opposition violence, but as the activists witnessed the nonviolent successes of their Egyptian and Tunisian counterparts, the movement came to adopt similar techniques. After two days of growing protests, February 16 saw activists storm Pearl Square in central Manama. The "square" is in fact a massive traffic roundabout and normally not home to pedestrians. But having observed the utility of Tahrir Square in Cairo (which is also not a "true" square in the European sense) and lacking large public gathering places, youth activists decided that the roundabout would have to do (Colombo 2013: 165; Lynch 2016: 70; Matthiesen 2013: 47).

As in many other places throughout the region in the early months of 2011, the protesters' initial pleas were relatively limited. Chants called for the reform – rather than the fall – of the regime, and the more specific demands pointed to the usual causes of dissatisfaction in authoritarian settings: the release of political prisoners, a new constitution, jobs and economic improvements, reduced powers for the king and other unelected officials, lifting of travel bans, and, of course, the introduction of real democracy and respect for human rights (Ambrosio 2014: 336; Colombo 2013: 165; Katzman 2015: 5; Lynch 2016: 69; Matthiesen 2013: 12).

Despite these moderate demands, the regime responded with immediate repression. In the early hours of February 17, that is, less than 24 hours after the roundabout had been captured by the protesters, the government ordered security forces to clear Pearl Square with the help of tear gas and rubber bullets. Three protesters died that morning and many more were injured (Matthiesen 2013: 16). In response to this heavy-handedness, *Wifaq*, at the time the main Shia opposition party in the Bahraini parliament, withdrew all eighteen of its delegates in protest. On February 19, partly in response to American pressure, the government withdrew its forces from Pearl Square and allowed the opposition to resume its peaceful protests (Noueihed and Warren 2012: 153). On the following day, a general strike was called that reportedly attracted the support of over 80% of Bahraini workers (Lynch 2016: 70). As a result of the building momentum, February 22 and 25 saw the largest demonstrations in Bahraini history take place (Katzman 2015: 6; Matthiesen 2013: 36).

The regime coupled concessions with reforms and the dismissal of a few government officials. Under the leadership of Crown Prince Salman, a dialogue was established between the regime and the protesters, which resulted in the prince's "Seven Principles" reform plan. This national roadmap contained promises of representative government and voting districts that would not, as the current ones did, favor Sunni parties. King Hamad, Salman's father, supplemented his son's efforts by releasing or pardoning more than 300 Bahrainis, including several opposition figures. Notwithstanding these promises and concrete actions, which gave some opposition actors hope that reform rather than the messier option of revolution could indeed be achieved, the concurrent use of government force against the protesters that still camped out in Pearl Square caused demands for the end of the monarchy to emerge (Katzman 2015: 6; Mabon 2012; Matthiesen 2013: 38). It seems that these absolutist demands against an absolutist regime soon forced the hand of more powerful international actors who were arguably more determined than the Bahraini monarchy.

Concerned by the continued strength of the protests, which by March 13 had reached Manama's financial district and begun to threaten the country's economy, the Bahraini government requested assistance from its Gulf Cooperation Council (GCC) partners. The GCC, composed of the six Gulf monarchies (besides Bahrain, Saudi Arabia, the United Arab Emirates, Kuwait, Qatar, and Oman), had already at the start of the protests committed $20 billion to Bahrain and Oman in order to quench the protesters' thirst for change, but in response to Manama's call for help assistance was about to become significantly more tangible. On March 14, more or less exactly one month into the protests, GCC troops, officially known as the Peninsula Shield Force, entered Bahrain via the causeway that connects the island nation to Saudi Arabia. The force, made up of 1,000–1,200 Saudi soldiers, was soon joined by 600 policemen from the United Arab Emirates (Colombo 2013: 168–169; Katzman 2015: 6; Lynch 2016: 72; Matthiesen 2013: 50–51). Although GCC officials later claimed that the troops, whose mission was "to support the government against its domestic challengers and deter Iran from becoming embroiled in the conflict" (Mabon 2012), never saw action and were immediately stationed at Bahraini barracks, some commentators report otherwise (Matthiesen 2013: 50–51). Regardless of the extent to which the Peninsula Shield Force was employed, its mere presence in Bahrain must have reinforced the message sent by the extensive repression that took place that day as Bahraini security forces attacked the demonstrators and destroyed religious structures belonging to the Shia community, including at least thirty-eight mosques (Mabon 2012). There could be little doubt among the activists that the regime and, importantly, its regional allies had run out of patience.

The following day King Hamad declared a three-month state of emergency that, combined with increased repression and military presence, succeeded in putting an end to large demonstrations. In a highly symbolic move on March 18, Bahraini forces, supported by their GCC counterparts, followed up the clearing of Pearl Square by tearing down the structure that had given the roundabout its popular name – a massive monument made up of six arches supporting a large globe. Rather ironically (or perhaps appropriately), the six arches represented the six members of the GCC, and the destruction of the monument made it clear that the GCC would not assist Bahraini demonstrators in their pursuit of rights and democracy (Katzman 2015: 6; Matthiesen 2013: 50).

Understanding Bahraini repression

As noted in the introduction, scholars seeking to explain the outcome of the Bahraini protests have pointed to the country's sectarian divisions as a plausible explanation for the regime's ability and willingness to suppress the uprising (Bellin 2012: 133–134; Gause 2011: 84; Nepstad 2013: 344). Bahrain is one of just a few countries in the Middle East where the ruling elite comes from a different religious grouping than the majority of the population. While no definitive number exists, a recent study estimates that between 53% and 62% of the Sunni monarch's subjects are Shia Muslims (Gengler 2015: 31). Despite being the majority, the Shia community finds itself subjugated by the Sunni minority and frequently complains about discrimination. Among other grievances, Shias claim that the current system favors Sunnis when it comes to economic and professional opportunities, political representation, access to housing, and inclusion in the upper government ranks. Their sense of being discriminated against is exacerbated by the fact that the regime has offered, and granted, Bahraini citizenship to Sunnis from other countries in an apparent effort to counter the country's sectarian imbalance and demographic trends (Ambrosio 2014: 335; Gengler 2015).

Notwithstanding these legitimate concerns, the protests that broke out in February 2011 were not initially fueled by sectarian motivations, nor were they driven solely by Shia activists (Lynch 2016: 69; Mabon 2012). As Matthiesen (2013: 12) points out, the majority of the protesters were indeed Shias, but since Shias make up a majority of the overall population of the country, "the demographic mix should not come as a surprise." Furthermore, and as noted previously, rather than focusing on sectarian issues, protesters emphasized broader economic, social, and political concerns, and the early days of the protests were thus characterized by a mixed crowd in terms of sectarian identities. However, it did not take long for Shia Islamist groups to make their voices heard in Pearl Square. This development did not only serve to put the government on high alert, but it also dissuaded Sunni protesters from taking further part in the movement (Matthiesen 2013: 43).

Unlike in Egypt where Islamist groups, especially the Muslim Brotherhood, shrewdly opted to remain in the background of the demonstrations against Hosni Mubarak, their Bahraini counterparts made different strategic choices. It should be noted that those Shia organizations that had fought hard to carve out a place for themselves on Bahrain's political stage, such as the *Wifaq*, worked hard to downplay the sectarian dimensions of the conflict. Other, more radical groups were less concerned with the messages their discourse was sending. One such group, the Shirazis (named after their ideological muse, the late Ayatollah Shirazi), sought to exploit the political opportunity represented by the protest movement. Consequently, they created a physical space for themselves in Pearl Square where they put up a large screen to project videos of their leader Hadi al-Mudarrisi, who "was speaking out in the harshest ways against the Al Khalifa ruling family and, slowly, also against the Saudi ruling family" (Matthiesen 2013: 41). As a result, and again very much unlike the developments in both Tunisia and Egypt, the Bahraini movement slowly but surely morphed from being a pro-democracy, pro-human rights movement into becoming a Shia movement. This transformation not only affected the way in which it could be treated by the regime, but also how Sunni Bahrainis came to perceive of it. Shia chants such as "With our soul, with our blood, we will defend you, Oh Hussayn," became increasingly common and made Sunni protesters feel unwelcome and ultimately fearful of the movement (Matthiesen 2013: 67–68).[2]

Noting the emerging sectarian nature of the uprising, scholars have connected it to the behavior of the armed forces and, by extension, to the demise of the movement. In brief, the argument has been that since the Bahraini military is made up mainly of Sunni soldiers and the protesters were principally Shia, the former was willing to repress the latter. To complicate matters further, many of the soldiers were of Pakistani or Jordanian origins and had been granted Bahraini citizenship as a result of serving in the armed forces, meaning that their loyalty was to the regime directly (Bellin 2012; Gause 2011; Gengler 2015: 96; Lynch 2016: 71; Nepstad 2013; also see Johnston's chapter in this volume, which discusses how autocratic regimes often use foreign mercenaries and thugs to ensure efficient repression by avoiding hesitant troops). This explanation makes some sense but is problematized by two factors. First, in other countries we encounter the opposite outcome where the sectarian composition of the armed forces and the protesters did not matter significantly. For instance, Iran's homogenous population did not prevent security forces in that country from repressing the Green Movement in 2009. On the other hand, in equally homogenous Tunisia, Ben Ali could not rely on the security forces to crush the uprising against him (Ritter 2015). Second, and perhaps more critically, it is possible that the question of military loyalty is an altogether moot point. The core assumption underlying any military-focused explanation of revolutionary success is that dictators under attack actually order soldiers to repress protesters. However, neither Tunisian nor Egyptian courts were able to confirm that Ben Ali or Mubarak issued such orders in the first place (Ritter 2015: 156). Consequently, what is distinctive about the Bahraini situation – and which therefore makes it more similar to Iran than to Egypt or Tunisia – is that the regime ordered naked repression to take place.

Does this mean that Bahrain's long-standing sectarian divide was a nonfactor during the uprising? No, but the sectarian dynamic may well have operated differently from how most scholars have approached the topic. It may not have been that the protesters were Shia and the troops Sunni that mattered for the outcome of the Bahraini uprising, but rather that the sectarian narrative – embraced by protesters and the grateful regime alike – came to substitute the pro-democracy narrative that had dominated the media reports from the streets of Tunis and Cairo. This meant that the Bahraini regime could accuse the protesters of being Iranian agents, and that it was therefore Iran – not Bahraini citizens – that was behind the unrest. This in turn allowed both the government and its foreign allies to offset international human rights concerns by justifying its heavy-handed response to the uprising as a legitimate response to an external threat to the country's sovereignty (Kamrava 2012: 102).

The notion that sectarian explanations of the Bahraini uprisings needed to be nuanced by international considerations is supported by Matthiesen's analysis that the pro-status quo geopolitical actors in the region (Bahrain, Saudi Arabia, the GCC), and beyond (the United States)

> adopted the sectarian threat narrative as a key discourse to delegitimize popular protest [and it is therefore] more useful to look at how religion is used and manipulated by elites to political ends, rather than explain the conflicts plaguing the region solely through references to an age-old schism at the heart of Islam.
>
> (Matthiesen 2013: 20)

I suggest that this rhetorical effort to frame the Bahraini movement – correctly or not – as a Shia, pro-Iranian effort to oust a Sunni government and thereby increase Iran's influence in the region is crucial to understanding the failed uprising. By invoking geopolitical concerns, the Bahraini government unshackled itself and its allies to make decisive repression of protesters possible. Let us examine the responses to the conflict of Bahrain's two most important allies, Saudi Arabia and the United States.

Saudi Arabia

Saudi Arabia's involvement in the uprising was officially justified as aiding a GCC partner faced by an externally backed attempt to overthrow it. But notwithstanding Saudi claims of altruistic concerns, the rulers in Riyadh had at least three reasons of their own to interfere. First, Saudi Arabia is indeed engaged in a power struggle with Iran over regional supremacy. If the Bahraini government would fall, or even permit a fair, representative political system in the country, it is likely that the next government of the country would come to be Shia-dominated, regardless of whether Iran had anything to do with the unrest in the country. Such a development would not be to the Saudis liking: they see competition with Tehran as a zero-sum game (Cooper et al. 2014: 374–375) and therefore have a strong vested interest in preserving the Bahraini status quo. To that end, in April 2011, the GCC, and Saudi Arabia especially, asked "the international community and the Security Council to take the necessary measures to stop flagrant Iranian interference and provocations aimed at sowing discord and destruction" in the region (quoted in Kamrava 2012: 99).

Second, Saudi Arabia sees in its poorer neighbor a reflection of itself, which leads Saudi rulers to draw a very specific and for it disconcerting conclusion. It is worth noting that Bahrain's ruling Al Khalifa family has its tribal roots in Saudi Arabia, and it benefits greatly from Saudi political and economic backing. To some extent Bahrain repays this debt by providing its neighbor with a much-needed outlet, as many Saudis regularly cross the causeway that connects the two countries to frequent bars and clubs that are not permitted in much more conservative Saudi Arabia (Downs 2012: 217–218; Mabon 2012). More importantly, Saudi

Arabia also has a sizable Shia population that, while not a religious majority, similarly finds itself discriminated against economically, politically, and socially. Thus, despite the fact that Saudi Shias do not make up the religious majority in the country, any sign of Shia empowerment in Bahrain would, from Riyadh's perspective, send all the wrong signals at home (Colombo 2013: 173; Mabon 2012).

Third, and perhaps most significant, Saudi Arabia sees in the Bahraini uprising not only a geopolitical and sectarian challenge, but also a systemic one (Downs 2012: 217). In fact, all five of the other GCC monarchies were desperate to see the Bahraini rulers remain in power. The reason for this is that the demise of one monarchy would bring into question the legitimacy of all, as each of the six GCC countries is characterized by the dynastic rule of royals with questionable, but absolute, claims to power. Consequently, it makes sense that what are most frightening to the Saudis are not sectarian demands or increased Iranian influence in the region, but that pro-democracy movements challenge, almost by definition, the very foundation on which the Saudi ruling family has built its power. While the Saudi's were unhappy to see Mubarak forced out of office, they did not perceive their own system to be similar enough to Egyptian, Tunisian, or even Yemeni republicanism for those countries' revolutionary movements to result in a systemic challenge to their own form of government. However, if Bahrain would fall, then the very notion of the Arab Gulf monarchy could be brought into question (Colombo 2013: 172).

The United States

Some commentators have criticized the US government for its reluctance to consistently chastise its Bahraini counterpart throughout the 2011 protests (Abrams 2015; Ambrosio 2014). Although Obama took a relatively active approach to the situation in the early stages of the uprising (Noueihed and Warren 2012: 153), including calling on the regime to recognize the importance of "respecting the universal rights of the people of Bahrain and reforms that meet the aspirations of all Bahrainis" (Obama 2011b), his muted response in the later phases of the uprising was unusual when compared to his engagement with other pro-democracy movements in the region. In contrast to the critical position of the US on Mubarak during the later stages of the protests in Egypt and its outright hostility toward Libya's Gaddafi, keen observers have noted that "the United States' official response initially indicated some degree of neutrality, but as the conflict in Bahrain intensified, there was increased support for the Bahraini government" (Cooper et al. 2014: 363). This means that in contrast to Gause's (2011: 84) prediction that "the United States will have a hard time supporting democracy in one Arab country, such as Egypt, while standing by as other allies, such as Bahrain, crush peaceful democratic protests," Washington has indeed been able to respond differently to similar challenges faced by different allies in the region. To understand how Obama managed to remain outside of the Bahraini spotlight, it is necessary both to examine the US-Bahraini relationship and to place it within a larger geopolitical context.

The US-Bahraini relationship dates back to the end of World War II. Like Egypt, Bahrain is an important US ally in the Middle East, and like Cairo, Manama provides the US with important strategic benefits, foremost among which is the hosting of the US Fifth Fleet that is responsible for the Persian Gulf and the maritime zones surrounding it. In 1991, the US and Bahrain signed a Defense Cooperation Agreement (DCA), and in 2002 President George W. Bush designated Bahrain as a "Major Non-NATO Ally," thus entitling the country to purchase the same US arms that NATO members can buy from Washington. More than 8,000 US soldiers are stationed in Bahrain where they, thanks to a Status of Forces Agreement, are subject to American rather than Bahraini law (Ambrosio 2014: 335; Katzman 2015: 19–21; Nepstad 2013: 344).

While Bahrain benefits from the US presence in the sense that it discourages any mischief Iran might be tempted to engage in, it seems that American benefits clearly overshadow those that Bahrain reaps from the relationship. One might therefore expect that the US makes up for this discrepancy by providing Bahrain, like it did Egypt, with large amounts of military and economic aid. However, this is not the case. Although Bahrain and the US signed a free trade agreement in 2004, the US provides more exports than it takes imports, and thus enjoys a positive trade balance (Katzman 2015: 31; Noueihed and Warren 2012: 147). When it comes to military aid, the US only grants Bahrain "relatively small amounts" of assistance (Katzman 2015: 22). For instance, in 2010, the US provided Bahrain with less than $25 million in what was a fairly average year (Weisgerber 2015). This amount can be compared to the $1.3 billion Egypt received on an annual basis for the better part of three decades. Furthermore, between 2000 and 2013, Bahrain purchased $1.4 billion worth of American arms, which amounts to roughly $100 million per year, thus greatly exceeding American military aid (Katzman 2015: 22).

In short, the US appears to benefit significantly more from the two countries' relationship than Bahrain does, which I suggest worked to Obama's advantage in 2011. In contrast to its relationship with Cairo, Washington could not reasonably be expected to dictate Bahraini domestic policy, due to its lack of leverage (and arguably even dependence on Manama). In this sense, the pressure on Obama was less intense than it had been in the case of Egypt, which was a high-profile ally with more intimate links to the US government than those enjoyed by Bahrain. In addition, Obama was helped by the fact that the US was not even Bahrain's most important or influential ally, with that dubious honor instead befalling Saudi Arabia. Indeed, the latter's role in Bahraini politics is so central that when Manama signed its free trade agreement with Washington in 2004 without first consulting Riyadh, the Saudis, "outraged by the display of independence," penalized its neighbor by withholding the 50,000 daily barrels of oil it donates to Bahrain (Noueihed and Warren 2012: 147).

Despite the absence of consistent US pressure, the Bahraini government still felt obliged to maintain a respectable image before the international community. The Obama administration was naturally embarrassed by the heavy-handedness of its Bahraini allies, as the crackdown made manifest Washington's double standards when it comes to promoting democracy in enemy lands while seeking to remain silent when similar demands are hurled at friendly regimes. Thus, in order "to appease its backers in the United States and Europe, the Bahraini ruling family undertook a number of 'reconciliatory' steps after the crackdown in mid-March 2011" (Matthiesen 2013: 68). The government established both a "national dialogue" with opposition elements and the Bahrain Independent Commission of Inquiry (BICI). Although the Commission was relatively independent and its findings turned out to be more critical of the regime than many had expected, it was nonetheless paid for by the king and had as its task to report back to him directly. Thus, while the Commission found that the security forces had committed human rights abuses and engaged in torture, it did not place the responsibility for such violations with high government officials. It also did not reject the notion that Iran was behind the unrest. With the help of PR companies, the regime managed to smooth out the BICI report and issued a report of its own a year later in which it claimed that the country was on the path of reform (Katzman 2015: 8–10; Matthiesen 2013: 68–70).

These purportedly liberalizing steps taken by the regime might have been enough for the US to wash its hands on the Bahraini repression of protesters, but it still had a trump up its sleeve. The fact that the Bahrainis and their GCC allies blamed Iran for the uprising by pointing to the sectarian nature of it as evidence thereof meant that Washington too could reasonably approach the Bahraini uprising as an external attack on the regime rather than as a domestic pro-democracy movement. Matthiesen (2013: xiii) argues that "while the West has not directly taken up the sectarian rhetoric, it has accepted the sectarian logic of marginalizing the Shia and by default Iran," as was evidenced by President Obama's remarks in May 2011, a point in time when the Bahraini government had reasserted its control of the situation and matters had more or less returned to normal. Speaking about the regional situation as large, Obama noted that although

> mass arrests and brute force are at odds with the universal rights of Bahrain's citizens . . . and such steps will not make legitimate calls for reform go away. . . . Bahrain is a longstanding partner, and we are committed to its security. *We recognize that Iran has tried to take advantage of the turmoil there* [emphasis added], and that the Bahraini government has a legitimate interest in the rule of law.
>
> (Obama 2011a)

Concluding thoughts

Unlike similar movements in Egypt and Tunisia, the Bahraini attempt at unarmed revolution came to an abrupt end when the regime, with international support, cracked down violently on the predominantly peaceful protesters. Much of the existing literature on civil resistance would have sought for explanations for this negative outcome in the strategies espoused by the movement. For instance, one conceivable voluntaristic explanation would be that by embracing a sectarian discourse, the protesters alienated both potential allies and the security forces, thus leading to the movement's defeat. This chapter, on the other hand, has sought to situate the protests in their relevant geopolitical context. Consequently, this chapter suggests that in order to understand the outcomes of civil resistance mobilization, scholars should pay more attention to the international and discursive contexts that surround episodes of revolutionary contention. This furthermore necessitates an analytical sensitivity to the fact that uprisings are not only affected by the strategic ingenuity of its activists, but also by how different countries are affected differently by the international relationships in which they find themselves. This means that rather than focusing exclusively on the concrete realities of each individual country, such as its sectarian divisions and the composition of its security forces, we might benefit from examining how international norms and relationships impacted developments throughout the region (Keck and Sikkink 1998). The fact that Tunisia and Egypt are relatively homogenous societies might explain why the military did not intervene in those two countries. However, this chapter suggests that homogeneity serves another, equally important role: taking religion and sectarianism out of the equation complicates government efforts to discredit pro-democracy movements. Furthermore, without sectarian conflict to point to, underlying foreign conspiracies cannot as easily be attributed as the true sources of the unrest. As the Bahraini case makes painfully clear, one of the great tools available to governments under popular attack is the ability to blame the turmoil on external actors. Doing so not only implicates foreign governments, but it also serves to vilify domestic actors and cast them as agents of enemy powers. This in turn has the potential of discrediting an entire movement.

To be clear, my intention here has not been to refute the importance of strategic decisions and choices made by activists in struggles against repressive regimes. On the contrary, such decisions have been crucial for the success of nonviolent movements around the globe over the past four decades, and there is little to suggest that they will not remain so in future struggles. However, it appears to me that we commit a grave mistake if we equate "strategy" with unrestrained human agency. For while activists certainly have the ability to make strategic choices they believe will lead to movement success, we should not assume that such strategic decisions are taken in domestic or international political vacuums. "Strategy," after all, is by definition context dependent. What makes a strategy effective is its compatibility with, and its ability to exploit, preexisting situations. Without context, there can be no strategy. Consequently, if we wish to understand why certain civil resistance strategies and tactics have been effective in past struggles, we must place them within their respective domestic and international contexts, rather than suggesting that certain ways of "doing" civil resistance are inherently powerful.

In the Bahraini case examined here, the border between domestic and international politics is severely blurred. One of the reasons why it is difficult to separate domestic aspects from international ones is the fact that the sectarian issue breaches both of them. Domestically, the relative deprivation of the Shia majority is the source of an infected conflict between Shias and Sunnis (Gengler

2015). Internationally, this conflict manifests itself in Iran's avowed concern for the Shia majority and Saudi Arabia's desire to maintain the Sunni regime. One might therefore suggest that the domestic sectarian conflict results in a regional proxy-conflict at the international level, which in turn threatens to contaminate domestic political struggle: any complaint against the regime can be cast by it as an attempt by Iran to sow discord and conflict within Bahrain with the ultimate goal of regime change – not for the sake of the duped Bahraini protesters, but for Iran's own nefarious purposes on the international stage.

For the outcome of the protest movement, the internationalization of its struggle can be either a blessing or a curse (Ritter 2015). For Bahraini activists, the international context in which they challenged the Al Khalifa regime proved detrimental. Unlike their Tunisian and Egyptian counterparts, the Bahraini protesters' target did not need to justify its actions to Western patrons concerned that human rights violations on the ground might bring into question their support for the regime. Quite on the contrary, the Al Khalifa family is backed by a Saudi regime even less democratic and liberal than itself. This means that Bahraini leaders faced very little pressure to respond to the protesters in a restrained manner. Unshackled by the approval of its patron, the Al Khalifas ordered brutal repression of the activists and thus managed to neutralize the threat the protests posed.

Operating within this type of internationalized context in which the struggle came to be framed as an Iranian conspiracy against Bahrain, I argue that there was little by means of effective strategizing that could have led to movement success. For an unarmed revolution to come about, the regime under attack needs to refrain from outright repression. As I have argued elsewhere, this is only likely to happen if the government feels prohibited from unleashing its repressive machinery due to international pressures. This is what happened in Tunisia and Egypt, where political elites could not afford to lose the support of the Western powers that sustained them. In Syria, on the other hand, al-Assad could rely on Russian and Chinese support regardless of how he handled the nonviolent protests that challenged his regime in early 2011. Unsurprisingly, brutal repression followed. The implicit question posed in this chapter has therefore been how a US ally like Bahrain could behave in a manner as unrestrained as Libya, Iran, or Syria. The answer has been that while aligned with Washington, more important support has historically been provided by Saudi Arabia, and because of that the Al Khalifas were under no pressure to treat its unarmed opponents in the street in accordance with human rights norms. In such a context, no strategic genius was ever likely to overcome the government's repressive advantage.

Notes

1 By nonviolent success, I simply mean the predominantly unarmed overthrow of an authoritarian leader and/or regime. Longer-term objectives, such as democratization, are thus not part of this definition.
2 Husayn ibn Ali, a grandson of the Prophet Muhammad, was the third Shia Imam. He was killed in the Battle of Karbala in 680 AD at the hands of the Umayyad caliph Yazid I. To

Shias, Husayn's martyrdom exemplifies struggling and dying for a just cause. The chant thus invokes rather violent and sectarian sentiments.

References

Abrams, Elliott. 2015. "How Obama Caved on Bahrain." *Foreign Policy.* February 27. https://foreignpolicy.com/2015/02/27/how-obama-caved-on-bahrain-manama-human-rights/ (Accessed June 15, 2017).

Ackerman, Peter, and Jack DuVall. 2000. *A Force More Powerful: A Century of Nonviolent Conflict.* New York: St. Martin's Press.

Ackerman, Peter, and Christopher Kruegler. 1994. *Strategic Nonviolent Conflict: The Dynamics of People Power in the Twentieth Century.* Westport, CT: Praeger.

Ackerman, Peter, and Beral Rodal. 2008. "The Strategic Dimensions of Civil Resistance." *Survival* 50(3): 111–126.

Ambrosio, Thomas. 2014. "Democratic States and Authoritarian Firewalls: America as a Black Knight in the Uprising in Bahrain." *Contemporary Politics* 20(3): 331–346.

Beck, Colin J. 2014. "Reflections on the Revolutionary Wave in 2011." *Theory and Society* 43: 197–223.

Beissinger, Mark R. 2007. "Structure and Example in Modular Political Phenomena: The Diffusion of Bulldozer/Rose/Orange/Tulip Revolutions." *Perspectives on Politics* 5(2): 259–276.

Bellin, Eva. 2012. "Reconsidering the Robustness of Authoritarianism in the Middle East: Lessons from the Arab Spring." *Comparative Politics* 44(2): 127–149.

Calvert, Peter. 1996. *Revolutions and International Politics*, 2nd edition. New York: Pinter.

Carter, April. 2009. "People Power and Protest: The Literature on Civil Resistance in Historical Context." Pp. 25–42 in *Civil Resistance and Power Politics: The Experience of Non-Violent Action from Gandhi to the Present*, edited by A. Roberts and T. Garton Ash. New York: Oxford University Press.

Chenoweth, Erica, and Maria J. Stephan. 2011. *Why Civil Resistance Works: The Strategic Logic of Nonviolent Conflict.* New York: Columbia University Press.

Chenoweth, Erica, and Jay Ulfelder. 2017. "Can Structural Conditions Explain the Onset of Nonviolent Uprisings?" *Journal of Conflict Resolution* 61(2): 298–324.

Clark, Howard, ed. 2009. *Unarmed Resistance and Global Solidarity.* London: Pluto.

Colombo, Silvia. 2013. "The GCC Countries and Arab Spring: Between Outreach, Patronage and Repression." Pp. 163–178 in *The Arab Spring and Arab Thaw: Unfinished Revolutions and the Quest for Democracy*, edited by J. Davis. Farnham, UK: Ashgate.

Cooper, Andrew F., Bessma Momani, and Asif B. Farooq. 2014. "The United States and Bahrain: Interpreting the Differentiated US Responses to the Arab Spring." *Digest of Middle East Studies* 23(2): 360–384.

della Porta, Donatella, and Mario Diani. 2006. *Social Movements: An Introduction*, 2nd edition. Malden, MA: Blackwell.

Downs, Kevin. 2012. "A Theoretical Analysis of the Saudi-Iranian Rivalry in Bahrain." *Journal of Politics and International Studies* 8: 203–237.

Dudouet, Véronique. 2011. "Nonviolent Resistance in Power Asymmetries." Pp. 237–264 in *Advancing Conflict Transformation: The Berghof Handbook*, edited by B. Austin, M. Fischer, and H. J. Giessman. Berlin: Berghof Foundation.

Foran, John. 2005. *Taking Power: On the Origins of Third World Revolutions.* New York: Cambridge University Press.

Gause, F. Gregory III. 2011. "Why Middle East Studies Missed the Arab Spring: The Myth of Authoritarian Stability." *Foreign Affairs* 90: 81–90.

Gengler, Justin. 2015. *Group Conflict and Political Mobilization in Bahrain and the Arab Gulf: Rethinking the Rentier State*. Bloomington: Indiana University Press.

Goodwin, Jeff. 2001. *No Other Way Out: States and Revolutionary Movements, 1945–1991*. New York: Cambridge University Press.

Halliday, Fred. 1999. *Revolution and World Politics*. Basingstoke: Palgrave Macmillan.

Halliday, Fred. 2001. "War and Revolution." Pp. 63–74 in *Revolutions: International Dimensions*, edited by M.N. Katz. Washington, DC: CQ Press.

Helvey, Robert L. 2004. *On Strategic Nonviolent Conflict: Thinking About the Fundamentals*. Boston, MA: The Albert Einstein Institution.

Kamrava, Mehran. 2012. "The Arab Spring and the Saudi-Led Counterrevolution." *Orbis* 56(1): 96–104.

Katzman, Kenneth. 2015. "Bahrain: Reform, Security, and U.S. Policy." Congressional Research Service 7-5700. www.fas.org/sgp/crs/mideast/95-1013.pdf

Keck, Margaret E., and Kathryn Sikkink. 1998. *Activist beyond Borders: Advocacy Networks in International Politics*. New York, NY: Cornell University Press.

Johnston, Hank. 2011. *States and Social Movements*. Cambridge, UK: Polity.

Katz, Mark N., ed. 2001. *Revolutions: International Dimensions*. Washington, DC: CQ Press.

Lawson, George. 2005. *Negotiated Revolutions: The Czech Republic, South Africa, and Chile*. Aldershot, UK: Ashgate.

Lawson, George. 2015a. "Revolutions and the International." *Theory and Society* 44(4): 299–319. DOI: 10.1007/s11186-015-9251-x

Lawson, George. 2015b. "Revolution, Nonviolence, and the Arab Uprisings." *Mobilization* 20(4): 453–470.

Lynch, Marc. 2016. *The New Arab Wars: Uprisings and Anarchy in the Middle East*. New York: Public Affairs.

Mabon, Simon. 2012. "The Battle for Bahrain: Iranian-Saudi Rivalry." *Middle East Policy* 19(2): 84–97.

Matthiesen, Toby. 2013. *Sectarian Gulf: Bahrain, Saudi Arabia, and the Arab Spring That Wasn't*. Stanford: Stanford University Press.

Nepstad, Sharon Erickson. 2004. *Convictions of the Soul: Religion, Culture, and Agency in the Central America Solidarity Movement*. New York: Oxford University Press.

Nepstad, Sharon Erickson. 2011. *Nonviolent Revolutions: Civil Resistance in the Late 20th Century*. New York: Oxford University Press.

Nepstad, Sharon Erickson. 2013. "Mutiny and Nonviolence in the Arab Spring: Exploring Military Defections and Loyalty in Egypt, Bahrain, and Syria." *Journal of Peace Research* 50(3): 337–349.

Nepstad, Sharon Erickson. 2015. *Nonviolent Struggle: Theories, Strategies, and Dynamics*. New York: Oxford University Press.

Noueihed, Lin, and Alex Warren. 2012. *The Battle for the Arab Spring: Revolution, Counter-Revolution and the Making of a New Era*. New Haven, CT: Yale University Press.

Obama, Barack H. 2011a. "Remarks by the President on the Middle East and North Africa." Published May 19, 2011. www.whitehouse.gov/the-press-office/2011/05/19/remarks-president-middle-east-and-north-africa (Accessed September 14, 2015).

Obama, Barack H. 2011b. "Statement by the President on Bahrain." Published February 27, 2011. https://obamawhitehouse.archives.gov/the-press-office/2011/02/27/statement-president-bahrain (Accessed January 3, 2018).

Ritter, Daniel P. 2012. "Inside the Iron Cage of Liberalism: International Contexts and Nonviolent Success in the Iranian Revolution." *Research in Social Movements, Conflicts and Change* 34: 95–121.

Ritter, Daniel P. 2015. *The Iron Cage of Liberalism: International Politics and Unarmed Revolutions in the Middle East and North Africa*. Oxford: Oxford University Press.

Schock, Kurt. 2005. *Unarmed Insurrections: People Power Movements in Nondemocracies*. Minneapolis: University of Minnesota Press.

Schock, Kurt. 2013. "The Practice and Study of Civil Resistance." *Journal of Peace Research* 50(3): 277–290.

Schock, Kurt. 2015. *Civil Resistance Today*. Cambridge, UK: Polity.

Sharp, Gene. 1973. *The Politics of Nonviolent Action*, 3 volumes. Boston: Extending Horizons.

Sharp, Gene. 2002. *From Dictatorship to Democracy: A Conceptual Framework for Liberation*. Boston, MA: The Albert Einstein Institution.

Sharp, Gene. 2005. *Waging Nonviolent Struggle: 20th Century Practice and 21st Century Potential*. Boston: Extending Horizons.

Skocpol, Theda. 1979. *States and Social Revolutions: A Comparative Analysis of France, Russia, and China*. New York: Cambridge University Press.

Smith, Jackie, and Dawn Wiest. 2012. *Social Movements in the World System: The Politics of Crisis and Transformation*. New York: Russell Sage Foundation.

Snyder, Robert S. 2001. "The U.S. and Third World Revolutionary States: Understanding the Breakdown in Relations." Pp. 75–113 in *Revolutions: International Dimensions*, edited by M.N. Katz. Washington, DC: CQ Press.

Stephan, Maria J., ed. 2009. *Civilian Jihad: Nonviolent Struggle, Democratization, and Governance in the Middle East*. New York: Palgrave Macmillan.

Stephan, Maria J., and Erica Chenoweth. 2008. "Why Civil Resistance Works: The Strategic Logic of Nonviolent Political Conflict." *International Security* 32(4): 7–40.

Tarrow, Sidney. 1998. *Power in Movement: Social Movements and Contentious Politics*, 2nd edition. New York: Cambridge University Press.

Tarrow, Sidney. 2005. *The New Transnational Activism*. New York: Cambridge University Press.

Walt, Stephen M. 2001. "A Theory of Revolution and War." Pp. 32–62 in *Revolutions: International Dimensions*, edited by M.N. Katz. Washington, DC: CQ Press.

Weisgerber, Marcus. 2015. "US Restores Bahrain Military Aid Despite Human Rights." *Defense One*. Published June 29, 2015. www.defenseone.com/politics/2015/06/us-restores-bahrain-military-aid-despite-human-rights/116560/ (Accessed September 8, 2015).

Zunes, Stephen, Lester R. Kurtz, and Sarah B. Asher, eds. 1999. *Nonviolent Social Movements: A Geographical Perspective*. Malden, MA: Blackwell.

10 Nonviolent civil resistance

Beyond violence and nonviolence in the age of street rebellion

Benjamin S. Case

In the past decade, uprisings have rocked the world. Globally, there have been civilian rebellions from Tunisia to Turkey to Thailand. Why are so many social movements engaging similar civil repertoires? How have they mobilized and what has made so many of them successful in their short term goals? These questions are enormously important and have significant implications for the ways activists will organize themselves today and tomorrow. One of the most prominent answers has been the use of *nonviolence* (Chenoweth and Stephan 2011; Nepstad 2015a; Schock 2013).

The field of civil resistance studies has stepped up to provide and explain this answer. Civil resistance studies, led by social scientists, activist-scholars, and think tanks such as the International Center on Nonviolent Conflict (ICNC), has been fast growing in influence in both academic (Nepstad 2015b) and social movement (Engler and Engler 2016) circles. Civil resistance scholars contend that there are certain identifiable strategies that mass movements can pursue to greatly enhance their chances of success. Main areas of scholarly focus include the importance of mass participation, polarization, strategic escalation of disruptive tactics, regime defections, and the backfiring effect of repression (Ackerman and Kruegler 1994; Chenoweth and Stephan 2011; Helvey 2004; Sharp 1973; Nepstad 2015a). Key to all of these, the argument goes, is that a movement maintains *nonviolent discipline* (Schneider 2012: 148).

The idea that revolutionary struggle, or protest of any kind, takes on two basic forms – violent or nonviolent – has become a paradigm in social movement studies. While many allow for nuance, the underlying dichotomy is often taken for granted by activists and analysts alike. This paradigm emerged in the mid-twentieth century, an "age of revolution" (Goodwin 2001: 3) when the proliferation of political uprisings demanded an explanation for what appeared to be two fundamentally different types of collective struggle: warfare and violent insurgencies on the one hand, and civil disobedience and nonviolent protest on the other. Warfare appeared to center on the application of violence, seizing territory, and holding it, while mass civil protest appeared to rely on an entirely different set of social dynamics. Violence and nonviolence, respectively, were understood to best capture an underlying divide in strategic logics. Since then, it is fair to say that it has become standard practice to categorize protest actions and even entire movements as either violent or nonviolent in nature, to the point that the two can be compared with one another to discover which method is more effective (e.g., Chenoweth and Stephan 2011; Schock 2005).

In this chapter, I will argue that in an age when civilian-based street rebellion has become the standard for revolutionary social movement mobilizations, abstract categories of "violence" and "nonviolence" are neither mutually exclusive nor inherently antagonistic in movement repertoires. The concept of *civil* resistance is an important analytic category as distinguished from *martial* resistance, but it must be critically disentangled from strict nonviolence. From an overarching analytical standpoint, whether a movement takes up arms to go to war with the state or takes up signs to march in the street is highly important, while whether or not some rocks get thrown at police in the second scenario is less important. Civil resistance – which is to say the general unarmed civilian-based protest repertoire – contains a variety of strategies and tactics, including some that could be considered nonviolent and others that could be considered violent. Different repertoires might operate differently in different circumstances, with successes and failures contingent on a host of factors, but there is no conceptual physics in which "violent" and "nonviolent" actions function as polar opposites in civil struggle.

The violent/nonviolent dichotomy creates two mutually constitutive problems for social movement analysis: (1) problems of movement classification, and (2) problems of theory-building and theoretical interpretation. The first problem relates to our ability to abstractly conceptualize different types of social-strategic formations or configurations of collective political action. A protest in which some people throw rocks at police is far more similar to a protest in which people do not throw rocks at police than it is to warfare. To classify the former as "violent," along with warfare, and the latter in a separate category of "nonviolent" is to subjugate all other axes of analysis to the single factor of rock throwing. On the other hand, to classify the former as "nonviolent" is to ignore the potential significance of the rock throwing – an action that is likely not inconsequential, especially concerning police responses (Earl and Soule 2006). Through the violent/nonviolent lens, we are faced with the problem of either analyzing protestor violence together with warfare as the same broad type of collective struggle or explaining away protestor violence in civil resistance movements. The second problem has to do with the ways we theorize the dynamics of contentious collective actions. Theories of nonviolent struggle identify a variety of leverage points associated with civil resistance, but these purport to describe nonviolent actions specifically in opposition to any violent action. This approach leads to an assumption that any violent actions in civil resistance movements must necessarily be detrimental to the processes that lead to movement success, foreclosing exploration of dynamic relationships between more and less violent actions within civil resistance movements.

The proliferation of heated debates (both among movement activists and among scholars) about protestor violence, property destruction, collective self-defense, and the parameters of nonviolent discipline prompt an examination of the analytic tools we as social scientists use to understand social movements. This chapter aims to probe the violence/nonviolence dichotomy, and in doing so, perhaps open a space to analyze social movements and revolutions in terms that are more empirically accurate and appropriate for how protests actually unfold in the twenty-first century. I will present evidence of the failures of the violence/ nonviolence approach to accurately capture the realities of social movement formations. In order to do this, I will draw on the most prominent quantitative study of civil resistance to date, Erica Chenoweth's Nonviolent and Violent Conflicts and Outcomes (NAVCO) dataset (Chenoweth and Stephan 2011), as well as a variety of recent examples. I will then explore the violence/nonviolence dichotomy in terms of Kuhnian paradigmatic science and its development based in a previous era of revolutionary political struggle. Overall, I argue that the categorical differences that the violence/nonviolence dichotomy attempt to describe can be more accurately framed as the difference between armed *martial struggle* and unarmed *civil struggle*, and that this analytic switch allows for a richer exploration of salient interactions between "violent" and "nonviolent" aspects of civilian-based social movement uprisings.

The violence in nonviolent movements

First, let us tackle the problem of categorization. Grouping actions and movements in a dichotomous analytic framework based on whether they involve any violence makes sense if the object of study is the phenomenon of collective violence (see Tilly 2003). If social movements are the object of study, however, this is not the most appropriate sociological distinction.

So what counts as a nonviolent movement? Social movements are a form of contentious politics that involve collective claims and sustained campaigns aimed at authorities and that employ public displays and repertoires of contention in pursuit of those claims (Staggenborg 2007; Tilly 2004; Tilly 2006). A campaign extends beyond a single event and links three parties: self-designated claimants, an object of claims, and a public (Tilly 2004: 4). Movements are "sustained" phenomena in that they "consist of multiple campaigns or at least multiple episodes of collective action within a single campaign" (Staggenborg 2007: 5). Movements and campaigns have *repertoires of contention*, which refers to the various familiar tools that are available to activists to pursue collective claims, or the recognizable things movement actors do to demonstrate their existence and pursue their goals (Tilly 2006). Social movement repertoires can range from rigid (i.e., the same types of action used over and over) to flexible (i.e., types of action are not closely linked to one another), meaning that different types of collective actions associated with similar claims against authorities can be understood as part of the same social movement (ibid.; Wada 2016) – regardless of whether all participants approve of each other's methods.

In civil resistance studies, nonviolent actions are actions taken by groups and individuals that do not injure or threaten to injure persons, and to a lesser degree of agreement, that do not destroy property, as means to achieve their political goals (Chenoweth and Stephan 2011: 13–17; Sharp 2012: 193–194). Some see this negative approach as overly simplistic in that it fails to consider "constructive nonviolence" and "hides the multidimensional character of nonviolent struggle" (Vinthagen 2015: 101), but nevertheless the definition of nonviolent action as action that does not harm or threaten persons or property is widely accepted and can be easily operationalized. So is a nonviolent movement one that includes only nonviolent repertoires, or can nonviolent movements involve violent actions? According to Chenoweth and Stephan, a campaign can be classified as nonviolent if it is *primarily* nonviolent (2011: 12), implying that a campaign can be considered nonviolent even if its participants use some violence. Indeed, if the category of "nonviolent movement" were to be restricted to movements with repertoires that included exclusively and incontrovertibly nonviolent actions, there would be very few nonviolent movements to study. Prominent civil resistance theorists admit that there is "virtually no case" of a purely nonviolent movement (Ackerman and Kruegler 1994: 9). The idea that movements can be nonviolent has become a kind of "master frame" (Benford and Snow 2000) understood by activists and onlookers alike, giving it great rhetorical significance, but nevertheless it does not accurately reflect what movements actually do. How then do we understand the violent actions that take place within nonviolent movements?

This problem is not limited to case studies and anecdotal evidence but is built into even the field's most thorough and respected databases. The NAVCO dataset (Chenoweth and Stephan 2011) is to date the most sophisticated and widely popularized statistical research in the field of civil resistance. The study attempts to quantify the violence/nonviolence debate, comparing success rates of primarily violent and primarily nonviolent campaigns between 1900 and 2006 and, in doing so, argues that nonviolent struggle is more effective than violent struggle. NAVCO data are restricted to campaigns with "maximalist" political goals, which include those that attempt to overthrow a government, oust a foreign occupation, or secede from a state (ibid.: 13; Chenoweth and Lewis 2013: 417). These criteria constitute a pared-down definition of a *revolutionary social movement*, or a movement that advances "exclusive competing claims to control of the state, or some segment of it" (Tilly 1993: 10). It also implicitly includes an element of Skocpol's (1979: 4) classic definition in that it applies to revolts "from below" as opposed to coups d'état and other elite conspiracies. Not all movements from below have revolutionary politics, and some are ambiguous as to their nature of their claims vis-à-vis the state (Goodwin 2001: 10), making cross-pollination of social movement studies and revolution studies highly useful (Goldstone 2001: 142). Many definitions of revolution also include the restructuring of political institutions, rapid cultural shifts, and other transformations in social processes and popular consciousness (Epstein 1993; Goldstone 2001; Paige 2003; Skocpol 1979), and of course many social movements advance nonrevolutionary claims. Such elements are not considered in NAVCO; the dataset relates to a particular subset of social movements, i.e., those making explicit claims to state control.[1]

Analysis of NAVCO data finds that nonviolent resistance is almost twice as likely to achieve full or partial success as violent resistance (Chenoweth and

Stephan 2011: 7). The quantitative study has enabled civil resistance advocates to validate their claims with hard numbers, but it also exposes the gaps in the violence/nonviolence framing. Remarkably, NAVCO omits data on property destruction, sabotage, unarmed street fighting, and even riots – precisely the types of "violent" actions that activists argue over in the violence/nonviolence debate today. In NAVCO, violent resistance means literal warfare. The violent struggles in NAVCO are drawn from existing datasets on intrastate war in which fighting between two armed parties results in at least 1,000 battle-related casualties per year (Chenoweth and Stephan 2011: 13; Sarkees 2010).[2] NAVCO contains variables for "radical flanks," or simultaneous armed campaigns and civil resistance campaigns taking place in the same country at the same time (see Chenoweth and Schock 2015), but this still relates to violence as armed struggle. One example of a radical flank in NAVCO data is the South African anti-apartheid movement in the 1960s, when Umkhonto we Sizwe was launched as an armed wing of the nonviolent African National Congress. Another example is the New People's Army in the Philippines, a communist armed insurgency that co-existed with the nonviolent "People Power Revolution" that ousted Ferdinand Marcos in the 1980s (ibid.). The radical flank variable accounts for contemporaneous armed challenges, but the dataset contains no variables for any type of violent action that falls below the threshold for war.

In fact, civilian-organized violent action is incredibly common in "nonviolent" movements. Cross-national data on low-level collective violence are sparse, but several prominent datasets on contentious political actions include data on major riots.[3] When matched with NAVCO, the results are striking. Nearly 85% of "nonviolent" campaigns – and more than 80% of successful cases – involved at least one major riot (Case 2018). Furthermore, these data only include large-scale riots and almost certainly involve underreporting errors due to limited data collection methods (Wilson 2013: 18), so it is highly likely that the true number of fully nonviolent cases is even smaller than 15%. The vast majority of civil resistance campaigns catalogued in NAVCO, including the vast majority of campaigns that achieved full or partial success, either involved major riots or took place in a context where major riots were occurring.[4]

Even excluding smaller or less physically destructive actions and focusing on the presence of major riots, the vast majority of civil resistance movements include violent actions. Of course, some campaigns are explicitly nonviolent and may dissociate themselves from rioters when protest violence occurs. Certainly, these types of inter- and intra-movement dynamics are crucial to our understandings of civil resistance movements. But ignoring the violent actions or assuming *a priori* that they must harm a movement's chances of success takes us further from this understanding, not closer. Neither a campaign's strategy nor its success or failure can be reasonably analyzed independently of political context, as David Meyer's chapter in this volume points out. Nor should analysts demure from accounting for other contentious political actions occurring in the same country at the same time.

The NAVCO dataset therefore tells us something about the comparative success rates between armed *martial struggle* and unarmed *civil struggle*, but it does not tell us anything about the comparative efficacy between violent civil actions and nonviolent civil actions. This is because in the NAVCO data, civil resistance campaigns involving riots, sabotage, and other protestor violence are not distinguished from civil resistance campaigns conforming to traditional models of nonviolent action. However, the use of the term "nonviolent action" as synonymous with "civil resistance" gives the impression that the study validates strict nonviolent discipline – with serious ramifications for the application of their findings on the ground. Chenoweth and Stephan's work is widely read among activists (Stoner 2012), with many interpreting their findings as pertaining to the violence/nonviolence debate as it is engaged with today, i.e., within the Sharpian nonviolence master frame. For example, readers might come away from their study with the notion that engaging in property destruction or throwing rocks at police make a movement statistically less likely to succeed, when in fact the research contains no data on the effects of these types of actions.

The omissions and limitations in analyses drawn from NAVCO data[5] are particularly clear because the quantitative method requires operationalizing nonviolent struggle in numerical terms, but the shortcomings are emblematic of an inability in the field at large to account for violent protest actions. This intervention is therefore not meant as a critique of the NAVCO dataset as such, but rather to complicate our understanding of civil resistance movements by pointing to the inadequacy of the violence/nonviolence framework as an analytic tool.

Examples abound of the failure of the stark civil resistance-as-nonviolence versus violence-as-warfare frameworks to effectively relate to contemporary civil resistance uprisings. Consider attempting to study the Black Lives Matter (BLM) movement (see Garza 2014) or the broader Movement for Black Lives without discussing the 2015 riots in Baltimore. Black Lives Matter as an organization has engaged in disruptive but nonviolent protest, and the city of Baltimore does not have an official BLM chapter.[6] But the Baltimore uprising, which followed the police killing of Freddie Gray, corresponded to the same collective action frame (Benford and Snow 2000) as BLM, which started as a Twitter hashtag in 2013 following the acquittal of George Zimmerman for fatally shooting Trayvon Martin, and was popularized after the 2014 police killings of (and subsequent acquittals of police for killing) Michael Brown, Eric Garner, and many others. The Baltimore uprising was widely perceived as part of the BLM social movement (see Rickford 2016) and was a flashpoint for "official" – and nonviolent – BLM mobilizations around the country. The impact that the Baltimore uprising had on the movement can be debated, but either way it would be deeply misleading to skip over those events altogether in telling the story of Black Lives Matter. In theory, it is for this reason that NAVCO includes data on the radical flank effect – to measure the impact that simultaneous political actions of a different type have on civil resistance campaigns – precisely because this context is important for a robust analysis. The problem is that the radical flanks variable does not capture the types of actions that are relevant to the current violence/nonviolence debate, i.e., unarmed, civilian-based violence.

Or consider the protests that marked Donald Trump's inauguration in Washington, DC. On January 20, 2017, a coalition of protestors, some using the hashtag

#DisruptJ20, organized permitted and unpermitted marches and rallies through-out the city and blockaded entrances to the inauguration ceremony. The different actions involved differing levels of contention and in some cases low-level violence resulting in smashed bank windows, a torched limousine, and projectiles thrown at riot police. In other cases, protestors engaged in disruptive nonviolent direct action, while others still rallied in a park and marched along a permitted route. Police used pepper spray, "non-lethal" grenades, and rubber bullets on demonstrators, injuring many and eventually rounding up and arresting more than 200 protestors and journalists (*The Washington Post* 2017). The following day, the Women's March drew millions around the country, including perhaps 500,000 in Washington, DC. Extrapolating from NAVCO and other civil resistance research, Chenoweth (2017) argued that the presence of protestor violence on January 20th would hurt the anti-Trump movement by diverting news coverage from nonviolent actions and reducing movement participation.[7] However, there is no evidence that the images of inauguration protests that went viral worldwide would have had such reach without the broken windows, flames, and concussion grenades. In fact, research suggests that radical actions and property destruction are often helpful components in attracting media attention (McCarthy et al. 1996). Neither did the violence on January 20 appear to reduce participation in what was "likely the largest single-day demonstration in recorded US history" (Chenoweth and Pressman 2017) on January 21. Importantly, this is not to say that the violent disruption on January 20 necessarily helped the Trump resistance either. Rather, the co-presence of more and less violent actions points to the insufficiency of the violence/nonviolence framework in comprehending real-world civil resistance dynamics.

One of the most conspicuous examples illustrating the failures of the violence/nonviolence dichotomy is the treatment of the 2011 Egyptian Revolution. Civil resistance scholars, nonviolence advocates, and journalists hailed this episode as a nonviolent revolution (e.g., Chenoweth and Stephan 2014; Engler and Engler 2016; Lawson 2015; Mallat 2015; Nepstad 2011). Inspired by the dramatic ouster of the Tunisian government by a powerful and spontaneous civil rebellion, Egyptians seized on the momentum, infusing pre-planned anti-police rallies with a sense that anything was possible (Bayat 2017: 9). Egyptians flooded to the streets and public squares, and in only seventeen days, the crowds forced the removal of President Hosni Mubarak. In addition to its swift success, civil resistance scholars applauded the Egyptian movement for creating a nonviolent "global sensation" (Engler and Engler 2016: 252) and "accomplish[ing] what years of violent rebellion could not" (Chenoweth and Cunningham 2013: 272). Incredibly, one journalist even suggested that Gene Sharp, the founding theorist of civil resistance studies, had fomented the revolt himself (Arrow 2011). This story of the Egyptian Revolution as an exemplary nonviolent movement emerged despite the uprising clearly involving widespread civil violence.

One of the early events in the Egyptian uprising was an anti-police protest in which dozens of police stations were burned and prisoners liberated by force (Ismail 2012: 446). Throughout the three-week rebellion, there were extended physical confrontations between revolutionaries on one side and police and government-backed gangs on the other, involving arson, massive street fights, and the heavy exchange of thrown projectiles (Shokr 2012). According to El-Ghobashy (2012: 22), it was the "four continuous days of street fighting, January 25–28, that pitted people against police all over the country" that transformed an episode of protest into a "revolutionary situation." The January 25 Revolution certainly involved spectacular acts of nonviolent resistance and contained wide-spread nonviolent sentiment, including moments when protestors attempted to restrain comrades from escalating to physically violent acts (Ketchley 2017: 25). At the same time, evidence from interviews and police records indicates that riots played a significant role in opening space for the nonviolent protests to grow and spread (ibid.). Nonviolent protest worked in large part the way it is supposed to, with all of the mechanisms civil resistance scholars identify, from the dramatic scenes of mass mobilization to the backfiring effect of repression[8] to the frater-nization between protestors and soldiers undermining the authority of a regime. However, it might not have been so if police had been able to continuously focus their repressive force on demonstrators. The police were unable to fully respond to the ongoing protests in part because they were busy fighting rioters and try-ing to protect their stations and vehicles from being burned. And in many cases, rioters attacked police stations in direct retaliation for police violence commit-ted against peaceful protestors (ibid.: 38). Regardless of the presence or absence of coordination between the more and less violent contingents, one cannot be examined in isolation from the other. Ketchley concludes that it was a combina-tion of security forces "underestimating the intensity and scale of street protest on 25 January" and the subsequent civilian "attacks on police stations and other security installations [which] averted a crackdown on anti-regime opposition, and in the process fatally undermined the Interior Ministry's coercive reach" that col-lapsed the Mubarak regime (ibid.: 44).

To the extent that the seventeen days between January 25 and the day Mubarak was deposed can be viewed as a bounded episode, that episode was *civil* – in the sense that the contentions were between civilians and state forces, not between armed militants and state forces – but it was not *nonviolent*. What made the Egyp-tian Revolution recognizable to civil resistance theorists was its civil character, i.e., its lack of armed combat and military maneuvers. Through this lens, the civil-ian violence that took place was deemphasized and/or glossed over, making it easier to fit the episode into the violence/nonviolence framework and portray the uprising as being nonviolent (Case 2018).

In cases where civil resistance scholars do acknowledge the co-presence of violent tactics alongside nonviolent actions, some mention the former in passing, but then proceed without engaging with it (e.g., Engler and Engler 2016; Paulson 2012). Others have seen fit to classify actions like throwing rocks at soldiers and tanks, setting up street barricades, and arson as forms of nonviolent action (e.g., Høigilt 2015: 5; Williams 2009: 118–121). But to ignore violent actions in civil resistance struggles is to present only a partial picture of those movements. Clas-sifying "relatively" nonviolent movements as *nonviolent* encourages the assump-tion that any violent acts that took place within a civil resistance struggle were alien to the movement and either inconsequential or detrimental to it. In a dichotomous framework in which a movement must ultimately be categorized as either violent or nonviolent, "relative" nonviolence either gets disregarded or ends up being included in the category of nonviolent. Rather than ignoring these potentially significant actions, making assumptions about their impact, or being cornered into claiming that throwing rocks at people is nonviolent, it would be both more productive and more conceptually consistent to reassess our understanding of what civil resistance actually constitutes.

The violence/nonviolence paradigm

Thomas Kuhn describes a paradigm shift as a change in worldview (1962). Society places importance on certain problems based on historical conditions and the needs of the time. In the search for answers, scientists end up with a system – a paradigm – for interpreting these problems, formulating questions, and providing the needed answers. Kuhn calls a paradigmatic lens, or the standardized lens through which problems are viewed in order to find solutions, the "normal science" of a given era. When eras shift, new questions emerge, and anomalies threaten the coherence of normal science, many experts remain stuck in the previous worldview. It is often easier to ignore that which does not appear to fit the model, or attempt to force the new reality to fit the modes of thinking that we are comfortable with, than it is to jettison the analytic system itself.

The broad question of how ordinary people can collectively resist oppression and successfully topple brutal regimes has likely been around as long as theories of the state have. The particular conditions of different historical eras, however, have shaped this question in different ways at different times. (Kuhn himself analogized the scientific revolution to the political revolution [1962: 93].) For most of the twentieth century, the standard for revolutionary movements was armed struggle (see Goodwin 2001). The archetype of the revolutionary was Che Guevara – the scrappy guerrilla soldier fighting in the remote mountains or the jungles. Of course, there were debates over the use of violence and nonviolence in previous eras, but it was in this twentieth century context that the violence/nonviolence dichotomy and the terms of the strategic debate as we know them emerged. While guerrilla war in the model of national liberation insurgencies became the standard for revolutionary struggle, many social movement mobilizations were distinctly different; they were civilian-based, unarmed, sometimes explicitly eschewed violent action, and were organized around a fundamentally different logic from that of warfare. For both analysts and participants, the problem was how to understand the difference between these basic types.

As collective strategies designed to liberate people from oppressive regimes, guerrilla war and nonviolent struggle actually share many commonalities (see Carter 2012). While Vietnamese guerrilla strategist Vo Nguyen Giap (1961) considered having a *just cause* the key to a revolutionary movement, Mohandas Gandhi (1927) believed the key was *truth force* – two starting points that are not so dissimilar. Modern guerrilla war theories, most closely associated with Mao

(1937) and Guevara (1963), emerged from Marxian analyses of material conditions focusing on the contradictions in the Japanese occupation of China and in the Batista dictatorship in Cuba, respectively. Both regimes were oppressive and unpopular, and while both commanded powerful militaries, neither had the capacity to observe or control large swaths of their claimed territory. On the other hand, although Gandhi's philosophy of change centers on the refusal to do harm (Cortright 2009: 16), his political strategy was also based on a social power analysis focusing on the material contradictions in British colonial rule, namely its reliance on the complicity and participation of Indian workers and consumers (Ackerman and Duvall 2000).

Though one strategy derives from communist political theory and the other from principled nonviolence, both base their strategic logic in a material analysis of political conditions and on the exploitation of structural weaknesses embedded in militarily formidable regimes. Civil resistance scholars claim that mass popular support and the backfiring effect of government repression are inherent to nonviolent strategies (Chenoweth and Stephan 2011; Chenoweth and Schock 2015), but in fact both are primary factors for success in guerrilla war as well. Let me explain. In guerrilla strategy, insurgents operate in remote, rural areas that are all but out of reach for the state in order to provide space to organize and time to establish trust and rapport with local populations. According to the strategy, in the initial phase of struggle, guerrillas are not equipped to fight in open battle and prefer to retreat or melt into the local population when confronted. The government, eager to eliminate the insurgency but unable to distinguish militants from civilians or supporters from the rest, are forced to retaliate against locals in guerrilla base areas more or less indiscriminately. However, the repression only validates the liberation movement and convinces regular people that the regime is their enemy. In this way, guerrilla strategy exploits its adversary's perceived strength by maneuvering the state into over-applying violent force, thereby driving popular support toward the rebels (Arreguín-Toft 2001). The "backfiring mechanism" is therefore not necessarily tied to nonviolent protest,[9] perhaps having more to do with the perception of unjust or disproportionate repressive force on the part of authorities than with the absence of violence on the part of activists (Case 2017).

For Gandhi, meanwhile, forcing authorities to violently repress protestors through disruptive nonviolent disobedience would eventually win the hearts of the authorities themselves, convincing them of their subjects' humanity and of the inhumanity of the colonial situation. For civil resistance theorists, however, the real strength in this aspect of Gandhi's strategy lay in the popular sympathy generated for a movement when police are seen violently attacking people who clearly refuse to do harm in return. As the theory of nonviolent direct action goes, by disrupting the status quo nonviolently, protestors put police in a "decision dilemma" (Boyd and Russell 2012), whereby they are obliged to use force in order to end the disruption, but where that repressive force will backfire and generate increased support for the movement (Sharp 1979). In other words, both guerrilla war in its early phases and nonviolent civil resistance strategies see the public, not the regime, as their primary audience, aiming to achieve leverage over their more powerful enemies by putting them in what chess strategists call *zugzwang* – a situation in which the opponent must act, but where any action they take worsens their position.

With these similarities in mind, the major difference between these two different approaches to political revolution had to do with their respective dispositions toward the use of naked violence to achieve their goals. One strategy ultimately relied on military force; the other relied on noncooperation and civil disobedience (Carter 2012: 27–29). It therefore made sense to distinguish between the military strategy and its civilian-based alternative in terms of "violent struggle" and "nonviolent struggle." Sharp, whose analysis of Gandhi's political strategy is credited with launching the field of civil resistance studies (Nepstad 2015b), began by exploring the dynamics of the latter type, which had received much less attention in terms of strategy than had the dominant model of revolutionary warfare. But despite jettisoning the moral pacifism, Sharp retained the notion that nonviolent action is fundamentally "contrasted" with violent action, and that "[t]hese are the two main classes of ultimate sanctions" available to a movement (2012: 194). Civil resistance studies therefore grew from the idea that "violent struggle" and "nonviolent struggle" are not only different in terms of their strategic approaches to social change, but that *they are ideal types that are inherently antagonistic* (Schock 2013). Faced with social science that often discussed violence as being a crucial component to revolutionary struggle, civil resistance scholars attempted to demonstrate the superior efficacy of nonviolent action compared with violent action, leading to the "violence versus nonviolence" debate as we know it today, and resulting in empirical research projects such as the NAVCO dataset.

This differentiation between "violent" and "nonviolent" forms did not answer all questions perfectly, but it was a useful shorthand for distinguishing between two different approaches to sociopolitical revolution. Still, the dichotomy conceals a great deal of salient information about both methods of resistance. Guerrilla war strategy depends on a logic of violent struggle, but it also includes a great deal of activity that does not involve violence. Contrary to the simplistic view that participation in guerrilla war necessitates "taking up weapons and killing" (Chenoweth and Stephan 2011: 34–38), participation can include sheltering, feeding, supplying, informing, spreading propaganda, functions of governance in liberated territories, organizing allied student or workers groups in cities, legal solidarity work, fundraising, or simply participating actively in the daily life of guerrilla base areas. These aspects of "violent" struggle have received appropriate attention in many studies of guerrilla war.[10]

Meanwhile, anomalies in the normal science of the violence/nonviolence paradigm in studies of nonviolent struggle have been noticeable for some time. Chabot and Sharifi (2013) problematize the violence/nonviolence dichotomy based on the violent outcomes that have often followed "successful" nonviolent uprisings. Seferiades and Johnston (2012) analyze dynamics of rioting and violence in social movements with a focus on relational interactions between more and less violent elements of movements – a notable exception to the focus on tactics of war and terrorism in much of the literature on political violence. Johnston (2014) also identifies emotional and relational mechanisms associated with the escalation of political violence in movements. Meckfessel (2016) discusses the important role of riots, or "unarmed insurrection" in civil uprisings, as do Dupuis-Déri (2010) and Thompson (2010), and Ketchley's study of the Egyptian Revolution (2017) makes a similar, more focused claim that violent protest in Egypt interacted symbiotically with nonviolent mobilizations to create conditions for Mubarak's removal. Bray's (2017) timely explication of the militant antifascist movement, or *antifa*, discusses the effective role that civil violence has played in leftist efforts to combat far right movements. And Auyero's (2003) excellent biographical history of contentious protests in northwestern Argentina brings out the social, political, and experiential dynamism in different types of disruptive action.

But mainly, scholars have struggled with how to account for the obvious reality that violent actions are a common occurrence during "nonviolent" movements. For example, in an edited volume that defines civil resistance as synonymous with nonviolent action (Roberts and Garton Ash 2009: 2), Williams's chapter on the 1989 "Velvet Revolution" in Czechoslovakia includes "more confrontational" actions such as "pelting tanks with rocks and bottles" and using commandeered buses to barricade streets in what he calls "full scale civil resistance" (2009: 118–121). In his participant observation of nonviolent Palestinian mobilization in the West Bank, Høigilt (2015: 5) footnotes his inclusion of stone throwing as being within the nonviolent repertoire based on the context in which it takes place. Using standard social science and civil resistance studies definitions of collective political violence (e.g., Gamson 1975: 74; Sharp 2012: 307; Tilly 2003: 12), throwing rocks at people is a violent act. At the very least, it is not a nonviolent act. However, despite the conceptual awkwardness, in the case of Palestinian resistance dominated by nonviolent action, a civil resistance scholar deemed it necessary to force those actions into the repertoire of nonviolent civil resistance. Indeed, in NAVCO, the First Palestinian *Intifada* is classified as nonviolent because it was "relatively nonviolent," despite stone throwing being an iconic tactic of that revolt (Chenoweth and Stephan 2011: 19).

Until recently, few social movement scholars and even fewer civil resistance scholars paid much attention to the role of unarmed collective violence in political struggles (Bosi et al. 2014: 1). Some have noted the "troublesome" terminology of violence/nonviolence in the study of civil resistance movements (e.g., Markoff 2013: 235; Carter 2012; Roberts and Garton Ash 2009; Schock 2013). However, in the absence of an alternative to the violence/nonviolence dichotomy, most have persisted in using it anyway. Carter (2012) and Schock (2005) deploy the terms "unarmed resistance" and "unarmed insurrection," respectively, which are intended to account for some repertoire flexibility around low-level violence, but both scholars also continue to use the term "nonviolent" as essentially synonymous. Meckfessel (2016) too uses the term "unarmed insurrection," but his focus (riots) is quite different from Schock's (nonviolent civil resistance). In his edited volume on *The Future of Revolutions* (2003), Foran and many contributing authors appear to wrestle with terminology to discuss what seem to be different types of movements with variously more and less violent aspects to them, but they too adopt the word "nonviolent" to describe civilian-based revolts. Pinckney (2016: 57), in struggling to classify a civil resistance movement in which "violent unarmed clashes were endemic," describes the 2005 Tulip Revolution in Kyrgyzstan as "barely nonviolent," a term which makes it clear that the line between "violent" and "nonviolent" in academic civil resistance research is not drawn at the point when movement actors use violent tactics. Indeed, the violence/nonviolence dichotomy has become so taken for granted that scholars such as Jack Goldstone use terms like "relatively non-violent" (2001: 141), while Asef Bayat can label Arab Spring participants as "non-violent rebels" (2017: 10) directly after recounting the early days of the Egyptian Revolution, which "saw the largest crowd in the nation's streets, where protestors fought security forces, attacked police stations, burned government buildings, and chanted, 'bread, freedom, justice'" (ibid.: 7). The cracks in this paradigm have been growing, and with globally shifting norms for social movements and revolutions, they are becoming unsustainable. It is time to rethink the application of these terms.

Times change

Paradigms emerge because they solve particularly well certain problems that are deemed important at a particular time (Kuhn 1962: 23). The problem in this case is how to understand the difference between types of revolutionary social movements. For most of the twentieth century, the standard for revolutionary struggle was guerrilla warfare; its alternative was civil resistance. Since warfare necessarily involved the application of violence, and since early proponents of the alternative (i.e., Gandhi) were principled nonviolentists, the difference was understood as the difference between violence and nonviolence. This framework was based on the major philosophical and strategic difference between dominant models of these two strategies for collectively pursuing revolutionary change from below. It left some things out of the picture, but was useful insofar as it applied to those particular types of struggle in that particular era.

Today, the theoretical standard for revolutionary movements has shifted from rural guerrilla insurgencies to mass protest insurrections in city centers. Advances in surveillance and military technology, increased state visibility in remote geographic areas of the world, the end of the Cold War, and the deflation of ideological Marxism-Leninism-Maoism all contributed to the declining potential for revolutionary guerrilla war as it had been constituted a half-century ago (Goodwin 2001; Robinson 2014). Of course, armed struggle for liberation has certainly not disappeared, with some decades-old guerrilla insurgencies hanging on in *de facto* stalemate, for example in India and the Philippines. More recent armed campaigns, for example the Zapatistas in southern Mexico (Esteva 1999; Foran 2003) and later the Rojava Revolution in northern Syria (Üstündağ 2016), are evolving in form and adopting a posture of armed self-defense rather than armed conquest of the state. But despite the waning feasibility of armed revolution, the capitalist world system (Wallerstein 2004), specifically its neoliberal variant (Seferiades and Johnston 2012), and authoritarian political regimes have continued to reproduce social tensions that produce revolutionary outbursts. In the neoliberal, urbanized twenty-first century, these outbursts have predominantly taken the form of civilian-based mass uprisings in city centers (Bayat 2017).

This leads us to the theoretical problem. The face of the revolutionary is no longer the guerrilla in the mountains facing off against the army; it is the protester in the streets facing off against lines of police, plainclothes agents, and, sometimes, gangs of state-employed thugs[11] (see Johnston's chapter in this volume). Whereas the image of the revolution had been the Sierra Maestra, now it is Tahrir Square. Looking at this shift through the violence/nonviolence lens, it appears as a trend away from violent and toward nonviolent uprisings (see Chenoweth and Stephan 2014; Lawson 2015). Indeed, these movements have not been characterized by the strategic logic of warfare, and by and large have not included the body counts that accompanied most guerrilla wars. However, they have also not been non-violent in any absolute sense, nor have they been *nonviolent* in the Gandhian sense. Among participants in these contemporary movements, the debates over violence and nonviolence have not been over whether to take up arms against the state; they have been over property destruction, thrown projectiles, physical defense against police and non-state political opponents, and other actions of that sort. In other words, the operational meanings of violence and nonviolence "on the street" have shifted based on changing norms for revolutionary social movements, while the terms have continued to follow a paradigm that is based in a previous era. The new wave of uprisings does not mark a shift from violent to nonviolent resistance, because many of them have involved significant acts of collective violence. *Rather, it marks a shift from martial resistance toward civil resistance.* Whereas armed warfare and unarmed civil resistance have fundamentally different strategic logics, unarmed civilian movements that involve little property destruction and unarmed civilian movements that involve a lot of property destruction do not; they are different versions of the same type of contentious collective mobilization.

Goldstone (2001) identifies a typological shift in revolutionary struggle beginning in the 1970s with the Iranian Revolution, followed by the anti-Marcos civilian uprising in the Philippines in the 1980s and the collapse of the Eastern Bloc in the late 1980s and early 1990s. The movements that drove these transitions, while revolutionary at least in the political sense, showcased a different type of revolution. In an "age of revolutions" dominated by guerrilla warfare (Goodwin 2001: 3), the "unthinkable" 1977–1979 revolution in Iran (Kurzman 2004) was both an innovation and a harbinger of civil resistance revolutions to come, its dynamics anticipating a revolutionary model that would become the standard for collective revolt in a new era. Charles Kurzman famously called this revolution "unthinkable" because US intelligence agencies and foreign policy experts had been convinced of its impossibility beforehand, but it was also unthinkable in terms of its method. An unarmed civilian uprising succeeded in toppling a seemingly stable regime backed by the US government in a matter of months. An escalating combination of massive street protests, labor strikes, and riots eroded state control, and mass defections eventually collapsed the regime (Kurzman 2004).

The Iranian Revolution thus confronted analysts with the first major anomaly in the violence/nonviolence paradigm. For the most part, its participants did not apply military strategy, nor did they organize around armed combat and seizure of territory. However, unlike the Indian struggle against British colonialism, this revolution was not led by committed nonviolentists. The Iranian Revolution included many acts of collective political violence – alongside massive nonviolent marches, protests, and strikes, there were at least twenty-three major riots in Iran between 1977 and 1979.[12] The revolution was not nonviolent. But it was not warfare either; it involved less violence than an intrastate war likely would have and a different type of violence too. As a contentious episode led by civilian mobilizations, it resembled the nonviolent model more closely than it did warfare. Because of this, it was eligible to be labeled a nonviolent revolution (e.g., Chenoweth and Stephan 2011: 116; Nepstad 2011; Schock 2005). Since then, similar civil resistance struggles involving mass urban civilian mobilizations and including varying amounts of violence have emerged as the new norm for revolutionary struggle.

Despite the changing norms for revolutionary movements, the violence/ nonviolence dichotomy has remained the normal science of movement analysis. Whether or not it is acknowledged or consciously subscribed to, the framework is near universally applied as though it makes sense. This is not to say that there is no difference between a "violent" protest and a "nonviolent" one – quite the opposite, in fact. It is to say that the application of the violence/nonviolence dichotomy as it has been constituted inhibits social scientific examination of the processes, mechanisms, relationships, and experiences embedded in the different approaches *within* civil resistance uprisings. In other words, we are faced with an incomplete conceptualization that constrains analysis of contemporary social movements. The old approach to the question of how to classify methods of political revolution simply does not provide the analytic leverage that it used to.

Movement dynamics in the age of street rebellion

We are living in a time of unarmed insurrection (Meckfessel 2016). Moving from a violence/nonviolence distinction to a martial/civil distinction enables us to more accurately explore the dynamics of contemporary movements by allowing for the critical examination of different types of "violent" and "nonviolent" tactics within civil resistance movements – alongside one another rather than necessarily in opposition to one another. Certainly, there are many activists and groups that believe in nonviolence, and there are more still who do not wish to engage in violent political actions. These are important attitudes and behaviors, but they are not the only ones that are relevant to civilian mobilizations. Research that ignores violent actions, assumes they are harmful to movement success, or finds ways to include violent actions within the label of nonviolence is self-limiting in its potential to comprehend and to theorize real-world social movements.

Understanding civil resistance movements as civilian-based as opposed to as nonviolence-based has deep theoretical implications. The mechanisms of leverage that civil resistance scholars have identified in nonviolent movements, e.g., mass participation, dramatization, and polarization, defections, the backfiring effect of repression, etc., might not be contingent upon movement participants' complete abstinence from violent actions. The "complex dance" between more and less violent elements of a movement, and between those elements and authorities, could take on myriad exchanges involving complex dynamics that bear exploration (Seferiades and Johnston 2012). Accurately sorting out different versions of and approaches to civil resistance along these lines is an empirical question requiring fieldwork that goes inside the strategic and tactical discussions among groups and participants that are networked in these complex social movements.

If we do away with the violence/nonviolence dichotomy – not do away with the terms "violence" and "nonviolence," but do away with the dichotomy that posits them as ideal and antithetical types – there is a vast array of possibilities to extend relevant social movement research. How do different repertoires interact with differing or changing movement goals? How does the experience of participating in more or less physically confrontational actions shape activists' perception of movements and relate to their future participation? Do factors like culture, geography, gender, class, religion, or proximity to the issue at hand shape the ways people perceive different types of actions? And of course, which tactics are likely to give movements the greatest leverage under different sets of circumstances? These questions and more are crucial to studying contemporary social movements, but in order to fully leverage conceptual frameworks from civil resistance studies and social movement studies in pursuing them, we must move beyond the violence/nonviolence dichotomy. The field of civil resistance studies provides important insights into the dynamics that movements use to create leverage, but in order to accurately study unarmed uprisings we must look at them as they are.

Notes

1 Findings from this study, however – for example that nonviolent tactics are more effective than violent tactics and that no movement in which 3.5% of a national population actively participated failed to achieve its goals – have been interpreted by activists as applicable to social movements with sub-maximalist claims as well (see for example Engler and Lasoff 2017).

2 Chenoweth and Lewis (2013) have discussed reducing this threshold from 1,000 to 25 battle-related casualties. Nevertheless, 25 people dying in combat between two opposing armed forces constitutes a different contentious dynamic from civil violence such as unarmed street fighting, arson, and property destruction.

3 Data on riots come from the Arthur S. Banks's Cross-National Time Series Archive (CNTS) and the World Handbook of Political Indicators Series IV (WHIV) dataset. CNTS defines a riot as "Any violent demonstration or clash of more than 100 citizens involving the use of physical force," and derives its data from analysis of articles published in *The New York Times* (Wilson 2013: 12). The WHIV dataset defines a riot as "Civil or political unrest explicitly characterized as riots, as well as behavior presented as tumultuous or mob-like" including "looting, prison uprisings, crowds setting things on fire, general fighting with police (typically by protestors), lynch mob assemblies, ransacking, football riots, and stampedes," and is derived from computer analysis of Reuters articles (Jenkins et al. 2012). See Case (2018) for more.

4 See Pinckney (2016) for a discussion of the effects of breakdowns in nonviolent discipline in three of the "color revolutions." Pinckney argues that breakdowns in nonviolent discipline hurt movement success, but all three cases he analyzes are ultimately coded as successful, and some of the specific findings around violent dynamics do not fit the argument (ibid.: 70).
5 For further critical analysis of Chenoweth and Stephan's methodology, see Lehoucq (2016) and Case (2018).
6 See list of chapters on the Black Lives Matter website: https://blacklivesmatter.com/take-action/find-a-chapter/ (Accessed November 5, 2018).
7 It is not unlikely that the nonviolent discipline discourse denouncing the J20 protests in fact stunted solidarity with the hundreds of protestors who faced decades in prison for felony riot charges, despite little or no evidence.
8 In this case, initial repression of nonviolent protests was effective in temporarily demobilizing protestors, but anti-police riots provided space and time for activists to regroup and retake public squares, after which repression was ineffective (Ketchley 2017).
9 For examples, see Lindekilde (2014) on the backfiring mechanism as applied to terrorism, and Siebens (2015) on the backfiring effect of foreign state intervention in intrastate conflict.
10 For vivid accounts of life during guerrilla struggle, see for example Anderson (2004); Becerra (2017); and Roy (2011).
11 See Hassan (2015) on the discourse of the "thug" in revolutionary Egyptian politics.
12 Arthur S. Banks's Cross-National Time Series Archive data (2013).

References

Ackerman, Peter, and Jack Duvall. 2000. *A Force More Powerful: A Century of Nonviolent Conflict*. Basingstoke: Palgrave Macmillan.
Ackerman, Peter, and Christopher Kruegler. 1994. *Strategic Nonviolent Conflict: The Dynamics of People Power in the Twentieth Century*. Westport: Praeger.
Anderson, Jon Lee. 2004. *Guerrillas: Journeys into the Insurgent World*. London: Penguin Books.
Arreguín-Toft, Ivan. 2001. "How the Weak Win Wars: A Theory of Asymmetric Conflict." *International Security* 26(1): 93–128.
Arrow, Ruaridh. 2011. "Gene Sharp: Author of the Nonviolent Revolution Rulebook." *BBC News*. February 21. www.bbc.com/news/world-middle-east-12522848 (Accessed September 14, 2017).
Auyero, Javier. 2003. *Contentious Lives: Two Argentine Women, Two Protests, and the Quest for Recognition*. Durham: Duke University Press.
Bayat, Asef. 2017. *Revolution without Revolutionaries: Making Sense of the Arab Spring*. Stanford: Stanford University Press.
Becerra, Diana C. S. 2017. *Insurgent Butterflies: Gender and Revolution in El Salvador, 1965–2015*. (Doctoral Dissertation). ORCID iD: 0000-0003-4949-2539.
Benford, Robert, and David Snow. 2000. "Framing Processes and Social Movements: An Overview and Assessment." *Annual Review of Sociology* 26: 611–639.
Bosi, Lorenzo, Chares Demetriou, and Stefan Malthaner. 2014. "A Contentious Politics Approach to the Explanation of Radicalism." Pp. 1–23 in *The Dynamics of Political Violence*, Lorenzo Bosi, Chares Demetriou, and Stefan Malthaner, eds. Farnham: Ashgate.
Boyd, Andrew, and Joshua Kahn Russell. 2012. "Principle: Put Your Target in a Decision Dilemma." in *Beautiful Trouble: A Toolbox for Revolution*, edited by Andrew Boyd. New York: OR Books.
Bray, Mark. 2017. *Antifa: The Antifascist Handbook*. Brooklyn: Melville House.
Carter, April. 2012. *People Power and Political Change: Key Issues and Concepts*. New York: Routledge.

Case, Benjamin. 2017. "Between Violence and Nonviolence." *ROAR Magazine* 5: 108–118.

Case, Benjamin. 2018. "Riots as Civil Resistance: Re-Thinking the Dynamics of 'Nonviolent' Struggle." *Journal of Resistance Studies* 4(1).

Chabot, Sean, and Majid Sharifi. 2013. "The Violence of Nonviolence: Problematizing the Nonviolent Resistance in Iran and Egypt." *Societies without Borders* 8(2): 205–232.

Chenoweth, Erica. 2017. "Violence Will Only Hurt the Trump Resistance." *New Republic*. February 7. https://newrepublic.com/article/140474/violence-will-hurt-trump-resistance (Accessed June 21, 2017).

Chenoweth, Erica, and Kathleen G. Cunningham. 2013. "Understanding Nonviolent Resistance: An Introduction." *Journal of Peace Research* 50(3): 271–276.

Chenoweth, Erica, and Orion Lewis. 2013. Unpacking Nonviolent Campaigns: Introducing the NAVCO 2.0 Dataset. *Journal of Peace Research* 50(3): 415–423.

Chenoweth, Erica, and Jeremy Pressman. "This Is What We Learned by Counting the Women's Marches." *The Washington Post*. February 7. www.washingtonpost.com/news/monkey-cage/wp/2017/02/07/this-is-what-we-learned-by-counting-the-womens-marches/?utm_term=.7eb4e23d1364 (Accessed June 21, 2017).

Chenoweth, Erica, and Kurt Schock. 2015. "Do Contemporaneous Armed Challenges Affect the Outcomes of Mass Nonviolent Campaigns?" *Mobilization* 2(4): 427–451.

Chenoweth, Erica, and Maria Stephan. 2011. *Why Civil Resistance Works: The Strategic Logic of Nonviolent Conflict*. New York: Columbia University Press.

Chenoweth, Erica, and Maria Stephan. 2014. "Drop Your Weapons: When and Why Civil Resistance Works." *Foreign Affairs*. July/August.

Cortright, David. 2009. *Gandhi and Beyond*. Boulder, CO: Paradigm Publishers.

Dupuis-Déri, Francis. 2010. "The Black Blocs Ten Years after Seattle: Anarchism, Direct Action, and Deliberative Practices." *Journal for the Study of Radicalism* 4(2): 45–82.

Earl, Jennifer, and Sarah A. Soule. 2006. "Seeing Blue: A Police Centered Explanation of Protest Policing." *Mobilization* 11(2): 145–164.

El-Ghobashy, Mona. 2012. "The Praxis of the Egyptian Revolution." *The Journey to Tahrir*, edited by Sowers and Toensing. London: Verso.

Engler, Mark, and Paul Engler. 2016. *This Is an Uprising: How Nonviolent Revolt Is Shaping the Twenty-First Century*. New York: Nation Books.

Engler, Paul, and Sophie Lasoff. 2017. *Resistance Guide: How to Sustain the Movement to Win*. Self-published. www.guidingtheresistance.org.

Epstein, Barbara. 1993. *Political Protest & Cultural Revolution: Nonviolent Direct Action in the 1970s and 1980s*. Berkeley: University of California Press.

Esteva, Gustavo. 1999. "The Zapatistas and People's Power." *Capital & Class* 23(2): 153–182.

Foran, John, ed. 2003. *The Future of Revolutions: Rethinking Radical Change in the Age of Globalization*. New York: Zed Books.

Gamson, William. 1975. *The Strategy of Social Protest*. Homewood: The Dorsey Press.

Gandhi, Mohandas. 1927. *An Autobiography or the Story of My Experiments with Truth*. Trans. M. Desai. Ahmedabad: Navajivan Publishing House.

Garza, Alecia. 2014. "A Herstory of the #BlackLivesMatter Movement by Alecia Garza." *The Feminist Wire*. October 7. https://news.northseattle.edu/sites/news.northseattle.edu/files/blacklivesmatter_Herstory.pdf (Accessed September 21, 2017).

Giap, Vo Nguyen. 2001 [1961]. *People's War, People's Army: The Viet Cong Insurrection Manual for Underdeveloped Countries*. Honolulu: University Press of the Pacific.

Goldstone, Jack A. 2001. "Toward a Fourth Generation of Revolutionary Theory." *Annual Review of Political Science* 4: 139–187.

Goodwin, Jeff. 2001. *No Other Way Out: States and Revolutionary Movements 1945–1991*. New York: Cambridge University Press.

Guevara, Ernesto. 2006 [1963]. *Guerrilla Warfare*. New York: Ocean Press.

Hassan, Hatem M. 2015. "Extraordinary Politics of Ordinary People: Explaining the Microdynamics of Popular Committees in Revolutionary Cairo." *International Sociology* 30(4): 383–400.

Helvey, Robert. 2004. *On Strategic Nonviolent Conflict: Thinking About the Fundamentals*. Boston: The Albert Einstein Institution.

Høigilt, Jacob. 2015. "Nonviolent Mobilization between a Rock and a Hard Place: Popular Resistance and Double Repression in the West Bank." *Journal of Peace Research* 52(5): 636–648.

Ismail, Salwa. 2012. "The Egyptian Revolution Against the Police." *Social Research* 79(2): 435–462.

Jenkins, Craig J., Charles Lewis Taylor, Marianne Abbott, Thomas V. Maher, and Lindsey Peterson. 2012. *The World Handbook of Political Indicators IV*. Columbus, OH: Mershon Center for International Security Studies, The Ohio State University.

Johnston, Hank. 2014. "The Mechanisms of Emotion in Violent Protest." Pp. 28–49 in *Dynamics of Political Violence*, edited by Bosi et al. Burlington: Ashgate Publishing Company.

Ketchley, Neil. 2017. *Egypt in a Time of Revolution: Contentious Politics and the Arab Spring*. Cambridge: Cambridge University Press.

Kuhn, Thomas. 1962. *The Structure of Scientific Revolutions*. Chicago: University of Chicago Press.

Kurzman, Charles. 2004. *The Unthinkable Revolution in Iran*. Cambridge: Harvard University Press.

Lawson, George. 2015. "Revolution, Nonviolence, and the Arab Uprisings." *Mobilization* 20(4): 453–470.

Lehoucq, Fabrice. 2016. "Does Nonviolence Work?" *Comparative Politics*. 48(2): 269–287.

Lindekilde, Lasse. 2014. "A Typology of Backfire Mechanisms." Pp. 51–69 in *Dynamics of Political Violence*, edited by Bosi et al. Burlington: Ashgate Publishing Company.

Mallat, Chibli. 2015. *Philosophy of Nonviolence: Revolution, Constitutionalism, and Justice beyond the Middle East*. New York: Oxford University Press.

Mao, Zedong. 1978 [1937]. *On Guerrilla Warfare*. Trans. Samuel Griffith. New York: Anchor Press.

Markoff, John. 2013. "Opposing Authoritarian Rule with Nonviolent Civil Resistance." *Australian Journal of Political Science* 48(2): 233–245.

McCarthy, John D., Clark McPhail, and Jackie Smith. 1996. "Images of Protest: Dimensions of Selection Bias in Media Coverage of Washington Demonstrations, 1982 and 1991." *American Sociological Review* 61(3): 478–499.

Meckfessel, Shon. 2016. *Nonviolence Ain't What It Used To Be: Unarmed Insurrection and the Rhetoric of Resistance*. Chico, CA: AK Press.

Nepstad, Sharon E. 2011. *Nonviolent Revolutions: Civil Resistance in the Late 20th Century*. Oxford: Oxford University Press.

Nepstad, Sharon E. 2015a. *Nonviolent Struggle: Theories, Strategies, and Dynamics*. New York: Oxford University Press.

Nepstad, Sharon E. 2015b. "Nonviolent Resistance Research." *Mobilization* 20(4): 415–426.

Paige, Jeffrey. 2003. "Finding the Revolutionary in the Revolution." Pp. 19–29 in *The Future of Revolutions: Rethinking Radical Change in the Age of Globalization*, edited by Foran. New York: Zed Books.

Paulson, Joshua. 2012. "Case Study: Serbia, 1996–2000." Pp. 10–33 in *Sharp's Dictionary of Power and Struggle: Language of Civil Resistance in Conflicts*, edited by Sharp. Oxford: Oxford University Press.

Pinckney, Jonathan. 2016. *Making or Breaking Nonviolent Discipline in Civil Resistance Movements*. International Center on Nonviolent Conflict Monograph Series. Washington, DC: ICNC Press.

Rickford, Russell. 2016. "Black Lives Matter: Toward a Modern Practice of Mass Struggle." *New Labor Forum* 25(1): 34–42.

Roberts, Adam, and Timothy Garton Ash. 2009. *Civil Resistance and Power Politics: The Experience of Non-Violent Action from Gandhi to the Present*. New York: Oxford University Press.

Robinson, William. 2014. *Global Capitalism and the Crisis of Humanity*. New York: Cambridge University Press.

Roy, Arundhati. 2011. *Walking with the Comrades*. New York: Penguin Books.

Sarkees, Meredith Reed. 2010. "The COW Typology of War: Defining and Categorizing Wars (Version 4 of the Data)." *The Correlates of War Project*. http://cow.dss.ucdavis.edu/data-sets/COW-war/non-state-wars-codebook-1 (Accessed July 31, 2015).

Schneider, Nathan. 2012. "Principle: Maintain Nonviolent Discipline." in *Beautiful Trouble: A Toolbox for Revolution*, edited by Boyd. New York: OR Books.

Schock, Kurt. 2005. *Unarmed Insurrections: People Power Movements in Nondemocracies*. Minneapolis: University of Minnesota Press.

Schock, Kurt. 2013. "The Practice and Study of Civil Resistance." *Journal of Peace Research* 50(3): 277–290.

Seferiades, Seraphim, and Hank Johnston. 2012. *Violent Protest, Contentious Politics, and the Neoliberal State*. London: Routledge.

Sharp, Gene. 1973. *The Politics of Nonviolent Action*. Boston: Porter Sargent Publishers Inc.

Sharp, Gene. 1979. *Gandhi as a Political Strategist*. Boston: Porter Sargent Publishers Inc.

Sharp, Gene. 2012. *Sharp's Dictionary of Power and Struggle: Language of Civil Resistance in Conflicts*. Oxford: Oxford University Press.

Shokr, Ahmad. 2012. "The Eighteen Days of Tahrir." in *The Journey to Tahrir*, edited by Sowers and Toensing. London: Verso.

Siebens, James A. 2015. *The Intrusion Factor: Insurrection and the Effects of Foreign Military Intervention*. (Master's Thesis). Retrieved from ProQuest Dissertations Publishing: https://search.proquest.com/docview/1707902228

Skocpol, Theda. 1979. *States and Social Revolutions: A Comparative Analysis of France, Russia, and China*. Cambridge: Cambridge University Press.

Staggenborg, Suzanne. 2007. *Social Movements*. New York: Oxford University Press.

Stoner, Eric. 2012. "Participation Is Everything: A Conversation with Erica Chenoweth." *Waging Nonviolence*. https://wagingnonviolence.org/feature/participation-is-everything-a-conversation-with-erica-chenoweth/ (Accessed September 15, 2017).

Thompson, AK. 2010. *Black Bloc, White Riot: Anti-Globalization and the Genealogy of Dissent*. Oakland: AK Press.

Tilly, Charles. 1993. *European Revolutions, 1492–1992*. Oxford: Blackwell.

Tilly, Charles. 2003. *The Politics of Collective Violence*. Cambridge: Cambridge University Press.

Tilly, Charles. 2004. *Social Movements, 1768–2004*. Boulder: Paradigm Publishers.

Tilly, Charles. 2006. *Regimes and Repertoires*. Chicago: Chicago University Press.

Üstündağ, Nazan. 2016. "Self Defense as Revolutionary Practice in Rojava, or How to Unmake the State." *South Atlantic Quarterly* 115(1): 197–210.

Vinthagen, Stellan. 2015. *A Theory of Nonviolent Action: How Civil Resistance Works.* London: Zed Books.

Wada, Takeshi. 2016. "Rigidity and Flexibility of Repertoires of Contention." *Mobilization* 21(4): 449–468.

Wallerstein, Immanuel. 2004. *World Systems Analysis: An Introduction.* Durham: Duke University Press.

The Washington Post. 2017. "Inauguration Protesters Vandalize, Set Fires, Try to Disrupt Trump's Oath, as Police Arrest More Than 200. By Theresa Vargas, Taylor Hartz, and Peter Hermann. January 20. www.washingtonpost.com/local/protesters-bring-shouts-skirmishes-and-shutdowns-to-inauguration-celebration/2017/01/20/00ea4c72-df11–11e6-acdf-14da832ae861_story.html?utm_term=.ecda7fa1a603 (Accessed September 15, 2017).

Williams, Kieran. 2009. "Civil Resistance in Czechoslovakia: From Soviet Invasion to 'Velvet Revolution'." Pp. 110–126 in *Civil Resistance and Power Politics: The Experience of Non-Violent Action from Gandhi to the Present*, edited by Robert and Garton Ash. New York: Oxford University Press.

Wilson, Kenneth A. 2013. User's Manual for Cross-National Time Series Archive. Databanks International. Jerusalem, Israel.

11 Authoritarianism, nonviolent resistance, and Egypt's Kefaya movement

Killian Clarke

In the square in front of the Egyptian Supreme Court, a black wall of state security forces confronted several hundred men and women on December 12, 2004. The protesters were peaceful, standing in silence on the steps of the court building with yellow stickers on their mouths and chests, emblazoned with the slogan "*Kefaya*" (the Arabic word for "Enough"). They were calling for an end to then-President Hosni Mubarak's 23-year reign as Egypt's head of state. Some protesters carried green banners, the color of Egypt's Islamist opposition groups. Others had signs with slogans of Marxist revolutionary groups. Others were from Nasserist organizations, or liberal political parties. Six years before the Arab Spring, the Kefaya movement united the ideologically disparate actors of Egypt's major opposition groups into a political coalition that sustained nonviolent protests for ten months. The movement focused on three events during 2005 to reform the government: a constitutional referendum in May, a presidential election in September, and parliamentary elections in November.

By many accounts the Kefaya movement should never have existed. Not only did it bring together a group of political rivals who had never meaningfully collaborated before, but it also persisted in taking on a far more powerful authoritarian regime for the better part of a year. How was this movement able to mobilize and sustain its nonviolent confrontational activity in the repressive environment of Mubarak's Egypt? And how was it able to draw in such a diverse range of groups whose ideological positions were both disparate and polarized? As it turns out, these two questions are linked – the Kefaya coalition's unlikely success was actually facilitated by the authoritarian context in which it operated. This observation points to a paradox that is largely overlooked in the literature on nonviolent movements in authoritarian regimes: that the authoritarian context can actually *facilitate* the formation of social movements.

In this chapter, I argue that in situations of limited political openings, when authoritarian regimes are less able or willing to control and coerce opposition groups, mechanisms that generate social movement mobilization can actually operate more effectively than they do in democratic settings. I discuss three specific mechanisms that facilitate limited, reform-oriented mobilization: (1) the ability to generate least-common-denominator goals; (2) the presence of incentives for existing organizations to mobilize; and (3) the elevation of protest events as catalysts for movement cohesion. Though all three of these mechanisms facilitate movement mobilization in both democratic and nondemocratic settings, the manner in which they operate differs across these contexts. In particular, authoritarian regimes with limited political openings actually may allow them to operate more effectively than in democracies. In this sense, this chapter proposes a new way of thinking about movements in authoritarian regimes: rather than conceiving of these states as unequivocally hostile to mobilization, these three mechanisms may make it easier for social movements to form.

The Kefaya movement sought relatively limited political reform, and such movements are not uncommon under dictatorships, despite the odds they face. Although their frequency may be less and their chances of success lower, they can and do play critical roles in stimulating reform in states that are seen as resistant to change from below. And perhaps most critically, these reform-oriented movements can sometimes sow the seeds for later waves of nonviolent mobilization that may eventually culminate in broader movements or even revolutions – much like the one that toppled Hosni Mubarak in February of 2011.

The Egyptian political context

Since 1970, when President Anwar Sadat came to power, it is fair to say that Egypt's political opposition had never formed a sustained and nonviolent movement to confront the regime directly. When mobilization in Egypt had occurred, it took the form of either grassroots organizing that targeted gradual, bottom-up reform, or intense – but brief – protests and rioting. The first form of mobilization had been championed by the Muslim Brotherhood, which was originally formed in 1928 to Islamize Egyptian society through social outreach campaigns and educational programs. Since then the Brotherhood more or less remained true to this vision, and over the three decades preceding Kefaya it had built up a vast network of social welfare programs that reached out to Egypt's poor and provided an alternative model of society and governance from that of the former regime (Wickham 2002; Clark 2004; Brooke 2017). However, this strategy differed in obvious ways from those employed by Kefaya. It was explicitly nonconfrontational, as the Brotherhood traditionally took great precautions not to incite the ire of the regime. Indeed, as I explain later, the Brotherhood refused to participate in most Kefaya activities in part because of its reluctance to adopt any kind of confrontational politics. Moreover, the Brotherhood was a tightly controlled and close-knit religious movement with none of the organizational diversity that Kefaya exhibited.

The second form of mobilization witnessed in Egypt – street protesting and rioting – occurred in two major instances after 1970: first, with the outbreak of student riots in January 1972, and then with the January 1977 bread riots. The bread riots erupted following the government's decision to lower subsidies on bread and other basic goods. Although they lasted several weeks and resulted in massive arrests and seventy-nine deaths, they were primarily outcries over economic policies; unlike Kefaya, they were not sustained over time or directed toward political reform (Beattie 2000; Brownlee 2007). The other example of street activism occurred in 1972, when students responded to the failures of then-President Anwar Sadat by marching out of the gates of Cairo University to stage a massive citywide rally. After five days of rioting, facilitated by lax state policing, Sadat finally cracked down, ordering army units to invade university campuses and arrest student leaders (Abdallah 1985; Erlich 1989). Though these riots, particularly the student protests, bear some resemblance to Kefaya, it would be a stretch to call them part of any sustained social movement. In the case of the student demonstrations, the protests lasted only a week and participation was limited primarily to university students.

Kefaya was also unique for its composition. For the first time in recent Egyptian history, the diverse members of Egypt's fragmented opposition factions came together in a unified social movement. The closest the opposition had ever come to genuine cross-ideological cooperation was in 1984, when a coalition between the Muslim Brotherhood and the liberal New Wafd party was formed for the purpose of contesting parliamentary elections. A marriage of political expediency, the coalition held together just long enough for the two parties to win a quarter of the Parliament's seats. But the alliance fragmented when parliamentary sessions began, as ideological differences prevented the parties from collaborating on legislative initiatives. For every election after that, opposition parties guarded their small political territories and competed against each other almost as vehemently as against the regime (Springborg 1989; Kepel 1993; Baker 2003; El-Ghobashy 2005; Bradley 2008). Collaboration among these groups was infrequent and unsustained. Thus, within the context of recent Egyptian history, Kefaya was unique on two fronts: it was a sustained, confrontational, reform-oriented social movement, and it brought together disparate factions within Egypt's opposition.

That being said, Kefaya did not emerge from a political vacuum. Between 2000 and 2004, Egypt witnessed a wave of political activism that helped provide the opposition with the momentum to ultimately form a social movement. This activity focused on two regional developments: the start of the second Palestinian Intifada in 2000 and the run-up to the US-led invasion of Iraq in 2003. The widespread feelings of outrage and anger triggered by these events sparked a flurry of political activism, as various factions within the Egyptian opposition joined forces to form committees of solidarity, action campaigns, and opposition conferences. Among the most important events during this period was a massive demonstration on March 20, 2003, in which 20,000 protestors gathered in Cairo's Tahrir Square to denounce the United States' invasion of Iraq. Many Kefaya activists, particularly in the younger generation, cited this protest as their first involvement in political activism and explained that it was a critical moment of convergence for the members of Egypt's opposition. The demonstration was supposed to be an anti-US and antiwar rally. But given Mubarak's close alliance with the United States, the crowds began to air some tentative criticisms about the regime as well (Shadid 2007).

After the protests, activists continued to meet in secret, weighing their options for further expressions of opposition and protest. The administration of US President George W. Bush was putting great pressure on Mubarak to implement liberalizing reforms, and the opposition began to recognize that this pressure might yield a rare opportunity to act. At a gathering in November 2003, twenty-two elites from a number of parties and political groups gathered over a Ramadan *iftar* at the house of Abu Elela Mady, a moderate Islamist. They discussed their options for effecting political reform and pressuring President Mubarak to release his grip on the state. By the end of the evening, they had selected six individuals with allegiances to various leftist, Islamist, Nasserist, and liberal groups to draft a document stating the aims of their new initiative. In August 2004, they released their manifesto and received supporting signatures from 300 prominent intellectuals and professionals. Then, on September 21, 2004, they invited these 300 individuals to a conference at a Christian NGO where they announced the formation of a movement for political reform. They adopted the name "The Egyptian Movement for Change" and declared George Ishak, a Coptic Christian on good terms with many Islamists, as their coordinator.

Kefaya staged its first public protest, described at the outset of this chapter, the following December. Emboldened by the relatively benign security response, the Kefaya leaders began to set up a permanent body to organize further protests. They established a Coordinators' Committee of thirty-six leaders and a Daily Works Committee to run day-to-day operations. Then on February 4, 2005, they gathered at the annual Cairo Book Fair to raise their anti-Mubarak chants again. These demonstrations and those that took place in the coming weeks and months were responses to two political events scheduled for 2005: a parliamentary election and a presidential referendum.[1] Kefaya and many other Egyptian elites were outraged when they heard that Mubarak was planning to return for a fifth six-year term. In February, the president responded to these and other criticisms (some of which came from abroad) with an amendment to Article 76 of the Constitution, subject to approval in a popular referendum, that would allow for (sham) multicandidate presidential elections.[2]

With the referendum for this amendment set for May and the presidential election for September, Kefaya redoubled its protest efforts, sustaining a campaign of heightened street activity from February to September. This momentum was fueled by support from many members of Cairo's student population and certain pockets of the urban professional classes. Initially drawn into the movement through the protests, these subgroups created their own affiliated satellite movements: Youth for Change, Journalists for Change, Workers for Change, Artists for Change, and Lawyers for Change. Although these submovements participated in the Kefaya protests and chanted the same slogans as Kefaya, some of them also held their own meetings, recruited their own members, and organized their own demonstrations.

It is difficult to estimate how big Kefaya's ranks were at any given time, especially with so many spin-off movements and individuals whose participation was partial or intermittent. People would drift in and out of involvement and membership was a nebulous category.[3] However, based on reports by the movement's leaders, turnout at major protests, and registration on the Kefaya website, a plausible estimate is that Kefaya's membership was between 10,000 and 20,000 individuals. These members primarily came from Cairo, although as the movement gained momentum it began to set up chapters in all of Egypt's governorates, and significant protests were orchestrated in Alexandria, Suez, Mansoura, and Port Said.

The political environment in Egypt became feverish through the summer as two other candidates entered the presidential race and campaigned against Mubarak. One of them, Ayman Nour from the Ghad Party, seemed to present a real challenge, and he was unofficially supported by Kefaya. But on the day of the election, September 7, 2005, ballot rigging and voting fraud resulted in Mubarak's winning by a landslide margin of 88.6%. Nour came in a distant second with 7.8% and the third candidate from the Wafd Party, Noaman Goma'a, took 2.8%. Although turnout was low (officially 22.9%, though some independent agencies claim it was much lower), Mubarak declared that the people had spoken and accepted the seat of the presidency for the fifth time. After the results were released, many of Kefaya's members turned away from public protesting and increased their involvement with specific political parties, campaigning in advance of the upcoming parliamentary elections. Diversity, in this case, turned out to be a liability, as each of the organizations in the coalition found it in their interests to go it alone in a quest for greater parliamentary representation rather than maintain the coalition and present a united front (a tactic that some attempted, but that ultimately failed). Although Kefaya would continue to exist in name and form, Mubarak's presidential victory marked the effective end of its activity in the streets.

The challenge of building movement coalitions

Kefaya's uniqueness in recent Egyptian history corroborates the overwhelming consensus among social movement scholars that mobilization is difficult in states where political organizations, information flows, and resources are dominated by an authoritarian regime and whose citizens live in fear of repression (Goodwin 2001; Wickham 2002; Schock 2005; Tilly 2006; O'Brien and Li 2006; Osa and Schock 2007; Almeida 2008; Robertson 2010; Trejo 2012). Only revolutions are expected to generate the necessary momentum to overcome the profound structural barriers to mobilization under these conditions. Scholars rarely consider how and why nonviolent reform-oriented social movements might manage to mobilize under conditions that would seem to preclude their emergence.

There are some exceptions to this tendency. For example, some scholars have explored how direct repression can catalyze mobilization (Della Porta 1995; Loveman 1998; Goodwin 2001; Davenport et al. 2005; Francisco 1996, 2005). Though repression often breeds broader, revolutionary movements, there are also examples of nonviolent, reform-oriented collective action emerging from acts of repression (Loveman 1998). Yet Kefaya suffered little violence (at least in its early stages), and so these arguments do little to help us understand how this reform-oriented movement was able to get off the ground in the first place.

Other scholars have pointed out that authoritarian states can unintentionally shift the locus of political activity to grassroots arenas, stimulating civil society and generating new participatory organizational structures. Oxhorn (1995) has shown that the military regime in Chile generated an array of democratic and participatory structures among the rural poor. Similarly, a group of Middle East scholars have drawn on the tools of social movement theory to study how authoritarian regimes encourage the mobilization of Islamist organizations and movements (Wiktorowicz 2001, 2004; Wickham 2002; Bayat 2007). Wickham (2002), in her study of the Muslim Brotherhood, shows that Mubarak's regime actually encouraged the Brotherhood's grassroots activity by providing it with an opportunity to offer social services to Egypt's poor. Yet these arguments are better for explaining broad, grassroots organization and activism than the confrontational politics of the Kefaya movement.

These studies aside, scholars of mobilization have mostly concluded that it is overwhelmingly difficult for activists to form social movements under authoritarian regimes. Scholars tend to agree that for collective action to occur in nondemocracies there must be some degree of political opening – created, perhaps, by diplomatic or economic pressure from an outside actor, internal regime fragmentation that hamstrings the repressive apparatus, or recent defeat in an external war – which provides the space in which mobilization can occur. Theda Skocpol (1979) became an early champion of this model in her explanation of three major social revolutions. She claimed that revolutions are not "made," but "come" – they emerge to fill the vacuum created when a weak state begins to collapse. Later reformulations of this theory argue that structural openings are critical to mobilization in authoritarian contexts because the barriers to collective action are normally so high (Goldstone 1998; Almeida 2003, 2008; Hafez 2003; Boudreau 2004; Osa and Corduneanu-Huci 2005; Schock 2005; Osa and Schock 2007). Goldstone (1998) claims that opportunities have different causal implications in nondemocracies than they do in democracies. In liberal contexts, a political opening defines the *nature* of collective action, but in authoritarian regimes a political opportunity determines whether a movement can mobilize at all.

I do not disagree with these conclusions – the Kefaya movement likewise confirms that a political opening is often an important precursor to mobilization in an authoritarian regime. However, the argument that when a regime opens up a movement or revolution will simply "come" is insufficient. Even in democratic settings, forming a social movement is no easy feat, and scholars have devoted much time and effort to debating how this happens. It is therefore worth taking the question of social movements in nondemocracies one step further: when a political opening does create a mobilization opportunity, what factors in the political environment make it likely that a movement will emerge? In essence, why is it that in cases of political opening social movements tend, simply, to "come?"

To answer these questions I turn to a literature on social movement coalitions. This is a literature infrequently invoked in nonviolence studies, but which is helpful for illuminating how the mechanisms that facilitate movement formation function differently in authoritarian versus democratic regimes. As noted earlier, Kefaya was noteworthy not only for its audacity in taking on the Mubarak regime but also because it brought together a multitude of diverse actors. Mobilization scholars often point out that social movements are inherently coalitional affairs. For example, David Meyer says that "although it is a grammatical convenience to speak of 'the' movement or 'a' movement, social movements are comprised of coalitions of actors" (2001: 11–12). Recognizing this fact, a number of scholars have taken to studying social movements less as unitary phenomena and more as constructed coalitions of preexisting social movement organizations, or SMOs (Van Dyke and McCammon 2010). Given the deeply coalitional nature of Kefaya, I suggest that if we focus on social movements as coalitions and take seriously the ways in which coalitions tend to form, we may be able to better understand how reform movements in nondemocracies come together.

In fact, this is a question of altering the lens, rather than the subject matter, for there is little difference between a "social movement" and a "social movement coalition." It is therefore no surprise to find that many theories of coalition formation echo ideas from social movement theory. However, one key difference between the literature on social movements and coalitions is that coalition scholars tend to focus more on the obstacles that keep SMOs apart, rather than mechanisms that facilitate collective action. This presents a useful framework for thinking about movements in nondemocracies. Indeed, because coalition scholars tend to study instances of mobilization in the democratic West, their research yields valuable insights about the obstacles that prevent coalitions from forming in liberal democracies. Examining how significant these obstacles were to the formation of the Kefaya coalition allows us to discern how such a movement ever got off the ground and how mechanisms that facilitate collective action might function differently in an authoritarian environment.

It is worth pointing out that many scholars of revolutions also take on the question of coalition formation (Goodwin and Skocpol 1989; Parsa 2000; Goodwin 2001; Kurzman 2004; Foran 2005; Almeida 2005; Schock 2005; Beissinger 2013). Successful revolutions are almost always precipitated by coalitions that draw together diverse sectors of society, particularly the kinds of nationwide or social revolutions that have received so much attention in the literature. Goodwin and Skocpol (1989) introduce the argument that successful revolutions are generally precipitated by a combination of urban "professional revolutionaries" and broad collections of rural peasants, laborers, and artisans, often brought together by particularly exclusionary authoritarian regimes. Tilly (2006) develops a typology of revolutionary coalitions, emphasizing two key axes that determine their nature: the basis of participating groups (either territorial or interest-based) and the directness of relations between the groups. However, if anything, these studies only emphasize the differences between Kefaya and such revolutionary coalitions. Kefaya never gained the scope, scale, or national ambitions of most revolutionary coalitions, and its members were largely drawn from a single social sector – what Goodwin and Skocpol (1989) would term "professional revolutionaries." In fact, Kefaya more closely resembles those Western, reform-oriented social movements that coalition scholars have examined. Moreover, the revolution literature tends to draw on broad structural factors – like regime type, nature of repression, and degrees of social isolation – in explaining how these coalitions come about, rather than on the meso- and micro-level organizational aspects of coalition formation.

The coalition literature discusses three obstacles relevant to Kefaya's mobilization: the struggle to define widely appealing goals, the challenge of providing incentives for different SMOs to join a coalition, and the difficulty of building cohesion among diverse participants. Within any multiorganizational field, there are always groups that maintain some common and some conflicting goals (Zald and McCarthy 1980, 1987; Klandermans 1990, 1992; Gerhards and Rucht 1992). As a result, activists seeking to build coalitions are challenged to select specific goals and frame them so that a wide array of SMOs find them appealing (Ferree and Roth 1998; Rose 2000; Armstrong 2002; Croteau and Hicks 2003; Levi and Murphy 2006). Some scholars argue that coalition formation is contingent on leaders being able to define a set of simple, least-common-denominator goals (Kleidman and Rochon 1997; Meyer and Corrigall-Brown 2005). Kleidman and Rochon (1997) contrast the effectiveness of this technique to that of the "laundry list" approach, in which coalition leaders adopt all the principal issues around which participating SMOs are oriented. While some have argued that such diversity in goals is effective (Olzak and Ryo 2007), Kleidman and Rochon (1997) contend that the "least-common-denominator" approach is more likely to generate the support of a broad range of actors.

A second key obstacle that coalition leaders face is convincing and inducing individual SMOs to join their movements. Scholars agree that SMOs tend to view coalition involvement through a utilitarian lens and undertake a cost-benefit analysis before deciding to join (Zald and McCarthy 1987; McCammon and Campbell 2002; Murphy 2005; Meyer and Corrigall-Brown 2005; Levi and Murphy 2006). They weigh what they can potentially gain against what they are likely to lose and ultimately make the decision that contributes most to their long-term preservation. The literature emphasizes two factors that shape these calculations: identity and resources. The desire of organizations to preserve their identity and autonomy is one of the primary reasons that they choose to refrain from coalition involvement (Staggenborg 1986; Hathaway and Meyer 1997; Dalton 1994; Hojnacki 1997; Kleidman and Rochon 1997; Obach 2004). SMOs do not want to appear to their constituencies as though they are compromising their values, straying from core goals, or giving up crucial decision-making rights. But SMO leaders balance this wariness against a desire to guarantee their SMO's survival through access to new resources.[4] Scholars disagree over whether an abundance or a dearth of resources is more likely to motivate SMO involvement. Some studies argue that a wealth of resources is more likely to motivate coalition formation, because when resources are scant SMOs compete rather than cooperate to obtain larger shares of the pie (Zald and McCarthy 1987; Kleidman 1993). In contrast, other scholars have shown that a lack of resource availability provides a strong incentive for coalition involvement, as organizations seek access to pooled resources (Arnold 1994; Van Dyke 2003; Obach 2004; Levi and Murphy 2006). These scholars argue that if SMOs are ultimately concerned with their own organizational maintenance, they are more likely to seek out partners when their resources are scarce and their survival is in jeopardy.

Finally, the literature on coalitions notes a third challenge to coalition formation – building cohesion. Van Dyke (2003), for example, identifies the experience of participating in a protest as important for building feelings of solidarity and collective identity. Similarly, Ansell (2001) examines the reasons why coalitions break into schisms and then reconsolidate, developing a concept of "strike waves," which serve as "triggering events" for motivating feelings of solidarity. The social movement literature also provides some insight into how activists overcome the obstacle of movement solidarity. Like coalition scholars, some find that protest events and incidents of collective action help to build collective identity (Melucci 1989; Gamson 1992; Taylor and Whittier 1992; Gould 1995; Jasper 1997; Klandermans and de Weerd 2000; Jasper and Polletta 2001). The shared experience of participating in a protest, particularly one of heightened intensity, draws the members of a movement together and increases the resonance of an otherwise constructed collective identity. Other studies have identified a specific form of collective identity, termed "oppositional consciousness," which arises when social movements of oppressed actors build a collective identity around their subordinated status (Mansbridge 2001; Wieloch 2002; Chowdhury 2006). Whatever the approach, coalition leaders will always struggle to construct identities that are appealing and resonant to all the diverse members of their coalitions.

Movement formation in authoritarian contexts

Scholars have convincingly demonstrated that authoritarian regimes present structural obstacles to activists seeking to foment protest and organize collective action. Such activity is not only dangerous but also greatly inhibited by the lack of a free press, state control of institutions, a robust internal security apparatus, and the limited availability of resources. And yet, I argue that certain structural features of authoritarian contexts can actually facilitate coalition formation. By reducing some of the obstacles that keep potential coalition partners apart in democratic settings, these states paradoxically facilitate opposition actors' mobilization efforts.

The argument has four components: (1) following the opening of a political opportunity, (2) a set of broad least-common-denominator goals and (3) strong incentives for SMO involvement bring together activists who then (4) cohere into a unified social movement through intense protest events. First, scholars agree that a political opening is often a necessary precondition for mobilization in non-democracies. A political opening creates the structural conditions that allow for the possibility of mobilization. Once that political opening has taken place, activists find themselves in an environment that is surprisingly conducive to collective action.

Second, formulating least-common-denominator goals that many different SMOs can embrace is a central problem for coalitions in democratic settings. Authoritarian regimes differ in that they grant opposition leaders an obvious and widely palatable platform for rallying support. Regardless of ideological affiliation, historical background, or political beliefs, a great number of SMOs in a nondemocracy can agree over opposition to the ruling regime. Here, the revolutions literature reinforces the point, as a number of scholars have pointed out that opposition to a despicable autocrat offers a particularly effective platform around which many diverse groups can mobilize (Parsa 2000; Bieber 2003; Foran 2005; Beissinger 2011, 2013).

Third, although incentives for SMOs to join coalitions are highly variable in liberal states, there are strong incentives for SMOs in authoritarian states to join a coalition. Autocratic regimes make a point of limiting access to resources. As the literature suggests, SMOs that lack access to resources may be more drawn to a coalition where they can share pooled resources and enhance their own organizational durability.[5] They will seek to form coalitions not only out of their joint desire to oppose the regime but also for the self-interested purposes of accessing greater financial resources, recruiting new members, and elevating their own political positions.

Once they have generated some momentum, a final aspect of authoritarian settings helps social movements endure. Scholars have identified protest events as important forums for building cohesion and have suggested that more intense moments of collective action will yield stronger feelings of solidarity. Moreover, as is suggested by the notion of oppositional consciousness, protest events at which a threatening and palpable enemy is present are likely to promote even stronger cohesion. I therefore argue that protests in authoritarian regimes, where the intensity is high and large numbers of security forces are often present, promote strong feelings of solidarity among activists.

Methodology and fieldwork

I traveled to Cairo for five weeks in August 2008 and carried out thirty-five interviews with thirty-eight leaders, members, and affiliates of Kefaya.[6] Twenty-one of my interviews were conducted with the older members and leaders of the movement, while seventeen were with youth and student members. I interviewed members of all the major ideological factions: five independents, five Nasserists, seven Islamists, six socialists/communists, twelve liberals, and three who identified themselves as Islamists and socialists. I also interviewed members of affiliated groups who collaborated with Kefaya but never formally joined the movement. One area in which my pool lacked diversity was gender: of my thirty-eight respondents, only four were women and the rest were men. However, this reflected the broader demographic breakdown of Kefaya, which was a movement largely composed of men.

I arrived in the field with the names of forty-five Kefaya members and affiliates taken from Arabic and English news articles, as well as several policy and academic papers. Drawing on preexisting contacts in Egypt, I arranged a set of initial interviews with individuals from this list. After every interview, I inquired as to whether the respondent knew of other individuals with whom I ought to meet. Additionally, if there was someone on my list with whom I knew the interviewee was acquainted, I asked whether he or she could provide me with contact information. In addition to the interviews, I drew information from newspapers such as *Al*

Ahram Weekly, *Al Masry Al Youm*, *The Daily News Egypt*, *Al Ahram*, *Al Dostoor*, and certain foreign publications. I also reviewed internet-based sources, including statements, manifestos, and proposals on the Kefaya website and a number of political blogs.

To analyze the data, I developed twenty codes based on initial observations of patterns, my research questions, my hypotheses, and the literature on social movements. I then grouped the data into these categories and reread and recoded to identify more specific patterns. Finally, I looked for ways in which these patterns could help explain how the Kefaya movement had come about.

A political opening

In 2003 the administration of George W. Bush began pressuring Mubarak to take steps towards democracy. Given Egypt's dependence on US foreign aid, the regime was forced to shelve the harsh tactics of repression that had become a mainstay of its policies and allow for a more open political climate. This political opening created an opportunity for activism that Kefaya was able to exploit. Indeed, one activist said that the political environment in 2005 was "like a ripe piece of fruit that was waiting for whomever might come along and pick it" (interview with Amin Iskander, Kefaya founder and leader in the Karama Party, August 12, 2008). Still, in the early days of Kefaya's formation, its leaders were unclear how much the environment had really changed. Many of them had participated in the antiwar protests in 2003 where the security forces had stood by and warily allowed the demonstrations to occur. But they had also experienced or witnessed incidents of brutal attacks against some of these protests. There was strong disagreement among the founding members as to whether the movement ought to adopt protest tactics at all, with some contending that it would be more prudent to organize conferences and release opposition statements. Magdi Oror, the Assistant General Secretary of the Labor Party and a member of the Kefaya Coordinators' Committee, described the debate that occurred in these early stages:

> The Labor Party members were saying "No to Mubarak." And the Revolutionary Socialists started saying "*Yasqut Mubarak*." And some of the members of the Daily Committee of Kefaya feared this at the beginning, because they thought the police would crack down. They wanted silent protests. Or they wanted to criticize corruption, or the government, or Gamal Mubarak[7] – but not the President.
>
> (Interview with Magdi Oror, Assistant General Secretary of the Labor Party, August 25, 2008)

In the end, the moderates capitulated to the movement's more radical wing, which insisted that another indoor committee would simply wither away. Nevertheless, no one knew if the regime would respond to Kefaya's first protest with brutal repression or reluctant toleration.[8]

The nature of this protest reflected the activists' nervous attitudes. The moderates in the movement had insisted that it be a silent protest, with no chanting or shouting of slogans. But toward the end of the event, the leaders of two of the more radical member organizations – the Revolutionary Socialists and the Labor Party – began belting out chants against Mubarak. Although this infuriated the coalition's moderates, who were terrified that if the movement were too confrontational it would be crushed, the security forces remained impassive. Indeed, had it not been for the nerve of these hardliners, Kefaya might never have realized the true extent of the political opening that had emerged in 2004 and 2005. Many of Kefaya's members explained that had it not been for that first protest, which proved that the attitude of the regime toward opposition had indeed changed, the Kefaya movement might never have taken off. Through the remainder of 2005, the Mubarak regime continued to tolerate an unprecedented level of political activism and protest activity, though on several occasions it did crack down on Kefaya with police violence and attacks against protesters. Still, by normal Egyptian standards, it was a period of remarkable openness, and Kefaya capitalized on the opportunity, defying the regime in a way that had never been allowed before.

Defining a least-common-denominator goal

As 2005 progressed, Kefaya came to be defined by its slogans.[9] One of the reasons these chants had such resonance was that they referred to a very simple set of goals: remove the president, reform the regime. The movement espoused a clear, basic, and widely palatable program, which was able to draw in large swaths of Egypt's opposition and unite it toward a common end.

A least-common-denominator goal provides a useful theoretical concept for thinking about Kefaya's goal definition and framing challenges. Although the groups that joined its coalition had ideological backgrounds ranging from socialist to liberal to Islamist, all could agree that they hated the regime. Defining its goals along this axis is one of the principal reasons Kefaya was able to appeal to so many parties and groups.[10] As George Ishak, the cofounder and leader of the movement, put it, they were the "minimum acceptable issues, and we never went beyond them" (Interview with George Ishak, General Coordinator of Kefaya, August 11, 2008).

During early discussions, the movement's leaders agreed on the need to draft a program that would have broad appeal. The product of this discussion was a concise, two-page manifesto that was vaguely politically liberal and democracy-oriented, but focused primarily on civil and human rights. The founders knew that they had to decide on issues that would "be simple and at the same time have a wide and comprehensive scope" (Interview with Amin Iskander, Kefaya founder and leader in the Karama Party, August 12, 2008). Abou Elela Madi explained how the founders decided on the content for the platform:

> We spoke about political issues only, because we knew that we had all the radical currents in Egypt – liberal, Islamic, leftist, Marxist, Nasserist, nationalist.

So we knew we would have a lot of differences, especially on economic and social issues. So we looked only to issues of political reforms. And with this we could get much more acceptance.

(Interview with Abu Elela Madi, Kefaya founder and director of the Wasat Party, August 13, 2008)

As long as they limited the document's contents to political reforms and ending the president's reign, they knew that no one within the opposition would find much to contest.

But some disputes did occur, despite these widely palatable aims. For example, the Revolutionary Socialists and the Labor Party, both of whom took hard lines against Israel and the United States, insisted that the manifesto include a denouncement of the "odious [foreign] assault on Arab native soil." According to Madi, most of the founders did not feel strongly about this point, but they agreed to include it because they wanted these groups' support. Negotiating agreement around points like this prolonged the drafting of the manifesto and delayed its release to the general public. Yet even factoring in these delays, Kefaya navigated its goal development with surprising ease. Given the diversity of its members, it is remarkable that the most significant points of contention were disagreements over what language to use in condemning the United States and Israel.

In a democratic regime, goal development tends to be much more difficult, even among groups sharing values and interests. In contrast, Egypt's authoritarian system helped Kefaya's leaders by mitigating the challenge of generating appealing least-common-denominator goals.

Organizational incentives

Kefaya comprised a motley assortment of parties and organizations: a fledgling liberal party calling for free-market reforms, an underground group of Marxists and Trotskyites, and an Islamist party with socialist roots. What was it, besides agreement on a set of basic demands, that drew such disparate political organizations into a social movement that had little chance of achieving its goals? Though the literature on this question suggests conflicting answers – resource scarcity has been shown to help some coalitions in forming but hinder others – the case of Kefaya suggests that in an authoritarian context, where social movement organizations typically lack access to resources, these organizations may seek to participate in a social movement because of the possibility of gaining access to pooled resources. The parties in Kefaya chose to join the coalition, in part, to obtain two resources: new members and political legitimacy.

In normal times, the Mubarak regime ensured that opposition players in Egypt were kept divided and weak by severely limiting the availability of resources. This tactic was manifested in numerous ways: the regime refused to grant official party licenses; obstructed parties from opening bank accounts; periodically raided party headquarters, destroying equipment and harassing members; and monopolized information channels, preventing parties from receiving key news and from disseminating their own messages. During normal times, when the climate was toxic and the regime showed no tolerance for expressions of opposition, political parties grudgingly made do with the few resources they were granted. But in a situation of limited political opportunity, when the fear of repression had been dulled, the incentive to collaborate through the pooling of resources became more potent.

Both the nature of the groups that participated in Kefaya and their behavior once they became involved indicate that joining the coalition was, in part, a self-interested move to boost their access to resources and bolster their credibility. Kefaya was composed, by and large, of the weakest members of the Egyptian opposition. Although some of its members were independents, it secured the official support and participation of five political groups: the Labor Party, the Wasat Party, the Ghad Party, the Karama Party, and the Revolutionary Socialists. The Labor Party had had its party license revoked and its newspaper shut down in 2000 for touting an Islamist message. The Wasat and Karama parties were splinter factions of the Muslim Brotherhood and the Nasserists, respectively, and each had had their applications for official party status rejected on several occasions. The Ghad Party had been recognized by the government, but it was young and untested, with a small mass base and little public recognition. Finally, the Revolutionary Socialists did not claim to be a political party – they had emerged in the early 2000s from an underground communist society and had become active in organizing the street protests around the Intifada and the Iraq War. What these groups all shared was a severe lack of resources, minimal political credibility, low membership bases, and a marginal role in Egyptian politics. They had little to lose and much to gain in joining an opposition social movement.

What is also conspicuous about this list is the absence of several long-standing political groups within the Egyptian opposition, most notably the Tagammu Party, the Nasserist Party, the Wafd Party, and the Muslim Brotherhood.[11] Kefaya's founders sought the support of these groups but could not convince them to officially come on board. The Tagammu, Nasserist, and Wafd parties had a long history of working tacitly with the regime and had managed over the years to gain some small political concessions. They were all officially recognized, had an established membership, participated in parliamentary elections, and occasionally even won a handful of seats. Their cozy relationship with the government and the small gains that they received militated against them getting involved in the Kefaya coalition.

The Muslim Brotherhood had different reasons for not joining Kefaya, which ultimately were based on their long-term interests. Historically, the Brotherhood had had one of the most hostile relationships with the regime and had been the target of consistent political repression. But these painful experiences also caused the Brotherhood to prioritize survival over almost every other goal, which made them naturally reticent to directly confront the regime. Although some Brotherhood members sympathized with Kefaya's goals, they deemed Kefaya's street tactics too risky to officially adopt or consistently support. Moreover, the Brotherhood operated from a unique position of strength in Egyptian politics, a result of its well-developed network of grassroots support (Wickham 2002; El-Ghobashy 2005). They saw none of the resource benefits that other participants did and thus, as one activist put it, they "were always on the fence with regard to Kefaya" (Interview with anonymous Kefaya activist, August 5, 2008). As the literature on coalitions would predict, the Brotherhood was too wary of losing autonomy, identity, and control over its own resources to join a coalition in which it would not be in charge.[12]

More than just the nature of the parties that joined Kefaya, their behavior also demonstrated that they saw it as an opportunity to gain resources. The parties jockeyed for visibility, influence, and power and tried to recruit members of the youth movements. These actions must be understood in the context of these parties' marginal positions in Egyptian politics, where their voices were rarely heard and their influence over political debates hardly felt. For them, Kefaya represented an opportunity to demonstrate their authority and make their positions known. As they sought to increase their prominence, parties naturally competed over who would be the leader of the movement. One member of the Coordinators' Committee decried this petty bickering and jockeying for political advantage:

> The problem was not differences of opinion so much as it was the determination of certain people to dominate the movement. They would try to turn the debate in such a way as to pass a decision that corresponded to what they wanted . . . The issue did not matter. Any issue could be discussed, but then the leader of a particular group would come and would change the discussion completely so as to promote the preferences of his own party.
> (Interview with Mustafa Kemal Sayed, Member of the Kefaya Coordinators' Committee, August 21, 2008)

The parties were involved in the movement to promote their own interests and they debated and discussed issues, in part, to acquire influence. Some other respondents said that the fiercest debates occurred over the issue of media attention – every leader wanted to be the face of the movement because they had "a personal interest in becoming more visible through the media" (Interview with Mohamad Said Idris, Kefaya founder and member of the Coordinators' Committee, August 24, 2008). For these parties, involvement in Kefaya was a chance to gain credibility and political influence. It is worth noting that in the end this bickering and posturing may have contributed to the fracturing of the movement as the parties failed to find enough common ground to create a front for the parliamentary elections and so left the coalition to compete in the elections alone.

Another key incentive for joining Kefaya was the possibility of recruiting new members, particularly from the youth. Kefaya's youth wing was largely composed of independent students who were new to political activism and had no defined political identity. For the parties, these young independents were prime targets for recruitment as they sought to expand their limited memberships. One member of the Coordinators' Committee admitted, "some leaders considered that Kefaya might be a source for membership for their parties" (Interview with Abdel

Galeel Mustafa, member of the Kefaya Coordinators' Committee, August 25, 2008). Younger members of the movement, particularly independents, referred to these activities in more hostile terms: "They were trying to recruit their elements from within the movement. They came to Kefaya to recruit people, and this really pissed me off" (Interview with Ahmed Mahgoub, Kefaya activist, August 10, 2008). The persistence and tenacity with which these parties pursued even reticent or openly resistant independent youths shows that they aimed to use Kefaya to acquire new human resources.

The social movement organizations that participated in Kefaya were drawn to the movement by the prospect of acquiring both tangible human resources and intangible resources like legitimacy and visibility. Because the regime had kept these groups weak and marginal by consistently restricting their access to organizational resources, the parties saw coalition involvement as more advantageous than they might have if they had been operating in a more liberal context where resources were more accessible.[13] In this way, the authoritarian regime made it easier for Kefaya to draw in participating SMOs and build a durable coalition.

Protest events and building cohesion

Egypt's authoritarian regime also facilitated Kefaya's sustained mobilization by elevating the role of protest events in consolidating and uniting the coalition. The dominant opinion among Kefaya's members was that the movement was most united during protest events. While many respondents mentioned bickering and infighting during committee meetings, they all agreed that when Kefaya took to the streets, its members were unified in their opposition to the regime. One protester explained that "the factions would mostly dissolve when we got out into the street" (Interview with Ahmed Al Droubi, Kefaya activist, August 6, 2008); another said that they would "become 'one' in the streets" (Interview with Ahmed Seif Al Islam, Kefaya activist and Director of the Hisham Mubarak Law Center, August 24, 2008). One youth member said that his closest bonds had been formed with the people who stood beside him in the protests – "the people I was in the street with, regardless of their political currents" (Interview with Khaled Abdel Hamid, Kefaya activists and youth leader of the Revolutionary Socialists, August 7, 2008). In these and other comments, "the street" is widely referenced as the site where movement consolidation occurred and partisan differences dissolved.

Of course, as other scholars have pointed out, protest events are often intense, giving them the potential even in liberal contexts to bring a diverse coalition together. But the protests that Kefaya activists experienced were particularly effective in unifying the movement because of the overwhelming security presence. Kefaya demonstrations rarely drew more than one or two thousand protesters, and sometimes many fewer. Activists would usually arrive at a protest site to find a sea of security forces waiting for them with ominous black riot gear (it was almost impossible for Kefaya to plan a protest without the time and place leaking out to the authorities). Often the protesters were outnumbered by as much as ten to one. As the activists began chanting, the police would close in and surround them in a tightly contained ring. In this way, the security forces served as a constant reminder to Kefaya's activists of their relative weakness and vulnerability.

This intense and threatening atmosphere served as a powerful catalyst for cohesion. Ahmed Al Droubi explained how his relationships to members of the parties changed during protests: "In the street we were together, because we had a common enemy. But I really hated what they [my fellow protesters] stood for" (Interview with Ahmed Al Droubi, Kefaya activist, August 6, 2008). Not only does Droubi emphasize how the "common enemy" brought him closer to his fellow protesters, but he also reveals how ideologically divided they all were. Even passers-by and onlookers were drawn into the movement through this uniformity of treatment, as indicated by one activist's account: "They dealt with all of us in the same way. And so they made an activist out of me. Before that, I admired Kefaya. But that day [while watching the protest take place], they made me a Kefaya activist just by treating me like one" (Interview with Tariq Munir, Kefaya activist and journalist, August 9, 2008). These and other comments indicate that the Kefaya coalition was held together by more than just the self-interested concerns of diverse parties agreeing on broad goals. Because of the protest events, the coalition began to develop an identity and unity of its own. These findings suggest that when authoritarian forces monitor protest activities, moments of collective action will take on great significance in keeping a coalitional movement bound together. Again, the implication of this is that an authoritarian regime may paradoxically aid activists in their efforts to build and sustain a social movement.

Conclusions: Kefaya's legacy

At the time, many political analysts and commentators dismissed Kefaya for its failure to bring about real reform. But social movements can have effects in multiple and often unpredictable ways. Five and a half years after the apparent demise of the Kefaya movement, another wave of protest emerged in Egypt and quickly gained a momentum that Kefaya was never able to muster. Eighteen days after these protests began, President Hosni Mubarak ceded his powers to a military council and fled to his home in Sharm al-Sheikh. It was an ending about which the leaders and members of Kefaya had likely only dared to dream.

In the emerging scholarship on the 2011 uprising, several studies have pointed to the importance of the oppositional networks and movements that were built in the decade preceding 2011, including Kefaya, for creating the organizational wherewithal necessary to launch the initial protests of the 2011 uprising (El-Ghobashy 2011; Korany and El-Mahdi 2012; Abdelrahman 2014; Clarke 2014; Gunning and Baron 2014). These studies suggest that Kefaya's importance to Egypt was, perhaps, downplayed at the time of its activities. This underappreciated importance, moreover, may offer a lesson to scholars seeking to make sense of collective action in nondemocracies. Reform-oriented movements in authoritarian regimes may often fail to achieve their immediate goals, but this does not render them unimportant. Sometimes they can be critical agents of gradual democratic change, opening up new avenues of contention and participation, or pressuring a regime into making small but irreversible reforms. A number of scholars have demonstrated this potential with studies that identify a connection between protest movements and democratization (Garretón 1989; Adler and Webster 1995; Bermeo 1997; Bratton and van de Walle 1992, 1997; Collier and Mahoney 1997; Giugni et al. 1998; Markoff 1996; Wood 2000; Trejo 2012; LeBas 2013; Kadivar and Caren 2015; Brancati 2016).

More significant for the case of Egypt and Kefaya is the idea that protests can occur in waves. Sometimes even a small protest movement can establish the basis for a subsequent, more powerful wave (Tarrow 1983, 1989, 1995; Tilly 1995; Bieber 2003; Almeida 2008). Activists meet each other, form bonds and groups, develop political sensibilities, hone their protest tactics, and become accustomed to taking risks and confronting uncertainty. As political situations change, movements and activists may melt into the shadows, biding their time until a new political opportunity emerges. When it does, they can call upon their previous protest experiences to precipitate a new, and potentially more successful, wave of activism.

Consistent with this view, many interviewees responded to questions about Kefaya's legacy by saying that the movement had mattered most for the way it politicized a new generation of youth, introducing them to opposition politics and educating them in the art of protest. The activist Ahmed Maher is a fine case in point. He described to me how he joined Kefaya, showing up at one of its early protests after reading about it in the opposition press. After Kefaya's protests declined in 2005, Maher remained active in politics, exploring new forums to express his opposition to the regime. In April 2008, he formed a group on the social networking site Facebook called the 6 of April Youth, which sought to organize young activists to stand in solidarity with a series of labor strikes. He explained to me how he created organizing committees modeled off the Youth for Change committees and adopted the most successful protest tactics that he had witnessed during the Kefaya days. His friend and colleague Ahmed Salah likewise pointed to the influence Kefaya had on Maher:

> Ahmed Maher was in Youth for Change, though he was not that active. He was new to politics. But he saw a lot and he learned a lot and he took those lessons with him. And now he is showing great courage in being the leader of this new 6 April movement . . . And they are using the Kefaya slogans. Because Kefaya is an identity, it's an ideology that we have and that has carried through in the work Ahmed is doing with his 6 April Youth. And who knows where those ideas will take them next.
>
> (Interview with Ahmed Salah, Kefaya activist,
> August 4, 2008)

Two and half years later, it was Ahmed Maher and several other members of the 6 of April Youth that used Facebook to call for the first protest of the January 25 uprising.

Reform-oriented social movements in authoritarian regimes undoubtedly matter, and my aim has been to explain how they manage to emerge when strong autocratic states would seem to preclude their mobilization. Political opportunities are likely just as important for movement formation in these regimes as the literature suggests. However, the study also moves beyond the political opportunity framework, demonstrating that certain structural factors inherent to authoritarian regimes make it easier for activists to cobble together opposition coalitions. We should not be surprised to see small (even ostensibly insignificant) social movements arise in conditions of modest political liberalization. Their rise, it turns out, is facilitated by some of the very structures that normally hold them back.

Notes

1 In Egypt, the president was for many years selected in a referendum, rather than an election. In these presidential referendums, there was only one candidate and the people either voted "yes" or "no."

2 The amendment established unfair requirements for who could participate in the election. It required all presidential candidates to either come from government-recognized parties or receive supporting signatures from 250 members of the Shura Council. Most established government parties are controlled by the regime, and the Shura Council was dominated by the regime-sponsored National Democratic Party (NDP), making it unlikely for them to approve any independent candidates.

3 Of the individuals I interviewed, participation ranged from some who said they were going to two protests a day through the summer of 2005 to one who said he had been only to the three biggest protests.

4 Resources is a broadly defined term encompassing, among other things, money, equipment, expertise, information, memberships, political influence, and credibility.

5 In cases of major political openings, it may be the case that SMOs are able to access more resources. If this occurs then coalition formation will be more difficult. However, a political opening in an authoritarian regime is usually somewhat limited, entailing the reduced likelihood of repression. In these instances, SMOs' access to resources will remain low, as was the case with Kefaya.

6 Twenty-four interviews were conducted in English and eleven in Arabic. For five of the Arabic interviews I brought a local Egyptian translator. For the remaining six Arabic interviews, the services of the translator were not needed, as the interviewee spoke the formal Arabic dialect that I had learned.

7 Gamal Mubarak is Hosni Mubarak's son and at the time was the general secretary of the NDP's Policy Committee and the party's deputy secretary general. It is widely believed that he was being groomed to succeed his father as president and, as a result, he too came under attack by Kefaya during 2005.

8 Even George Ishak, who was leading the event, described being "very frightened" because of uncertainty about how the regime would respond (Interview with George Ishak, General Coordinator of Kefaya, August 11, 2008).

9 Kefaya's very name was appropriated from one of its most popular chants, in which a movement leader would call out a number of grievances (Corruption! The NDP! Hosni Mubarak!), and after each phrase the protesters would cry back: "Kefaya!" "Enough!" Other chants – "Yasqut, Yasqut, Hosni Mubarak" and "La li Tamdid! La li Tawrith!" (No to succession! No to inheritance!) – became common parlance among activist circles and the Egyptian public at large.

10 Of the thirty-eight interviewees, thirty-two cited this factor as critical to the coalition's cohesion. The issue was raised in fifty-five discrete instances.

11 Certain members of these groups did contribute to Kefaya's activities and some even sat on the Coordinators' Committee, but as individuals only. For example, one Muslim

Brotherhood leader, Sayed Abdel Sattar, helped draft the manifesto, and two others, Issam Al Ariyan and Muhammad Abdel Qudoos, participated in many Kefaya protests.

12 Another reason the Muslim Brotherhood remained outside of Kefaya may have stemmed from some Kefaya members' reticence toward collaborating with them. Many members of Kefaya wanted to work with the group because they believed this was the only way to make Kefaya an effective opposition front. Among those who opposed working with the Brotherhood were a small number who had ideological or personal problems with the group and a larger faction that were wary of joining with an organization that was much more powerful than any of the groups in Kefaya and might try to control the movement. In the end, Kefaya did reach out to the Brotherhood, just as it did to the other political opposition groups. But for the reasons outlined previously, no more than a handful of individual Brotherhood members became active.

13 This is not to say that the parties did not harbor some reservations about joining Kefaya. In fact, as the literature would predict, they worried about preserving their unique identities and organizational autonomy, and they required that their members maintain ultimate loyalty to the party, not Kefaya.

References

Abdallah, Ahmed. 1985. *The Student Movement and National Politics in Egypt*. London: Al Saqi Books.

Abdelrahman, Maha. 2014. *Egypt's Long Revolution: Protest Movements and Uprisings*. New York: Routledge.

Adler, Glenn, and Eddie Webster. 1995. "Challenging Transition Theory: The Labor Movement, Radical Reform, and the Transition to Democracy in South Africa." *Politics and Society* 23: 75–106.

Almeida, Paul D. 2003. "Opportunity Organizations and Threat-Induced Contention: Protest Waves in Authoritarian Settings." *American Journal of Sociology* 109(2): 345–400.

Almeida, Paul D. 2005. "Multi-Sectoral Coalitions and Popular Movement Participation." Pp. 63–99 in *Research in Social Movements, Conflicts and Change*, volume 26, edited by Patrick G. Coy. New York: Elsevier Science.

Almeida, Paul D. 2008. *Waves of Protest: Popular Struggle in El Salvador, 1925–2005*. Minneapolis: University of Minnesota Press.

Ansell, Christopher K. 2001. *Schism and Solidarity in Social Movements*. New York: Cambridge University Press.

Armstrong, Elizabeth A. 2002. *Forging Gay Identities: Organizing Sexuality in San Francisco, 1950–1994*. Chicago: University of Chicago Press.

Arnold, Gretchen. 1994. "Dilemmas of Feminist Coalitions: Collective Identity and Strategic Effectiveness in the Battered Women's Movement." Pp. 279–290 in *Feminist Organizations: Harvest of the New Women's Movement*, edited by Myra Marx Ferree and Patricia Y. Martin. Philadelphia, PA: Temple University Press.

Baker, Raymond William. 2003. *Islam without Fear: Egypt and the New Islamists*. Cambridge, MA: Harvard University Press.

Bayat, Asef. 2007. *Making Islam Democratic: Social Movements and the Post-Islamist Turn*. Stanford, CA: Stanford University Press.

Beattie, Kirk J. 2000. *Egypt during the Sadat Years*. New York: Palgrave Macmillan.

Beissinger, Mark R. 2011. "Mechanisms of Maidan: The Structure of Contingency on the Making of the Orange Revolution." *Mobilization* 16(1): 25–43.

Beissinger, Mark R. 2013. "The Semblance of Democratic Revolution: Coalitions in Ukraine's Orange Revolution." *The American Political Science Review* 107(3): 574–592.

Bermeo, Nancy. 1997. "Myths of Moderation: Confrontation and Conflict during Democratic Transitions." *Comparative Politics* 29: 305–322.

Bieber, Florian. 2003. "The Serbian Opposition and Civil Society: Roots of the Delayed Transition in Serbia." *International Journal of Politics, Culture, and Society* 17(1): 73–90.

Boudreau, Vincent. 2004. *Resisting Dictatorship: Repression and Protest in Southeast Asia*. Cambridge: Cambridge University Press.

Bradley, John R. 2008. *Inside Egypt: The Land of the Pharaohs on the Brink of Revolution*. New York: Palgrave Macmillan.

Brancati, Dawn. 2016. *Democracy Protests*. New York: Cambridge University Press.

Bratton, Michael, and Nicolas van de Walle. 1992. "Popular Protest and Political Reform in Africa." *Comparative Politics* 24: 419–442.

Bratton, Michael, and Nicolas van de Walle. 1997. *Democratic Experiments in Africa: Regime Transitions in Comparative Perspective*. Cambridge: Cambridge University Press.

Brooke, Steven. 2017. "From Medicine to Mobilization: Social Service Provision and the Islamist Reputational Advantage." *Perspectives on Politics* 15(1): 42–61.

Brownlee, Jason. 2007. *Authoritarianism in an Age of Democratization*. Cambridge: Cambridge University Press.

Chowdhury, Reshmi. 2006. "'Outsiders' and Identity Reconstruction in the Sex Workers' Movement in Bangladesh." *Sociological Spectrum* 26(3): 335–357.

Clark, Janine A. 2004. *Islam, Charity, and Activism: Middle-Class Networks and Social Welfare in Egypt, Jordan, and Yemen*. Bloomington, IN: Indiana University Press.

Clarke, Killian. 2014. "Unexpected Brokers of Mobilization: Contingency and Networks in the 2011 Egyptian Uprising." *Comparative Politics* 46(4): 379–397.

Collier, Ruth Berins, and James Mahoney. 1997. "Adding Collective Actors to Collective Outcomes: Labor and Recent Democratization in South America and South Europe." *Comparative Politics* 29: 285–303.

Croteau, David, and Lyndsi Hicks. 2003. "Coalition Framing and the Challenge of a Consonant Frame Pyramid: The Case of a Collaborative Response to Homelessness." *Social Problems* 50(2): 251–272.

Dalton, Russell J. 1994. *The Green Rainbow: Environmental Groups in Western Europe*. New Haven, CT: Yale University Press.

Davenport, Christian, Hank Johnston, and Carol McClurg Mueller, eds. 2005. *Repression and Mobilization*. Minneapolis: University of Minnesota Press.

Della Porta, Donatella. 1995. *Social Movements, Political Violence, and the State: A Comparative Analysis of Italy and Germany*. Cambridge: Cambridge University Press.

Earl, Jennifer. 2003. "Tanks, Tear Gas, and Taxes: Toward a Theory of Movement Repression." *Sociological Theory* 21: 44–68.

El-Ghobashy, Mona. 2005. "The Metamorphosis of the Egyptian Muslim Brothers." *International Journal of Middle East Studies* 37: 373–395.

Erlich, Haggai. 1989. *Students and University in 20th Century Egyptian Politics*. London: Frank Cass.

Ferree, Myra Marx, and Silke Roth. 1998. "Gender, Class, and the Interaction between Social Movements: A Strike in West Berlin Day Care Workers." *Gender and Society* 12: 626–648.

Foran, John. 2005. *Taking Power: On the Origins of Third World Revolutions*. Cambridge: Cambridge University Press.

Francisco, Ronald. 1996. "Coercion and Protest: An Empirical Test in Two Democratic States." *American Journal of Political Science* 40(4): 1179–1204.

Francisco, Ronald. 2005. "The Dictator's Dilemma." Pp. 58–81 in *Repression and Mobilization*, edited by Christian Davenport, Hank Johnston, and Carol McClurg Mueller. Minneapolis: University of Minnesota Press.

Gamson, William. 1992. "Social Psychology of Collective Action." Pp. 53–76 in *Frontiers in Social Movement Theory*, edited by Aldon D. Morris and Carol McClurg Mueller. New Haven, CT: Yale University Press.

Garretón, Manuel Antonio. 1989. *The Chilean Political Process*. Winchester, MA: Unwin Hyman.

Gerhards, Jurgen, and Dieter Rucht. 1992. "Mesomobilization: Organizing and Framing in Two Protest Campaigns in West Germany." *American Journal of Sociology* 98(3): 555–595.

Giugni, Marco G., Doug McAdam, and Charles Tilly. 1998. *From Contention to Democracy*. Lanham, MD: Rowman and Littlefield Publishers.

Goldstone, Jack A. 1998. "Social Movements or Revolutions? On the Evolution and Outcomes of Collective Action." Pp. 125–145 in *From Contention to Democracy*, edited by Marco G. Giugni, Doug McAdam, and Charles Tilly. Lanham, MD: Rowman and Littlefield Publishers.

Goodwin, Jeff. 2001. *No Other Way Out: States and Revolutionary Movements, 1945–1991*. New York: Cambridge University Press.

Goodwin, Jeff, and Theda Skocpol. 1989. "Explaining Revolutions in the Contemporary Third World." *Politics and Society* 17(4): 489–509.

Gould, Roger. 1995. *Insurgent Identities: Class, Community, and Protest in Paris from 1848 to the Commune*. Chicago, IL: University of Chicago Press.

Gunning, Jeroen, and Ilan Zvi Baron. 2014. *Why Occupy a Square? People, Protests and Movements in the Egyptian Revolution*. London: Hurst.

Hafez, Mohammad M. 2003. *Why Muslims Rebel: Repression and Resistance in the Islamic World*. Boulder, CO: Lynne Rienner Publishers.

Hathaway, Will, and David S. Meyer. 1997. "Competition and Cooperation in Movement Coalitions: Lobbying for Peace in the 1980s." Pp. 61–79 in *Coalitions and Political Movements: The Lessons of the Nuclear Freeze*, edited by Thomas Rochon and David S. Meyer. Boulder, CO: Lynne Rienner Publishers.

Hojnacki, Marie. 1997. "Interest Groups' Decisions to Join Alliances or Work Alone." *American Journal of Political Science* 41(1): 61–87.

Jasper, James M. 1997. *The Art of Moral Protest: Culture Biography and Creativity in Social Movements*. Chicago, IL: University of Chicago Press.

Jasper, James M., and Francesca Polletta. 2001. "Collective Identity and Social Movements." *Annual Review of Sociology* 27(1): 283–305.

Kadivar, Mohammad Ali, and Neal Caren. 2015. "Disruptive Democratization: Contentious Events and Liberalizing Outcomes Globally, 1990–2004." *Social Forces* 94(3): 975–996.

Kepel, Gilles. 1993. *Muslim Extremism in Egypt: The Prophet and Pharaoh*. Berkeley, CA: University of California Press.

Klandermans, Bert. 1990. "Linking the 'Old' and 'New': Movement Networks in the Netherlands." Pp. 122–136 in *Challenging the Political Order*, edited by Russell J. Dalton and Manfred Kuechler. Cambridge: Polity Press.

Klandermans, Bert. 1992. "The Social Construction of Protest and Multiorganizational Fields." Pp. 77–103 in *Frontiers in Social Movement Theory*, edited by Aldon D. Morris and Carol McClurg Mueller. New Haven, CT: Yale University Press.

Klandermans, Bert, and Marga de Weerd. 2000. "Group Identification and Political Protest." Pp. 68–90 in *Self, Identity, and Social Movements*, edited by Sheldon Stryker, Timothy J. Owens, and Robert W. White. Minneapolis: University of Minnesota Press.

Kleidman, Robert. 1993. *Organizing for Peace: Neutrality, the Test Ban, and the Freeze.* Syracuse, NY: Syracuse University Press.

Kleidman, Robert, and Thomas Rochon. 1997. "Dilemmas of Organization in Peace Campaigns." Pp. 47–60 in *Coalitions and Political Movements: The Lessons of the Nuclear Freeze*, edited by Thomas Rochon and David S. Meyer. Boulder, CO: Lynne Rienner Publishers.

Korany, Bahgat, and Rabab El-Mahdi, eds. 2012. *Arab Spring in Egypt: Revolution and Beyond.* Cairo: American University in Cairo Press.

Kurzman, Charles. 1996. "Structural Opportunity and Perceived Opportunity in Social Movement Theory: The Iranian Revolution of 1979." *American Sociological Review* 61: 153–170.

Kurzman, Charles. 2004. *The Unthinkable Revolution in Iran.* Cambridge, MA: Harvard University Press.

LeBas, Adrienne. 2013. *From Protest to Parties: Party-Building and Democratization in Africa.* New York: Oxford University Press.

Levi, Margaret, and Gillian H. Murphy. 2006. "Coalitions of Contention: The Case of the WTO Protests in Seattle." *Political Studies* 54(4): 651–670.

Loveman, Mara. 1998. "High-Risk Collective Action: Defending Human Rights in Chile, Uruguay, and Argentina." *American Journal of Sociology* 104(2): 477–525.

Mansbridge, Jane. 2001. "The Making of Oppositional Consciousness." Pp. 1–19 in *Oppositional Consciousness: The Subjective Roots of Social Process*, edited by Jane Mansbridge and Aldon D. Morris. Chicago: The University of Chicago Press.

Markoff, John. 1996. *Waves of Democracy: Social Movements and Political Change.* Thousand Oaks, CA: Pine Forge Press.

McCammon, Holly J., and Karen E. Campbell. 2002. "Allies on the Road to Victory: Coalition Formation between the Suffragists and the Women's Christian Temperance Union." *Mobilization* 7(3): 231–251.

Melucci, Alberto. 1989. *Nomads of the Present: Social Movements and Individual Needs in Contemporary Society.* Philadelphia: Temple University Press.

Meyer, David S. 2001. "Social Movements and Public Policy: Eggs, Chicken, and Theory." Paper presented at the Annual Meeting of the American Political Science Association, San Francisco, CA.

Meyer, David S., and Catherine Corrigall-Brown. 2005. "Coalitions and Political Contexts: US Movements against the Wars in Iraq." *Mobilization* 10(3): 327–346.

Murphy, Gillian. 2005. "Coalitions and the Development of the Global Environmental Movement: A Double-Edged Sword." *Mobilization* 10(2): 235–250.

Obach, Brian K. 2004. *Labor and the Environmental Movement: A Quest for Common Ground.* Cambridge, MA: MIT Press.

O'Brien, Kevin J., and Lianjiang Li. 2006. *Rightful Resistance in Rural China.* New York: Cambridge University Press.

Olzak, Susan, and Emily Ryo. 2007. "Organizational Diversity, Vitality, and Outcomes in the Civil Rights Movement." *Social Forces* 85(4): 1561–1592.

Osa, Maryjane, and Cristina Corduneanu-Huci. 2005. "Linking Economic and Political Opportunities in Nondemocracies." Pp. 171–201 in *Economic and Political Contention in Comparative Perspective*, edited by Maria Kousis and Charles Tilly. London: Paradigm Publishers.

Osa, Maryjane, and Kurt Schock. 2007. "A Long Hard Slog: Political Opportunities, Social Networks, and the Mobilization of Dissent in Nondemocracies." Pp. 123–153 in *Research in Social Movements, Conflicts and Change*, volume 27, edited by Patrick G. Coy. New York: Elsevier Science.

Oxhorn, Philip. 1995. *Organizing Civil Society: The Popular Sectors and the Struggle for Democracy in Chile.* University Park, PA: Penn State Press.

Parsa, Misagh. 2000. *States, Ideologies, and Social Revolutions: A Comparative Analysis of Iran, Nicaragua, and the Philippines.* Cambridge: Cambridge University Press.

Robertson, Graeme B. 2010. *The Politics of Protest in Hybrid Regimes: Managing Dissent in Post-Communist Russia.* New York: Cambridge University Press.

Rose, Fred. 2000. *Coalitions across the Class Divide: Lessons from the Labor, Peace, and Environmental Movements.* Ithaca, NY: Cornell University Press.

Schock, Kurt. 2005. *Unarmed Insurrections: People Power Movements in Nondemocracies.* Minneapolis, MN: University of Minnesota Press.

Shadid, Anthony. 2007. "Egypt Shuts Door on Dissent as US Officials Back Away." *Washington Post.* May 19.

Skocpol, Theda. 1979. *States and Social Revolutions.* Cambridge: Cambridge University Press.

Springborg, Robert. 1989. *Mubarak's Egypt: Fragmentation of the Political Order.* London: Westview Press.

Staggenborg, Suzanne. 1986. "Coalition Work in the Pro-Choice Movement: Organizational and Environmental Opportunities and Obstacles." *Social Problems* 33: 374–390.

Tarrow, Sidney. 1983. *Struggle, Politics and Reform: Collective Action, Social Movements and Cycles of Protest.* Ithaca, NY: Cornell University Press.

Tarrow, Sidney. 1989. *Democracy and Disorder: Protest and Politics in Italy, 1965–1975.* Oxford: Oxford University Press.

Tarrow, Sidney. 1995. "Mass Mobilization and Elite Exchange: Democratization Episodes in Italy and Spain." *Democratization* 2: 221–245.

Taylor, Verta, and Nancy E. Whittier. 1992. "Collective Identity in Social Movement Communities: Lesbian Feminist Mobilization." Pp. 169–194 in *Frontiers in Social Movement Theory*, edited by Aldon D. Morris and Carol McClurg Mueller. New Haven, CT: Yale University Press.

Tilly, Charles. 1995. *Popular Contention in Great Britain, 1758–1834.* Cambridge, MA: Harvard University Press.

Tilly, Charles. 2006. *Regimes and Repertoires.* Chicago, IL: University of Chicago Press.

Trejo, Guillermo. 2012. *Popular Movements in Autocracies: Religion, Repression, and Indigenous Collective Action in Mexico.* New York: Cambridge University Press.

Van Dyke, Nella. 2003. "Crossing Movement Boundaries: Factors That Facilitate Coalition Protest by American College Students." *Social Problems* 50(2): 1930–1990.

Van Dyke, Nella, and Holly J. McCammon, eds. 2010. *Strategic Alliances: Coalition Building and Social Movements.* Minneapolis, MN: University of Minnesota Press.

Wickham, Carrie Rosefsky. 2002. *Mobilizing Islam: Religion, Activism, and Political Change in Egypt.* New York: Columbia University Press.

Wieloch, Neil. 2002. "Collective Mobilization and Identity from the Underground: The Deployment of 'Oppositional Capital' in the Harm Reduction Movement." The Sociological Quarterly 43(1): 45–72.

Wiktorowicz, Quintan. 2001. *The Management of Islamic Activism: The Salafis, the Muslim Brotherhood, and State Power in Jordan.* Albany, NY: State University of New York Press.

Wiktorowicz, Quintan, ed. 2004. *Islamic Activism: A Social Movement Theory Approach.* Bloomington: Indiana University Press.

Wood, Elisabeth Jean. 2000. *Forging Democracy from Below: Insurgent Transitions in South Africa and El Salvador.* New York: Cambridge University Press.

Zald, Mayer N., and John D. McCarthy. 1980. "Social Movement Industries: Competition and Cooperation among Movement Organizations." Pp. 120 in *Research in Social Movements, Conflict, and Change*, volume 3, edited by Louis Kriesberg. Greenwich, CT: JAI Press.

Zald, Mayer N., and John D. McCarthy. 1987. *Social Movements in an Organizational Society*. New Brunswick, NJ: Transaction.

Index